Lyman Coleman

The Apostolical and Primitive Church

popular in its government, informal in its worship : a manual on prelacy and

ritualism carefully revised and adapted to these discussions

Lyman Coleman

The Apostolical and Primitive Church
popular in its government, informal in its worship : a manual on prelacy and ritualism
carefully revised and adapted to these discussions

ISBN/EAN: 9783337285395

Printed in Europe, USA, Canada, Australia, Japan

Cover: Foto ©Lupo / pixelio.de

More available books at **www.hansebooks.com**

THE

APOSTOLICAL

AND

PRIMITIVE CHURCH

POPULAR IN ITS GOVERNMENT,

INFORMAL IN ITS WORSHIP.

A

MANUAL

ON

PRELACY AND RITUALISM

CAREFULLY REVISED

AND ADAPTED TO THESE DISCUSSIONS.

BY

LYMAN COLEMAN, D.D.

PROFESSOR IN LAFAYETTE COLLEGE,

AUTHOR OF "ANCIENT CHRISTIANITY EXEMPLIFIED," "HISTORICAL TEXT-BOOK AND ATLAS OF BIBLICAL GEOGRAPHY," &c.

PHILADELPHIA

J. B. LIPPINCOTT & CO.

1869.

Entered according to Act of Congress, in the year 1869, by
LYMAN COLEMAN, D.D.,
In the Clerk's Office of the District Court of the United States for the Eastern District of Pennsylvania.

LIPPINCOTT'S PRESS,
PHILADELPHIA.

PREFACE.

THE object of the author in the following work is to commend to the consideration of the reader the admirable simplicity of the government and worship of the primitive church, in opposition to the polity and ceremonials of prelacy.

In the prosecution of this object he has sought, under the direction of the best guides, to go to the original sources, and first and chiefly to draw from them. On the constitution and government of the church none have written with greater ability, or with more extensive and searching erudition, than Mosheim, Planck, Neander and Rothe. These have been his principal reliance: and after these a great variety of authors.

The work has been prepared with an anxious endeavor to sustain the positions advanced, by references sufficiently copious, pertinent and authoritative; and yet to guard against an ostentatious affectation in the accumulation of authorities. Several hundred have indeed been entered in these pages; but many more that have fallen under the eye of the writer have been rejected. Much labor, of which the reader probably will make small account, has been expended in an endeavor to authenticate those that are retained, and to give him an explicit direction to them. The whole has been written with studied brevity, and a uniform endeavor to make it at once concise, yet complete and suggestive of principles.

The translation of the Introduction was made in Berlin; and after a careful comparison with the original by Dr. Neander, received his unqualified approbation. It is, therefore, to be regarded as an authentic expression of his sentiments on the several topics to which it relates.

In the preparation of this work the author has studiously sought to write neither as a Congregationalist nor as a Presbyterian exclusively; but as the advocate of a free and popular government in the church; and of simplicity in worship, in harmony with the free spirit of the Christian religion. It is enough for the author, and, as he would hope, for both Congregationalists and Presbyterians, if the church is set free from the bondage of a prelatical hierarchy, and trained, by simple and expressive rites, to worship God in spirit and in truth. In opposition to the assumptions of prelacy, there is common ground sufficient for all the friends of popular government in the church of Christ to occupy. In the topics discussed in the following pages they have equal interest, whether they would adopt a purely democratical or a representative form of government as the best means of defending the popular rights of the church. We heartily wish indeed for all true churchmen a closer conformity to the primitive pattern in government and in worship; but we have no controversy even with them on minor points, provided we may still be united with them in the higher principles of Christian fellowship and love. The writer has the happiness to number among the members of the Episcopal Church some of his most cherished friends, to whose sentiments he would be sorry to do violence by anything that may appear in these pages.

The great controversy of the day is not with true Protestant Episcopacy, but with High Church Episcopacy, Popery, Ritualism, Formalism. Formalism, by whatever name it is known, is the great antagonist of spiritual Christianity. Here the church is brought to a crisis, great and fearful in prospect, and momentous, for good or for evil, in its final results. The struggle at issue is between a spiritual and a formal religion—against a religion which substitutes the outward form for the inward spirit; which exalts sacraments, ordinances and rites into the place of Christ himself; and disguises, under the covering of imposing ceremonials, the great doctrines of the cross. Dr. Pusey himself declares that on the issue of this controversy "hangs the destiny of the Church of England;" and the Tractarians again— "that two schemes of doctrine, the Genevan and the Catholic, are probably for the last time struggling within that church." This "great Catholic movement," this "Catholic revival" of the Ritualists, with its endless ceremonials, costumes and "histrionic representations," is the great religious controversy of the age. It has often engaged the notice of the highest primates of the church in England, and of the prime ministers in the British Parliament, as "a grave and serious evil," requiring the attention both of church and of state. The ritualistic party themselves claim to be the predominant party and the only true representatives of the Church of England, which, dissevered by the Reformation, is soon to be "reingrafted into the true Catholic Church."

In this country the periodical literature and the voluminous productions of the press are charged with this ritualistic controversy. The last literary labor of the late Bishop of Vermont was an elaborate effort to establish "the Law of Ritualism" on the authority of the Scriptures, as the "glory and beauty of the church." This law he gave at the request of a large committee of "sons in the church," who appear to follow, "with a glad mind and will, his godly admonitions, and submit themselves to his godly judgments." The House of Bishops, in their late convention, gave to the high church party the sanction of their silent approval by refusing all official action in relation to it. This "masterly inactivity" is highly commended as the surest means of establishing the law of ritualism in their churches.

Ritualism is the aggressive heresy of our churches. The taint of this ritualistic movement has already infected even our Congregational and Presbyterian churches. An American bishop several years since publicly stated that of "*two hundred and eighty persons* ordained by him, *two hundred and seven* came from other denominations." Another says: "From the most accurate investigation that can be made, I am led to believe that about *three hundred* clergymen and licentiates of other denominations have, within the last *thirty years*, sought the ministerial commission from the hands of bishops of that church; and that at least *two-thirds* were not originally, by education, Episcopalians, but have come from other folds." Not a few in our churches, both of the clergy and the laity, openly advocate or silently approve a qualified or partial liturgy. The controversy is upon us, and the public, the ministry especially, and candidates for the ministry, are required to be prepared for the conflict. Those *two hundred* who have gone from other folds into the Episcopal Church, "not originally by education Episcopalians," were they, *by education*, anything else? Had they been duly educated in the ecclesiastical polity of their Pilgrim forefathers? Are the principles of this polity duly inculcated either in our Congregational and Presbyterian churches, or in their theological seminaries? In this eventful crisis we are urgently pressed to a renewed examination of the apostolic and primitive polity of the church in government and in worship; for under cover of these the warfare of ritualism is now waged. These are the prominent points, both of attack and of defence, to which the eye of the minister, the theological student, and the intelligent Christian of every name, should be turned. Let them fall back on that spiritual Christianity which Christ and his apostles taught. Let them, in doctrine, in discipline, and in worship, entrench themselves within the stronghold of this religion; and here, in calm reliance upon the great Captain of our salvation, let them await the issue of the contest.

In accordance with these views the following manual, studiously adapted to this conflict, is respectfully submitted to the consideration of the public. The former editions have been the subject of frequent and careful revisions. Much has been added, and more, by omissions and a severe condensation, has given place to these additions. The authorities, as far as practicable, have been revised and verified anew by the kind aid of gentlemen having access to the libraries of the Theological Seminaries at Andover, at Princeton and in New York. Candidates for the ministry in our theological seminaries, may find this a convenient manual for reference or for study, in connection with their recitations and the lectures delivered on kindred topics. And clergymen who have neither time nor opportunity for such investigations may find here authorities laboriously collected and collated for the defence of the several arguments by which we earnestly protest that Christ and his apostles established the primitive church without a bishop, and ordained its worship without a ritual. God is a Spirit; and they that worship him must worship him in spirit and in truth—in the inward spirit, not by an outward form; least of all, by "the mysterious and symbolical pomp" of modern ritualism. Can these "carnal ordinances" ever make him that does "the service perfect as pertaining to the conscience?" Sons of the Pilgrims! Ministers of grace to Puritan churches! "Are ye so foolish? Having begun in the Spirit, are ye now made perfect by the flesh?"

LAFAYETTE COLLEGE, *Easton, Penn.*, 1869.

CONTENTS.

	PAGE
INTRODUCTION TO THE FIRST EDITION, BY NEANDER	15

PART FIRST.

THE PRIMITIVE CHURCH—POPULAR IN ITS GOVERNMENT.

CHAPTER I.

PRELIMINARY REMARKS ON THE GOVERNMENT AND WORSHIP OF THE CHURCH INSTITUTED BY CHRIST AND HIS APOSTLES... 25

CHAPTER II.

THE PRIMITIVE CHURCHES FORMED AFTER THE MODEL OF THE JEWISH SYNAGOGUE... 37

CHAPTER III.

THE INDEPENDENCE OF THE PRIMITIVE CHURCHES... 45

CHAPTER IV.

	PAGE
ELECTIONS BY THE CHURCHES	50
1. Scriptural Argument	51
2. Historical Argument	61
Loss of the Right of Suffrage	68
Remarks: Results upon the Church, the People and the Ministry	79

CHAPTER V.

DISCIPLINE BY THE CHURCHES	87
1. Argument from the Scriptures	88
2. Argument from the Ancient Fathers	95
3. Argument from Modern Ecclesiastical Writers	107
4. Argument from Analogy	109
Mode of Admission	114
Usurpation by the Priesthood	115
Remarks: Results on the Purity and Efficiency of the Church	119
Objections to Episcopacy	121

CHAPTER VI.

EQUALITY AND IDENTITY OF BISHOPS AND PRESBYTERS	126

Scriptural Argument.

Identity of their Titles	128
Identity of their Qualifications	131
Identity of their Duties	133
Identity of their Clerical Order or Rank	137

CONTENTS.

	PAGE
James not Bishop of Jerusalem	139
Nor Timothy, of Ephesus	142
Nor Titus, of Crete	145
The Angels of the Seven Churches not Bishops	146

Historical Argument.

According to the Ancient Fathers, Bishops and Presbyters are—

Identical in Names	151
Identical in Rank or Office	153
Identical in Official Duties	162
Parochial Episcopacy	163
Divine Right of Episcopacy Disowned	171
Groundless Assumptions of Episcopacy	177

CHAPTER VII.

APOSTOLICAL SUCCESSION	178
Apostolical Succession—Groundless, Impossible	181

CHAPTER VIII.

PRESBYTERIAN ORDINATION	185
Laying on of Hands	186
Historical Authorities	192
Episcopal Concessions	203
Divine Right first Asserted in the English Church	204
Remarks: Efficiency of Primitive Church Government	207
Encumbrances of the Episcopal Ritual	212
The Puritans and their Principles	215

CHAPTER IX.

	PAGE
THE RISE OF EPISCOPACY	219
Ascendency of Churches and Clergy in the Cities	221
Presiding Presbyter a Bishop	224
Jerome, Hilary and Stillingfleet on the Origin of Episcopacy.	228
American Episcopacy	232

CHAPTER X.

THE PROGRESS OF EPISCOPACY	235
Means of its Development	235
Results	239
METROPOLITAN GOVERNMENT	242
Means of its Establishment	243
Results in regard to the Laity	244
Results in regard to the Clergy	248
Degeneracy under the Hierarchy	259
THE PATRIARCHAL GOVERNMENT	264
THE PAPAL GOVERNMENT	265
Remarks: Objections to Prelacy	268
A Corrupt Compromise with Paganism	272

PART SECOND.

THE PRIMITIVE CHURCH—INFORMAL IN ITS WORSHIP.

CHAPTER XI.

PRAYERS OF THE PRIMITIVE CHURCH	275
Forms of Prayer—	
Opposed to the Spirit of the Christian Dispensation	275

CONTENTS.

	PAGE
Opposed to the Example of Christ	277
Opposed to the Instructions of Christ and his Apostles	279
The Lord's Prayer	283
The Freedom of Primitive Worship	285
Liturgical Forms unknown to the Primitive Church.	288
Origin of Liturgies	304
Remarks: Objections to Liturgies	308
Popish Origin and Tendencies of the English Liturgy	314
Doctrinal Errors of the Prayer-Book	316
The Ritualists of England	319

CHAPTER XII.

PSALMODY OF THE PRIMITIVE CHURCH	321
Argument from Reason	321
Argument from Analogy	322
Argument from Scripture	322
Argument from History	324
Mode of Singing	328
Changes in the Psalmody of the Church	333
Remarks on Congregational Singing	338
Power of Sacred Psalmody	341

CHAPTER XIII.

HOMILIES IN THE PRIMITIVE CHURCH	351
Discourses of Christ and the Apostles	351
Expository Preaching	357
Homilies in the Greek Church	360
Homilies in the Latin Church	365
Episcopacy an Encumbrance to the Preacher	368

CHAPTER XIV.

	PAGE
THE BENEDICTION	373
Origin and Import of the Rite	374
Mode of Administering it	379
Superstitious Perversions of the Benediction	382
Episcopacy a Vicarious Religion	384
APPENDIX	389

INDEXES.

Index of Texts	399
Index of Authorities	401
Index of Subjects	406

INTRODUCTION,

BY

Dr. AUGUSTUS NEANDER,

PROFESSOR OF THEOLOGY IN THE UNIVERSITY OF BERLIN, CONSISTORIAL COUNSELOR, ETC.

In compliance with the request of my worthy friend, the Rev. Mr. Coleman, I am happy to accompany his proposed work, on the Constitution and Worship of the apostolical and primitive church, with some preliminary remarks. I regard it as one of the remarkable signs of the times, that Christians, separated from each other by land and by sea, by language and government, are becoming more closely united in the consciousness that they are only different members of one universal church, grounded and built on the rock Christ Jesus. And it is with the hope of promoting this catholic union that I gladly improve this opportunity to address my Christian brethren beyond the waters on some important subjects of common interest to the church of Christ.

This is not the proper place to express in detail, and to defend my own views upon the controverted topics which, as I have reason to expect from the respected author, will be the subject of an extended, thorough and impartial examination in his proposed work. My own sentiments have already been expressed, in a work which, I am happy to learn, is offered to the English reader in a translation by my friend, the Rev. Mr. Ryland, of Northampton, in England.[1] I have only time and space, in this place, briefly to express the results of former inquiries, which, with the reasons for them, have on other occasions already been given to the public.

It is of the utmost importance to keep ever in view the difference between the economy of the Old Testament and that of the New. The neglect of this has given rise to the grossest errors, and to divisions, by which those who ought to be united together in the bonds of Christian love have been sundered from each other. In the Old Testament, everything relating to the kingdom of God was estimated by *outward forms*, and promoted by specific *external rites*. In the New, everything is made to depend upon what is *internal* and *spiritual*. Other foundation, as the apostle Paul has said, can no man lay than that is laid. Upon this the Christian church at first was grounded, and upon this alone, in all time to come, must it be reared anew and compacted together. Faith in Jesus of Nazareth, the Saviour of the world, and union with him, a participation in that salvation which cometh through him,—this is that inward principle, that unchangeable foundation, on which the Christian church essentially rests. But whenever, instead of making the existence of the church to depend on this inward principle alone, the necessity of some outward form is asserted as an indispensable means of grace, we readily

---

[1] History of the Planting and Training of the Christian Church, by the Apostles, by Dr. A. NEANDER, Ordinary Professor of Theology in the University of Berlin, Consistorial Counselor; translated from the third edition, by J. E. Ryland.

perceive that the purity of its character is impaired. The spirit of the Old Testament is commingled with that of the New. Neither Christ nor the apostles have given any unchangeable law on the subject. Where two or three are gathered together in my name, says Christ, there am I in the midst of them. This coming together in his name, he assures us, alone renders the assembly well pleasing in his sight, whatever be the different forms of government under which his people meet.

The apostle Paul says indeed, Eph. iv. 11, that Christ gave to the church certain offices, through which he operated with his Spirit and its attendant gifts. But assuredly Paul did not mean to say that Christ, during his abode on earth, appointed these offices in the church, or authorized the form of government that was necessarily connected with them. All the offices here mentioned, with the single exception of that of the apostles, were instituted by the apostles themselves, after our Lord's ascension. In making these appointments, they acted, as they did in everything else, only as the organs of Christ. Paul, therefore, very justly ascribes to Christ himself what was done by the apostles in this instance as his agents. But the apostles themselves have given no law requiring that any such form of government as is indicated in this passage should be perpetual. Under the guidance of the Spirit of God, they gave the church this particular organization, which, while it was best adapted to the circumstances and relations of the church at that time, was also best suited to the extension of the churches in their peculiar condition, and for the development of the inward principles of their communion. But forms may change with every change of circumstances. Many of the offices mentioned in that passage either were entirely unknown at a later period, or existed in relations one to another entirely new.²

Whenever at a later period, also, any form of church government has arisen out of a series of events according to the direction of divine providence, and is organized and governed with regard to the Lord's will, he may be said, himself, to have established it, and to operate through it, by his Spirit; without which nothing pertaining to the church can prosper. The great principles which are given by the apostle, in the passage before us, for the guidance of the church,—these, and these only, remain unchangeably the same; because they are immediately connected with the

---

² One peculiar office, that of the prophets, in process of time ceased in the church, while something analogous to the gift of prophecy still remained; indeed it might be easily shown that the prophetic office continued at that early period so long as it was necessary for the establishment of the Christian church, under its peculiar exigencies and relations. Pastors and teachers are mentioned in this passage, in the same connection. Their office, which related to the government of particular churches, is distinguished from that of those who had been mentioned before, and whose immediate object was the extension of the Christian church in general. And yet a distinction is also made between these pastors and teachers, inasmuch as the qualifications for the outward government of the church, κυβέρνησις, were different from those which were requisite for the guidance of the church by the preaching of the word, διδασκαλία. The first belonged especially to the presbyters or bishops who stood at the head of the organization for the outward government of the church. Certain it is, at least, that they did not all possess the gift of teaching as διδάσκαλοι, teachers. On the other hand, there may have been persons endowed with the gift of teaching, and qualified thus to be teachers, who still belonged not to the class of presbyters. The relations of these offices to one another seem not to have been the same in all stages of the development of the apostolical churches.

nature of the Christian church, as a spiritual community. All else is mutable. The form of the church remained not the same, even through the whole course of the apostolic age, from the first descent of the Spirit, on the day of Pentecost, to the death of John the apostle. Particular forms of church government may be more or less suited to the nature of the Christian church; and we may add, no one is absolutely perfect, neither are all alike good under all circumstances. Would then that all, in their strivings after forms of church government, would abide fast by those which they believe to be best adapted to promote their own spiritual edification, and which they may have found, by experience, to be best suited to the wants of their own Christian community. Only let them not seek to impose upon all Christians any one form as indispensably necessary. Only let them remember, that the upbuilding of the church of Christ may be carried on under other forms also; and that the same Spirit, on which the existence of the church depends, can as truly operate in other churches as in their own. Would that Congregationalists, Presbyterians and Episcopalians, Calvinists and Lutherans, would abide by that only unchangeable foundation which Christ has laid. Would that on such a foundation, which no man can lay, they would meet as brethren in Christ, acknowledging each other as members of one catholic church, and organs of the same Spirit, co-operating together for the promotion of the great ends indicated by the apostle Paul in Eph. iv. 13–16.

It must indeed be of great importance to examine impartially the relations of the apostolical church; for, at this time, the Spirit of Christ, through the apostles, wrought in its purest influence; by which means the mingling of foreign elements was prevented in the development of this system of ecclesiastical polity. In this respect we must all admit that the apostolical church commends itself to us as a model of church government. But, in the first place, let us remember, agreeably to what has already been said, that not all the forms of church government which were adapted to the exigencies of the church at this early period can be received as patterns for the church at other times; neither can the imitation be pressed too far. Let us remember that it is only that same Spirit which is imparted to us through the intervention of the apostles, which, at all times, and under all possible relations, will direct to the most appropriate and most efficient form of government, if, in humility and sincerity, we surrender ourselves up to its teaching and guidance. And secondly, let us remember that, after true and faithful inquiry on these subjects, men may honestly differ in their views on those minor points, without interrupting the higher communion of faith and love.

In the apostolical church there was one office which bears no resemblance to any other, and to which none can be made to conform. This is the office of the apostles. They stand as the medium of communication between Christ and the whole Christian church, to transmit his word and his Spirit through all ages. In this respect the church must ever continue to acknowledge her dependence upon them, and to own their rightful authority. Their authority and power can be delegated to none other. But the service which the apostles themselves sought to confer, was to transmit to men the word and the Spirit of the Lord, and, by this means, to establish independent Christian communities. These communities, when once established, they refused to hold in a state of slavish dependence upon themselves. Their object was, in the Spirit of the Lord, to make the churches free and independent of their guidance. To the churches their language was, "Ye beloved, ye are made free; be ye the servants of no man." The churches were taught to govern themselves. All the members were made to co-operate together as organs of one Spirit, in connection with which spiritual gifts were imparted to each as he might need. Thus they whose prerogative it was to rule among the brethren demeaned themselves as the servants of Christ and his church. They acted in the name of Christ and his church, as the organs of that Spirit with which all were inspired, and from which they derived the consciousness of their mutual Christian fellowship.

The brethren chose their own officers from among themselves. Or if, in the first organization of the churches, their officers were appointed by the apostles, it was with the approbation of the members of the same. The general concerns of the church were managed by the apostles in connection with their brethren in the church, to whom they also addressed their epistles.

The earliest constitution of the church was modeled, for the most part, after that religious community with which it stood in closest connection, and to which it was most assimilated—the Jewish synagogue. This, however, was so modified as to conform to the nature of the Christian community, and to the new and peculiar spirit with which it was animated. Like the synagogue, the church was governed by an associated body of men appointed for this purpose.

The name of *presbyters*, which was appropriated to this body, was derived from the Jewish synagogue. But in the Gentile churches, formed by the apostle Paul, they took the name of ἐπίσκοποι, *bishops*, a term more significant of their office in the language generally spoken by the members of these churches. The name of *presbyters* denoted the dignity of their office. That of *bishops*, on the other hand, was expressive rather of the nature of their office, ἐπισκοπεῖν τὴν ἐκκλησίαν, *to take the oversight of the church*. Most certainly no other distinction originally existed between them. But, in process of time, some one, in the ordinary course of events, would gradually obtain the pre-eminence over his colleagues, and by reason of that peculiar oversight which he exercised over the whole community, might come to be designated by the name ἐπίσκοπος, *bishop*, which was originally applied to them all indiscriminately. The constant tumults, from within and from without, which agitated the church in the times of the apostles, may have given to such a one opportunity to exercise his influence the more efficiently; so that, at such a time, the controlling influence of one in this capacity may have been very salutary to the church. This change in the relation of the presbyters to each other was not the same in all the churches, but varied according to their different circumstances. It may have been as early as the latter part of the life of John, when he was sole survivor of the other apostles, that one, as president of this body of presbyters, was distinguished by the name of ἐπίσκοπος, *bishop*. There is, however, no evidence that the apostle himself introduced this change; much less that he authorized it as a perpetual ordinance for the future. Such an ordinance is in direct opposition to the spirit of that apostle.[3]

[3] In the angels of the churches in the seven epistles of the Apocalypse, I cannot recognize the שָׁלִיחַ צִבּוּר of the Jewish synagogue transferred to the Christian church. The application appears to me

This change in the mode of administering the government of the church, resulting from peculiar circumstances, may have been introduced as a salutary expedient, without implying any departure from the purity of the Christian spirit. When, however, the doctrine is—as it gradually gained currency in the third century—that the bishops are, by divine right, the head of the church, and invested with the government of the same; that they are the successors of the apostles, and by this succession inherit apostolical authority; that they are the medium through which, in consequence of that ordination which they have received, merely in an outward manner, the Holy Ghost, in all time to come, must be transmitted to the church—when this becomes the doctrine of the church, we certainly must perceive, in these assumptions, a strong corruption of the purity of the Christian system. It is a carnal perversion of the true idea of the Christian church. It is falling back into the spirit of the Jewish religion. Instead of the Christian idea of a church, based on inward principles of communion, and extending itself by means of these, it presents us with the image of one, like that under the Old Testament, rest-

to be altogether arbitrary. Nor again can I discover in the angel of the church, the bishop, addressed as the representative of this body of believers. How much must we assume as already proved, which yet is entirely without evidence, in assigning to this early period the rise of such a monarchical system of government, that the bishop alone can be put in the place of the whole church? In this phraseology I recognize rather a symbolical application of the idea of guardian angels, similar to that of the Ferver of the Parsees, as a symbolical representation and image of the whole church. Such a figurative representation corresponds well with the poetical and symbolical character of the book throughout. It is also expressly said that the address is to the whole body of the churches.

ing in outward ordinances, and, by external rites, seeking to promote the propagation of the kingdom of God. This entire perversion of the original view of the Christian church was itself the origin of the whole system of the Roman Catholic religion,—the germ from which sprung the popery of the dark ages.

We hold, indeed, no controversy with that class of Episcopalians who adhere to the episcopal system above mentioned as well adapted, in their opinion, to the exigencies of their church. We would live in harmony with them, notwithstanding their mistaken views of the true form of the church, provided they denounce not other systems of church government. But the doctrine of the absolute necessity of the episcopal as the only valid form of government, and of the episcopal succession of bishops above mentioned, in order to a participation in the gifts of the Spirit, all this we must regard as something foreign to the true idea of the Christian church. It is in direct conflict with the spirit of protestantism; and is the origin, not of the true catholicism of the apostle, but of that of the Romish church. When, therefore, Episcopalians disown, as essentially deficient in their ecclesiastical organization, other protestant churches which evidently have the Spirit of Christ, it only remains for us to protest, in the strongest terms, against their setting up such a standard of perfection for the Christian church. Far be it from us, who began with Luther in the spirit, that we should now desire to be made perfect by the flesh, Gal. iii. 3.

DR. A. NEANDER.

BERLIN, *April* 28, 1843.

THE PRIMITIVE CHURCH.

PART FIRST.

POPULAR IN ITS GOVERNMENT.

CHAPTER I.

PRELIMINARY REMARKS.

THE Christian church derived its earliest form from a small society of believers, who were united together by no law but that of the love which they felt to one another and to their common Lord.[1] After his ascension they continued to meet, in singleness of heart, for the mutual interchange of sympathy and love, and for the worship of their Lord and Master. The government which, in process of time, the fraternity adopted for themselves, was free and voluntary. Each individual church possessed the rights and powers inherent in an independent popular assembly; or, to adopt the language of another, "The right to enact their laws, and the entire government of the church, was vested in each individual association of which the church was composed, and was exercised by the members of the same, in

[1] Neander's Apost. Kirch. Vol. I. c. 1. Rothe, Anfänge der Christ. Kirch. I. S. 141-2.

connection with their overseers and teachers, and, when the apostles were present, in common also with them."² This general exposition of the government of the primitive church, it will be our business to illustrate and defend in the following pages. The course of our inquiries will lead us to examine the popular government of the apostolical and primitive church, to trace the gradual extinction of this form of government, and the rise of the episcopal system; and also to consider the simplicity of primitive worship in its several parts.

The arguments for the popular government of the apostolical and primitive church may be arranged under the following heads:

1. It harmonizes with the primitive simplicity of all forms of government.

The multiplication of offices, the adjustment of the gradations of rank and power, and a complicated system of rites and forms, are the work of time. At first, the rules of government, however administered, are few and simple. The early Christians, especially, associating together in the confidence of mutual love, and uniting in sincerity of heart for the worship of God, could have had only a few conventional rules for the regulation of their fraternity.

2. It is, perhaps, the only organization which the church could safely have formed, at that time, under the Roman government.

The Romans tolerated, indeed, different religious sects, and might have extended the same indulgence to the primitive Christians. But they looked with suspicion upon every organization of party or sect, and punished with cruel jeal-

² Cited in Allgemeine Kirch. Zeitung, 1833. No. 103.

ousy every indication of a confederacy within the empire. The charge of treasonable intentions prevailed with the Roman governor against our Lord. And under Trajan, A. D. 103, a bloody persecution was commenced against the church, on the suspicion that it might be a secret society, formed for seditious purposes. Under these circumstances, it is difficult to conceive how a diocesan consolidation of the churches could have been established by the apostles without bringing down upon them the vengeance of the Roman government. Their harmless and informal assemblies, and the total absence of all connection one with another, was, according to Planck, the means of saving the early churches so long and so extensively from the exterminating sword of Roman jealousy.[3]

<blockquote>Crevit occulto, velut arbor, aevo.</blockquote>

3. Such an organization must have been formed to unite the discordant parties in the primitive churches.

Here was the Jew, the Greek, the Roman, and Barbarians of every form of superstition; converts, indeed, to faith in Christ, but with all their partialities and prejudices still. What but a voluntary principle, guaranteeing to all the freedom of a popular assembly, could unite these parties in one fraternity? Our Lord himself employed no artificial bands to bind his followers together into a permanent body; and they were alienated from him upon the slightest offence. The apostles had still less to bind their adherents firmly to themselves. It required all their wisdom and address to reconcile the discordant prejudices of their converts and unite them in harmonious fellowship one with another. This difficulty met the apostles at the outset of their ministry, in the murmuring of the Greeks against the Jews, that

---

[3] Gesellschafts-Verfass, I. S. 40-50.

their widows were neglected in the daily ministration. This mutual jealousy was a continual trial besetting them on every side. Under such circumstances, they assumed not the responsibility of settling these controversies by apostolical or episcopal authority. Everything relating to the interests of each church they left to be publicly discussed and decided by mutual consent. In this manner they quieted these complaints of the Greeks respecting the distribution of alms, Acts vi. 1–8. And such, of necessity, became their settled policy in their care of the churches. Even the apostles were not exempt from these infirmities and misunderstandings, and might have found no small difficulty in arranging among themselves a more artificial and complicated system of church government.[4]

4. The same is inferred from the existence of popular rights and privileges in the early periods of the Christian church.

Had the doctrine of the rights of the people been totally lost in the second and third centuries, this would by no means warrant the inference that such rights were unknown in the days of the apostles. They all might have been swept away by the irresistible tide of clerical influence and authority. But they were not lost. They were asserted even in the fourth and fifth centuries, and long after the hierarchy was established in connection with the state, and its authority enforced by imperial power.

5. A popular form of church government harmonizes with the spirit, the instructions and the example of Christ.

[4] Schroeter und Klein, Für Christenthum Oppositionsschrift, I. S. 567. Siegel, Handbuch, II. 455–6. Arnold, Wahre-Abbildung der Ersten Christen, B. II. c. 5, seq. Schoene, Geschichtsforschungen d. Kirch. Gebräuch, I. S. 234–5.

(a) *With his spirit.* He was of a meek and lowly spirit unostentatious and unassuming. He shrank from the demonstrations of power, and refused the titles and honors that, at times, were pressed upon his acceptance. With such a spirit, that religious system must be congenial which, without any parade of titles and of rank, has few offices, and little to excite the pride or tempt the ambition of man.

(b) *With his instructions.* Ye know that the princes of the Gentiles exercise dominion over them, and they that are great exercise authority upon them, but it shall not be so among you; but whosoever will be great among you, let him be your minister; and whosoever will be chief among you, let him be your servant; even as the Son of man came, not to be ministered unto, but to minister, and to give his life a ransom for many, Matt. xx. 25–28; Comp. Mark x. 42–45.

(c) *With his example.* This was in perfect coincidence with his instructions, and a striking illustration of his spirit. His life was a pattern of humility, of untiring, unostentatious benevolence. He condescended to the condition of all; and, as one of the latest and most expressive acts of his life, washed his disciples' feet, giving them an example for their imitation, as the servants of all men. Has such a spirit its just expression in a hierarchy, which has often dishonored the religion of Christ by the display of princely pomp and the assumption of regal and imperial power?[5]

6. It equally accords with the spirit, the instructions and the example of the apostles.

(a) *With their spirit.* They had renounced their hopes of aggrandizement in the kingdom of Christ, and had im-

---

[5] The French infidels have an expression relating to our Saviour, which, though impious and profane, clearly indicates the nature of his instructions and example: "*Jesus Christ, the great Democrat.*"

bibed much of his spirit. The world took knowledge of them that they had been with Jesus, and had learned of him, who was meek and lowly of heart. This spirit must be foreign from the distinctions of rank and of office, as well as from the authority and power which are inherent in every form of the episcopal system.

(*b*) *With their instructions.* These were in coincidence with those of their Master. They disowned personal authority over the church; and instructed the elders not to lord it over God's heritage, but to be examples to the flock, 1 Pet. v. 3. If, in the discharge of his ministry, one has occasion to reprove sin in an elder, this he is charged, before God and the elect angels, to do with all circumspection, without prejudice or partiality, 1 Tim. v. 21.

(*c*) *With their example.* This is the best comment upon their instructions, and the clearest indication of that organization which the church received at their hands. They exercised, indeed, a controlling influence over the several churches which they established, as an American missionary does in organizing his Christian converts into a church, while he constitutes them a popular assembly under a Congregational or Presbyterian form. In like manner, it is observable that the apostles studiously declined the exercise of prelatical or episcopal authority.[6] The control which they at first exercised in the management of the affairs of the church was no part of their office. It was only a temporary expedient, resulting from the necessity of the case. In support of this position we offer the following considerations:

---

[6] Planck, Gesellschafts-Verfass, 1. S. 39. Spittler, Can. Recht, c. 1. § 3. Pertsch, Can. Recht, c. 1. § 5–8. Siegel, Kirchliche Verfassungsformen, in Handbuch, II. S. 455. Pertsch, Kirch. Hist. I. S. 156–170, 362–370.

(α) They addressed the members of the church as *brethren* and *sisters* and fellow-laborers. I would not have you ignorant, brethren, that oftentimes I purposed to come unto you, Rom. i. 13; Comp. 1 Cor. ii. 1; Rom. xvi. 1. The same familiar, affectionate style of address runs through all the epistles, showing in what consideration the apostles held all the members of the church. "The apostles severally were very far from placing themselves in a relation that bore any analogy to a mediating priesthood. In this respect they always placed themselves on a footing of equality. If Paul assured them of his intercessory prayers for them, he in return requested their prayers for himself."[7]

(β) The apostles remonstrated with the members of the church as with *brethren*, instead of rebuking them authoritatively. Now I *beseech* you, brethren, by the name of our Lord Jesus Christ, that ye all speak the same thing, and that there be no divisions among you, 1 Cor. i. 10; Comp. 1 Thess. iv. 1; James ii. 1. They spoke not by *commandment*, but in the language of mutual counselors, 1 Cor. xi. 13–16.[8]

(γ) They treated with the church as an independent body, competent to judge and act for itself. They appealed to the judgment of their brethren personally, 1 Cor. xi. 13–16; 1 Thess. v. 21. They reported their own doings to the church, as if amenable to that body, Acts xi. 1–18; xiv. 26, 27.

(δ) They exhorted the churches to deeds of charity and benevolence; but submitted to each individual the disposal of his goods and his charities, Acts v. 4; xi. 29, 30, etc.; 1 Cor. xvi. 1, seq.; 2 Cor. ix. 1, seq.

(ε) They addressed their epistles not to the pastors of the

---

[7] Neander, Apostol. Kirch., I. p. 161, 3d edit.; and in the sequel much more to the same effect. Trans. I. 150.

[8] Comp. Socrates, Hist. Eccl. Lib. 5. c. 22.

churches, but to the churches, or to the churches and pastors, collectively, giving precedence, in some instances, to the church, Phil. i. 1. Even the epistles which treat of controverted ecclesiastical matters are addressed not to the bishops and presbyters, but to the *whole body of believers*, indicating that the decision belonged to them.

(ζ) They recognized the right of the churches to send out their own religious teachers and messengers, as they might have occasion, Acts xi. 19–24; xv. 32, 33; 2 Cor. viii. 23; Phil. ii. 25; 1 Cor. xvi. 3, 4. These deputations, and the power of sending them, indicate the independent authority of the churches.

(η) They united with the church in mutual consultation upon doubtful questions. The brethren took part in the dissension with Peter, for having preached unto the Gentiles, Acts xi. 1–18. The apostles united with them in the discussion of the question which was submitted to them by the delegation from Antioch, and the result was published in the name of the apostles and the *brethren*, jointly, Acts xv. 1, seq.

(θ) They submitted to the church the settlement of their own difficulties. The appointment of the seven deacons, to obviate the murmurs of the Greeks, was made at the suggestion of the apostles, but the election was wholly the act of the church, Acts vi. 1–6. The apostles refused any authoritative arbitration in the case; and required the churches to choose arbitrators among themselves to settle their own litigations, 1 Cor. xi. 1, seq.

(ι) They entrusted the church with the important right of electing its own officers.[9] As in the case of the seven

---

[9] Clement of Rome, Ep. ad Cor., A. D. 98, § 44, states it as a rule received from the apostles, that the appointment of church officers should be with the consent of the whole church, συνευδοκησάσης τῆς ἐκκλησίας πάσης.

deacons, which we have just stated, the apostles refused even the responsibility of supplying, in their own number, the place of the traitor Judas, but submitted the choice to the assembly of the disciples, Acts i. 15, seq. In this connection should the appointment of elders, Acts xiv. 23, also be mentioned, as may hereafter appear.

(z) The apostles submitted to the church the discipline of its members; as in the case of the incestuous person, who was excommunicated and afterward restored to the church by that body. "The relation of presbyters to the church was not that of rulers with monarchical powers, but of the officers of an ecclesiastical republic. In all things they were to act in connection with the church, and to perform their duties as the servants, and not the lords of the church. The apostles recognized the same relation. The apostle Paul, when speaking of the excommunication of the incestuous person at Corinth, regards himself as united in spirit with the whole church, 1 Cor. v. 4, thus indicating the principle that their co-operation was required in all such cases of general interest." [10]

The churches, therefore, which were planted by the apostles, were under their sanction organized as independent popular assemblies, with power to elect officers, adopt rules, administer discipline, and to do all those acts which belong to such deliberative bodies.

7. The popular government of the primitive church is apparent from its analogy to the Jewish synagogue.

This and each of the following articles, under this head, will be the subjects of consideration in another place. They are assumed as so many separate heads of argumentation, so far as they may appear to be founded in truth. Comp. Chap. II.

[10] Neander, Allgem. Gesch., I. S. 324, 2d ed. Tr. I. p. 190.

8. The primitive churches were, severally, independent bodies, in Christian fellowship, but having no confederate relations one toward another.

"The power of enacting laws, of appointing teachers and ministers, and of determining controversies, was lodged in the people at large; nor did the apostles, though invested with divine authority, either resolve or sanction anything whatever without the knowledge and concurrence of the general body of Christians of which the church was composed." [11] Comp. Chap. III.

9. These churches severally enjoyed the inherent right of every independent body—that of choosing their own officers. Comp. Chap. IV.

10. In the apostolical and primitive churches the right of discipline was vested not in the clergy, but in each church collectively.[12]

Even the officers of the church were subject to the authority of the same. Clement recognizes this authority in his epistles to the Corinthians.[13] Comp. Chap. V.

11. The appropriate officers of the church were deacons

---

[11] De Rebus Christ., etc., § 1, 37. To the same effect, also, is the authority of Neander, Apost. Kirch. pp. 1, 161, 201, 214, 3d ed.

[12] Primo omnibus ecclesiae membris jus eligendi pastores et diaconos erat. Communicatio erat quaedam inter varios coetus christianos vel ecclesias; literae quas altera acceperat alteri legendae mittebantur. Pecunias ad pauperes sublevandos ecclesia ecclesiae donabat. De rebus fidei et disciplinae jam apostoli deliberaverunt. Quaequae ecclesia exercebat jus excommunicandi eos qui doctrinae et vitae christianae renunciaverant, eosque recipiendi quorum poenitentia et mentis mutatio constabat. Sic prima christianorum ecclesia libertate, concordia, sanctitate floruit. Sack Comment, ad Theol. Inst., p. 141.

[13] Epist. § 54, comp. 44. Also Pertsch, Kirch. Hist. I. 362.

and pastors. These pastors were denominated indiscriminately bishops, *overseers*, and elders, *presbyters*, and were at first identical.[14] Comp. Chap. VI.

Greiling, after going through with an examination of the government of the apostolical churches, gives the following summary: "In the age of the apostles there was no primate of the churches, but the entire equality of brethren prevailed. The apostles themselves exercised no kind of authority or power over the churches, but styled themselves their helpers and servants. The settlement of controverted points, the adoption of new rites, the discipline of the church, the election of presbyters, and even the choice of an apostle, were submitted to the church. The principle on which the apostles proceeded was, that the *church*, that is, the elders and the members of the church unitedly, were the depositaries of all their social rights; that *no others* could exercise this right but those to whom the church might entrust it, and who were accordingly amenable to the church. Even the apostles, though next to Christ himself, invested with the highest authority, assumed no superiority over the presbyters, but treated them as brethren, and styled themselves fellow-presbyters, thus recognizing them as associates in office." [15]

Finally, the worship of the primitive churches was remarkable for its freedom and simplicity. Their religious rites were few and simple, and restrained by no complicated ritual or prescribed ceremonials. This point is considered at length in a subsequent part of the work.

The government throughout was wholly popular. Every church adopted its own regulations and enacted its own laws. These laws were administered by officers elected by

[14] Neander, Apost. Kirch. I. p. 1, 184. Tr. I. p. 168.
[15] Apostol. Christengemeine. Halberstadt, 1819.

the church. No church was dependent upon another. They were represented in synod by their own delegates. Their discipline was administered not by the clergy, but by the people or the church collectively. And even after ordination became the exclusive right of the bishop, no one was permitted to preach to any congregation who was not approved and duly accepted by the congregation. All their religious worship was conducted on the same principles of freedom and equality.

Such was the organization of the Christian church in its primitive simplicity and purity. The national peculiarities of the Jewish and Gentile converts in some degree modified individual churches, but the form of government was substantially the same in all. We claim not for it authority absolutely imperative and divine, to the exclusion of every other system; but it has, we must believe, enough of precept, of precedent and of principle, to give it a sanction truly apostolic. Its advantages and practical results justly claim an attentive consideration.

CHAPTER II.

THE PRIMITIVE CHURCHES FORMED AFTER THE MODEL OF THE JEWISH SYNAGOGUE.

THE apostles and the first disciples were Jews, who, after their conversion, retained the prejudices and partialities of their nation. They observed still all the rites of their religion; and, firmly believing that salvation by Christ belonged only to the circumcision, they refused the ministry of reconciliation to the Gentiles. All their national peculiarities led them to conform the Christian to the Jewish church.

With the temple-service and the Mosaic ritual, however, Christianity had no affinity. The sacrificial offerings of the temple and the Levitical priesthood it abolished. But in the synagogue-worship the followers of Christ found a more congenial institution. It invited them to the reading of the Scriptures and to prayer. It gave them liberty of speech in exhortation and in worshiping and praising God. The rules and government of the synagogue, while they offered little, comparatively, to excite the pride of office and of power, commended themselves the more to the humble believer in Christ. The synagogue was endeared to the devout Jew by sacred associations and tender recollections. It was near at hand, and not, like the temple, afar off. He went but seldom up to Jerusalem, and only on great occasions joined in the rites of temple-service. But in the synagogue he paid his constant devotions to the God of his fathers. It met his eye in every place. It was constantly before him, and from infancy to hoary age he was accustomed to repair to that hallowed place of worship, to listen to the reading of his sacred books, to pray and sing praises unto the God of Israel. The reading of the Scriptures was followed with familiar remarks, and exhortations upon the portion read, by priests, elders, scribes, and intelligent members of the assembly, or strangers in attendance. Thus our Lord habitually taught in the synagogues as he journeyed from place to place, Luke iv. 15, 44; Matt. iv. 28; ix. 35; John xviii. 20.[1]

In accordance with this usage, the apostles also continued to frequent the synagogues of the Jews. Wherever they went they resorted to these places of worship, and strove to convert their brethren to faith in Christ, not as a new religion, but as a modification of their own. The freedom of synagogue-worship accorded to them everywhere a hearing. "Men and brethren, if ye have any word of exhortation for the people, say on," Acts xiii. 15. Thus, at Salamis, xiii. 5; at Iconium, xiv. 1; at Berea, xvii. 10; at Ephesus, xviii. 19, they reasoned in the synagogues with the Jews, preaching the gospel of Christ.

In their own religious assemblies they also conformed, as far as was consistent with the spirit of the Christian religion, to the same rites, and gradually settled upon a church-organization which harmonized in a remarkable manner with that of the Jewish synagogue. They even retained the same *name* as the appellation of their Christian assemblies. "If there come into your assembly, συναγωγήν—if there come into your *synagogue*—a man with a gold ring," etc, James ii. 2. Compare also ἐπισυναγωγήν, Heb. x. 25.

[1] Comp., also Philo., II. 458, 630, cited in Hertzog's Encyclop. 15, 311.

Their modes of worship were substantially the same as those of the synagogue. The *titles of their officers* they also borrowed from the same source. The titles bishop, pastor, presbyter, etc., were familiar to them as synonymous terms denoting the same class of officers in the synagogue. Their duties and prerogatives remained in substance the same in the Christian church as in that of the Jews.

So great was this similarity between the primitive Christian churches and the Jewish synagogues that by the Pagan nations they were mistaken for the same institutions. Pagan historians uniformly treated the primitive Christians as Jews.[2] As such they suffered under the persecutions of their idolatrous rulers. These, and many other particulars that might be mentioned, are sufficient to show that the ecclesiastical polity of the Jewish synagogue was very closely copied by the apostles and primitive Christians in the organization of their assemblies.

In support of the foregoing statements, authorities to any extent and of the highest character might easily be adduced. Let the following, however, suffice, from Neander: "The disciples had not yet attained a clear understanding of that call, which Christ had already given them by so many intimations, to form a church entirely separated from the existing Jewish economy; to that economy they adhered as much as possible; all the forms of the national theocracy were sacred in their esteem; it seemed the natural element of their religious consciousness, though a higher principle of life had been imparted, by which that consciousness was to be progressively inspired and transformed. As the believers, in opposition to the mass of the Jewish nation who remained hardened in their unbelief, now formed a community internally bound together by the one faith in Jesus

---

[2] Vitringa, De Synagog. Vet., Prolegom. pp. 3, 4.

as the Messiah, and by the consciousness of the higher life received from him, it was necessary that this internal union should assume a certain external form. And a model for such a smaller community within the great national theocracy already existed among the Jews, along with the temple worship, namely, *the synagogues.* The means of religious edification which they supplied took account of the religious welfare of all, and consisted of united prayers and the addresses of individuals who applied themselves to the study of the Old Testament. These means of edification closely corresponded to the nature of the new Christian worship. This form of social worship, as it was copied in all the religious communities founded on Judaism (such as the Essenes), was also adopted, to a certain extent, at the first formation of the Christian church. But it may be disputed whether the apostles, to whom Christ committed the chief direction of affairs, designed from the first that believers should form a society exactly on the model of the synagogue, and, in pursuance of this plan, instituted particular offices for the government of the church corresponding to that model; or whether, without such a preconceived plan, distinct offices were appointed, as circumstances required, in doing which they would avail themselves of the model of the synagogue with which they were familiar."[3] "We are disposed to believe that the church was at first composed entirely of members standing on an equality with one another, and that the apostles alone held a higher rank, and exercised a directing influence over the whole, which arose from the original position in which Christ had placed them in relation to other believers; so that the whole arrangement and administration of the affairs of the church proceeded from them, and they were first induced by particular cir-

---

[3] Apost. Kirch. 3d edit. p. 31. Trans. I. 33. Comp. 179, 198.

cumstances to appoint other church officers, as in the instance of deacons."⁴ To the same effect is also Neander's account of this subject in his Church History, where he shows that this organization of Christian churches was the most natural under existing circumstances, and the most acceptable not only to Jewish converts, but to those who were gathered from the subjects of the Roman government.⁵ If the reader require other authority on this subject, he has only to examine Vitringa, De Synagoga Vetere, especially his third book, to say nothing of Selden, Lightfoot and many others. Vitringa himself has fully sustained the bold title which he gives to his immortal work: "Three books on the ancient Synagogue; in which it is *demonstrated* that the form of government and of the ministry in the synagogue was transferred to the Christian church."

These views are fully avowed by Archbishop Whately with his usual independence and candor. "It is probable that one cause, humanly speaking, why we find in the Sacred Books less information concerning the Christian ministry and the constitution of church-governments than we otherwise might have found, is that these institutions had less of *novelty* than some would at first sight suppose, and that many portions of them did not wholly originate with the apostles. It appears highly probable—I might say, morally certain—that, wherever a Jewish synagogue existed, that was brought—the whole, or the chief part of it—to embrace the gospel, the apostles did not, there, so much *form* a Christian church (or congregation,* *ecclesia*), as

⁴ P. 33. Comp. 195, seq. So, also, Rothe, Anfänge, S. 146–148.
⁵ Kirchen. Gesch. I. S. 183–185. Trans. 184.

* The word "*congregation*," as it stands in our version of the Old Testament (and it is one of very frequent occurrence in the Books of Moses), is found to correspond, in the Septuagint, which was familiar to the New Testament writers, to *ecclesia*; the word which, in our ver-

make an *existing* congregation *Christian;* by introducing the Christian sacraments and worship, and establishing whatever regulations were requisite for the newly-adopted faith; leaving the machinery (if I may so speak) of government unchanged; the "rulers of synagogues, elders and other officers (whether spiritual or ecclesiastical, or both) being already provided in the existing institutions. And it is likely that several of the earliest Christian churches did originate in this way; that is, that they were *converted synagogues;* which *became* Christian churches as soon as the members, or the main part of the members, acknowledged Jesus as the Messiah.

"The attempt to effect this conversion of a Jewish synagogue into a Christian church seems always to have been made, in the first instance, in every place where there was an opening for it. Even after the call of the idolatrous Gentiles, it appears plainly to have been the practice of the apostles Paul and Barnabas, when they came to any city in which there was a synagogue, to go thither first and deliver their sacred message to the Jews and 'devout (or proselyte) Gentiles;' according to their own expression (Acts xiii. 17), to the 'men of Israel and those *that feared* God:' adding, that 'it was necessary that the word of God should first be preached to them.' And when they founded a church in any of those cities in which (and such were, probably, a very large majority) there was no Jewish synagogue that received the gospel, it is likely they would still conform, in a great measure, to the same model."[6]

"A Jewish synagogue or a collection of synagogues in the same neighborhood became at once a Christian church

sion of these last, is always rendered not "congregation," but "*church.*" This, or its equivalent, "kirk," is probably no other than "circle;" *i. e.*, assembly, *ecclesia.*

[6] Kingdom of Christ, pp. 83-85.

as soon as the worshipers or a considerable portion of them had embraced the gospel and had separated themselves from unbelievers."[7]

It is an admitted fact, as clearly settled as anything can be by human authority, that the primitive Christians, in the organization of their assemblies, formed them after the model of the Jewish synagogue. They discarded the splendid ceremonials of the temple-service, and retained the simple rites of the synagogue-worship. They disowned the hereditary aristocracy of the Levitical priesthood,[8] and adopted the popular government of the synagogue.[9]

We are here presented with an important fact in the organization of the primitive churches strongly illustrative of the popular character of their constitution and government. The synagogue was essentially a popular assembly, invested with the rights and possessing the powers which are essential to the enjoyment of religious liberty. Their government was voluntary, elective, free, and administered by rulers or elders elected by the people. The ruler of the synagogue was the moderator of the college of elders, but only *primus inter pares*, holding no official rank above them.[10] The people, as Vitringa has shown,[11] appointed

[7] Whately's Hist. of Relig. Worship, p. 114.

[8] The prelatical reference of the Christian ministry to the Levitical priesthood is a device of a later age, though it has been common from the time of Cyprian down to the present time.

[9] Totum regimen ecclesiasticum conformatum fuit ad synagogarum exemplar. Hugo Grotius, Comment. ad Act. xi. 30.

[10] Vitringa, De Vet. Syn. L. 3. c. 16.

[11] Comp. Vitringa, De Synagoga, Lib. 3. P. 1. c. 15, pp. 828–863. Nihil actum absque ecclesia, [*i. e.*, the synagogue] quae in publico consulta est, et quidem hac ipsa formula: וְהָגוּן עֲלֵיכֶם sive ἄξιος quam in vertere ecclesia in eligendis episcopis adhibitam meminimus, p. 829. In vita Josephi, ... publica omnia ibi tractari videmus in synagogis, *consulto populo,* p. 832.

their own officers to rule over them. They exercised the natural right of freemen to enact and execute their own laws, to admit proselytes, and to exclude, at pleasure, unworthy members from their communion. Theirs was "*a democratical form of government*," and is so described by one of the most able expounders of the constitution of the primitive churches.[12] Like their prototype, therefore, the primitive churches also embodied the principle of a popular government and of enlightened religious liberty.

Before the Babylonish captivity, the Jews were perpetually falling away into the prevailing idolatries of the age. The imposing ritual of the temple service failed to hold them fast in their allegiance to God. After their return from this captivity, synagogue worship was introduced, and, in time, became universal. In the age of Christ there were four hundred and sixty or four hundred and eighty synagogues in Jerusalem, and in like proportion in other cities. Here the Scriptures, divided into fifty-two lessons, were read every Sabbath day, so that the reading of the entire roll was completed every year. And by this reading of God's Word the Jews have held fast, with remarkable tenacity, the faith of their fathers; so that only by a miracle of sovereign grace is one of them converted to faith in Christ. Such is the power of divine truth to maintain the doctrines of our religion. The power of this truth, as presented in the synagogues of the Jews above the ceremonials of the Mosaic ritual, in maintaining the steadfastness of their faith, is worthy of profound consideration. It illustrates the inefficacy of ritualistic forms to defend the faith once delivered to the saints.

[12] Rothe, Anfänge der Christ. Kirch. S. 14.

CHAPTER III.

INDEPENDENCE OF THE PRIMITIVE CHURCHES.

The churches which were established by the apostles and their disciples exhibit a remarkable example of unanimity. One in faith and the fellowship of love, they were united in spirit as different members of one body, or as brethren of the same family.[1] This union and fellowship of spirit the apostles carefully promoted among all the churches. But they instituted no external form of union or confederation between those of different towns or provinces; nor, within the first century of the Christian era, can any trace of such a confederacy, whether diocesan or conventional, be detected on the page of history. Wherever converts to Christianity were multiplied they formed themselves into a church, under the guidance of their religious teachers, for the enjoyment of Christian ordinances. But each individual church constituted an independent and separate community. The society was purely voluntary, and every church so constituted was strictly independent of all others in the conduct of its worship, the admission of its members, the exercise of its discipline, the choice of its officers and the entire management of its affairs. They were independent republics. " Each individual church which had a bishop or presbyter of its own assumed to itself the form and rights of a little distinct republic or commonwealth; and with regard to its internal concerns was wholly regulated by a code of laws

---

[1] 1 Cor. xii. 12, 13; Eph. ii. 20; iv. 3.

that, if they did not originate with, had at least received the sanction of the people constituting such church." [2]

Particular neighboring churches may for various reasons have sustained peculiar fraternal relations to each other. Local and other circumstances may, in time, have given rise to correspondence between churches more remote, or to mutual consultations by letter and by delegates, as in the instance of the churches at Antioch and Jerusalem, Acts xv., and of Corinth and Rome;[3] but no established jurisdiction was exercised by one over the other. The church at Jerusalem, with the apostles and elders, addressed the church at Antioch, not in the language of authority, but of *advice*. Nor does ancient history, sacred or profane, relating to this early period, record an instance in which one church presumed to impose laws of its own upon another.

"On the contrary, several things occur therein which put it out of all doubt that every one of them enjoyed the same rights, and was considered as being on a footing of the most perfect equality with the rest. Indeed it cannot, I will not say be proved, but even be made to appear probable, from testimony human or divine, that in this age it was the practice for several churches to enter into and maintain among themselves that sort of association which afterward came to subsist among the churches of almost every province. I allude to their assembling by their bishops, at stated periods, for the purpose of enacting general laws and determining any questions or controversies that might arise respecting divine matters. It is not until the second century that any traces of that sort of association from whence councils took their origin are to be perceived." [4]

[2] Mosheim, De Rebus Christ., Saec. II. § 22. Comp. Neander, Allgemein. Gesch., I. 291, 2. Trans. p. 184.

[3] See Epistle of Clement of Rome to the Corinthians.

[4] De Rebus Christ., Saec. I. § 48.

INDEPENDENCE OF THE CHURCHES.

Indications of this original independence are distinctly manifest even after the rise of episcopacy. Every bishop had the right to form his own liturgy and creed, and to settle at pleasure his own time and mode of celebrating the religious festivals.[5] Cyprian strongly asserts the right of every bishop to make laws for his own church. Socrates assigns this original independence of the bishops as the principal cause of the endless controversies in the church respecting the observance of Easter and other festivals.[6]

But we need not enlarge. Nothing in the history of the primitive churches is more incontrovertible than the fact of their absolute independence one of another. It is attested by the highest historical authorities, and appears to be generally conceded by episcopal authors themselves. "At first," says the learned Dr. Barrow, "every church was settled apart under its own bishop and presbyters, so as independently and separately to manage its own concerns. Each was governed by its own head and had its own laws."[7]

"The apostles or their representatives exercised a general superintendence over the churches by divine authority, attested by miraculous gifts. The subordinate government of each particular church was vested in itself; that is to say, the whole body elected its ministers and officers, and was consulted concerning all matters of importance. All churches were independent of each other, but were united by the bonds of holy charity, sympathy and friendship."[8]

Similar views are also expressed by Archbishop Whately: "Though there was one Lord, one faith, one baptism, for all of these, yet they were each a distinct, independent com-

---

[5] Greiling, Apostol. Christengemeine, S. 16.
[6] Eccles. Hist. Lib. 5, c. 22.
[7] Treatise on Pope's Supremacy, Works, Vol. I. p. 662. Comp. King's Prim. Christ. c. 12, p. 14, also 136.
[8] Riddle's Chronology, Beginning of Second Century.

munity on earth, united by the common principles on which they were founded by their mutual agreement, affection and respect; but not having any one recognized head on earth, or acknowledging any sovereignty of one of those societies over others."⁹ "The apostles founded Christian communities, churches, all *based on the same principles* and having the same *object* in view, but quite independent of each other, and having no common head on earth.

"Besides the several churches in Judea, in Galilee, in Samaria and elsewhere, we find the apostle Paul himself founding many distinct churches, both in Asia and in Europe. And it does not appear that these have any common head on earth except himself; nor that he appointed any one to succeed him in having the care of all the churches."[10] Now what, according to these episcopal concessions, was the bishop at first, but the pastor of a single church, a *parochial bishop*, exercising only the jurisdiction and enjoying the rights of an independent pastor of a church? But more of this hereafter.

Several of the ancient churches firmly asserted and maintained their original religious liberty by refusing to acknowledge the authority of the ancient councils for a long time after the greater part of the churches had subjected themselves to the authority of these confederacies. The church in Africa, for example, and some of the Eastern churches, although they adopted the custom of holding councils, and were in correspondence with these churches, declined entering into any grand Christian confederation with them; and continued for some time inflexibly tenacious of their own just liberty and independence. This their example is an effectual refutation of those who pretend that these councils were divinely appointed and had, *jure divino*, authority over

---

[9] Kingdom of Christ. N. Y. 1842; p. 110, 136.
[10] Whately's Hist. of Relig. Worship, pp. 101-2.

INDEPENDENCE OF THE CHURCHES. 49

the churches. Who can suppose that these churches would have asserted their independence so sternly against an institution appointed by our Lord or his apostles?[11]

The early independence of the churches, then, is conceded even by Episcopalians themselves. It has both the sanction of apostolic precedent and the concurring authority of ecclesiastical writers, ancient and modern. This is a point strongly illustrative of the religious freedom which was the basis of their original polity. This independence of particular churches is the great central principle, the original element, of their popular constitution and government. It vests the authority and power of each church in its own members collectively. It guards their rights. It guarantees to them the elective franchise, and ensures to them the enjoyment of religious liberty under a government administered by the voice of the majority or delegated at pleasure to their representatives. The constitution of the churches and their mutual relations may not have been precisely Congregational or Presbyterian, but they involved the principles of the religious freedom and the popular rights which both are designed to protect.

[11] Even the council of Nice, in treating of the authority of the metropolitan bishops of Rome, Antioch and Alexandria, rests the dignity and authority of these prelates not on any *divine right*, but solely on ancient usage. Τὰ ἀρχαῖα ἔθη κρατείτω, etc., ἐπειδὴ καὶ τῷ ἐν τῇ Ῥώμῃ ἐπισκόπῳ σύνηθές ἐστιν, Can. 6. Comp. Du Pin, Antiq. Eccl. Disciplina, Diss. 1. § 7. Mosheim, De Rebus Christ., Saec. II. § 23, Note.

CHAPTER IV.

ELECTIONS BY THE CHURCH.

The right of suffrage is the first requsite of civil and religious liberty. Without it, in church or state, man is a serf, a vassal, a slave, restrained in the enjoyment of his inalienable rights of life, liberty and the pursuit of happiness. This right, early abridged and finally usurped and destroyed by the hierarchy, was from the beginning enjoyed in the Christian church. The first public act of this body was a formal recognition and a legitimate exercise of this right. First in importance among their popular rights, they maintained it with greater constancy than any other against the usurpations of prelatical power, and resigned it last of all into the hands of their spiritual oppressors. The subject of the following chapter leads us to consider,

I. The evidence that the right of suffrage was enjoyed by the primitive church.

II. The time and means of the extinction of this right.

I. The members of the primitive church enjoyed the right of electing, by a popular vote, their own officers and teachers. The evidence in support of this position is derived from the writings of the apostles and of the early fathers. In the former we have on record instances of the election of an apostle, and of deacons, delegates and presbyters of

ELECTIONS BY THE CHURCH.

the church, each by a popular vote of that body. From the latter we learn that the church continued for several centuries subsequent to the age of the apostles in the enjoyment of the elective franchise.

1. The scriptural argument, from the writings of the apostles.

(a) The election of an apostle.

The first public act of the church after our Lord's ascension was the choice of a substitute in the place of the apostate apostle, Judas. This election was made, not by the apostles themselves, but by the joint action of the whole body of believers. If, in any instance, the apostles had the right, by their own independent authority, to invest another with the ministerial office, we might expect them to exercise that prerogative in supplying this vacancy in their own body. That right, however, they virtually disclaimed, by submitting the election to the arbitration of the assembled body of believers. The *election* was the act of the assembly, and was made either by casting lots or by an elective vote. Mosheim understands the phrase, ἔδωκαν κλήρους αὐτῶν, to express *the casting of a popular vote* by the Christians. To express the *casting of lots*, according to this author, the verb should have been ἔβαλον, as in Matt. xxvii. 35; Luke xxiii. 34; John xix. 24; Mark xv. 24. Comp. Septuagint, Ps. xxii. 19; Joel iii. 3; Nah. iii. 10, which also accords with the usage of Homer in similar cases.[1] But the phrase, ἔδωκαν κλήρους, according to this author, expresses the casting of a popular vote; the term, κλῆρος, being used in the sense of ψῆφος, a *suffrage or vote*, so that what the evangelist meant to say was simply this: "and those who were present gave their votes."[2]

---

[1] Iliad, 23, 352. Odyss. 14, 209.
[2] De Rebus Christ., Saec. 1, § 14, Note.

The precise mode of determining the election, perhaps, cannot be fully settled. But the persons who gave the vote appear to have been the whole body of believers then present. When we compare this election with that of the deacons, which soon followed, and consider the uniform custom of the disciples to submit to the church the enacting of their own laws, and the exercise of their popular rights, in other respects, we must regard the election before us as the joint act of the brethren there assembled. For this opinion we have high historical authority. "The whole company of believers had a part in supplying the number of the apostles themselves, and the choice was their joint act."[3] "At the request of the apostles, the church chose, by lot, Matthias for an apostle, in the place of Judas."[4] "Without doubt, those expositors adopt the right view, who suppose that not only the apostles, but all the believers were at that time assembled; for, though in Acts i. 26, the apostles are primarily intended, yet the *disciples collectively* form the chief subject, Acts i. 15, to which *all* at the beginning of the next chapter successively refers."[5] This is said with reference to the assembly on the day of Pentecost, but the reasoning shows distinctly the views of the author respecting the persons who composed the assembly at the election of Matthias. "In all decisions and acts, even in the election of the twelfth apostle, the church had a voice."[6] Even after the rise of episcopacy the bishop was frequently chosen by lot from a number of candidates previously elected by the people.[7]

[3] Röhr, Kritischen Predigerbibliothek. Bd. 13. Heft. 6.

[4] D. Grossmann, Ueber eine Reformation der protestantischen Kirchenverfassung in Königreiche Sachsen. Leipzig, 1833, S. 47.

[5] Neander, Apost. Kirch. I. c. 1. Note.

[6] Greiling, Apostol. Kirchengemeine, S. 15.

[7] Bingham B. IV. Chap. i. § 1. Cotelerius II. App. p. 180. τὸν τῆς επισκοπῆς κλῆρον, Irenaeus.

Chrysostom's exposition of the passage, confirmed as it is also by Cyprian, may, without doubt, be received as a fair expression of the sentiments and usages of the early church on this subject. "Peter did everything here with the common consent; nothing, by his own will and authority. He left the judgment to the multitude, to secure the respect to the elected, and to free himself from every invidious reflection." After quoting the words, "they appointed two," he adds, "he did not himself appoint them, it was the act of all."[8]

The order of the transaction appears to have been as follows: Peter stands up in the midst of the disciples, convened in assembly to the number of one hundred and twenty, and explaining to them the necessity of choosing another apostle in the place of the apostate Judas, urges them to proceed to the election. The whole assembly then designate two of their number as candidates for the office, and after prayer for divine direction, all cast lots, and the lot falls upon Matthias;[9] or, according to Mosheim, all cast their *votes*, and the vote falls upon Matthias. Whatever may have been the *mode* of the election, it was a popular vote, and indicates the inherent right of the people to make the election.

(*b*) The election of the seven deacons, Acts vi. 1-6.

Here again the proposition originated with the apostles. It was received with approbation by the whole multitude, who immediately proceeded to make the election by a united and public vote. The order of the transaction is very clearly marked. The apostles propose to "the multitude of the disciples" the appointment of the seven, The proposal is favorably received by "the whole multitude,"

---

[8] Hom. ad locum, Vol. IX. p. 25. Comp. Cyprian, Ep. lxviii.; vi. 4.
[9] Rothe. Anfänge der Christ. Kirch. S. 149. Comp. Lange's Comm., Acts vi. 1-9.

who accordingly proceed to the choice of the proposed number, and set them before the apostles, not to ratify the election, but to induct them into office by the laying on of hands. This election is universally admitted to have been made by a popular vote, and may be passed without further remark. Indeed, "it is impossible," as Owen observes, "that there should be a more evident convincing instance and example of the free choice of ecclesiastical officers by the multitude or fraternity of the church, than is given us herein. Nor was there any ground or reason why this order and process should be observed, why the apostles would not themselves nominate and appoint persons, whom they saw and knew meet for this office to receive it, but that it was the right and liberty of the people, according to the mind of Christ, to choose their own officers, which they would not abridge or infringe."[10]

(c) The election of delegates of the churches.

These delegates were the fellow-laborers and assistants of the apostle, to accompany him in his travels, to assist in setting in order the churches, and generally to supply his lack of service to all the churches the care of which came upon him. Such, according to Rothe, was Timothy, whom he commends as his fellow-laborer, Rom. xvi. 21; 1 Thess. iii. 2, and associates with himself in his salutation to the churches, Phil. i. 1; 1 Thess. i. 1; 2 Thess. i. 1, etc. Such was Titus, 2 Cor. viii. 23; Silvanus, 1 Thess. i. 1; 2 Thess. i. 1; Mark, Coloss. iv. 10; 1 Peter v. 13; Clemens, Phil. iv. 3; Epaphras, Coloss. i. 7, etc.[11]

Whatever may have been the specific duties of this office, the appointment to it was made by a vote of the church. One such assistant Paul greatly commends, who was ap-

---

[10] Gospel Church, Chap. IV.
[11] Rothe, Anfänge, I. S. 305–307.

pointed by the church χειροτονηθεὶς ὑπὸ τῶν ἐκκλησιῶν, 2 Cor. viii. 19, as his traveling companion. To this and the election of the seven deacons Neander refers as evidence of the manner in which this popular right was exercised in the churches. "Inasmuch as the apostles submitted the appointment of the deacons to the vote of the church, and that of the delegates who should accompany them in the name of the churches, we may infer that a similar course was pursued also in the appointment of other officers of the church." [12]

Rothe appeals to the same example as a clear instance of a popular election, and adds, that it harmonizes with the authority of Clement of Rome, who states explictly that where the apostles had established churches they appointed bishops and deacons, "*with the approbation of the whole church*," συνευδοκησάσης τῆς ἐκκλησίας πάσης.[13]

(*d*) The election of presbyters or bishops.

That presbyters were elected by the church is a fair conclusion from the examples that have already been given. If the apostles submitted to the church the election of one of their number as an extraordinary and temporary minister, superior to presbyters, and of deacons as subordinates to them, much more may they be supposed to have submitted to the same body the election of their ordinary pastors and teachers, the presbyters or bishops. If there be any doubt as to the choice of Matthias by the church, there can be none of the election of the deacons and delegates by a popular vote. "That the presbyters of the primitive church of Jerusalem were elected by the suffrages of the people cannot, I think, well be doubted by any one who shall have duly considered the prudence and moderation

---

[12] Allgemein. Gesch. I. S. 290. Trans. 189.
[13] Anfänge, I. S. 151.

discovered by the apostles in filling up the vacancy in their own number and in appointing curators or guardians for the poor."[14] After having invested the churches with the right of electing their own officers, can the apostles be supposed to have invaded this sacred right by refusing to them the election of their own pastors and teachers?

These several instances of election chiefly relate to the church at Jerusalem. But wherever churches were planted by the apostles, they were, without doubt, organized after the original plan of that at Jerusalem; so that the above is a fair exhibition of the mode of appointment which generally prevailed in the churches. "The new churches everywhere formed themselves on the model of the mother church at Jerusalem."[15] "Since all these churches were constituted and formed after the model of that which was planted at Jerusalem, a review of the constitution and regulations of this one church alone will enable us to form a tolerably accurate conception of the form and discipline of all these primitive Christian assemblies."[16]

In the Gentile churches the popular principle is more strongly marked than in the Jewish, but the organization of all appears, at first, to have been essentially the same. At a later period, all may have been more or less modified by peculiar circumstances, and a greater difference may naturally appear in the government of different churches.

The conclusion therefore is, that the apostolical churches generally exercised the right of universal suffrage.

On the same principle, Paul and Barnabas may be presumed to have proceeded when, in their missionary tour,

---

[14] Mosheim, De Rebus Christ., Saec. I. § 39. Comp. Neander and Rothe, cited above.

[15] Gieseler. Cunningham's Trans. I. p. 56.

[16] Mosheim, De Rebus Christ., Saec. I. § 87. Comp. Whately's Hist. of Relig. Worship, p. 114.

they appointed presbyters in the churches which they visited, Acts xiv. 23. The question here turns wholly upon the interpretation of the term χειροτονήσαντες, "*when they had ordained;*" or, as in the margin, "*when with lifting up of hands they had chosen them.*"

If, according to the marginal reading, we understand, with our interpreters, the declaration to be, that the apostles made choice of these disciples, even this supposition does not necessarily exclude the members of the church themselves from participating in the election. It would imply, rather, that Paul and his companion proceeded in the usual way by calling the churches to the election of their own presbyters; just as in the instructions which Paul gives to Titus and to Timothy respecting the appointment of presbyters and deacons for the churches of Ephesus and Crete respectively, the participation of these churches in the appointment is of necessity presupposed. For, "from the fact that Paul, in committing to his pupils, as to Timothy and Titus, the organization of new churches or of those which had fallen into many distractions, committed to them also the appointment of the presbyters and deacons, and directed their attention to the qualifications requisite for such offices, *from this fact we are by no means to infer that they themselves effected this alone, without the participation of the churches.* Much more, indeed, does the manner in which Paul himself is elsewhere wont to address himself to the whole church and to claim the co-operation of the whole, authorize us to expect that, at least where there existed a church already established, he would have required their co-operation also in matters of common concern. But the supposition is certainly possible that the apostle in many cases, and especially in forming a new church, might think it best himself to propose to the church the persons best qualified for its officers, and such a nomination must naturally have had great weight. In the example of the family of Stephanas at Corinth, we see the members of the household first converted in the city becoming also the first to fill the offices of the church."[17] Neander also asserts that this mode of election, by the whole body of the church, remained unimpaired in the third century.[18]

The foregoing views of Neander, together with the following extract from Mosheim, give us a clear idea of the manner in which the elective franchise was exercised in the primitive church through the first three centuries of the Christian era. "To them (the multitude, or people) belonged the appointment of the bishop and presbyters, as well as of the inferior ministers; with them resided the power of enacting laws, as also of adopting or rejecting whatever might be proposed in the general assemblies, and of expelling and again receiving into communion any depraved or unworthy members. In short, nothing whatever, of any moment, could be determined on or carried into effect without their knowledge and concurrence."[19]

But the phrase itself, χειροτονήσαντες, may with great probability be understood to indicate that the appointment of these presbyters was by a public vote of the church.

(*a*) *This is the appropriate meaning of the term,* χειροτονεῖν, *which is here used.* It means, *to stretch out the hand, to hold up the hand,* as in voting; hence, *to give one's vote,* by holding up the hand, *to choose, to elect.* In this sense it is abundantly used in classic Greek. Demosthenes exhorts the Athenians in popular assemby to elect, χειροτονῆσαι, ten men to go on an embassy to the Thebans.* Again it is re-

---

[17] Apost. Kirch. Vol. I. c. 5, p. 194. Trans. I. 181.

[18] Neander, Allgem. Gesch. I. 323, seq. 340–342, 2d ed. Comp. Trans. p. 199, 211; II. p. 152.

[19] De Rebus Christ., Saec. I. § 45.

* Demos. on the Crown, § 178.

solved by the senate and people of Athens to choose, ἑλέσθαι, five of the people to go on an embassy, which embassadors, thus chosen, χειροτονηθέντες, shall depart, etc. The people, ὁ δῆμος choosing αἱρούμενος, a commissary, elected me, ἐμὲ ἐχειροτόνησαν, § 249.

Again, § 285, the people, ὁ δῆμος, choosing, χειροτονῶν, an orator, to pronounce a funeral oration over the dead bodies of those who fell at Chaeronaea, elected,—not you, οὐ σὲ ἐχειροτόνησε; but chose me, ἐχειροτόνησεν ἐμέ. In the same sense the term is frequently used by other Greek authors.

Robinson translates it, *to choose by vote, to appoint.* Suidas also renders it by ἐκλεξάμενοι, *having chosen.* Such is the concurring authority of lexicographers.

(β) *This rendering is sustained by the common use of the term by early Christian writers.* The brother who accompanied Paul in his agency to make charitable collections for the suffering Jews in Judea, was *chosen of the churches* for this service, where the same word is used, χειροτονηθείς. ἐπὸ τῶν ἐκκλησιῶν, 2 Cor. viii. 19. "It will become you," says Ignatius to the church at Philadelphia, "as the church of God, to *choose,* χειροτονῆσαι, some deacon to go there," *i. e.,* to the church at Antioch.[20]

Again, to the church at Smyrna, "It will be fitting, and for the honor of God, that your church *elect,* χειροτονῆσαι, some worthy delegate," etc.[21]

Again, in the Greek version of the Codex Ecclesiae Africanae, the heading of the nineteenth canon is, that a bishop should not be chosen, χειροτονεῖσθαι, except by the multitude, ἀπὸ πολλῶν.[22]

The above examples all relate, neither to an official ap-

---

[20] Ad Phil. c. 10.   [21] Ad Smyrn. c. 11.
[22] Cited by Suicer, ad verbum.

pointment or commission granted by another, nor to an *ordination* or consecration, but to an actual *election* by a plurality of voters. They justify, therefore, the supposition that Paul and Barnabas, like the apostles in the case of Matthias, and of the seven deacons, led the church to a popular election of their presbyters.

(γ) *This mode of appointment was the established usage of the churches*, to which it may be presumed that Paul and Barnabas adhered in the election of these presbyters. The appointment of Matthias the apostle, of the seven deacons, and of the delegates of the churches, as we have already seen, was by a public vote of the churches. And the same continued to be the authorized mode of appointment at the close of the apostolical age; as we learn from the epistle of Clement, cited above, who also rebukes the church of Corinth for rejecting from office those presbyters who had been chosen in this manner.[23] No other mode of appointment to any office in the church had, in any instance, been adopted, so far as we are informed; from all which the inference is, that presbyters, like all other ecclesiastical officers, were appointed by vote of the church.

(δ) This conclusion is sustained by the most approved authorities. According to Suicer, the primary and appropriate signification of the term is to denote *an election made by the uplifting of the hand*, and particularly denotes the election of a bishop by vote. "In this sense," he adds, "it continued for a long time to be used in the church, denoting not an *ordination* or *consecration*, but an election."[24] Grotius,[25] Meyer,[26] and De Wette[27] so interpret the passage, to say nothing of Beza, Böhmer, Rothe and others.

To the same effect is also the following extract from Tim-

---

[23] Ep. I. ad Corinth. § 44. See p. 65, note.
[24] Thesaurus, Eccl. v. χειροτονέω.
[25], [26], [27] Comment. ad locum.

dal: "We read only of the apostles, constituting elders *by the suffrages of the people*, Acts xiv. 23, which, as it is the genuine signification of the Greek word, χειροτονήσαντες, so it is accordingly interpreted by Erasmus, Beza, Diodati, and those who translated the Swiss, French, Italian, Belgic, and even English Bibles, till the episcopal correction, which leaves out the words, *by election*, as well as the marginal notes, which affirm that the apostles did not thrust pastors into the church through a lordly superiority, *but chose and placed them there by the voice of the congregation*."[28] Tyndale's translation is as follows: "And when they had ordened them seniours by eleccion, in every congregacion, after they had preyde and fasted, they commennd them to God, on whom they beleved."

In view of the whole, we must conclude, that presbyters, like all other ecclesiastical officers, were elected in the apostolic churches by the suffrages of the people,[29] even though the term χειροτονέω is occasionally used to denote either an official appointment, or the laying on of hands.

2. The historical argument, from the early Fathers.

When from the writings of the apostles we turn to the records of history, we find evidence sufficient to show that the churches continued, even after the rise of episcopacy, to defend and to exercise the right of election,—that great principle which is the basis of religious liberty.

The earliest and most authentic authority on this subject,

[28] Rights of the Church, p. 358.

[29] "It may not have occurred to some of our readers," says the Edinburgh Review, "that the Greek word, ἐκκλησία, which we translate *church*, was the peculiar term used to denote the general assembly of the people in the old democracies, and that it essentially expresses *a popularly constituted meeting*, and that such, in a great measure, was the original constitution of the Christian society."—*Baudry's Selections*, V., p. 319.

after that of the Scriptures themselves, is derived from Clement of Rome, contemporary with some of the apostles. This venerable father, in his epistle to the church at Corinth, about A. D. 96, speaks of the regulations which were established by the apostles for the appointment of others to succeed them after their decease. This appointment was to be made *with the consent and approbation of the whole church*, συνευδοκησάσης τῆς ἐκκλησίας πάσης, grounded on their previous knowledge of the qualifications of the candidate for this office. This testimony clearly indicates the active co-operation of the church in the appointment of their ministers.[30] It may have been the custom for the presbyters to propose one to supply any vacancy which occurred; but it remained for the church to ratify or to reject the nomination.[31]

Tertullian in his Apology for Christians against the heathen, A. D. 198 or 205, says that the elders came into their office *by the testimony* [*of the people*], that is, by *the approval*, the suffrage or election of the people.[32] Their free and in-

[30] The passage has been already cited, but it is here given at length, with the title of C. J. Hefele: "*Apostolorum institutio, ne de munere sacerdotali contentio fiat. Legitime electos ac recte viventes de munere suo dejicere nefas.*—Καὶ οἱ ἀπόστολοι ἡμῶν ἔγνωσαν διὰ τοῦ κυρίου ἡμῶν Ἰησοῦ Χριστοῦ, ὅτι ἔρις ἔσται ἐπὶ τοῦ ὀνόματος τῆς ἐπισκοπῆς. Διὰ ταύτην οὖν τὴν αἰτίαν πρόγνωσιν εἰληφότες τελείαν κατέστησαν τοὺς προειρημένους, καὶ μεταξὺ ἐπινομὴν δεδώκασιν, ὅπως, ἐὰν κοιμηθῶσιν, διαδέξωνται ἕτεροι δεδοκιμασμένοι ἄνδρες τὴν λειτουργίαν αὐτῶν. Τοὺς οὖν κατασταθέντας ὑπ' ἐκείνων, ἢ μεταξὺ ὑφ' ἑτέρων ἐλλογίμων ἀνδρῶν, σ υ ν ε υ δ ο κ η σ ά σ η ς τ ῆ ς ἐ κ κ λ η σ ί α ς π ά σ η ς, καὶ λειτουργήσαντας ἀμέμπτως τῷ ποιμνίῳ τοῦ Χριστοῦ μετὰ ταπεινοφροσύνης, ἡσύχως καὶ ἀβαναύσως μεμαρτυρημένους τε πολλοῖς χρόνοις ὑπὸ πάντων, τούτους οὐ δικαίως νομίζομεν ἀποβάλλεσθαι τῆς λειτουργίας. Ἁμαρτία γὰρ οὐ μικρὰ ἡμῖν ἔσται, ἐὰν τοὺς ἀμέμπτως καὶ ὁσίως προσενέγκοντας τὰ δῶρα τῆς ἐπισκοπῆς ἀποβάλωμεν."

[31] Neander, Allgemein. Gesch. I. S. 323, 2d ed. Trans. p. 189.

[32] *Praesident probati quique seniores honorem istum non pretio, sed testimonio, adepti.*—*Apol.* c. 39.

dependent suffrages were the highest testimony which the people could give of their approbation of their elders.

This interpretation of Tertullian is sustained by Cyprian, who requires the appointment of a bishop to be ratified by the approval and judgment of his colleagues and of the people, et collegarum ac plebis *testimonio et judicio* comprobato, Epist. 41. He must be designated in the presence of the people, and by their public judgment and *testimony* approved as worthy and suitable, ut sacerdos plebe praesente, sub omnium occulis deligatur, et dignus atque idoneus *publico judicio, ac testimonio* comprobetur. He is to be invested with the episcopal office, de universae fraternitatis suffragio et de episcoporum qui in praesentia convenerant, Ep. 68, c. 5. This will be a just and legitimate ordination, quae omnium suffragio et judicio fuerit examinatio. From these varied forms of expression it is sufficiently clear that the *testimonium* of the people was essential to the validity of an election. Their suffrages were the highest testimony which they could give of their approbation of their elders.

Origen, in his last book against Celsus, about A. D. 240, speaks of the elders and rulers of the churches as ἐκλεγόμενοι, *chosen to their office.* In his sixth homily on Leviticus, he asserts that the presence of the people is required in the ordination of a priest; and the reason assigned for their intervention is to secure an impartial election and the appointment to this office of one who possessed the highest qualifications for it. The whole passage implies the active co-operation of the people in the appointment of their ministers.[33]

---

[33] Requiritur enim in ordinando sacerdote et praesentia populi ut sciant omnes, et certi sint, quia qui praestantior est ex omni populo, qui doctior, qui sanctior, qui in omni virtute eminentior—ille eligitur ad sacerdotium, et hoc, adstante populo, ne qua postmodum, retractatio cuiquam, ne quis scrupulus resideret.

Even Cyprian, A. D. 258, with all his high-church pretensions, most fully accords to the people the right of suffrage in the appointment of their spiritual teachers, declaring that they have the highest authority to choose those who are worthy of this office and to refuse such as may be unworthy. It was, according to this father, an *apostolic usage*, preserved by a *divine* authority in his day, and observed throughout the churches of Africa (*apud nos*), that a pastor, *sacerdos*, should be chosen publicly, in the presence of the people; and that by their decision thus publicly expressed, the candidate should be adjudged worthy to fill the vacant office, whether of deacon, presbyter or bishop. In accordance with these views, it was his custom, on all such occasions, to consult his clergy and the people before proceeding to ordain any one to the office of the ministry.[34]

So universal was the right of suffrage, and so reasonable, that it attracted the notice of the emperor, Alexander Severus, who reigned from A. D. 222 to 235. In imitation of the custom of the Christians and Jews in the appointment of their priests, as he says, he gave to the people the right of rejecting the appointment of any procurator, or chief

[34] Plebs obsequens praeceptis dominicis et Deum metuens, a peccatore praeposito separare se debet, nec se ad sacrilegi sacerdotis sacrificia miscere, quando ipsa maximè habeat potestatem vel *eligendi dignos sacerdotes, vel indignos recusandi*. Quod et ipsum videmus de divina auctoritate descendere ut sacerdos, *plebe presente,* sub omnium oculis deligatur, et dignus atque idoneus publico judicio ac testimonio comprobetur,—Diligentur, de traditione divina et apostolica observatione servandum est et tenendum quod apud nos quoque, et fere per provincias universas tenetur, ut ad ordinationes rite celebrandas ad eam plebem cui praepositus ordinatur, episcopi ejusdem provinciae proximi quique conveniant et episcopus deligatur plebe praesente.—*Ep*. 68. Comp. Ep. 7; Ep. 9, 3–4; Ep. 5; Ep. 13.

president of the provinces, whom he might nominate to such an office.³⁵ Their votes, however, in these cases, were not merely testimonial, but really judicial and elective.

Even the Apostolic Constitutions, fabricated toward the end of the third century to support the fictitious pretensions of bishops and to assist the growth of episcopal power, required that a bishop shall be "a select person *chosen by the whole people.*" ³⁶

The authorities above cited indicate that the suffrages of the church were directed by a previous nomination of the clergy. But there are on record instances in which the people, of their own accord and by acclamation, elected individuals to the office of bishop or presbyter without any previous nomination. Athanasius of Alexandria, A. D. 328, was chosen by the suffrages of the people, Ψήφῳ τοῦ λαοῦ παντός,³⁷ and Fabian also, A. D. 236.³⁸ Ambrose, bishop of Milan, was elected in this manner, A. D. 374.³⁹ Martin of Tours, A. D. 375, was appointed in the same manner.⁴⁰ So also were Eustathius at Antioch, A. D. 310,⁴¹ Chrysostom at Constantinople, A. D. 398,⁴² Eraclius at Hippo,⁴³ and Miletius at Antioch.⁴⁴ It is also observable that these examples belong to a later age, the fourth century. They are therefore important as evidence that the

---

[35] Lampridius, in Vit. Alexandri Severi, c. 45.
[36] Book viii. 4. Comp. 16.
[37] Greg. Nazianz. Orat. 21, Tom. I. p. 377.
[38] Euseb. Hist. vi. c. 29.
[39] Paulin., Vit. Ambros, Rufin., Hist. Eccl. Lib. 2, c. 11; Theodoret, Hist. Eccl. Lib. 4, c. 6, p. 666; Sozomen, Hist. Eccl. Lib. 6. c. 24.
[40] Sulpic. Sev., Vit. e. Martini, c. 7.
[41] Theodoret, Hist. Eccl. Lib. 1, c. 6.
[42] Socrat., Hist. Eccl. Lib. 6, c. 2.
[43] Augustin., 4 Ep. 110, al. 213.
[44] Theodoret, Hist. Eccl. Lib. 2, c. 27.

people continued even at this late period to retain their rights in these popular elections.

It has been asserted that the people were denied the right of suffrage by the fourth canon of the council of Nice. But Bingham has clearly shown that the people were not excluded by this canon from their ancient privilege in this respect.[45] And both Riddle[46] and Bishop Pearson, as quoted by him, concur with Bingham in opinion on this subject. Indeed the assertion is sufficiently refuted by the fact that Athanasius, bishop of Alexandria, and others were elected by popular vote immediately after the session of that council.

Daillé sums up the evidence on this subject in the following terms: "It is clear that in the primitive times they [popular elections and ordinations] depended partly on the people, and not wholly on the clergy; but every company of the faithful either chose their own pastors, or else had leave to consider and to approve of those that were proposed to them for that purpose. Pontius, a deacon of the church of Carthage, says that "St. Cyprian, being yet a neophyte, was elected to the charge of pastor and the degree of bishop by the judgment of God and the favor of the people."[47] Cyprian also tells us the same in several places. In his fifty-second epistle, speaking of Cornelius, he says, "That he was made bishop of Rome by the judgment of God and of his Christ, by the testimony of the greatest part of the clergy, by the suffrage of the people who were there present, and by the college of pastors or ancient bishops, all good men."[48]

---

[45] Book 4, chap. 2, § 11.   [46] Christ. Antiq. p. 286.

[47] Judicio Dei, et plebis favore, ad officium sacerdotii, et episcopatus gradum adhuc neophytus, ut putabatur, novellus electus est.—*Pont. Diac. in vita Cypr.*

[48] Factus est autem Cornelius episcopus, de Dei et Christi ejus judi-

"It appears clear enough, both out of St. Hierome [49] and by the acts of the council of Constantinople [50] and of Chalcedon,[51] and also by the *Pontificale Romanum* [52] and several other productions, that this custom continued a long time in the church." [53]

This right in question is clearly admitted even in the Roman pontifical, in which the bishop, at the ordination of a priest, is made to say: "It was not without good reason that the fathers had ordained that the advice of the people should be taken in the election of those persons who were to serve at the altar; to the end that having given their assent to their ordination, they might the more readily yield obedience to those who were so ordained." [54] This passage is cited by Daillé, who remarks that an honest canon of Valencia very gravely proposed to the council of Trent that this and all such authorities should be blotted out, so that no trace or footstep of them should remain in future, for heretics to bring against them for having taken away this right!

cio, de clericorum penè omnium testimonio, de plebis, quæ tunc adfuit suffragio, et de sacerdotum antiquorum, et bonorum virorum collegio.—*Cyprian, Ep.* 52, c. 8.

[49] Hieron., Com. 10 in Ezech. c. 33 Tom. III. p. 935 et Com. in Agg. Ed. Basil, 1537, T. 6, p. 280, A.

[50] Conc. Const., 1 in Ep. ad Damas, p. 94 et 95, t. 1, Conc. Gener.

[51] Conc. Chalced., act. 11, p. 375, t. 2 Conc. Gen., et act. 16, p. 430, etc.

[52] Pontific. Rom. in Ordinat. Presbyter. fol. 38, vide supr. l. 1, c. 4.

[53] Comp. also Leo. Epist. 9, c. 6; 12, c. 5.

[54] Neque enim frustra à patribus institutum, ut de electione illorum qui ad regimen altaris adhibendi sunt, consulatur etiam populus; quia de vita et conversatione praesentandi, quod nonunquam ignoratur a pluribus, scitur à paucis; et necesse est, et facilius ei quis obedientiam exhibeat ordinatio cui assensum praebuerit ordinando.—*Pontif. Rom. De Ordinat. Pres.* fol. 38.

Bingham [55] and Chancellor King,[56] and multitudes of the most respectable writers in the communion of the Episcopal Church, fully sustain the foregoing representations of the right of suffrage as enjoyed by the primitive churches. They are clearly supported by the late Dr. Burton [57] and by Riddle, both of Oxford University, and by the best authorities, both ancient and modern. "The mode of appointing bishops and presbyters has been repeatedly changed. Election by the people, for instance, has been discontinued. This is indeed, in the estimation of Episcopalians, a great improvement; but still, as they must allow, it is a change."[58]

For what term of time the several churches continued in the full enjoyment of the right of suffrage we are not distinctly informed. We can only say with Mosheim, "This power of appointing their elders continued to be exercised by the members of the church at large as long as primitive manners were retained entire, and those who ruled over the churches did not conceive themselves at liberty to introduce any deviation from the apostolic model."[59] The reader will find an elaborate discussion of this whole subject, with an extended citation of authorities, through the several centuries of church history, in Blondell's treatise, De Plebis in Electionibus jure.[60]

II. Abridgment and final extinction of the right of suffrage.

The sovereign rights of the people in their free elective

---

[55] Book 4 c. 6.   [56] Part I. c. 3–c. 6.
[57] Church History, c. 12.
[58] Riddle, Christ. Antiq., Preface, p. 76.
[59] De Rebus Christ., Saec. I. § 39. Comp. Clarkson, No Evidence for Diocesan Churches.
[60] Apologia pro. St. Hieron, pp. 379–549. Comp. Böhmer, Altherthum, 240; Conc. Cathar., iv. c. 22.

franchise began at an early period to be invaded. The final result of these changes was a total disfranchisement of the laity and the substitution of an ecclesiastical despotism in the place of the elective government of the primitive church. Of these changes one of the most effective was the attempt, by means of correspondence and ecclesiastical synods, to consolidate the churches into *one church universal,* to impose upon them a uniform code of laws, and establish an ecclesiastical polity administered by the clergy. The idea of a holy catholic church, and of an ecclesiastical hierarchy for the government of the same, was wholly a conception of the priesthood. Whatever may have been the motives with which this doctrine of the unity of the church was promulgated, it prepared the way for the overthrow of the popular government of the church.

Above all, the doctrine of the *divine right* of the priesthood aimed a fatal blow at the liberties of the people. The clergy were no longer the servants of the people, chosen by them to the work of the ministry, but a privileged order, like the Levitical priesthood; and, like them, by divine right invested with peculiar prerogatives. Elated with the pride of their divine commission, a degenerate and aspiring priesthood sought by every means to make themselves independent of the suffrages of the people. This independence they began by degrees to assert and to exercise. The bishop began, in the third century, to appoint at pleasure his own deacons and other inferior orders of the clergy. In other appointments also he endeavored to disturb the freedom of of the elections and to direct them agreeably to his own will.[61]

And yet Cyprian, even in the middle of that century, apologized to the laity and clergy of his diocese for appoint-

[61] Pertsch. Kirch. Gesch., drit. Jahrhund. S. 439–452. Planck, Gesell. Verfassung, I.183.

ing one Auretius to the office of reader. In justification of this measure he pleads the extraordinary virtues of the candidate, the urgent necessity of the case, and the impossibility of consulting them, as he was wont to do on all such occasions.[62] Such, however, was the progress of episcopal usurpation, that, by the middle of the fourth century, elections by the people were nearly lost;[63] and from the beginning of the fifth century the bishop proceeded to claim the appointment even of the presbyters, together with the absolute control of all ecclesiastical offices subordinate to his own episcopate. But down to the fourth century the bishops were not at liberty even to license one to perform the duties of a presbyter without first obtaining the approbation of the people. Such at least was still the rule in many places.[64]

Against these encroachments of ecclesiastical ambition and power the people continued to oppose a firm but ineffectual resistance. They asserted, and in a measure maintained, their primitive right of choosing their own spiritual teachers.[65] The usage of the churches of Africa has been already mentioned. Examples are given by Böhmer,[66] in evidence that this right was still recognized in the churches of Spain and of Rome.[67] Later still, in the fourth century,

---

[62] In ordinationibus clericis, Fratres carissimi, solemus vos ante consulere, et mores ac merita singulorum, communi consilio ponderare, Ep. 33.

[63] Pertsch. 4, Jahrhund. S. 263.

[64] Riddle's Eccl. Chron., A. D. 350, 400. Planck, Vol. I. p. 183.

[65] Gieseler, Vol. I. 272. For a more full and detailed account of these changes of ecclesiastical policy and of the means by which they were introduced, the reader is referred to the first volume of J. G. Planck, Gesch. der Christ. kirch. Gesellschaftsverfassung, Bd. I. 149–212, 433, seq.

[66] Christ. kirch. Alterthumswissenschaft, I. S. 144, seq.

[67] Presbyterio vel episcopatui, si eum cleri ac *plebis* vocaverit *electio*,

an instance occurred in the Eastern church, in Cappadocia, of the controlling influence of these popular elections. The people, after having been divided in their choice between different candidates, united their suffrages in the election of an individual high in office in the state, who had not even been baptized. He accordingly received this ordinance at the hands of the bishops present, and was duly invested with his office. In the Western church, the election of Martin of Tours, A. D. 375, above mentioned, was carried by the popular voice against the decided disapprobation of the bishops present. Ambrose, bishop of Milan, A. D. 374, was appointed by the unanimous acclamation of the multitude, previously even to his baptism. On the other hand, there are on record instances in the fourth, and even in the fifth century, when the appointment of a bishop was effectually *resisted* by the refusal of the people to ratify the nomination of the candidate to a vacant see.[68]

But notwithstanding all these examples in which the people successfully asserted their ancient right of suffrage, it became, as early as the fifth century, little else than an empty name. The elections degenerated into a tumultuous and unequal contest with a crafty and aspiring hierarchy, who had found means so to trammel and control the elective franchise as practically to direct at pleasure all ecclesiastical appointments. The rule had been established by decree of council, and often repeated, requiring the presence and *unanimous concurrence of all the provincial bishops* in the election and ordination of one to the office of bishop. This afforded them a convenient means of defeating any popular election, by an affected disagreement among them-

non immerito societur.—Siricius, bishop of Rome, A. D. 384. Ep. I. ad Himer. c. 10.

[68] Greg. Naz., Orat. 10. Comp. Orat. 19, p. 308; 21, p. 377. Bingham, B. IV. c. 1, § 3. Planck, I. 440, n. 10.

selves. The same canonical authority had made the *concurrence of the metropolitan* necessary to the validity of any appointment. His veto was accordingly another efficient expedient by which to baffle the suffrages of the people, and to constrain them into a reluctant acquiescence in the will of the clergy.[69]

Elections to ecclesiastical offices were also disturbed by the interference of secular influence from without, in consequence of that disastrous union of church and state which was formed in the fourth century under Constantine the Great.

"During this century," the fourth, "1. The emperors convened and presided in general councils; 2. Confirmed their decrees; 3. Enacted laws relative to ecclesiastical matters by their own authority; 4. Pronounced decisions concerning heresies and controversies; 5. Appointed bishops; 6. Inflicted punishment on ecclesiastical persons.

"Hence arose complaints that the bishops had conceded too much to the emperors; while, on the other hand, some persons maintained that the emperors had left too much in the hands of the bishops. The bishops certainly did possess too much power and influence, to the prejudice of the other clergy, and especially to the disadvantage of Christians at large.

"Thus the emperor and the bishops share the chief government of the church between them. But the limits of their authority were not well defined. Great part of the power formerly possessed by the general body of Christians, the laity, had passed into the hands of the civil governor."[70]

Agitated and harassed by the conflict of these discordant

---

[69] Conc. Nic. c. 4. Conc. Antioch, c. 1. Carthag. A. D. 390, c. 12. Planck, Vol. I. pp. 433-452.

[70] Riddle's Chronology, pp. 70, 71.

elements, the popular assemblies for the election of men to fill the highest offices of the holy ministry became scenes of tumult and disorder that would disgrace a modern political canvass. "Go and witness the proceedings at our public festivals, especially those in which, according to rule, the elections of ecclesiastical officers are held. One supports one man; another, another; and the reason is, that all overlook that which they ought to consider: the qualifications, intellectual and moral, of the candidate. Their attention is turned to other points, by which their choice is determined. One is in favor of a candidate of noble birth; another, of a man of wealth, who will not need to be supported by the revenues of the church; a third votes for one who has come over from some opposite party; a fourth gives his influence in favor of some relative or friend; while another is gained by the flatteries of a demagogue."[71] Repeated notices of similar disturbances occur in the ecclesiastical writers of that period.[72]

To correct these disorders, various but ineffectual expedients were adopted at different times and places. The council of Laodicea, A. D. 361, c. 13, excluded the multitude, τοῖς ὄχλοις, *the rabble*, from taking part in the choice of persons for the sacred office, apparently with the design of preventing these abuses, without excluding the better

---

[71] Chrysostom, A. D. 398, De Sacerdot. Lib. 3, c. 15.

[72] August., Ep. 22, § 7. Synessii, Ep. 67. Sidon, Apollinar. Lib. IV. Ep. 25, and other passages collected by Baronius, Annal. 303, n. 22, seq., and in Baluzii Miscell. tom. 2. Ammianus Marcellinus gives the following representation of the unholy contest of the two rival candidates, Damasus and Ursinus, for appointment to the episcopal see at Rome: "Supra humanum modum ad rapiendam episcopatus sedem ardentes, scissis studiis asperrime conflictabantur, ad usque mortis, vulnerumque discrimina adjumentis utriusque progressis. Et in certatione superaverat Damasus, parte quae ei favebat instante."—*Lib.* 28, *Ep.* 3.

portion of the laymen from a participation in the elections. The expedient, however, was of little avail.

In the Latin Church, and especially in that of Africa, an attempt was made to restore order and simplicity in these elections by means of *interventors*, or *visitors*, whose duty it was to visit the vacant diocese and influence the clergy and people to harmonize their discordant interests, that thus the way might be prepared for a quiet and regular election. By this means the visitor had a fair opportunity, as Bingham justly remarks, " to ingratiate himself with the people and promote his own interests among them, instead of those of the church." [73] This measure, though supported by Symmachus,[74] in the sixth century, and by Gregory the Great,[75] failed to produce the desired effect, and seems neither to have been generally adopted nor long continued.

Justinian, in the sixth century, sought, with no better success, to remedy the evils in question by limiting the elective franchise to a mixed aristocracy composed of the *clergy* and the *chief men* of the city. These were jointly to nominate three candidates, declaring under oath that in making the selection they had been influenced by no sinister motive. From these three the ordaining person was to ordain the one whom he judged best qualified.[76] But it was not defined who should be included among the chief men, and the result was the loss of the people's rights and an increase of the factions which the measure was intended to prevent. The council of Arles, A. D. 452, c. 54, in like manner ordered the *bishops to nominate three candidates*, from whom the clergy and the people should make the election; and that of Barcelona, A. D. 599, c. 3, ordered

---

[73] Book II. c. 15, § 1. Comp. Book IV. c. 11, § 7.

[74] Ep. 5, c. 6. [75] Ep. Lib. 9, Ep. 16.

[76] Justin., Novell. 123, c. 1, 137, c. 2d. Cod. Lib. 1, tit. 3. De Episcop. leg. 42.

the *clergy* and *people* to make the nomination, and the *metropolitan* and *bishops* were to determine the election by lot.

But even these ineffectual efforts to restore in some measure the right of the people, sufficiently show to what extent it was already lost. Indeed, the bishops had already assumed to themselves, in some instances, the independent and exclusive right of appointing spiritual officers.[77] The emperor Valentinian III. complains of Hilary of Arles that he unworthily ordained some in direct opposition to the will of the people; and that, when they refused those whom they had not chosen, he collected an armed body, and by military power forcibly thrust into office the ministers of the gospel of peace.[78] Leo the Great, A. D. 450, asserts the right of the people to elect their spiritual rulers.[79]

The government of the church, from a pure democracy, had changed first into an ambitious aristocracy, and then into a more oppressive oligarchy, which, assuming practically the sentiment of a crafty tyrant, οὐκ ἀγαθὸν πολυκοιρανίη,[80] directed its assaults against that most sacred principle both of civil and religious liberty—the right of every corporate body to choose its own rulers and teachers. This extinction of religious freedom was not effected in the church universally at the same time, nor in every place by the same means. Oppressed by violence, overreached by stratagem, or awed into submission by superstition, the churches severally yielded the contest at different and somewhat distant

---

[77] Sidon, Apollinar. Lib. IV. Ep. 25.

[78] Valentinian III. Nov. XXIV. ad calcem Cod. Theodos.

[79] Qui praefecturus omnibus, ab omnibus eligatur. Ep. 89. Comp. Ep. 84, c. 5.

[80] Iliad, II. 204. Paraphrased by Pope in the following lines:

> Be silent, wretch, and think not here allowed
> That worst of tyrants, *an usurping crowd*.—POPE.

intervals. In Rome the rights of the people were recognized under Coelestin, A. D. 422,[81] and Leo the Great, A. D. 440, which, as we have seen, Justinian attempted to restore in the century following. In Gaul these rights were not wholly lost until the fifth,[82] and even the sixth century.[83] In the East, Proclus, ordained by the bishops, was rejected by the people A. D. 426.

The doctrine that to the clergy was promised a divine guidance from the Spirit of God had its influence also in completing the subjugation of the people. This vain conceit, by ceaseless repetition on the part of bishops and councils, became an unquestionable dogma of the church. Once established, it had great influence in bringing the people into passive submission to their spiritual oppressors. Resistance to such an authority under the infallible guidance of God's Spirit was rebellion against high Heaven, which the laity had not the impiety to maintain.

"Thus everything was changed in the church. At the beginning it was a society of brethren; and now an absolute monarchy is reared in the midst of them. All Christians were priests of the living God, 1 Pet. ii. 9, with humble pastors for their guidance. But a lofty head is uplifted from the midst of these pastors. A mysterious voice utters words full of pride; an iron hand compels all men, small and great, rich and poor, freemen and slaves, to take the mark of its power. The holy and primitive equality of souls is lost sight of. Christians are divided into two strangely unequal classes. On the one side a separate class of priests daring to usurp the name of the church and claiming to be possessed of peculiar privileges in the sight of the Lord. On the other, timid flocks, reduced to a blind

---

[81] Ep. 2, c. 5.
[82] Sidon, Apollinar. Lib. IV. Ep. 25.
[83] Conc. Orleans, A. D. 549, c. 11.

and passive submission; a people gagged and silenced, and delivered over to a proud caste."[84]

The interference of the secular power with ecclesiastical appointments has been already mentioned. The civil magistrate often exercised the same arbitrary power in these matters which the priesthood had usurped over the people, so that the oppressor became in turn the oppressed. This secular interference began with Constantine. Both in the Eastern and the Western church it was often the means of disturbing and overruling the appointment of ecclesiastical officers, and finally itself completed the extinction of religious liberty. Valentinian III., A. D. 445, for example, enacted that all bishops of the Western empire should obey the bishop of Rome, and should be bound to appear before him at his summons.[85] Constantius appointed Liberius to be bishop of Rome A. D. 353, and the Gothic kings in the sixth century exercised the same arbitrary power over the churches of France and Spain.[86]

In the Eastern church, Theodosius I. also appointed Nectarius bishop of Constantinople A. D. 381;[87] and Theodosius II., in the same summary manner, appointed Proclus, A. D. 434, to succeed Maximian in the same place. Of the vehemence with which the church sometimes protested against these encroachments of secular power, we have a remarkable example in the sixth canon of the council of Paris, A. D. 557. "Seeing that ancient custom and the regulations of the church are neglected, we desire that no bishop be consecrated against the will of the citizens. And only such persons shall be considered eligible to this dignity who may be appointed not by command of the prince, but

---

[84] D'Aubigné's Hist. of the Reformation, I. p. 31.
[85] Riddle's Eccl. Chron. p. 103.
[86] Simonis, Vorlesungen über die christlichen Allerthümer, p. 106.
[87] Böhmer's Alterthumswissenschaft, Vol. I. p. 151.

by the election of the people and clergy; which election must be confirmed by the metropolitan and the other bishops of the province. Any one who may enter upon this office *by the mere authority of the king* shall not be recognized by the other bishops; and if any bishop should recognize him, he must himself be deposed from his office." [88] The eighth council of Rome also, A. D. 853, forbade, on pain of excommunication, "all lay persons whatsoever, even princes themselves, to meddle in the election or promotion of any patriarch, metropolitan, or any other bishop whatever, declaring withal, that it is not fit that lay persons should have anything at all to do in these matters; it becoming them rather to be quiet, and patiently to attend until such time as the election of the bishop who is to be chosen be regularly finished by the college of the church." [89]

Such demands for the institution of *apostolical* and *canonical elections*, as they were called,[90] were, however, but rarely made, and never with success. The clergy were brought to bow to a usurpation more absolute and despotic than that by which they had at first wrested from the laity those rights which, in their turn, they were reluctantly compelled to resign to the secular power, until at length the pope, that prince of tyrants, became the supreme head of all power, whether ecclesiastical or secular. Innocent III., at the close of the twelfth century, described himself as "the successor of St. Peter, set up by God to govern not only the

[88] Conc. Paris, c. 8.

[89] Neminem laicorum principum, vel Potentum semet inscrere electioni vel promotioni Patriarchae, vel Metropolitae, aut cujuslibet episcopi, etc., praesertim cùm nullam in talibus potestatem quenquam potestativorum, vel ceterorum laicorum habere conveniat, sed potiùs silere, ac attendere sibi, usque quò regulariter à collegio ecclesiae suscipiat finem electio futuri pontificis.—*Conc.* 8, *Con.* 12, t. 3, *Conc.* p. 282.

[90] Gregory Naz. Orat. 21.

church, but the whole world. As God," said he, " has placed two great luminaries in the firmament, the one to rule the day and the other to give light by night, so has he established two great powers, the pontifical and the royal; and as the moon receives her light from the sun, so does royalty borrow its splendor from the papal authority!"

REMARKS.

The right of suffrage involves all the great principles of a popular government. The rights and privileges belonging to such a government the apostles, under the guidance of wisdom from on high, studiously sought to protect in framing the constitution which they gave to the churches; as the following remarks may serve to show:

1. The right of suffrage is the first element of a popular government in the church.

The right to elect our rulers and teachers presupposes the right to adopt our own form of government, to frame our constitution, to enact our laws, to exercise the prerogatives and enjoy the privileges of a free and independent body. The enjoyment of this right constitutes freedom; the absence of it, slavery. All just government is based on the participation or consent of the governed.

2. The right to elect their own pastors and teachers is the inherent right of every church.

If it be true that all men are endowed by their Creator with certain inalienable rights, among which are "life, liberty and the pursuit of happiness," then much more is liberty of conscience and the pursuit of future blessedness the inherent, inalienable right of man. What is the life that now is to that which is to come? or the happiness of earth to the bliss of heaven? Such are the religious to the civil rights of any people, all of which are involved in the enjoyment of the elective franchise, and are lost to a disfranchised laity. This consideration was lately urged in the hearing of the writer, with great pertinency and force, by the Marquis of Breadalbane, in the House of Lords, on a motion relating to the religious liberty of the church of Scotland. "The choice of a pastor is really a measure of more importance, and, by the members of that church is regarded as an event more interesting, than the election of a member of Parliament; for it affects their religious interests—interests to them and to their children high as Heaven and lasting as eternity."

3. The right of suffrage preserves a just balance of power between the lay members of the church and the clerical order—between the laity and the clergy.

The sacred office of the clergy, coupled with learning and talents, gives them, under any form of government, a controlling influence. If to all this be added the exclusive right of making and executing the laws, and of electing the officers, the balance of power between the clergy and the people is destroyed. The restraints and checks which the clergy ought to feel against the exercise of arbitrary power are removed. The history of the church shows that the dangerous prerogatives of prelatical power cannot with safety be entrusted to any body of men, however great or good. Accordingly, as in all free governments, the sovereign power is vested in the people, so in the primitive church, this great principle of religious as well as of civil liberty was carefully observed. The people were made the depositaries of the sovereign power. The enactment of the laws and the appointment of their officers belonged to them.[91]

[91] Riddle, Eccl. Chr. p. 13.

4. The loss of this right brings with it the extinction of religious liberty.

The free church of Scotland, by their secession, had the magnanimity to resign the heritage of their ancestors and go out from the sanctuary where their fathers worshiped, taking joyfully the spoiling of their goods rather than submit to the loss of their religious rights. In the manifesto which they published as their declaration of independence, they complain that their religious liberty has been invaded by the civil courts; whereas the church of Christ is, and of right ought to be, free, and independent of all spiritual jurisdiction from the state. We subjoin an extract from this manifesto, which clearly sets forth the wrongs that they must suffer under this spiritual bondage to which they nobly refused to bow:

(*a*) "That the courts of the church as now established, and members thereof, are liable to be coerced by the civil courts in the exercise of their spiritual functions; and in particular in their admission to the office of the holy ministry, and the constitution of the pastoral relation, and that they are subject to be compelled to intrude ministers on reclaiming congregations in opposition to the fundamental principles of the church, and their views of the word of God, and to the liberties of Christ's people.

(*b*) "That the said civil courts have power to interfere with and interdict the preaching of the gospel, and administration of ordinances as authorized and enjoined by the church courts of the establishment.

(*c*) "That the said civil courts have power to suspend spiritual censures pronounced by the church courts of the establishment against ministers and probationers of the church, and to interdict their execution as to spiritual effects, functions and privileges.

(*d*) "That the said civil courts have power to reduce and

set aside the sentences of the church courts of the establishment, deposing ministers from the office of the holy ministry, and depriving probationers of their license to preach the gospel, with reference to the spiritual states, functions and privileges of such ministers and probationers, restoring them to the spiritual office and status of which the church had deprived them.

(*e*) "That the said civil courts have power to determine on the right to sit as members of the supreme and other judicatories of the church by law established, and to issue interdicts against sitting and voting therein, irrespective of the judgment and determination of the said judicatories.

(*f*) "That the said civil courts have power to supersede the majority of a church court of the establishment in regard to the exercise of its spiritual functions as a church court, and to authorize the minority to exercise the said functions, in opposition to the court itself and to the superior judicatories of the establishment.

(*g*) "That the said civil courts have power to stay processes of discipline pending before courts of the church by law established, and to interdict such courts from proceeding therein.

(*h*) "That no pastor of a congregation can be admitted into the church courts of the establishment and allowed to rule as well as to teach, agreeably to the institution of the office by the Head of the church, nor to sit in any of the judicatories of the church, inferior or supreme, and that no additional provision can be made for the exercise of spiritual discipline among members of the church, though not affecting any patrimonial interests, and no alteration introduced in the state of pastoral superintendence and spiritual discipline in any parish without the coercion of a civil court.

"All which jurisdiction and power on the part of the

said civil courts severally above specified, whatever proceedings may have given occasion to its exercise, is, in our opinion, in itself inconsistent with Christian liberty—with the authority which the Head of the church hath conferred on the church alone."

5. The free exercise of the elective franchise is one of the most effectual means of guarding against the introduction of unworthy men into the ministry.

The common people best know the private character of the minister. They have a deep interest in it. They seek the spiritual welfare of themselves and their children in the selection of their pastor. These are precisely the considerations assigned for continuing to the people the right of election in the ancient church, after the rise of episcopacy.[92]

On the contrary, he who has a living at his disposal is often ignorant of the true character of him who seeks a preferment. A thousand sinister motives may bias his judgment. He may be the most unsuitable man possible for such a trust.[93] In a word, the curse of a graceless ministry

---

[92] It was, according to Cyprian, a divine tradition and apostolical custom, observed by the African church and throughout almost all the provinces, that the election is to be performed in the presence of the people of the place, who fully know every man's life, and in their very intimate acquaintance have carefully observed his habitual conversation. Episcopus deligatur, plebe praesente, quae singulorum vitam plenissime novit, et uniuscujusque actum de ejus conversatione perspexerit... Coram omni synagoga jubet Deus constitui sacerdotem, id est, instruit atque ostendit ordinationes sacerdotales nonnisi, sub populi assistentis conscientia fieri opportere ut, *plebe praesente, vel delegantur malorum crimina, vel bonorum merita praedicentur,* ... Quod utique idciro tam diligenter et caute, convocata plebe, tota gerebatur, ne quis ad altaris ministerium, vel ad sacerdotalem locum *indignus obreperet.*—*Cyprian,* Ep. 68, c. 4, 5.

[93] Tracts for the Times, No. 59, p. 413.

has ever rested upon the church, to a greater or less extent, wherever they have not enjoyed the right of electing their own pastors. The rich and quiet livings of an establishment, especially if coupled with the authority, the distinction and emoluments of the episcopal office, will ever be an object of ambition to worldly men. "Make me a bishop," said an ancient idolater, "make me a bishop, and I will surely be a Christian."

6. The free enjoyment of the elective franchise is one of the best means of guarding the church against the inroads of error.

The Puseyism of the day is a delusion of the priesthood. The writer has often been assured in England that few, comparatively, of the common people are led away by it. And in this country we have lately seen the laity nobly struggling to resist diocesan despotism. So it has ever been; the delusions and heresies that have overrun the church have originated with the clergy.[94] In a ministry having no dependence upon the people will be found, if anywhere, irreligious and dangerous men, who, caring little for the real interests of their flocks, will substitute their own delusions[95] for those simple truths which an intelligent and

---

[94] "If you were to take the *great mass of the people* of England, you would find a burst of righteous indignation against them (the Tractarians). They would say, If we are to have popery, let us have honest old popery at once. If you are right, you do not go far enough; and if you are wrong, you go too far."—*Rev. Mr. Stowell, cited in Letters to the Laity,* p. 34. Comp. Jerome Hieron. on Hos. ix. Vol. 6. Ed. Basil. 1537, p. 40.

[95] "When the prerogative and pre-eminence of any single person in the church began to be in esteem, not a few who failed in their attempts of attaining it, to revenge themselves on the church, made it their business to invent and propagate pernicious heresies. So did Thebuthis, at Jerusalem, Euseb., lib. 4, cap. 22, and Valentinus, Tertul. adv. Val., cap. 4, and Marcion, at Rome, Epiphan. Haeres. 42.

virtuous people delight to hear, and which a godly ministry would desire to preach. Leave, then, the choice of the clergyman in the hands of the people. They will most carefully seek for one who is sound in the faith and devoted to the sacred work; they will soonest reject one who may seek to pervert the truth of God. Upon the laity alone can we rely for the appointment of ministers who shall be the best defenders of the faith by the authority of their learning and the piety of their lives.

7. The right of suffrage promotes mutual attachment between pastor and people, and the spiritual edification of the church.

The people receive instruction with affectionate interest and confidence from the lips of the preacher whom they have appointed over themselves, the man of their own choice; while he in turn speaks to them in the fullness and confidence of reciprocal love. On the other hand, the ministrations of a priesthood which is imposed upon a people are felt to be a hireling service, in which neither speaker nor hearer can have special interest.

Finally. It produces the most efficient ministry.

This is a general conclusion, drawn from the foregoing considerations, and a position established by the whole history of the church. It contradicts all history and all the

---

Montanus fell into his dotage on the same account; so did Novatianus at Rome, Euseb. lib. 6, cap. 43, and Arius at Alexandria. Hence is that censure of them by Lactantius, lib. 4, cap. 30: 'Ii quorum fides fuit lubrica, cum Deum nosse se et colere simularent, augendis opibus et honori studentes, affectabant maximum sacerdotium, et a potioribus victi, secedere cum suffragatoribus maluerunt, quam eos ferre praepositos quibus concupierant ipsi ante praeponi."—*Owen, Works,* Vol. XX. p. 169.

principles of human conduct to suppose that an independent establishment, in which the priesthood are settled down at ease in their livings, can have the efficiency and moral power of a clergy the tenure of whose office depends upon their activity and usefulness.

CHAPTER V.

DISCIPLINE BY THE CHURCHES.

The discipline of the primitive church was administered by each body of believers collectively; and continued to be under their control until the third or fourth century. About this period the simple and efficient discipline of the primitive church was exchanged for a complicated and oppressive system of penance administered by the clergy. But the church itself possesses the only legitimate authority for the administration of discipline. Its members have the right to enact their own laws, and to prescribe such conditions of membership with themselves as they may judge expedient and agreeable to the word of God. The right to administer ecclesiastical discipline was guaranteed to the churches from their first organization under the apostles; but was finally lost by the usurpation of the priesthood under the episcopal hierarchy.

I. The right to administer ecclesiastical discipline was originally vested in the church itself.

The argument in support of this proposition is derived—

1. From the Scriptures.
2. From the early Fathers.
3. From the authority of modern ecclesiastical writers.
4. From the fact that the entire government of the church was vested in that body itself.

1. The argument from Scripture.

Our Lord himself is supposed to teach, in Matt. xviii. 15–18, that the public discipline of offenders should be administered by the authority of the church.

These instructions are understood to have been given prospectively, and to contain the rules by which the discipline of the Christian church should be administered. But whether given with reference to the Christian church which was about to be established, or designed to exhibit the proper mode of procedure in the discipline of the Jewish synagogue, they doubtless develop the *principle* on which ecclesiastical censure should be conducted under the Christian dispensation. Vitringa has clearly shown that the directions of our Lord, in this instance, accord with the established usage of the synagogue, which was the pattern of the primitive church, both in its government and forms of worship. He has shown that this sentence was to be pronounced in accordance with a popular vote in public assembly; and that the same course of procedure was to be the rule of the Christian church. The church, therefore, like the synagogue,[1] is the ecclesiastical court of impeachment for the trial of offences. If private remonstrance proves ineffectual, the case is to be brought before the church, to be adjudged by a public vote of that body, after the manner of the Jewish synagogue.

This rule of discipline was also established in the Christian church by *apostolical* authority.

We have on record one instance of a trial before the church which was instituted by the command of the apostle Paul, and conducted throughout agreeably to his instructions. A Christian convert in Corinth, and a member of

---

[1] Vitringa, De Synagoga Vet. Lib. 3. p. 1, c. 9. Angusti. Denkwürdigkeiten, IX. S. 43, seq. Pfaff, De Originibus Juris Eccles. p. 99.

the church which had recently been established in that city, had maintained an incestuous connection with his father's wife. This shocking sin, unexampled even among the Gentiles, the apostle rebukes with righteous abhorrence. The transgressor ought to be put away from among them; and, uniting with them as if present in their assembly convened for the purpose, Paul resolves to deliver him unto Satan, in the name, and with the power of the Lord Jesus Christ, *i. e.*, by the help and with the authority of the Lord. 1 Cor. v. 3–5.

Upon this passage we remark:

(*a*) The decision was not an official act of the apostle, a sentence pronounced by his authority alone. It was the act of the church. Absent in body, but present in spirit with them when assembled together, the apostle pronounces his decision *as if acting and co-operating with them.* By this parenthetic sentence, "When ye are gathered together, and my spirit," he indicates the intervention and co-operation of the church in the sentence pronounced upon the transgressor. "The apostle qualifies the earnestness with which he speaks in the third verse, by reference, first, to the authority of Christ, and secondly, to the co-operation of the church; agreeably to the republican spirit of ancient Christianity, personating himself as present in spirit in their assembly."[2] "When the apostle speaks of an excommunication from the church, he regards himself as united in spirit with the whole church, 1 Cor. v. 4, setting forth the rule that their action is requisite in all such concerns of general interest."[3] Even in this very chapter, he refuses to be himself the judge in such cases, submitting them to the church themselves: "What have I to do to judge them

---

[2] De Wette, Comment. ad locum.

[3] Neander, Allgem. Gesch. I. S. 292. Tr. I. 190. Comp. S. 350. Apost. Kirch. I. pp. 319, 320. Tr. I. p. 170.

that *are without?*" men of the world, "Do not ye judge them that *are within?*" members of the church. "But them that are without God judgeth," κρίνει, or rather κρινεῖ, *will judge,* which is the approved reading. "*Therefore put away from among yourselves that wicked person,*" vs. 12, 13.

The severe censure with which the apostle reflects upon the Corinthians for tolerating the offender so long, shows that the responsibility rested with them. They should have put away this offence from among them.[4] But if it was wholly the act of the apostle, why censure them for neglecting to do that which they had no right or authority to do? Are the members of the Episcopal Church blameworthy for the general neglect of discipline in their communion, while the clergy have the sole power of administering that discipline? Neither could the Corinthians deserve censure, unless they had authority to administer the discipline which they had neglected. Both here, and in 2 Cor. ii. 3–11, the apostle refers distinctly to their neglect in this matter.

Again, in 2 Cor. ii. 6, he speaks of the excommunication as the act of the church. The punishment was inflicted, ὑπὸ τῶν πλειόνων, by *the many,* the majority. Bilroth paraphrases this in connection with the preceding verse, as follows: "Whether he, or the offender, have caused grief to me, comes not into consideration. It is not that *I* must suffer for him, but *you;* at least, a part of you; for I will not be unjust, and charge you *all* with having been indifferent concerning his transgressions. Paul proceeds still further, verse 6; he calls those who had reprehended the transgressor, *the majority,* who had condemned his vice and been grieved by it."

Once more, the apostle does not himself restore the transgressor, now penitent for his sin; *but exhorts the Corinthians to do it.* But if the church had themselves the authority

[4] Mosheim, Institutiones Majores, P. II. c. 3, § 14.

to receive him again to their communion, had they not also the right of censure? "The punishment which they had extended over him, by excluding him from their communion, is declared to be sufficient, since he had reformed himself (on ἱκανόν, see Winer, p. 297). The apostle himself, therefore, proposes, v. 7, that they should again treat him in a friendly manner, and comfort him, in order that he might not be worn away by over-much grief."[5] In v. 10, again, he signifies his readiness to assent to their decisions; whom they forgive, he forgives also, and because *they* had forgiven him.

(b) *This sentence was an actual excommunication;* not a judicial visitation analogous to that upon Simon Magus, Acts xiii. 11. By this sentence the offender was removed from the church of Christ and reduced to his former condition as a heathen man. This, according to the most approved commentators, is the full meaning of the phrase, παραδοῦναι τῷ Σατανᾷ. The world, in the angelology of the Jews, and agreeably to the Scriptures, comprises two great divisions: the kingdom of Christ and the kingdom of Satan. By this sentence of excommunication, the incestuous person is transferred from the visible kingdom of our Lord to the dominion of Satan, and in this sense delivered unto him.

(c) *The ultimate object of this discipline was the reformation of the offender;* the destruction of the flesh, that *the spirit may be saved* in the day of the Lord Jesus. It was not a penance, an arbitrary, prelatical infliction of pains and penalties, but a disciplinary process for the spiritual benefit of the individual.

(d) *It is questionable, perhaps, whether the sentence was accompanied with the judicial infliction of any disease whatever.* Many of the most respectable commentators understand by the delivering "to Satan for *the destruction of the*

---

[5] Bilroth, Comment. ad locum.

flesh," the visitation of some wasting malady. The phraseology doubtless admits of such a construction, and the language of the apostle on other occasions seems to favor it. Comp. 1 Cor. xi. 30; 1 Tim. i. 20. But the consequences of this excommunication were of themselves sufficient, it may be, to justify this strong expression, *the destruction of the flesh.* To the Jews, under the old dispensation, and to primitive Christians under the new, the sentence of excommunication was no light matter. It was a withering curse, a *civil death.* It involved a total exclusion from kindred, from society, from all those charities of life which Christians were wont to reciprocate even with the heathen.[6] This construction, again, is given to the passage by commentators of high authority.

But is any *bodily disease* intended? Flesh, σάρξ, often denotes *the carnal propensities,* the *sinful appetites* and *passions,* Gal. v. 17, 19; vi. 8; Eph. ii. 3; Col. ii. 11. The subjugation, the putting away of these, is distinctly implied in the ultimate design of this discipline—the salvation of the spirit—and is not this all that is intended in the ὄλεθρον τῆς σαρκός, *the destruction* of the flesh? However that may be, it is not essential to our present purpose. Whatever may have been to the guilty person the consequences of the sentence of excommunication, that sentence proceeded from the church, acting at the suggestion and with the advice of the apostle.

[6] Josephus relates that those who were excommunicated from the Essenes often died after a miserable manner, and were therefore, from motives of compassion, received again when at the point of death. In this instance, the oath of the Essenes obliged them to refuse such food as the excommunicated person might find; but was not the case equally bad when all were bound not only to refuse him subsistence, but every expression of kindness and charity? Comp. Jahn's Archäology, § 528; Horne's Introduction, B. II. c. 3, § 4; Neander, Allgem. Gesch. I. 373, 2d edit.; Tr. I. p. 218.

An excommunication somewhat similar is described briefly in 1 Cor. xvi. 22: "If any man love not the Lord Jesus Christ, let him be anathema maran-atha." The word anathema corresponds to the Hebrew חֵרֶם, which denotes either anything given up to God or devoted to destruction. It was a form of excommunication familiar to the Jews, which was pronounced publicly upon the offender, and excluded him from all communion whatever with his countrymen.[7] Such was the *anathema*, a solemn sentence of excommunication, publicly pronounced upon the transgressor. The phrase *Maran-atha* is the Syro-Chaldaic מָרָנָא אֲתָה, *The Lord cometh*, i. e., *to judgment*. The whole, taken together, implies that the transgressor is separated from the communion of the church, and abandoned to the just judgment of God. All that the apostle seems to demand of the Corinthians respecting the offender is, that they should exclude him from their society, so that he might cease to be a member of the church, verses 12, 13. He pronounces no further judgment upon him, but expressly refers to the future judgment of God.

In review, therefore, of these important passages, several things are worthy of particular remark:

(α) The sentence of exclusion proceeded not from the pastor of the church, but *from the church collectively*.

(β) The excommunication is styled a punishment, ἐπιτιμία. But the apostle distinguishes it both from the civil penalties which attended the ban of excommunication among the Jews and from the judicial sentence of God, regarding the whole transaction as an ecclesiastical act intended to express just abhorrence of the crime and merited censure of it.

(γ) The reason assigned for the restoration of the offender

---

[7] Jahn's Archäology, § 258. Du Pin, De Antiqua Disciplina, Diss. 3, c. 2, p. 272.

was repentance—λύπη—*sorrow for his sin*, to which the apostle probably refers in a subsequent passage, vii. 10, when he says, "Godly sorrow worketh repentance to salvation not to be repented of."

(*δ*) He was restored to the communion and fellowship of the church, as he had been excluded, *by the public consent*, the vote of that body. In accordance with these views, the apostle exhorts the Corinthians to separate from them any other immoral person, any man that is called a brother, whether he be a fornicator, or covetous, or an idolater, or a railer, or a drunkard, or an extortioner, 1 Cor. v. 11. And the Galatians he exhorts to restore, in the spirit of meekness, one who may have been overtaken in fault. Now this right of judging and acting, both in the expulsion of the immoral and the restoration of the penitent, obviously vests in the church the power of ecclesiastical censure.[8] Comp. 2 Thess. iii. 14 and Rom. xvi. 17.

It was therefore the privilege of the apostolical church to administer its own discipline—a right which accords with every just principle of religious liberty, while it clearly illustrates the popular character of the primitive constitution of the church. For, as in their elections so in their discipline, the apostolical churches were doubtless in harmony one with another, and may justly be presumed to have observed the same rules of fellowship. Based on the same principles and governed by similar laws, one example may suffice to illustrate the policy of all.[9]

---

[8] Rights of the Church, by Tindal, p. 39.
[9] On this whole subject, comp. Vitringa, De Synagoga, Lib. 3, p. 1, c. 10; Pertsch, Kirch. Hist. I. 4to. S. 469, seq.; Recht. Eccles. Kirchenbanns, Vorrede, Ausgab, 1738, 4, C. M. Pfaff, De Originibus Juris Eccl. pp. 10–13; Neander's Allgem. Gesch. S. 349, seq., 71, 98, etc.; Dr. W. D. Killen's Ancient Church. p. 223, seq.; Lange and Schaff on Apost. Ch.

The following passages may be consulted in relation to the duty of the church to maintain its watch and discipline over its members: 2 Thess. iii. 14; Matt. xviii. 15-17; Rom. xvi. 17; Gal. ii. 11, seq.; 2 Epist. John 10; 1 Tim. i. 20; Rev. ii. 14, 20.

2. Argument from the early fathers

Few passages, comparatively, occur in their writings relating immediately to the point under consideration. But enough can be derived from them to show that the church continued for two or three centuries to regulate her own discipline by the will of the majority, as expressed either by a direct popular vote or through a representative delegation chosen by the people.

Clemens Romanus, the only apostolical father belonging strictly to the first century, and contemporary with several of the apostles, throughout his epistle treats the church of Corinth as the only court of censure. He addresses his epistle, A. D. 68 or 98, not to the bishop, but to the entire body of believers. This circumstance is worthy of particular notice, inasmuch as the epistle is written in relation to a case of discipline, and not to enforce the practical duties of religion. The church at Corinth was recognized as having authority in the case under consideration.

Clement in his epistle reflects severely upon the Corinthians for their treatment of their religious teachers, some of whom they had rejected from the ministry. To do this without good reason, he assures them, "would be no small sin" in them,[10] and earnestly exhorts them to exercise a charitable, orderly and submissive spirit. But he offers no hint that they had exceeded the limits of their legitimate authority, even in deposing some from the ministry; on the contrary, he recognizes the right of the church to regulate,

[10] Chauncey's Episcopacy, pp. 77, 78.

at their discretion, their own discipline, and the duty of all to acquiesce in it. "Who among you is generous? who is compassionate? who has any charity? Let him say whether this sedition, this contention, and these schisms be on my account. I am ready to depart, to go whithersoever you please, and *to do whatsoever ye shall command me*, only let the flock of Christ be in peace with the ministers that are set over them."[11]

The above passage is twice quoted by Chancellor King in proof that the laity were members of the ecclesiastical court for the trial of offences, "and judges therein."[12] "Clement recommends those on whose account the dissensions had arisen, to retire and to submit to the will of the majority."[13] These censures to which Clement urges them to submit, he characterizes as "*the commands of the multitude*, τὰ προστασσόμενα ὑπὸ τοῦ πλήθους."

The epistle of Polycarp to the Philippians, A. D. 117–120, affords us, indirectly, a similar example of the deportment of the church toward a fallen brother. This venerable father was greatly afflicted at the defection of Valens, a presbyter of that church, who had fallen into some scandalous error. But he entreats the charitable consideration of the church toward the offender, urging them to exercise moderation toward him; and on similar occasions to seek to reclaim the erring, and to call them back, in the spirit of kindness and Christian charity.[14] The address and exhortation, throughout, proceed on the supposition that the duty of mutual watchfulness belongs to the brethren of the

[11] Εἰ διὰ ἐμὲ στάσις καὶ ἔρις καὶ σχίσματα ἐκχωρῶ, ἄπειμι, οὗ ἐὰν βούλησθε, καὶ ποιῶ τὰ προστασσόμενα ὑπὸ τοῦ πλήθους.—Ep. ad Cor. c. 54. Comp. § 44.

[12] Primitive Church, B. I. c. 11, § 6, 7, § 2.

[13] Riddle, Christian Antiquities, p. 9.   [14] Comp. Ep. c. 11.

church collectively. It is not, however, a clear case of church discipline, though this may be implied.

At the beginning of the second century, A. D. 103 or 104, Pliny the Younger instituted a severe examination, by torture and the rack, into the character of the Christians in his province in Asia Minor. As the result, he reports to the Emperor Trajan, that under this terrible alternative some abjured their profession as Christians; others, with inflexible obstinacy, maintained it; but all of those who denied their faith affirmed that the sum of their fault or error was, that they were accustomed, on a stated day, to assemble before the dawn of the morning to sing a hymn to Christ as to God, and to bind themselves by an oath neither to commit theft, robbery or adultery, nor to swerve from the faith or disown a trust committed to them."[15]

The report of Eusebius respecting these covenant vows is that these Christians, "for the purpose of maintaining their discipline, prohibited adultery, murder, overreaching, fraud, and all crimes like them."[16]

Tertullian also represents Pliny to have said, that besides their obstinacy in refusing to offer sacrifices, he discovered nothing more concerning their secret vows than that they were accustomed to meet before the dawn of the morning to sing to Christ and to God; and to enter into a mutual disciplinary covenant, forbidding murder, adultery, fraud, perfidy and other crimes."[17]

---

[15] Omnes affirmabant autem hunc esse summum vel culpae suae, vel erroris, quod essent soliti, stato die, ante lucem convenire, carmenque Christo, quasi Deo dicere secum invicem; seque sacramento, non in scelus aliquod, obstringere, sed ne furta, ne latrocinia, ne adulteria, committerent ne fidem, fallerent, depositum appellati abnegarent. Epist. ad Traj.

[16] Hist. Book III. 33.

[17] Allegans, praetor obstinationem non sacrificandi nihil aliud se de

Tertullian wrote his Apology for the Christians a hundred years after these persecutions in Bithynia, at the beginning of the third century. From him we learn that the discipline of the church remained unchanged at this period, the members of the church sustaining the same covenant relations, exercising the same mutual watchfulness and maintaining the same discipline in the exclusion of the unworthy from their fellowship and communion. "We Christians are a confederate body by our agreement in religion, our uniformity in discipline and in the bonds of hope. From the Sacred Oracles we nourish our faith and inspire our hopes; and, by inculcating the precepts of religion, enforce our discipline. There are administered also admonitions, reproofs and the *divine censure*. For it is regarded as a transaction of great solemnity in the sight of God, and a most impressive anticipation of the future judgment, when one so sins as to be excluded from all fellowship in the prayers, the assemblies and the sacred communion of saints."[18]

None can doubt that this divine sentence of excommunication is the action of the church collectively. Certain approved elders preside, probati quique seniores praesident, acting in co-operation with the church. This authoritative action of the church becomes undeniably evident from the

sacramentis corum comperisse quam coetus antelucanos ad canendum Christo et Deo, et ad confoederandam disciplinam homicidium, adulterium, fraudem, perfidiam et caetera scelera prohibentes."—*Apol.* c. 2.

[18] Corpus sumus de conscientia religionis et disciplinae unitate et spei foedere. . . . . . Certe fidem, sanctis vocibus pascimus, spem erigimus, fiduciam figimus, disciplinam praeceptorum nihilominous inculcationibus, densamus; ibidem etiam exhortationes, castigationes, et *censura divina*. Nam et judicatur magno cum pondere, ut apud certos de Dei conspectu; summumque futuri judicii praejudicium est, si quis ita deliquerit ut, a communicatione orationis et conventus et omnis sancti commercii relegetur.—*Apol.* 39.

example of Cyprian, who, while sternly defending his episcopal prerogatives, does nothing without the counsel of the clergy and the consent of the people.[19] Böhmer has illustrated this action of the church at great length in his incomparable Dissertation on the confederate discipline of these primitive Christians.[20]

Both Chancellor King,[21] and the "great Du Pin,"[22] though himself a Roman Catholic, cite the above passage as evidence that the discipline of the church continued to be administered, as from the beginning it had been, *by public vote of the church;* the clergy being understood to have a joint action and influence in their deliberations.

On another occasion Tertullian remarks that the crimes of idolatry and of murder are of such enormity that the charity of the *churches* is not extended to such as have been guilty of these offences.[23]

The authority of the church again is manifest in the case of Alexander, A. D. 180–193, an impostor who sought to join himself to the faithful; but " the *church of the place whence he sprang* would not receive him because he was a robber."[24]

The strict caution observed by the church in the admission of members to their communion is fully described by Origen, who lived after Tertullian, near the close of the first half of the third century: "Strict inquiry is made into the life and carriage of the candidates, ἐξετάστειν τοὺς βίους

---

[19] A primordio episcopatus mei statuerim nihil sine consilio vestro et sine, consensu plebis. mea privatim sententia gerere.—Epist. 5.
[20] Diss. III., de Confoederata Christianorum Disciplina.
[21] Prim. Christ. P. I. c. VII. § 4.
[22] Du Pin's Antiqua Disciplina, Diss. 3, c. 1.
[23] Neque idololatriae, neque sanguini pax ab ecclesiis redditur.—De Pudicit. c. 12.
[24] Euseb. Hist. B. V. c. 18.

καὶ τὰς ἀγωγὰς τῶν προσιόντων, requiring of them repentance and a better life; then we admit them to our mysteries."[25] Again, in his second book, he says that "they make private and public examinations of such as present themselves, that they may guard their communion from such as indulge in forbidden offence." "Toward transgressors their discipline is peculiarly severe, especially toward the licentious. On their repentance they are restored to the communion of the church, but never received to any ecclesiastical office."[26] This restoration is sought from the church, δεηδῆναι τοῦ ἐπὶ πάσης ἐκκλησίας, as being the party in whom this authority is vested.

Cyprian, ever ready to assert the prerogatives of the bishop, uniformly recognizes and fully asserts the right of the church to direct in the discipline of its members. About the year 250, the emperor Decius issued an edict commanding the Christians to sacrifice to the gods. To escape the requisitions and penalties of this edict, Cyprian, then bishop of Carthage, was compelled to fly for his life, and continued in exile about sixteen months. But many of his church, under the relentless persecution that ensued, yielded an apparent compliance with the emperor's impious command. Others, without compliance, had the address to obtain a certain certificate from the prosecuting officer, which freed them from further molestation. All such persons, however, were denominated the lapsed, *lapsi*, and were excommunicated as apostates. The system of canonical penance, as it was called, was so far established at this time that this class of offenders were required to fulfill the forms of a pre-

---

[25] Contra Celsum, Lib. 3.

[26] Comp. Stillingfleet. Irenicum, p. 161, Phil. ed. Böhmer, pp. 105–110. Comp. Chrysost. Comment. in Math., Tom. 13, pp. 612–613. Comp. Blondell. De jure plebis in regimine ecclesiastico, where are given many other authorities.

scribed and prolonged penance before they could be restored to the communion of the church. Many of the lapsed, touched with a sense of their guilt, pleaded for an abatement of the rigor of these austerities, and an earlier and easier return to the communion of the church. To this course a party in the church were, for various reasons, strongly inclined; and some were actually restored in the absence of the bishop. This irregularity was severely censured by Cyprian, who often recognizes the right of the people to be a party in the deliberations and decisions respecting them. The clergy who had favored this abuse, he says, "shall give an account of what they have done, to me, to the confessors,"[27] and *to the whole church.*"[28]

In a letter, addressed to the church, he says, "When the Lord shall have restored peace unto us all, and we shall all have returned to the church again, we shall then examine all these things, *you also being present and judging of them.*" In the conclusion of the same epistle he adds, " I desire then that they would patiently hear our counsel and wait for our return, that then, when many of us bishops shall have met together, we may examine the certificates and desires of the blessed martyrs, according to the discipline of the Lord, in the presence of the confessors, and *according to your will.*"[29]

---

[27] " It was the privilege of the *confessors*, that is, of persons who had suffered torture, or received sentence of death, to give to any of the lapsed a written paper, termed *a letter of peace;* and the bearer was entitled to a remission of some part of the ecclesiastical discipline."—*Burton's History of the Church,* chap. 15.

[28] Acturi et apud nos et apud confessores ipsos et *apud plebem universam* causam suam, cum, Domino permittente, in sinum matris ecclesiae recolligi coeperimus.—*Ep.* 10, al. 9.

[29] Cum, pace nobis omnibus a Domino prius data, ad ecclesiam regredi coeperimus, tunc examinabuntur singula, *praesentibus et judicantibus vobis.*—Audiant quaeso, patientur consilium nostrum, expectent regressionem nostram; ut cum ad vos, per Dei misericordiam, veneri-

In his epistle to his people at Carthage, in which he laments the schism of Felicissimus, he assures them that on his return, he with his colleagues will dispose of the case *agreeably to the will of his people*, and the mutual council of both clergy and people.[30] The two offending sub-deacons and acolytes, he declares, shall be tried, not only in the presence of his colleagues, but *before the whole people*.[31] The above and other similar passages are often cited in evidence of the agency which the people still continued, in the middle of the third century, to exert in the administration of ecclesiastical censure.[32] Will any one presume to say, that in refusing to decide upon any case, or to exercise any authority, Cyprian only condescends kindly to regard the will of the people, without acknowledging their right to be consulted? We ask in reply, Is this the language and spirit of prelacy? Under such instructions as those of Cyprian, the church would learn but slowly the doctrine of passive obedience.

Enough has been said to illustrate the usage of the church at Carthage. Between this church and that at Rome, under Cornelius, there was, at this time, the greatest harmony of sentiment in relation to the discipline of the church. And, from the correspondence between the churches, which is recorded in the works of Cyprian, there is conclu-

mus, convocati episcopi plures secundum Domini disciplinam, et confessorum, praesentiam et vestram quoque sententiam martyrum litteras et desideria examinare possimus.—*Ep.* 12, al. 11.

[30] Cum collegis meis, quibus praesentibus, secundum arbitrium quoque vestrum et omnium nostrum commune consilium, sicut semel placuit ea quae agenda sunt disponere pariter et limare poterimus.—*Ep.* 40.

[31] Non tantum cum collegis meis, sed cum plebe ipsa universa.—*Ep.* 34, al. 28. Crimina—publice a nobis et *plebe* cognoscerentur.—*Ep.* 44, al. 41.

[32] Comp. Daillé, Right Use of the Fathers, B. 2, c. 6, pp. 328–330.

sive evidence that their polity was the same. This is so clearly asserted by Du Pin, that I shall dismiss this point by citing his authority. After making the extract from Tertullian, which has been given above, and others from Cyprian, similar to those which have already been cited, he adds, "From whence it is plain, that both in Rome and at Carthage, no one could be expelled from the church, or restored again, except with the consent of the people." This, according to the same author, was in conformity with apostolical precedent in the case of the incestuous person at Corinth.[33]

Origen, again, of Caesarea in Palestine, speaks of the conviction of an offender before the whole church, ἐπὶ πάσης τῆς ἐκκλησίας, as the customary mode of trial.[34] With the authority of Origen we may join that of Chrysostom at Constantinople. In commenting upon 1 Cor. v. 3–5, he represents the complaint of the apostle to be that the Corinthians had not put away that wicked person from among them; "showing that this ought to be done *without their teacher*,"[35] and that the apostle associates them with himself, "that his own authority might not seem to be too great" in the transaction. Theodoret also expresses much the same sentiments upon the passage under consideration.[36]

These authorities are derived both from the Eastern and

[33] De Antiqua Disciplina, Diss. 3, pp. 248, 249.

[34] Πρὸς δὲ τὸ δοκοῦν σκληρὸν πρὸς τοὺς τὰ ἐλάττονα ἡμαρτηκότας, εἴποι τις ἂν ὅτι οὐκ ἔξεστι δίς ἐξῆς μὴ ἀκούσαντα, τὸ τρίτον ἀκοῦσαι ὡς διὰ τοῦτο μηκέτι εἶναι ὡς ἐθνικὸν καὶ τελώνην, ἢ μηκέτι δεηθῆναι τοῦ ἐπὶ πάσης τῆς ἐκκλησίας.—*Comment, in Matt.*, Tom. 13, p. 612. Comp. 613.

[35] Δεικνὺς ὅτι δὲ χωρὶς τοῦ διδασκάλου τὸ γενέσθαι ἔδει ἵνα μὴ δόξῃ πολλὴ εἶτ ἡ αὐθεντία.—*Hom.* 15, ad 1 *Cor.*, Tom. 10, p. 126.

[36] Theodoret, Comment. ad locum, Opera, Tom. 10, p. 141. Comp. Blondell, De jure plebis in regimine ecclesiastico, where many other authorities are given. Comp. especially the masterly discussions of J. H. Böhmer, XII. Dissertationies Juris Ecclesiastici Antiqui.

the Western churches. As ancient expositions of the apostolical rule, and as examples of the usage of the churches in the ages immediately succeeding that of the apostles, they indicate that throughout this period ecclesiastical discipline was administered in accordance with the will of the people, and by their decision. The bishop and clergy, instead of holding in their own grasp the keys of the kingdom of heaven, co-operated with the church in its deliberations; and acted as the official organ of the assembly in executing its decisions. Neither was the ban of the church wielded in terror, as it has often been by an arbitrary priesthood to accomplish their own sinister ends.

The penitent was restored, also, in the spirit of kindness and Christian forgiveness, by the joint consent of the same body which had originally excluded him from its communion.

This point deserves distinct consideration, as another indication of the religious liberty enjoyed by the church. Paul submitted to the church at Corinth the restoration of the offender whom they had excluded from their communion. Tertullian makes it the duty of the penitent to cast himself at the feet of the clergy, and kneeling at the altar of God, to *seek the pardon and intercessions of all the brethren.*[37] Cyprian, in the passage cited above, declares, that the lapsed, who had been excluded from the church, must make their defence before all the people, *apud plebem universam.* "It was ordained by an African synod, in the third century, that, except in danger of death, or of a sudden persecution, none should be received unto the peace of the church, *without the knowledge and consent of the people.*"[38]

---

[37] Presbyteris advolvi, et caris [aris] Dei adgeniculari omnibus fratribus legationes deprecationis suae injungere.—*De Poenitentia,* c. 9.

[38] Cyprian, Epist. 59. The same fact is also asserted by Du Pin, in the passage quoted above.

Natalius, at Rome, in the first part of the third century, threw himself at the feet of the clergy and *laity*, and so bewailed his faults that *the church was moved with compassion for him*, and with much difficulty he was received into its communion.[39] The same is related of one of the bishops, who was restored to the church at Rome, under Cornelius, to lay communion, "*through the mediation of all the people then present.*"[40] Serapion, at Antioch, was also refused admission to that church, no one *giving attention to him.*"[41] At Rome, then, in Africa, in Asia, and universally, the penitent was restored to Christian communion by the authority of the church from which he had been expelled.

If it were necessary to adduce further evidence in vindication of the right of the people to administer the discipline of the church, it might be drawn from the acknowledged fact that the people, down to the third or fourth century, retained, and not unfrequently exercised, the right even of deposing from the ministry. The controversy of the people of Corinth with their pastors, as indicated in the epistle of Clement, has been already mentioned; and the case of Valens deposed from the ministry by the church at Philippi. To these may be added the instances of Martialis and Basilides, bishops of Leon and Astorga in Spain, who were deposed for idolatry. From this sentence they appealed to several bishops in Africa. These, after hearing the case in common council, A. D. 258, affirmed the act of the people. The result of their deliberations was communicated by Cyprian, from which decision the extract below is taken, in which he fully accords to the people the right both to choose the worthy and depose the unworthy: *eligendi dig-*

---

[39] Euseb. Eccl. Hist. Lib. 5, c. 28.
[40] Euseb. Eccl. Hist. Lib. 6, c. 43.
[41] Euseb. Eccl. Hist. Lib. 6, c. 44.

nos sacerdotes et indignos recusandi.[42] Cyprian, the father of old Catholic high-church episcopalianism, most explicitly declares that the church is *superior to* the bishops, *super episcopos;* the supreme power is vested in them—in all that are *in good and regular standing, omnibus stantibus,* all who have not apostatized. The bishop only acts as the moderator of the church. "Many other such like passages are found in that Synodical Epistle, which flatly asserts the people's power to depose a wicked and scandalous bishop."[43] And again, by Dr. Barrow, of the Episcopal Church: "No man can be bound to follow any one into the ditch, or to obey any one in prejudice to his own salvation. If any pastor should teach bad doctrine or prescribe bad practice, his people may reject and disobey him."[44]

From these censures of a popular assembly an appeal would be made, as in the case before us, to a synodical council or to the neighboring bishops. For this reason they are sometimes represented as the ecclesiastical court for the trial of the clergy. Such they were at a subsequent period; but in the primitive church it was, as appears from the foregoing authorities, the right of the church to exercise her discipline over both laity and clergy. The greater includes the less. The right to depose a scandalous bishop

---

[42] See p. 64, note. Mosheim, De Rebus. Cent. III. § 23.

[43] King's Prim. Chris. P. 1, c. 6. Inde per temporum et successionum vices episcoporum ordinatio et ecclesiae ratio decurrit ut *ecclesia super episcopos constituatur* et omnis actus ecclesiae per eosdem praepositos gubernetur. Cum hoc itaque *lege divina* fundatum sit, miror quosdam, audaci temeritate, sic mihi scribere voluisse ut ecclesiae nomine literas facerent, quando ecclesia in episcopo et clero et in omnibus stantibus [*i. e.,* who had not apostatized] sit constituta.—*Ep.* 33, al. 27. Comp. Bingham, Book 16, c. 1; Neander, Allgem. Kirch. Gesch. 11, S. 341; Tr. I. p. 200.

[44] Barrow's Works, Vol. I. p. 744. Comp. also Pertsch, Kirch. Hist. I. S. 370. Mosheim, Can. Recht, p. 60.

of necessity supposes the right to expel from their communion an unworthy member of humbler rank. The conclusion is irresistible, that, as in the highest act of ecclesiastical censure, so in smaller offences, the discipline of the church was conducted with the strictest regard to the rights and privileges of its members.

3. Argument from the authority of modern ecclesiastical writers.

Authority is not argument, but to some minds it is more satisfactory than argument. The opinion of those who have made ecclesiastical history the study of their lives is worthy of our regard. The concurring opinion of many such becomes a valid reason for our belief. What then is their authority?

Valesius, the learned commentator on Eusebius, says that "the people's suffrages were required when any one was to be received into the church who for any fault had been excommunicated." [45] This is said in relation to the usage of the church in the third century.

The authority of Du Pin, the distinguished historian of the Roman Catholic communion, whose opinion upon this point is worthy of all confidence, is to the same effect: that the discipline of the church continued, in the *third century*, to be administered by the church as it had been from the beginning.[46]

Simonis, profoundly learned on all points relating to ecclesiastical usage, declares that "this church discipline was so administered that not only the clergy, especially the bishops, and in important cases a council of them, but also the *church, in every case*, gave their decision and approbation, in order that nothing might be done through preju-

---

[45] Eccl. Hist. Lib. 6, 44. Com. Lib. 5, 28.
[46] Antiqua Disciplina, Diss. 3, c. 1.

dice and private interest by being submitted to the clergy and bishops alone."[47]

Baumgarten ascribes to the church alone the entire control of ecclesiastical censures, from the earliest periods of its history down to the time of Cyprian, when he supposes each case to have been first adjudicated by the church, and afterward by the clergy and bishop.[48]

Mosheim is full and explicit upon the same point. He not only ascribes to the church the power of enacting their own laws and choosing their own officers, but of excluding and receiving such as were the subjects of discipline, *malos et degeneros et excludendi et recipiendi.*[49]

Planck asserts that, so late as the middle of the third century, the members of the church still exercised their original right of controlling the proceedings of the church, both in the exclusion of offenders and in the restitution of penitents.[50]

Guerike also states that, in the third century, the duty of excluding from the church and of restoring to her communion still devolved upon the laity.[51]

The views of Neander are sufficiently apparent from quotations which have already been made in the progress of this work. More thoroughly conversant with the writings of the fathers, and more profoundly skilled in the government and history of the church, than any in his age, he not only ascribes the discipline of offenders originally to the deliberate action of the church, but states, moreover, that

---

[47] Vorlesungen über Christ. Alterthum, S. 426.

[48] Erläuterungen, Christ. Alterthum, § 122. Comp. also § 36, and S. 85.

[49] De Rebus Christ., Saec. Prim. § 45.

[50] Gesell. Verfass. 1, S. 180, 508. Comp. S. 129–140, and Fuchs, Bibliothek, 1, S. 43, seq.

[51] Kirch. Gesch. S. 94, 100, 101, 2d edit.

the right of controlling this discipline was retained by the laity in the middle of the third century, after the rise of the episcopal power and the consequent change in the government of the church. "The participation of the laity in the concerns of the church was not yet altogether excluded. One of these concerns was the restoration of the lapsed to the communion of the church. The examination which was instituted in connection with this restoration was also held before the whole church." [52]

These authorities might be extended almost indefinitely; but enough have been cited to show that, in the opinion of those who are most competent to decide, the sacred right of directing the discipline of the church was, from the beginning, exercised by the whole body of believers belonging to the community; and that they continued, in the third century, to exercise the same prerogative.

4. Argument from the fact that the entire government of the church was under the control of its members.

Government by the people characterized the whole ecclesiastical polity of the primitive church. The members of the church, unitedly, enacted their own laws, elected their own officers, established their own judicature, and managed all their affairs by their mutual suffrages. "With them resided the power of enacting laws, as also of adopting or rejecting whatever might be proposed in the general assemblies, and of expelling and again receiving into communion any depraved or unworthy members. In a word, nothing whatever of any moment could be determined on or carried into effect without their knowledge and concurrence." [53]

On this point, again, we must be permitted to adduce the authority of Neander. After showing at length that, agree-

[52] Allgem. Kirch. Gesch. 1, S. 342, 2d edit. Tr. I. p. 200.
[53] Mosheim, De Rebus Christ., Saec. 1, § 45.

ably to the spirit of the primitive church, all were regarded as different organs and members of one body, and actuated by one and the same spirit, he adds: "But from the nature of the religious life and of the Christian fellowship, it was hardly possible that the controlling influence should naturally have been entrusted to the hands of a single individual. *The monarchical form of government was not at all consistent with the spirit of the Christian community.*" [54]

Riddle gives the following sketch of the constitution and government of the church as it existed at the close of the first and at the beginning of the second century. "The subordinate government, etc., of each particular church was vested in itself; that is to say, the whole body elected its minister and officers, and was consulted concerning all matters of importance." [55]

Even the "judicious" Hooker, the great expounder of the ecclesiastical polity of the Episcopal Church, distinctly declares that "the general consent of all" is requisite for the ratification of the laws of the church. "Laws could they never be without the consent of the whole church to be guided by them; whereunto both nature and the practice of the church of God set down in the Scripture is found so consonant that God himself would not impose his own laws upon his people by the hands of Moses without their free and open consent." [56]

From all these authorities, in connection with what has already been said in the former part of this work, the popular administration of the government is an undeniable conclusion. Even the minute concerns of the church were submitted to the direction of the popular voice. Is a delegate to be sent out? He goes, not as the servant of the bishop,

---

[54] Allgem. Gesch. 1, S. 312, 2d edit. Tr. I. p. 183.
[55] Chronology, p. 13.
[56] Ecclesiastical Polity, B. VIII.

but as the representative of the church, chosen to this service by public vote.[57] Is a letter missive to be issued from one church to another? It is done in the name of the church; and, when received, is publicly read.[58] In short, nothing is done without the consent of the church. Even Cyprian, the great advocate for episcopal authority in the middle of the third century, protests to his clergy that, " from his first coming to his bishopric, he had ever resolved to do nothing according to his own private will without the advice of the clergy and the approbation of the people." [59]

The point now under consideration is very clearly presented by an old English writer of Cambridge, in England, whose work on Primitive Episcopacy evinces such a familiar acquaintance with the early history of the church as entitles his conclusions to great respect. "In the apostles' times, and divers ages after, all the people, under the inspection of one bishop, were wont to meet together, not only for worship, but for other administrations. All public acts passed at assemblies of the whole people. They were consulted with, their concurrence was thought necessary, and their presence required, that nothing might pass without their cognizance, satisfaction and consent. This was observed

---

[57] Ignatius, ad. Phil. c. 10.

[58] The letters of Clement and Polycarp were written by the authority of the respective churches. Comp. Euseb. Eccl. Hist. 4, c. 15; 5, c. 1, and c. 24. With the epistle of Clement, five delegates were sent also from the church at Rome to that at Corinth, to attempt to reconcile the dissensions in the latter church, § 59.

[59] Ad id vero quod scripserunt mihi compresbyteri nostri, Donatus et Fortunatus, Novatus et Gordius, solus rescribere nihil potui; quando a primordio episcopatus mei statuerim nihil sine consilio vestro, et sine consensu plebis meae privatim sententia gerere; sed cum ad vos per Dei gratiam venero, tunc de eis quae vel gesta sunt, vel gerenda sicut honor mutuus poscit in commune tractabimus.—*Cyprian, Ep.* 5. Comp. Ep. 3, 55. *Daillé on the Fathers*, p. 330. London.

not only in elections of officers, but in ordinations and censures, in admission of members and reconciling penitents, and in debates and consultations about other emergencies. There is such evidence of this, particularly in Cyprian, almost in every one of his epistles, that it is acknowledged by modern writers of all sorts, such as are most learned and best acquainted with antiquity."[60]

If then the sanction of the church was sought in the minutest matters, transactions of such solemnity as those of expelling the guilty and of restoring the penitent must have been submitted to their direction. Was a Christian salutation to a sister church communicated by public authority, commending a faithful brother to communion and fellowship, and had they no voice in rejecting a fallen and reprobate member from their own communion? Was the sanction of the whole body requisite before one from another church could be received to their communion, and had they no voice in restoring the penitent who returned confessing his sins and entreating the enjoyment of the same privileges?

All this fully accords with the usage of the apostolical churches, and is a continuation of the same policy. Whether deacons are to be appointed, or an apostle or presbyters chosen, it is done by vote of the church. A case for discipline occurs; it is submitted to the church. A dissension arises, Acts xv; this also is referred to the church. The decision is made up as seemeth good *to the whole church*. The result is communicated by the apostles, the elders and the brethren jointly. The brethren of the church have a part in all ecclesiastical concerns; nothing is transacted without their approbation and consent. The sovereign

---

[60] Clarkson's Primitive Episcopacy, Works, p. 236. The authority of the Magdeburg Centuriators is also to the same effect. Comp. Chap. 7, Cent. II. and III.

power is vested in the people. They are constituted by the apostles themselves the guardians of the church, holding in their hands the keys of the kingdom, to open and to shut, to bind and to loose at their discretion. Neither Peter nor any apostle, nor bishop, nor presbyter, but each and every disciple of Christ, is the rock on which he would build his church. Such is Origen's interpretation of the passage in Matt. xvi. 18: "Every disciple of Christ is that rock, and upon all such the whole doctrine of the church and of its corresponding polity is built. If you suppose it to be built upon Peter alone, what say you of John, that son of thunder? and of each of the apostles? Will you presume to say that the gates of hell will prevail against the other apostles and against all the saints, but not against Peter? Rather is not this and that other declaration, 'On this rock I will build my church,' applicable to each and every one alike?"[61]

Such are the arguments which we offer in defence of the proposition, that any body of believers, associated together for the enjoyment of religious rights and privileges, was also originally an ecclesiastical court, for the trial of offences.[62] This is asserted by the great Du Pin, of the Roman Catholic Church. It is admitted by respectable authorities, King Cave, Riddle, etc., of the Episcopal Church. It is generally acknowledged by Protestants of other religious denominations. It is implied or asserted in various passages from the early fathers. They speak of it, not as a controverted point, but as an admitted principle. The sanction of the

---

[61] Comment. in Matt. Tom. 3, p. 524.

[62] It was a doctrine of Tertullian, that where three are assembled together in the name of Christ, there they constitute a church, though only belonging to the laity. Three were sufficient for this purpose. Ubi tres, ecclesia est, licet laici.—*Exhort. ad Castitat.* c. 7, 522. *De Fuga,* c. 14.

members of the primitive church was sought in all the less important concerns of the church. They controlled, also, the highest acts of ecclesiastical censure, and frequently exercised their right of deposing those of their own pastors and bishops who proved themselves unworthy of the sacred office. And, finally, the church was from the beginning authorized and instructed by the apostle Paul to administer discipline to an offending member. With the approbation of the great apostle, they pronounced upon the transgressor the sentence of excommunication, and again, on receiving satisfactory evidence of penitence, restored him to their communion and fellowship.

With the question of expediency, in all this, we have now no concern. If any prefer the episcopal system of church government to one more free and popular, we shall not here dispute their right to submit themselves to the control of the diocesan. But when they assert that the exercise of such authority belongs to him by the divine right of episcopacy, we rest assured that they have begun to teach for doctrine the commandments of men. From the beginning it was not so. "Full well ye reject the commandment of God, that ye may keep your own tradition."

MODE OF ADMISSION.

This was at first extremely simple; consisting only in the profession of faith in Christ, and baptism. The churches, however, at an early period, learned the necessity of exercising greater caution in receiving men into their communion. Taught by their own bitter experience, they began to require, in the candidate for admission to their communion, a competent acquaintance with religious truth, and a trial of his character for a considerable space of time. From undue laxness they passed into the opposite extreme of excessive rigor, in prescribing rules and qualifications for communion. These austerities gave rise to the order of catechumens toward the close of the second century, and to a long train of formalities preliminary to a union with the church.

In immediate connection with these rites, and as a part of the same discipline, began the system of penance in the treatment of the *lapsed*—persons who had incurred the censure of the church. By this their return to the church was rendered even more difficult than had been their original entrance. The system was rapidly developed. In the course of the third century it was brought into full operation, while the people still retained much influence over the penal inflictions of the church upon transgressors.[63] But it is not our purpose to treat upon this subject. The system is described at length in the author's Ancient Christianity, chap. xxii., to which the reader is referred for information in relation to the offences which were the subject of discipline, the penalties inflicted and the manner of restoring penitents.

The entire regimen, however, passed, in process of time, from the hands of the people into those of the clergy, especially of the bishops. It was lost in the general extinction of the rights and privileges of the church, and the overthrow of its primitive apostolical constitution; upon the ruins of which was reared the episcopal hierarchy, first in the form of an "ambitious oligarchy," and then, of a tyrannical despotism.

II. Usurpation of discipline by the priesthood.

In the fourth century, the clergy, by a discipline peculiar to themselves, and applicable only to persons belonging to

[63] Planck, Gesellschafts-Verfass. 1, S. 129–140. Fuchs, Bibliothek, 1, S. 43, 44, 45–50, 403.

their order, found means of relieving themselves from the penalties of the protracted penance which was exacted of those who fell under the censure of the church. Suspension and the lesser excommunication or degradation, and the like, were substituted as the penalties of the clergy, instead of the rigorous penance of the laity. And though in some respects it was claimed that the discipline of the clergy was more severe than that of the laity, the practical effect of this discrimination was to separate the clergy from the laity, and to bring the latter more completely under the power of the priesthood.[64] It was at once the occasion of intolerance in the one, and of oppression to the other.

The confederation of the churches in synods and councils had also much influence in producing the same result. In these conventions, laws and regulations were enacted for the government and discipline of the churches of the province. And though the churches, severally, still retained the right of regulating their own polity as circumstances might require, they seldom claimed the exercise of their prerogative. The law-making power was transferred, in a great degree, from the people to the provincial synods, where again the authority of the people was lost in the overpowering influence of bishops and clergy. These claimed at first only to act as the representatives of their respective churches, by authority delegated to them by their constituents.[65] But they soon assumed a loftier tone.

[64] Planck, Gesellschafts-Verfass. 1, S. 342–346. Comp. c. 8, S. 125–141.

[65] Tertullian describes such assemblies as bodies *representative* of the whole Christian church. Ipsa repraesentatio totius nominis Christiani.—*De Jejun.* c. 13, p. 552.

In the infancy, indeed, of councils, the bishops acknowledged that they appeared there merely as the ministers or legates of their respective churches, and were, in fact, nothing more than representatives acting under instructions; but this humble language began, by little

Claiming for themselves the guidance of the Spirit of God, they professed to speak and act according to the teachings of this divine agent. Their decisions, therefore, instead of being the judgment of ignorant and erring men, were the dictates of unerring wisdom. And the people, in exchange for the government which they had been accustomed to exercise for themselves, were provided with an administration which claimed to be directed by wisdom from above.[66] Taught thus and disciplined in that great lesson of bigotry and spiritual despotism,—*passive submission to persons ordained of God for the good of the church*,—they were prepared to resign their original rights and privileges into the hands of the hierarchy.

There is the fullest evidence that the action of the laity was requisite, as late as the middle of the third century, in all disciplinary proceedings of the church. By the beginning of the fourth, however, this cardinal right was greatly abridged; and soon after, wholly lost. This fact strongly illustrates the progress of the episcopal hierarchy. While the right of the laity was yet undisputed, the power of the bishop began to be partially asserted, and occasionally admitted; the people occupying a neutral position between submission and open hostility. But, from disuse to denial, and from denial to the extinction of neglected privileges and powers, the descent is natural, short and rapid. From about the middle of the fourth century the bishops assumed the control of the whole penal jurisdiction of the laity, opening and shutting at pleasure the doors of the church, inflicting sentences of excommunication, and prescribing, at

and little, to be exchanged for a loftier tone. They at length asserted that they were the legitimate successors of the apostles themselves, and might, consequently, of their own proper authority, dictate laws to the Christian flock.—*Mosheim, De Rebus Christ., Saec. II., § 23.*

[66] Planck, Gesellschafts-Verfass. 1, S. 448–452.

their discretion, the austerities of penance; and again absolving the penitents, and restoring them to the church by their own arbitrary power.[67] The people, accordingly, no longer having any part in their trial of offences, ceased to watch for the purity of the church, connived at offences, and concealed the offenders; not caring to interfere with the prerogatives of the bishop, in which they had no further interest. The speedy and sad corruption of the church was but the natural consequence of this loose and arbitrary discipline.

The ecclesiastical discipline, if such indeed it can be called, now appears in total contrast with that of the church under the apostles. Then, the supreme authority was vested in the people; now, in the clergy. The church then enacted her own laws, and administered her discipline; the pastor, as the executive officer, acting in accordance with her will for the promotion of her purity and of her general prosperity. The clergy are now the supreme rulers of the church, from whom all laws emanate, and are also the executioners of their own arbitrary enactments. The church is no longer a free and independent republic, extending to its constituents the rights and privileges of religious liberty; but a spiritual monarchy under the power of an ambitious hierarchy, whose will is law, and whose mandates the people are taught to receive, as meting out to them, with wisdom from on high, the mercy and the justice, the goodness and severity of their righteous Lawgiver and Judge. The people are wholly disfranchised by the priesthood, who have assumed the prerogatives of that prophetic Antichrist, who "as God sitteth in the temple of God, showing himself that he is God."

[67] Planck, Gesellschafts-Verfass. 1, 509.

REMARKS.

1. It is the right and the duty of the members of every church themselves to administer the discipline of their own body.

Each church is a voluntary association, formed for the mutual enjoyment of the privileges and ordinances of religion. To its members belongs the right to prescribe the conditions of a connection with their communion, or of exclusion from it, as may seem good to them, in conformity with the principles of the gospel.

The duty of carefully exercising a Christian watch and fellowship, one toward another, and of excluding those who walk unworthily, is most clearly enforced in the Scriptures. It is one important means of preserving the purity of the church and promoting the interests of religion.

2. Ecclesiastical censure is not a penal infliction, but a *moral discipline* for the reformation of the offender and the honor of religion.

This thought has been already presented, but it should be borne distinctly in mind. Church discipline seeks, in the kindness of Christian love, to recover a fallen brother, to aid him in his spiritual conflicts, and to save him from hopeless ruin. In its simplicity and moral efficacy, if not in principle, the discipline of the apostolical and primitive churches differed totally from that complicated system of penance into which it degenerated under the hierarchy. The austerities of this system, with its pains and privations, have more the appearance of penal inflictions to deter others from sin, than of Christian efforts to reclaim the guilty. The system itself was often, in the hands of the priesthood, an engine of torture, with which to molest an adversary or to gratify private resentment. But the Christian love that administers ecclesiastical censure, in the spirit of the apostolical rule seeks only the reformation of the offender, and the honor of that sacred cause upon which he has brought reproach.[68]

3. This mode of discipline is the best safeguard against the introduction of bad men into the church.

The members of the church who are associated with the candidate in the relations and pursuits of private life, best know his character. Commit, therefore, the high trust of receiving men into the sacred relations of the church of Christ, neither to bishop, nor presbyter, nor pastor, but to the united, unbiased decision of the members of that communion.

4. Discipline administered by the brethren of the church is the best means of securing the kind and candid trial of those who may be the subjects of ecclesiastical censure.

Cases of this kind are often involved in great difficulty, and always require to be treated with peculiar delicacy and impartiality. These ends of impartial justice the wisdom of the world seeks to secure by the *verdict of a jury*. The brethren of the church, in like manner, are the safest tribunal for the impeachment of those who walk unworthily.

5. The mode of discipline now under consideration relieves the pastor from unwelcome responsibilities, both in the admission of members and in the treatment of offences.

He has a delicate and responsible duty to perform toward those who present themselves for admission to the church. He is not satisfied, it may be, with regard to the qualifications of the candidate, and yet this is only an impression received from a great variety of considerations which cannot well be expressed. But to refuse the applicant without assigning good and sufficient reasons may expose him to the charge of uncharitableness, and involve him in great difficulty. But no railing accusation, however, can be

[68] Venema, Institutiones Hist. Eccles. III. § 188, p. 214, seq.

brought against him, provided the case is submitted to the impartial decision of the church.

And again, in the treatment of offences, the pastor should always be able to take shelter under the authority of the church. Like Paul, in the case of the Corinthians, he may be obliged to rebuke them for their neglect, and to urge them to their duty. But he should never appear as the accuser and prosecutor of his people. The trial should begin and end with the church, who ought always to be ready to relieve their pastor from duties so difficult and delicate, which belong not to his sacred office.

6. Discipline so administered serves to promote the peace of the church.

In every communion may be found men of hasty, restless spirits, who are ever ready to rally at the cry of bigotry, intolerance, persecution, however unjustly raised. The contention may rise high and rend the whole church asunder if the minister alone becomes the object of attack. The only safe appeal is to the calm, deliberate decision of the whole body of the church. Here the case is open for a full discussion and a fair decision, which, more than anything else, has power to silence the rage of faction and to calm the tumults of party. Thus a church may gather about their pastor for the defence of his character, for his encouragement in the faithful discharge of his duty, and for the preservation of their own peace, by silencing the clamors of restless malcontents.

7. The only mode that has ever been devised for preserving the discipline of the church is to submit it to the control not of the clergy, but of the members themselves.

In consequence of depriving the members of the church of a participation in its discipline soon after the rise of episcopacy, they became remiss in their attention to the scandals of their brethren, and withdrew their watch over each other.[69] And since that day, when has any just discipline been maintained in any church under a national establishment and an independent priesthood? What is the discipline of the Episcopal Church even in this country, where, without a state religion or an independent priesthood, the laity have little or no concern with the admission of members to their communion or the exclusion of them from it? Let the reader weigh well this consideration. It suggests one of our strongest and most important objections to the ecclesiastical polity of the Episcopal Church.[70]

According to one of the most able historians of the Episcopal Church in this country, and one of its most eminent divines, there is no power of "excommunication" now residing in the church. I refer to the authority of the Rev. Dr. Hawks:

"Who ever heard of the excommunication of a layman by our branch of the apostolic church? Neither the General Convention nor any State Convention have ever provided any 'rules or process' for excommunication. There is not a clergyman in the church, who, if he were desirous to excommunicate an offender, would know how to take the very first step in the process. It certainly is not to be done according to his mere whim; and if it were so done, it is as

[69] Planck, Gesell. Verfass. 1, S. 509, seq.

[70] Some of the clergy of that communion, we understand, are accustomed to keep a private list of those who are wont to receive the sacred elements at their hands, and if any are found to walk unworthily, their names are silently stricken off from the roll, and their communion with the church is dropped in this informal manner. Such pastoral fidelity, duly exercised, is worthy of all consideration. But can it be expected, as a general rule, to accomplish the high ends of faithful Christian discipline? Is it the discipline of the New Testament? Or can it be expected of any class of men that they will have the independence to be faithful here? A magnanimity how rare! Comp. Barnes' Reply to Dr. Tyng.

certainly invalid. Shall then the presbyter alone do it, or shall it be done by his bishop, or by a conclave of bishops, or of bishops and presbyters, or by a State Convention including the laity, or by the General Convention including the laity again? No man can answer it, for there is no rule on the subject." "There are very few of the dioceses in which *any* provision is made by canon for investigating or trying the case of a *layman*."—Constitution and Canons of the Protestant Episcopal Church in the United States, pp. 359, 360, 362.

"Every churchwarden in every parish in England is called upon once a year to attend the visitation of his archdeacon. At this time oaths are tendered to him respecting his different duties; and among other things he swears that he will present to the archdeacon the names of all such inhabitants of his parish as are leading notoriously immoral lives. This oath is regularly taken once a year by every churchwarden in every parish in England; yet I believe that such a thing as any single presentation for notoriously immoral conduct has scarcely been heard of for a century."[71] Another of the Tractarians complains in the following terms of this total neglect of discipline in the Episcopal Church: "I think the church has in a measure forgotten its own principles, as declared in the sixteenth century; nay, under stranger circumstances, as far as I know, than have attended any of the errors and corruptions of the Papists. Grievous as are their declensions from primitive usage, I never heard, in any case, of their practice directly contradicting their services; whereas we go on lamenting, once a year, the absence of discipline in our church, yet do not even dream of taking any one step toward its restoration."[72]

A clergyman of our own country, in assigning his "Reasons for preferring Episcopacy," admits that "in no Chris-

[71] Tracts for the Times, No. 59, p. 416. [72] Ibid. No. 41, p. 297.

tian denomination of the country is there so great a diversity of opinion [as in the Episcopal Church] about doctrines, church polity, etc. But we hear," he adds with great complacency, "of no discipline on account of this diversity. The probability is, that discipline on these accounts would rend and break up the church." . . . "There is no church in the world that has in fact so great a diversity of opinion in her own bosom as the Church of England, and not a little of downright infidelity. And yet no one can reasonably doubt that, if she continue to let discipline for opinion alone, etc. . . . . . . that most important branch of Protestantism will ere long be redeemed from her past and present disadvantages, and recover the primitive vitality of Christianity, so as to have it pervading and animating her whole communion. Nor is it less certain, that by attempting discipline for opinion, she would for ever blight all these prospects." [73]

In the Lutheran Church in Germany, Christian discipline has fallen into equal neglect. So totally is it disregarded that persons of abandoned character, known to be such, and the most notorious slaves of lust, are publicly and indiscriminately received to the sacrament of the Lord's Supper.[74] What ecclesiastical hierarchy or national establishment was ever known to maintain, for any long period, the purity of the church?

8. This mode of discipline gives spiritual life and power to the church.

---

[73] Thoughts on the Religious State of the Country; with Reasons for preferring Episcopacy. By Rev. Calvin Colton, pp. 199, 200.

[74] Liebetrut, Tag des Herrn, S. 331. One of the faithful pastors in Germany informed the writer that he refused to receive to the communion such as were known to be immoral. But the refusal was a civil offence, for which he had often been prosecuted, and suffered the penalties of the statute law!

The moral efficiency of any body of believers depends not upon their number, but upon the purity of their lives and their fidelity in duty. A church composed of men who are a living exemplification of the power of the Christian religion by their holy lives and by the faithful discharge of their duties,—such a church, and such only, is what the Lord Jesus designed his church should be—the pillar and ground of the truth, the most efficient means of defending the honor of the Christian name, and of promoting pure and undefiled religion. Without intending any invidious reflection, may we not request of the reader a careful consideration of this subject? Let him remember that a single case of discipline, rightly conducted, gives renewed energy to the whole body, quickening every member into newness of life in the service of the Lord. Let him estimate the moral efficacy of a living church, quickened into healthful, holy action compared with one which has a name to live and is dead. Let him ponder well these considerations before he decides to go over to a communion that tolerates a general neglect of the Christian duty which we have been contemplating.

11 *

CHAPTER VI.

EQUALITY AND IDENTITY OF BISHOPS AND PRESBYTERS.

Soon after the ascension of our Lord, it became expedient for the brethren to appoint a certain class of officers to superintend the secular concerns of their fraternity. These were denominated διάκονοι, *servants, ministers, deacons.* In process of time, another order of men arose among them, whose duty was to superintend the religious interests of the church. These were denominated οἱ προιστάμενοι, Rom. xii. 8; 1 Thess. v. 12; οἱ ἡγούμενοι, Heb. xiii. 7, 17, 24; πρεσβύτεροι, Acts xx. 17; ἐπίσκοποι, Acts xx. 28, equivalent to the terms, *presidents, leaders, elders, overseers.* These terms all indicate one and the same office, *that of a presiding officer, a ruler, in their religious assemblies.* Officers of this class are usually designated, by the apostles and the earliest ecclesiastical writers, as *presbyters* and *bishops,*—names which are used interchangeably and indiscriminately to denote one and the same office. By the apostles and the apostolic fathers they are designated in the *plural number.* As in the synagogue there was a plurality of rulers, so in the churches there was a plurality of presbyters, or bishops, like the modern presbyterian session.

The appropriate duty of the bishops or presbyters at first was, not to teach, or to preach, but to preside over the church, and to preserve order in their assemblies. "They were originally chosen as in the synagogue, not so much for the instruction and edification of the church, as for taking the lead in its general government."[1] The necessity of such a presiding officer in the church at Corinth is sufficiently apparent from the apostle's rebuke of their irregularities, 1 Cor. xiv. 26. The apostle, however, allows all to prophesy, to exercise their spiritual gifts; and only requires them to speak "one by one," that all things may be done decently and in order. The ordinary officers of the apostolical church, then, comprised two distinct classes or orders. The one was known by the name of deacons; the other, designated by various titles, of which *presbyters* and *bishops* were the most frequent.

Bishops and presbyters, according to the usages of the apostles and of the earliest ecclesiastical writers, are identical and convertible terms, denoting officers of one and the same class. In this proposition we join issue with the episcopalians, who assert that bishops were divinely appointed as an order of men superior to presbyters. We, on the other hand, affirm that presbyters were the highest grade of permanent officers known in the apostolical and primitive churches; and that the title of bishop was originally only another name for precisely the same officer. Even after a distinction began to be made between presbyters and bishops, the latter were not a peculiar order distinct from presbyters and superior to them. The bishop was merely one of the presbyters appointed to preside over the college of his fellow-presbyters. Like the moderator of a modern presbytery or association, he still retained a ministerial parity with his brethren, in the duties, rights and privileges of the sacred office. Our

---

[1] Neander's Apost. Kirch. I. p. 44, seq. Comp. Siegel, Handbuch, IV. S. 223. Ziegler, Versuch, der kirchlichen Verfassungsformen, S. 3–12. Rothe, Anfänge, I. S. 153. So, also, Giesler, Rheinwald, Böhmer, Winer, etc.

sources of argument in defence of this general proposition are two-fold,—Scripture and history.

I. The scriptural argument for the equality and identity of bishops and presbyters may be comprised under the following heads:

1. The appellations and titles of a presbyter are used indiscriminately and interchangeably with those of a bishop.

2. A presbyter is required to possess the same qualifications as a bishop.

3. The official duties of a presbyter are the same as those of a bishop.

4. There was, in the apostolical churches, no ordinary and permanent class of ministers superior to that of presbyters.

1. The appellations and titles of a presbyter are used interchangeably with those of a bishop.

One of the most unequivocal proof-texts in the Scriptures is found in Acts xx. 17, compared with verse 28. Paul, on his journey to Jerusalem, sent from Miletus and called the *presbyters*, πρεσβυτέρους, *elders*, of Ephesus, to meet him there. And to these presbyters, when they had come, he says, in his affectionate counsel to them, "Take heed to yourselves, and to all the flock over which the Holy Ghost hath made you *bishops*, ἐπισκόπους, to feed the church of God which he hath purchased with his own blood." Both terms are here used in the same sentence with reference to the same men. It is remarkable that bishops and presbyters are never mentioned *together* by the apostles as two orders of the ministry.

We have another instance, equally clear, of the indiscriminate use of the terms, in the first chapter of Paul's epistle to Titus: "For this cause I left thee in Crete, that thou shouldst set in order the things that are wanting, and ordain *presbyters*, πρεσβυτέρους, in every city, as I had appointed thee." Then follows an enumeration of the qualifications which are requisite in these presbyters, one of which is given in these words: "A *bishop* must be blameless, as the steward of God."

Again, it is worthy of particular attention that the apostle, in his instructions to Timothy, 1 Tim. iii. 1–7, after specifying the qualifications of a *bishop*, proceeds immediately to those of *deacons*, the *second class* of officers in the church, without making the least allusion to *presbyters*, though giving instructions for the appointment of the appropriate officers of the church. This omission was not a mere oversight in the writer; for he subsequently alludes to the *presbytery*, iv. 14, and commends those that rule well, v. 17. In these passages the apostle has in mind the same offices, and uses the terms bishop and presbyter, as identical in meaning.

To all the saints in Christ Jesus which are at Philippi, the apostle addresses his salutation,—to the saints, with the *bishops* and *deacons*, that is, to the church and the officers of the church. Here, again, as in all his epistles, these officers are divided into two classes.

The supposition that these were bishops of the episcopal order involves the absurdity of a plurality of bishops *over the same church;* a supposition at variance with the first principles of diocesan episcopacy, which admits of but *one* in a city.[2] This difficulty appears to have forcibly im-

---

[2] "Epiphanius tells us that Peter and Paul were both bishops of Rome at once: by which it is plain he took the title of bishop in another sense than now it is used; for now, and so for a long time upward, two bishops can no more possess one see, than two hedge-sparrows dwell in one bush. St. Peter's time was a little too early for bishops to rise."—*Hales' Works*, Vol. I. p. 110.

F *

pressed the mind of Chrysostom. "How is this?" exclaims the eloquent patriarch. "Were there many bishops in the same city? By no means; but he calls the presbyters by this name [bishops]; for at that time this was the common appellation of both."³

Finally, we appeal to 1 Pet. v. 2, 3, where the apostle, as being also an elder, exhorts the elders to feed the flock of God, *taking the oversight of them*, ἐπισκοποῦντες, *acting the bishop, performing the duties of a bishop over them*, requiring of them the same duties which the apostle Paul enjoins upon the presbyter-bishops of Ephesus. As at Ephesus, where Paul gave his charge to those presbyters, so here there could have been no *bishop* over those whom Peter commits to the oversight of these *presbyters*. "That the terms *bishop* and *presbyter*, in their application to the first class of officers, are perfectly convertible, the one pointing out the very same class of rulers with the other, is as evident as the sun 'shining in his strength.' To a man who has no turn to serve, no interest in perverting the obvious meaning of words, one would think that a mathematical demonstration could not carry more satisfactory evidence."⁴

These terms are also precise and definite, descriptive of a peculiar office, which cannot be mistaken for any other in the apostolic church. The original identity of bishops and presbyters is now conceded by many episcopalians themselves. "That presbyters were called bishops I readily grant; that this proves that the officer who was then called a bishop, and consequently the office, was the same."⁵

---

³ Σὺν ἐπισκόποις καὶ διακόνοις. Τί τοῦτο ; μιᾶς πόλεως πολλοὶ ἐπίσκοποι ἦσαν ; Οὐδαμῶς, ἀλλὰ τοὺς πρεσβυτέρους οὕτως ἐκάλεσε· τότε γὰρ τέως ἐκοινώνουν τοῖς ὀνόμασι.—*In Phil.* 1, 1, p. 188, seq. Tom. 11.

⁴ Mason's Works, Vol. III. pp. 41–43. Comp. King, Prim. Christ. pp. 67, 68.

⁵ Bowden, Works on Episcop. Vol. 1. p. 161.

"The episcopalian cannot be found who denies the interchangeable employment of the terms bishop and presbyter in the New Testament."[6] Bishop Burnet admits that they "are used promiscuously by the writers of the first two centuries;" to which might be added authorities without limit.

The scriptural title of the office under consideration is usually that of presbyter or elder. It had long been in use in the synagogue. It denoted an office familiar to every Jew. It conveyed a precise idea of a ruler whose powers were well defined and perfectly understood. When adopted into the Christian church, its meaning must have been easily settled; for the office was essentially the same in the church as previously in the synagogue. Accordingly, it constantly occurs in the writings of the apostle, to denote an officer familiarly known, but having no resemblance to a modern diocesan bishop. The term, bishop, occurs but five times in the New Testament; and, in each instance, in such a connection as to be easily identified with that of presbyter. The former is derived from the Greek language, the latter has a Jewish origin. Accordingly, it is worthy of notice, that the apostles, when addressing Jewish Christians, use the term presbyter; but in their addresses to Gentile converts, they adopt the term *bishop*, as less obnoxious to those who spoke the Greek language.[7]

2. A presbyter is required to possess the same qualifications as a bishop.

The apostle has specified at length the qualifications both for a bishop and a presbyter, which, for the sake of comparison, are here set in opposite columns:

---

[6] Chapman, cited in Smyth's Pres. and Prelacy, p. 111.

[7] Rothe, Anfänge, I. 218, 219. Neander, Apost. Kirch. I. 178, 179. Schoene, Geschichtsforschungen, I. 247-249. Comp. Bishop Croft, in Smyth's Apost. Succ. p. 159.

QUALIFICATIONS.

For a bishop, 1 Tim. iii. 2–7:

A bishop must be blameless, the husband of one wife,[8] one that ruleth well his own house, having his children in subjection with all gravity. For if a man know not how to rule his own house, how shall he take care of the church of God? vs. 2, 4, 5.

Vigilant, νηφάλεον, *circumspect*, sober, of good behavior, given to hospitality, apt to teach. v. 2.

Not given to wine, no striker, not greedy of filthy lucre, but patient, ἐπιεικῆ, *gentle, not soon angry*, not a brawler, not covetous, not a novice, lest, being lifted up with pride, he fall into the condemnation of the devil. Moreover, he must have a good report of them which are without, lest he fall into reproach and the snare of the devil. vs. 3, 6, 7.

For a presbyter, Tit. i. 6–10:

If any be blameless, the husband of one wife, having faithful children, (who are) not accused of riot, or unruly. v. 6.

A lover of hospitality, a lover of good men, sober, just, holy, temperate, holding fast the faithful word as he hath been taught, that he may be able by sound doctrine both to exhort, and to convince the gainsayers. vs. 8, 9.

A bishop must be blameless, as the steward of God, not self-willed, not soon angry, not given to wine, no striker, not given to filthy lucre. v. 7.

The qualifications are identical throughout. Is a blameless, sober and virtuous life, a meek and quiet spirit, required of a bishop? So are they of a presbyter. Whatever is needful for the one is equally essential for the other.

---

[8] In utraque epistola sive episcopi sive presbyteri (quanquam apud veteres iidem episcopi et presbyteri fuerint quia illud nomen dignitatis est, hoc aetatis) jubentur monogami in clerum eligi.—Jerome, *Ep.* 83, *ad Oceanum*, Tom. 4, p. 648.

If, then, there be this wide and perpetual distinction between the two which episcopacy claims, how extraordinary that the apostle, when stating the qualifications of a humble presbyter, should not abate an iota from those which are requisite for the high office of a bishop?

3. The duties of a presbyter are the same as those of a bishop.

Their duties, severally and equally, are to rule, to counsel and instruct, to administer the ordinances, and to ordain.

(*a*) Both exercised the same authority over the church.

If bishops were known in the apostolical churches as a distinct order, the right of government confessedly belonged to them. We have, therefore, only to show that presbyters exercised the same right. This exercise of authority is denoted in the New Testament by several terms, each of which is distinctly applied to presbyters.

(*a*) Such is ἡγέομαι, *to lead, to guide*, etc. In Heb. xiii. 7 and 17 this term occurs. Remember them that have the rule over you, τῶν ἡγουμένων ὑμῶν. Obey them that have rule over you, τοῖς ἡγουμένοις ὑμῶν.

(*β*) Another term expressive of authority over the church is προΐστημι, *to preside, to rule*. Xenophon uses this verb to express the act of leading or ruling an ancient chorus and an army.[9] The apostle Paul uses the same to express the authority which the presbyters exercised as *rulers* of the church.

"We beseech you, brethren, to know them which labor among you and *are over you*, προϊσταμένους, in the Lord," 1 Thess. v. 12. Prelates of the church these *presbyters* cannot have been; for there were several, it appears, in this single city, a circumstance totally incompatible with the

---

[9] Οὐδὲν ὅμοιόν ἐστι χοροῦ τε καὶ στρατεύματος προεστάναι. "Between the *taking the lead* of a chorus and *the command* of an army," both expressed by προεστάναι, "there is no analogy."—*Mem.* 3, 4, 3.

organization of diocesan episcopacy. The whole, taken together, is descriptive not of a bishop in his see, but of a presbyter, a pastor, in the discharge of his parochial duties. Again, "Let the elders, presbyters, that *rule well* be accounted worthy of double honor," οἱ καλῶς προιστῶτες πρεσβύτεροι, 1 Tim. v. 17. Here are *presbyters* ruling over the church of Ephesus, where, according to the episcopal theory, Timothy, as bishop, had established the seat of his apostolical see.

(γ) Another term of frequent occurrence, in writers both sacred and profane of approved authority, is ποιμαίνω, *to feed;* metaphorically, *to cherish, to provide for, to rule, to govern.* It expresses the office, and comprehends all the duties of a shepherd. This term the apostle uses in his exhortation to the *presbyters* of Ephesus at Miletus: "Take heed to yourselves, and to all the flock over which the Holy Ghost hath made you *bishops, to feed,* ποιμαίνειν, the church of God." Beyond all question, this term, both in classic and hellenistic Greek, expresses the power of government. Both this and ἡγούμενος, above mentioned, are used in the same passage to express the government of Christ, the chief Shepherd, over his people Israel: "Thou, Bethlehem, in the land of Juda, art not the least among the princes of Juda, for out of thee shall come a governor, ἡγούμενος, who shall rule, ποιμανεῖ, my people Israel," Matt. ii. 6. Without further illustration, we have sufficient evidence that the presbyters were invested with all the authority to guide, govern and provide for the church which the bishop himself could exercise. The very same terms which express the highest power of government and which are applied to the office even of the great Head of the church, are used to express the authority of presbyters, and to set forth the power with which they are invested to rule and feed the church.

EQUALITY OF BISHOPS AND PRESBYTERS. 135

(b) Presbyters were the authorized *counselors of the church;* and, in connection with the apostles, constituted the highest court of appeal for the settlement of controversies in the church.

About the year 50, a spirited controversy arose at Antioch, which threatened to rend the church, and to hinder the progress of that gospel which Paul and Barnabas had begun successfully to preach to the Gentiles. It was of the utmost importance that this dispute should be immediately and finally settled. For this purpose, a delegation, consisting of Paul, and Barnabas, and others, was sent from the church at Antioch on an embassy to Jerusalem, to submit the subject under discussion to the examination and decision of the church, with the apostles and presbyters. This delegation was kindly received by the members of the church at Jerusalem, with their officers, the apostles, πρεσβύτεροι, and *elders,* and to them the whole subject of the dissension at Antioch was submitted. Peter and James were, at this time, at Jerusalem, and members of this council. The subject was discussed at length on both sides, but the concurring opinions of Peter and James finally prevailed, and the council united harmoniously in the sentiments expressed by these apostles. It is observable, however, that the *result of the council* was given, not in the name of James[10] or any

---

[10] That James did not draw up this decree as "the head of the church at Jerusalem," and as his "authoritative sentence," is unanswerably shown by Rev. Dr. Mason, in his Review of Essays on Episcopacy. The amount of the argument is, that James *simply expresses his opinion,* verse 19; just as Peter had done before. So the word, κρίνω, *in the connection in which it is used,* implies, and so it was understood by the sacred historian, who, in Acts xvi. 4, declares, that the "authoritative sentence," the decrees, were ordained by the *apostles and presbyters.* Comp. also Acts xxi. 25. The case was not referred to James, neither could it be submitted to him as bishop of Jerusalem, Antioch lying entirely without his diocese, even on the supposition

one of the apostles, but conjointly, by the apostles, and *presbyters*, and brethren, Acts xv. 23. Throughout the whole narrative the presbyters appear as the authorized counselors of the church, and *the only ordinary officers of the church*, whose opinion is sought in connection with that of the apostles, without any intimation of an intermediate grade of bishops.[11]

(*c*) To administer the ordinances of the church was the appropriate office of the presbyters.

The performance of these duties could not have been restricted to the apostles. The sacrament was at first administered daily;[12] and afterward, on each Lord's day as a part of public worship. The frequency and universality of the ordinance of necessity required that it should be administered by the ordinary ministers of the church. Baptism, by a like necessity, devolved upon them. The numerous and far-spreading triumphs of the gospel utterly forbid the idea that the apostles, few in number, and charged with the high commission of preaching the gospel, and giving themselves wholly to this as their appropriate work, could have found time and means for going everywhere, and baptizing with their own hands all that believed on the Lord Jesus Christ. Besides, they appear expressly to have disclaimed this work, and to have entrusted the service chiefly to other hands. "I thank God that I baptized none of you but Crispus and Gaius. And I baptized

that Jerusalem was the seat of his episcopal see. The authority of this decree was also acknowledged in all the churches of Asia. The supposition that it was the official and authoritative sentence of James as bishop, exalts him above all the other apostles who were members of the council, and gives him a power far-reaching and authoritative beyond that which belonged to St. Peter himself, the prelatical head of the church.

[11] Comp. Rothe, Anfänge, Vol. I. S. 181, 182.
[12] Neander, Apost. Kirch. 1, p. 30.

EQUALITY OF BISHOPS AND PRESBYTERS. 137

also the household of Stephanas; besides, I know not whether I baptized any other. For Christ sent me, not to baptize, but to preach," 1 Cor. i. 14–17. Cornelius, again, was baptized, not by Peter, but by some Christian disciple, agreeably to his command. The apostles seldom baptized. The inference therefore is, that this service was by them committed to the presbyters, the ordinary officers of the church. "In the earliest times, when no formal distinction between ἐπίσκοποι, *bishops*, and πρεσβύτεροι, *presbyters*, had taken place, the presbyters, especially the προεστῶτες, *presiding presbyters*, 1 Tim. v. 17, discharged those episcopal functions, which, afterward, when a careful distinction of ecclesiastical officers had been made, they were not permitted to discharge, otherwise than as substitutes or vicars of a bishop. Instances, however, do sometimes occur, in later times, of presbyters having officiated in matters which, according to the canon-law, belonged only to the episcopal office."[13]

(d) To ordain is the right and prerogative of presbyters.

Episcopacy claims this as the exclusive prerogative of bishops. We, on the contrary, claim for presbyters precisely the same duty, right and prerogative, and offer it as evidence of the ministerial parity of bishops and presbyters. The argument for the validity of presbyterian ordination is reserved for consideration under a separate head.

4. There was in the apostolical churches no *ordinary* class of ministers superior to that of presbyters or bishops.

We deny that Timothy or Titus, or any other person or class of persons named in Scripture, represents an order of ministers in the churches planted by the apostles who were invested with prerogatives superior to those of presbyters, and whose office was to be perpetuated in the church of

---

[13] Riddle, Chr. Antiquities, p. 233.

Christ. In opposition to these episcopal pretensions, we remark:

(*a*) That no distinct appellation is given to the supposed order, and no class of religious teachers represents them in the Scriptures.

If there were such an order, how extraordinary that it should have been left without a name or a distinctive appellation of any kind! Here is the highest grade of officers possessed exclusively of certain ministerial rights and powers, from whom all clerical grace has been transmitted by episcopal succession, age after age, down to the present time; and yet this grade is distinguished by no peculiar appellation, and represented by no single class or order of men. The inferior orders, presbyters and deacons, are specified with great distinctness, but the highest and most important has no definite name, no distinct and single representative. Yet the modern bishop, with astonishing credulity, traces back his spiritual lineage almost through a thousand generations, in strange uncertainty all the while to whom he shall at last attach himself or with whom claim kindred. If Peter fails him, he flies to Paul, to James, to Timothy, to Titus, to the angel of the church, to—he knows not whom. He is, however, a legitimate descendant and successor of some apostolical bishop, but that bishop—nobody knows who he was, or what, precisely, his office may have been!

(*b*) The Scriptures give no authority for ascribing either to the apostles or to their assistants and fellow-laborers the exercise of episcopal authority.

The *fathers* do indeed assign episcopal sees to several of the apostles and to their helpers. And modern episcopalians refer us with great confidence to James, to Timothy, to Titus, and to the angels of the churches in the epistles of the Apocalypse, as instances of primitive bishops. Now we

EQUALITY OF BISHOPS AND PRESBYTERS. 139

deny that either of these exercised the rights and prerogatives of an episcopal bishop.

(*a*) James was not bishop of Jerusalem.

We have already seen [14] with what care the apostles guarded against any assumption of authority over the churches. They taught, they counseled, they admonished, they reproved, indeed, with the authority belonging to ambassadors of God and ministers of Christ. But they assumed not to rule and to govern with the official power of a diocesan. The evidence of this position is already before the reader, and to his consideration we submit it without further remark.

But James, it is said, resided at Jerusalem, as bishop of that church and diocese, and in this capacity offers us a scriptural example of an apostolical bishop. The episcopal functions of this bishop, therefore, require a particular consideration.

In the days of Claudius Caesar arose a dearth throughout Judea so distressing that a charitable contribution was made, and relief sent by the hands of Barnabas and Saul to the brethren in Judea residing in the supposed diocese of this bishop of Jerusalem. To whom was this charity sent? Not to the bishop, but to the *presbyters*, the appropriate officers of that church, Acts xi. 30.

The delegation sent from Antioch to Jerusalem for counsel were received, not by the bishop, but by the church, the apostles and the presbyters, Acts xv. 4. They compose this council and make up the result. *It seemed good to the apostles and presbyters, with all the church.* Where is our diocesan all this time? Plainly he has no official character; no existence in this church. The idea of a diocesan bishop over this community, just now living together in the sim-

---

[14] Chapter 1.

plicity of their mutual love, is an idle fancy, devoid of all reality.[15]

James appears to have chiefly resided at Jerusalem for good and sufficient reasons, but not as the prelatical head of that church or diocese. As a Jew, as the brother of our Lord, as well as by his personal characteristics, he was eminently qualified to serve as mediator between the opposite parties of Jewish and Gentile converts, and to counsel and to act for the peace of the church. But in all this he acted not as a bishop, but as an apostle, in that divine character and by that authority which he possessed as an apostle of the Lord Jesus Christ, and which, as Neander has well observed, could be delegated to none other.[16]

But do not Clement of Alexandria,[17] Hegesippus,[18] the Apostolical Constitutions,[19] Eusebius,[20] Cyril of Jerusalem,[21] Epiphanius,[22] Chrysostom,[23] Jerome,[24] Augustine,[25] and many others of later date, all agree that James was bishop of Jerusalem? Grant it all. But their declaration only relates to a disputed point in the history of the Acts of the Apostles, upon which we, perhaps, are as competent to decide as

[15] Rothe, Anfänge, I. S. 267, seq.
[16] Introduction, p. 20. Also, Apost. Kirch. 2, c. 1, p. 14, seq. Comp. Euseb. Eccl. Hist. Lib. 2, c. 23.
[17] Euseb. Eccl. Hist. 2, c. 1.
[18] Euseb. Eccl. Hist. 2, c. 23.
[19] Lib. 6, Ep. 14, p. 346.
[20] Lib. 2, c. 1; 2, c. 23; 3, c. 5; 7, c. 19. Comment. in Hesai. xvii. 5, Vol. II. p. 422. Montfaucon, Collec. Nov. Pat. et Scrip. Graec. ed. Paris, 1706.
[21] Catech. 4, Ep. 28, p. 65, ed. Touttée.
[22] Haer. 78. Antidicomarianitar. § 5, p. 1039.
[23] Hom. 38, in Ep. ad Corinth, Vol. X. p. 355.
[24] Catal. Script. Eccl. s. v. Jacob, frater Domini, Vol. I. p. 170. Comment. in Ep. ad Gal. i. 19; Vol. IV. p. 236. Ed. Paris.
[25] Contra literas Petiliani, L. 2, c. 51, § 118, Vol. IX. p. 172.

they. With the same historical data in view, why cannot a judgment be made upon them as safely in the nineteenth century as in the third or the fifth? With what propriety these ancient fathers denominate James bishop of Jerusalem let the reader himself judge in view of the foregoing considerations.

But Hegesippus lived in the second century, within one hundred years of the apostolic age, and must be an unexceptionable witness. What then is his testimony? Simply that James took charge of the church *in connection with the apostles*, for such must the term μετά imply. This preposition not unfrequently expresses the relation of co-operation or concomitancy, μετὰ βοιωτῶν ἐμάχοντο, Il. 13, 700. They engaged in this contest μεθ ὑμῶν, *with you*, says Demosthenes, rather than against you. This personal association is implied in John iii. 22; Matt. xii. 42; Acts ix. 39, as in the text διαδέχεται δὲ—τὴν ἐκκλησίαν μετὰ τῶν ἀποστόλων. He remained chiefly at Jerusalem, the centre of operations for all of the apostles, and had, if you please, the immediate supervision of this church in connection with the other apostles. After the rise of the hierarchy, the episcopal fathers that have been mentioned may have interpreted the testimony of this author into a declaration of the episcopal office of James. If so, we are at liberty to challenge the authority of these fathers on the point under consideration. Like them, we have the historical record before us, and the means of forming an independent opinion.[26]

Indeed, antiquity itself, in the language of Milton, "hath turned over the controversy to that sovereign Book which we had fondly straggled from." After refuting other traditions, he adds: "As little can your advantage be from Hegesippus, an historian of the same time, not extant, but

---

[26] Rothe, Anfänge der Christ. Kirch. I. 263–272.

cited by Eusebius. His words are, 'that in every city all things so stood in his time as the law and the prophets, and our Lord did preach.' If they stood so, then stood not bishops above presbyters. For what our Lord and his disciples taught, God be thanked, we have no need to go learn of him." [27]

The churches, besides their union of faith and fellowship of spirit, had one bond of union in the instruction, care and oversight which the apostles exercised in common over all the churches. What care the apostle Paul took to encourage this fellowship of the churches is manifested in the salutations which he sends in their behalf: *All the churches in Christ salute you,* Rom. xvi. 16; *The churches of Asia salute you. All the brethren greet you,* 1 Cor. xvi. 19, 20.

This oversight the apostles constantly exercised; caring for all and watching for all as they had opportunity, that thus they might, as far as possible, supply the place of their Lord and fulfill the ministry which they had received from him. In the distribution of their labors, by mutual consent, they occupied, to a great extent, separate fields. Some went to the heathen, and others to the circumcision, Gal. ii. 7–9. But none had any prescribed field of labor bearing the remotest analogy to a modern diocese. "The apostles were constituted of God rulers not over a separate nation or city, but all were entrusted with the world." [28]

(3) Timothy at Ephesus was not a bishop.

Timothy was one of a class of religious teachers who

---

[27] Prose Works, Vol. I. p. 86.

[28] Εἰσὶν ὑπὸ θεοῦ χειροτονηθέντες ἀπόστολοι ἄρχοντες, οὐκ ἔθνη καὶ πόλεις διαφόρους λαμβάνοντες, ἀλλὰ πάντες κοινῇ τὴν οἰκουμένην ἐμπιστευθέντες.—*Chrysostom, cited by Campbell, Lectures,* p. 77. Comp. Rothe, Anfänge, Christ. Kirch. I. S. 297–310.

acted as itinerant missionaries, the assistants and fellow-laborers of the apostles. Their assistance was employed as a necessary expedient, to enable the apostles to exercise through them a supervision over the infant churches which sprang up in the different and distant countries in which Christianity was propagated. Over churches widely separated the apostles could personally exercise but little supervision.

Such assistants and delegates of the apostles are of frequent occurrence in the Scriptures. And this view of their office affords at once a natural and easy explanation of the peculiar and somewhat anomalous rank which they seem to have held. Bishops they certainly were not, in the episcopal sense of that term.[29] Neither were they merely presbyters; for though in many respects their office was analogous to that of presbyters, in others it was widely different. Timothy, Paul styles his fellow-laborer, $\sigma \upsilon \nu \epsilon \rho \gamma \acute{o} \varsigma$, Rom. xvi. 21; 1 Thess. iii. 2. In the salutations of his epistles he often couples the name of Timothy with his own, Phil. i. 1; 1 Thess. i. 1; 2 Thess. i. 1, etc. Accordingly, Timothy was the traveling companion of the apostle, and his fellow-laborer.

At different times he had the superintendence of several churches in various places. Comp. 1 Cor. iv. 17; 1 Tim. i. 3, and 1 Thess. iii. 2, from which it appears that he was sent to Corinth, to Ephesus and to Thessalonica as a fellow-laborer and assistant of the apostle. From what is said of his influence at Corinth, he might, with almost equal propriety, be styled the bishop of that city as of Ephesus. The whole history of the Acts of the Apostles and the language of the epistles prove that, like the other fellow-travelers of St. Paul, Timothy had no settled abode, no fixed station,

---

[29] Bishop Onderdonk only claims this distinction for Timothy, and many others of that communion give up this point.

but assisted him as an evangelist in setting the churches in order and in the accomplishment of any special object which the apostle had in view, and to which he could not personally attend. This itinerating life of Timothy sufficiently proves that he was not the bishop of Ephesus. When both the epistles to the Thessalonians were written, A. D. 62, Timothy was with Paul at Corinth, having lately returned from Thessalonica, where he had spent some time in ministering to that church.

When Paul wrote the first epistle to the Corinthians, A. D. 57, from Ephesus, Timothy was absent again on a mission to Macedonia and Achaia, from whence he was expected soon to return, 1 Cor. xvi. 10.

The year following, when Paul wrote his second epistle from Macedonia, Timothy was with him there, and Titus, whom Paul had met in Macedonia, was again one of the messengers by whom the letter was forwarded to the church.

Some months later, A. D. 58, when he wrote his epistle to the Romans from Corinth, Timothy was with him there.

The epistle to the Ephesians was written from Rome, A. D. 61, subsequently to the time when Timothy is alleged to have been made bishop of Ephesus; yet he is not named in it, nor is there any allusion in it to any head of the church there. The address is only to "the saints and faithful brethren." Indeed it is certain, from the epistles to the Colossians and to Philemon, written about the same time from Rome, that Timothy was at this time in that city; so that he could scarcely have been in his supposed diocese at all.

"The expression in 1 Tim. i. 3, 'As I besought thee to abide still at Ephesus when I went into Macedonia,' marks but a temporary purpose, and bears little similitude to a settled appointment and establishment of him as head of the church there—the bishop, in the modern acceptation of the term. When the second epistle to Timothy was written, he was not in his supposed diocese at Ephesus, but the apostle had sent Tychicus there, a fellow-servant, a beloved brother and fellow-minister of the Lord (Eph. vi. 21), as Timothy himself was."[30] The absurdity of beseeching Timothy as a diocesan bishop to abide at Ephesus, 1 Tim. i. 3, is forcibly presented by Daillé: "Why *beseech* a bishop to remain in his diocese? Is it not to beseech a man to stay in a place to which he is bound? I should not think it strange to beseech him to leave it, if his services were needed elsewhere. But to beseech him *to abide* in a place where his charge obliges him to be, and which he cannot forsake without offending God and neglecting his duty, is, to say the truth, not a very civil entreaty; as it plainly presupposes that he has not his duty much at heart, seeing one is under the necessity of *beseeching* him to do it."[31]

He was endowed with peculiar gifts, which qualified him to serve the churches as a fellow-laborer with the apostle, who accordingly charges him not to neglect this gift.[32]

(γ) Titus was not bishop of Crete.

Like Timothy, Titus was an evangelist, a traveling missionary. He received similar instructions and performed similar labors. Like Timothy, he traveled too much to be a stationary prelate. From Syria we trace him to Jerusalem; thence to Corinth; thence to Macedonia; back again to Corinth; thence to Crete; thence to Dalmatia; and

---

[30] Bowdler's Letters on Apost. Succession, pp. 25, 26.

[31] Daillé, *ci-dessus*, p. 23. Cited in Mason's Works, Vol. III. p. 197.

[32] Comp. Neander, Apost. Kirch. 1, c. 10. Rothe, Anfänge, I. S. 160, 161 and 263; also, J. H. Böhmer, Diss. Jur. Eccl. Antiq. p. 424. seq., where is given an able discussion of the points under consideration, in relation to Timothy, Titus and the angel of the churches. Barnes' Apost. Church, pp. 99-107, and Smyth's Presbytery and Prelacy, chap. 12, § 3. Wilson on Church Government, § 25, p. 251-263.

whether he ever returned to Crete is wholly uncertain. He was left at Crete, therefore, not as bishop of that diocese, but as an assistant of the apostle, to establish the churches and to continue the work which the apostle had begun. "After Paul had laid the foundation of the Christian church in Crete, he left Titus behind to complete the organization of the churches, to confirm the new converts in purity of doctrine, and to counterwork the influence of the false teachers." [33]

Dr. Whitby, himself a zealous advocate of Episcopacy, assures us that he could find *nothing in any writer of the first three centuries concerning the episcopate of Timothy and Titus; nor any intimation that they bore the name of bishop.* "Certain it is," says Campbell, "that in the first three centuries neither Timothy nor Titus is styled bishop by any writer."

Of the same general character was Silvanus, 1 Thess. i. 1; 2 Thess. i. 1; comp. 1 Pet. v. 12; and Mark, Col. iv. 10; 1 Pet. v. 13; and Clemens, Phil. iv. 3, and several others. Silas is first the companion of Paul and Barnabas in Asia Minor; then of Paul in his second missionary tour through Asia Minor, Macedonia and Achaia; and, at a later period, of Peter in the Parthian empire. Mark, too, was first the companion of Paul and Barnabas; then, after their separation, of Barnabas in Cyprus, and afterward of Peter in the Parthian empire, from whence also they journeyed in company to Rome.[34]

(*δ*) The angel of the church in the apocalyptic epistles was not a bishop.

On this subject we shall present the reader with the exposition of several distinguished scholars, and submit it to

---

[33] Neander, Apost. Kirch. Vol. I. p. 401. Trans. 1.

[34] Comp. Rothe, Anfänge, I. S. 305, seq. Comp. Wilson on Church Government, § 26, p. 263–270.

EQUALITY OF BISHOPS AND PRESBYTERS. 147

him whether this phraseology supports the prelatical claims of episcopacy. The views of Neander are briefly given in his Introduction.[35]

"The seven angels have given occasion to much speculation and diversity of opinion. Are they *teachers, bishops, overseers?* or is some other office designated by the word ἄγγελος, angel, here?

1. "Old Testament usage, *viz.*, the later Hebrew, employs the word מַלְאָךְ=ἄγγελος, to designate a prophet, Hag. i. 13, also a priest, Mal. ii. 7, and Eccl. v. 6. As priests, in the appropriate sense of the word, did not exist in the Christian churches (for they had no Mosaic ritual of sacrifices and oblations), so we must compare ἄγγεγος here with מַלְאָךְ, prophet, in Hag. i. 13. Προφῆται, prophets, there were in the Christian church. See 1 Cor. xii. 28; Acts xiii. 1; 1 Cor. xiv. 29, 32, 37; Eph. ii. 20; iii. 5; iv. 11. Taken in this sense, the word designates here the leading teacher in the Asiatic churches. The nature of the case would seem to indicate a *leader* here, else why should he be especially addressed as the representative of the whole body in each of the Christian churches? But,

2. "Another exposition has been given. Vitringa[36] has compared the ἄγγελος of the Apocalypse with the שְׁלִיחַ צִבּוּר of the Jewish synagogues, which means *legatus ecclesiae, the representative or delegate of the church,* and compares well with ἄγγελος ἐκκλησίας, *angel of the church,* as to the form of the phrase. The office of the individual thus named was to superintend and conduct the worship of the synagogue; he recited prayers and read the Scriptures, or invited others to perform these duties; he called on the priests to pro-

---

[35] Page 22.

[36] De Vet. Synagoga. p. 910, seq. As an interpretation of the Hebrew phrase שְׁלִיחַ צִבּוּר, the English reader may read, as often as it occurs, *the ruler of the synagogue.*

nounce the final benediction in case he himself was not a priest; he proclaimed the sacred feasts, and, in a word, he superintended the whole concerns of religious worship, and evidently took the lead in them himself. He was a προεστώς, or an ἐπίσκοπος, a *superintendent* or *overseer*, and also a διδάσκαλος, *teacher*, in a greater or less degree. Comp. John iii. 10. The best account of his office is in Schoettgen, Horae Heb. p. 1089, seq., who has pointed out some errors and deficiencies of Vitringa. The nature of the case shows that the superior officer is, in this instance, and should be, addressed. He is probably called the angel of the church in conformity to the Hebrew Chaldee צִבּוּר שָׁלִיחַ (possibly in reference to Hag. i. 13, or Mal. ii. 7), and may be called *legatus ecclesiae*, because he is *delegatus ab ecclesia*, delegated by the church, to render their public devotions to God and superintend their social worship. Exactly the limits of the office and its specific duties neither the word ἄγγελος explains, nor does the context give us any particular information." [37]

The learned Origen affirms that the angels of the churches were the προεστῶτες, the presiding presbyters, the same of whom Justin, Tertullian and Clemens Alexandrinus speak, in the extracts which are given below, in their order.[38]

The exposition given below is from the learned Dr. Delitzsch, the associate of Dr. Fürst, in preparing his Hebrew Concordance. The writer is a man of profound erudition in all that relates to Hebrew and Rabbinical literature, and has furnished the article for us at our particular request:

"The ἄγγελοι τῆς ἐκκλησίας, *angels of the churches*, are the bishops; or, what in my opinion is the same in the apostolical churches, the presbyters of the churches. The expres-

[37] Stuart on Rev. ad locum.
[38] Προεστῶτας τινὰς τῶν ἐκκλησιῶν ἀγγέλους λέγεσθαι παρὰ τῷ Ἰωάννῃ ἐν τῇ ἀποκαλύψει.

sion, like many others in the New Testament, is derived from the synagogue, which may be regarded as the parent source of the Christian church, having remained essentially unchanged for a long time after the overthrow of the temple service. The office of the שְׁלִיחַ צִבּוּר corresponds entirely with that of bishop or presbyter of the apostolical churches.

1. "The שְׁלִיחַ צִבּוּר bears this name as the *delegatus ecclesiae*, the delegate of the church, who was elected by them to exercise and enjoy the privileges and prerogatives of a presiding officer in their assemblies. It was his duty to pray in the name of the assembly, to lead in the reading of the Scriptures, to blow the trumpet, the שׁוֹפָר, on the opening of a new year; and, in the absence of those who belonged to the priesthood, the כֹּהֲנִים, to pronounce the Aaronitic benediction. So far as the performance of this rite is concerned, the priests themselves are the שְׁלִיחֵי צִבּוּר. The original passages are given by Schoettgen.[39] So high and important was the office of this שְׁלִיחַ צִבּוּר, and so nearly did it correspond with that of bishop or presbyter, that the name of the former might be applied to the latter.

"The signification of the term may also be learned from the Aramaean term, the קָרְבָּא. This officer of the synagogue, the שְׁלִיחַ צִבּוּר, was regarded as bringing before God the prayers of the people, which were considered as their spiritual offerings. It appears from the Jerusalem Talmud that when one was invited to ascend the pulpit to offer public prayers, the language of the invitation was not 'Come and pray,' but 'Come hither and present our offering,' עֲשֵׂה קָרְבָּנִי."

"The office of the שְׁלִיחַ צִבּוּר did not, indeed, include the

---

[39] Horae Hebraicae et Talmudicae ad Apoc. 1, p. 1089, seq.
[40] Berachot, c. 4, f. 206. Comp. Zunz, Die gottesdienstlichen Vorträge der Juden.

duty of a public teacher; for the office of public preaching was not established as a permanent institution, but had its origin within the period of the Christian dispensation.

"I have thus shown that the appellation *angel of the church* was used to designate the presiding officer of the Christian church, with particular reference to the שְׁלִיחַ צִבּוּר of the synagogue. Still, as a name of an office, the angel of the church may have a meaning somewhat higher. Such a meaning it may have with reference, retrospectively, to the מַלְאַךְ יְהוָה of the Old Testament.[41] So that the angel of the church may, at the same time, denote the bishop or presbyter chosen by this Christian community to be the messenger or servant both of God and of the church. This call of the church is itself a *vocatio divina*, a *divine calling*; and, according to the New Testament view of the subject, unites the idea of both offices in the same person."

Bengel, also, is of opinion that the angel of the church corresponds to the שְׁלִיחַ צִבּוּר, of the synagogue. "The Hebrews had, in their synagogue, a שְׁלִיחַ צִבּוּר a *deputatum ecclesiae*, who, in reading, in prayer, etc., led the congregation; and such a leader, also, had each of the seven churches of the Apocalypse."[42]

The result is, that the angel of the churches, whatever view we take of the origin of the term, was not the representative of an order or grade superior to presbyters, but was himself merely a presbyter; or, if you please, *a bishop*—provided you mean by it simply what the Scriptures always mean—the pastor of a church, the ordinary and only minister. The New Testament never recognizes more than one church in a city. This fact of itself precludes the

---

[41] Comp. Malachi ii. 7, and Haggai i. 13.

[42] Erklärte Offenbarung, S. 216. For a further illustration of the opinions of the learned, the reader is referred to Campbell's Lectures on Eccl. Hist. pp. 82–88. Whately, Kingdom of Christ, pp. 246–250.

supposition that the angel of the church could have been a diocesan having in the same city several churches under his authority.

II. It remains to consider the historical argument for the original equality and identity of bishops and presbyters.

This equality and identity was fully recognized in the early church, and continued to be acknowledged as an historical fact, even after the establishment of the hierarchy, down to the time of the Reformation. The historical argument comprised in this proposition may be resolved into several particulars, each of which serves to show that both the early fathers and later historians regarded presbyters and bishops as belonging originally to the same grade or order of the clergy, and as being equal in their rights and privileges.

1. Presbyters are designated by the fathers by names and titles similar to those of bishops.
2. Presbyters, like bishops, are carefully distinguished from the deacons, the *second order* of the clergy; and in such a manner as to show that both presbyters and bishops are indiscriminately and equally the representatives of the first order.
3. Bishops, themselves, in their ministerial character, exercised only the jurisdiction, and performed merely the offices, of presbyters in the primitive churches.
4. The original equality of bishops and presbyters continued to be acknowledged from the rise of the episcopal hierarchy down to the time of the Reformation.

1. Presbyters are designated in the writings of the early fathers by names and titles similar to those of bishops.

They speak sometimes of bishops and sometimes of presbyters as the presiding officers of the church, and then again of both indiscriminately, as being one and the same in rank. To both they ascribe the same or similar names and titles, such as seniors, elders, chairmen, moderators, presidents, etc., all indicating identity of office and equality in rank. Even when the first place is assigned to the bishop, he is only chief among equals, just as in a modern presbytery or association one is promoted to the office of moderator, to which all are alike eligible.[43]

[43] We have brought together in parallel columns some of the names and titles which are ascribed to bishops and presbyters severally. The intelligent reader will readily perceive the similarity of the titles given to both, and the identity of their significations:

TITLES OF BISHOPS.	TITLES OF PRESBYTERS.
Ἐπίσκοποι, πρεσβύτεροι, πρόεδροι, προιστάμενοι, ἔφοροι, ἄρχοντες ἐκκλησιῶν, προεστῶτες.	Ἐπίσκοποι,* πρεσβύτεροι,† πρόεδροι,‡ προεστῶτες,§ προστάται.‖
Praesides, praepositi; praesidentes, superattendentes, superintendentes, pastores, patres ecclesiae, vicarii, praesules, antistites, antistites sacrorum, seniores, etc.	Praepositi, antistites, majores natu, seniores, seniores plebis, sacerdotes, etc.

These and several other titles are given in the author's Antiquities, pp. 70, 94; in Riddle, Christ. Antiq. pp. 161, 229; in Baumgarten, Erläuterungen, S. 75, 94; and in Rheinwald, S. 30, 45. Obviously the titles of both are synonymous, and are applied indiscriminately to both bishops and presbyters, to denote one and the same office. Riddle, Christ. Antiq. p. 230. Blondell justly remarks that "the use of such terms creates no difficulty, and for the reason that, even after a distinction was made between bishops and presbyters in the second century by the decision of the churches, both continued to be dis-

* Chrysost. Hom. 1, in Phil. I. p. 8. Hom. 11, in 1 Tim. 3. Theodoret, in Phil. i. 1; ii. 25. Jerome, ad Tit. 1, and Ep. 83, 85. Schol. in Epist. ad Nepotian.
† Greg. Naz. Orat. I. Basil, Reg. Morali, 71.
‡ Synesius, Ep. 12.
§ Greg. Naz. Orat. I. Basil, M. Regula Morali.
‖ Chrysost. Hom. 11, in 1 Tim. 4. Stillingfleet, Irenicum, p. 278, Phil. ed. Comp. Rom. xii. 8.

EQUALITY OF BISHOPS AND PRESBYTERS. 153

2. Presbyters, like bishops, are carefully distinguished from the deacons, the second order of the clergy, and in such a manner as to show that both presbyters and bishops are indiscriminately and equally the representatives of the first order.

Several of the earliest fathers distinctly recognize but two orders of the priesthood. Those of the first order are sometimes denominated presbyters, sometimes bishops, and then again bishops and presbyters indiscriminately. It is worthy of particular notice, that while bishops and presbyters are confounded one with another, they are uniformly distinguished from the deacons, the second order of the priesthood. Whatever be the title by which the clergy of the first order are called, we are in no danger of mistaking them for the second.

Clement of Rome, about A. D. 96, is our first authority. His epistle addressed to the Corinthians, is the earliest and most authentic of all the writings of the apostolical fathers. By the early Christians it was publicly read in their religious assemblies, in the same manner as the apostolical epistles." And, by ecclesiastical writers generally nothing that is not divine is admitted to be of higher authority. This revered father recognizes but *two orders* of the priesthood—*bishops* and *deacons*, ἐπισκόπους καὶ διακόνους. He gives not the least intimation of the existence of an individual diocesan bishop at Corinth; but uniformly speaks

---

tinguished indiscriminately by the same appellation."—*Apologia pro Hieron.* p. 92. Comp. Gieseler's Ch. Hist. Vol. I. pp. 90, 91. Tr.

Blondell has collected the following as the epithets applied to presbyters by Gregory Nazianzen, † 387: Ποιμένες, ἱερεῖς, πρέχοντες, προεστῶτες, προστάται, ἄρχοντες, νυμφίοι, νυμφαγωγοὶ τῶν ψυχῶν καὶ πρωμνήστορες, κεφαλὴ Χριστοῦ πληρώματος—all appropriate appellations of bishops, Apol. p. 64.

" Euseb. Eccl. Hist. Lib. 3, c. 13.

of the presbyters of that church, whom the Corinthians had rejected, as belonging to the highest order. "The apostles preaching in countries and cities appointed the first fruits of their labors to be *bishops* and *deacons*, having proved them by the Spirit."[45] These are the two orders of the ministry, as originally appointed by the apostles. "It were a grievous sin," he proceeds to say, "to reject those who have faithfully fulfilled the duties of their *episcopal office;*" and immediately adds, "blessed are those *presbyters* who have finished their course and entered upon their reward;"[46] blessed are those *presbyters*, who have thus faithfully performed the duties of *their episcopal office;* bishops and presbyters being used interchangeably as equally descriptive of the same order. This passage establishes the identity of bishops and presbyters in the opinion of this venerable author, who may be understood to express the prevailing opinion both at Rome and at Corinth. "Clement himself was not even aware of the distinction between bishops and presbyters—terms which in fact he uses as synonymous."[47]

Polycarp is our next witness. This father was familiar with those who had seen our Lord. He was the disciple of John the Apostle, and is supposed by many to be the angel of the church at Smyrna, in Rev. ii. 8. Such was the respect in which his epistle was held by the primitive Christians that it was publicly read in their churches until

---

[45] Κατὰ χώρας οὖν καὶ πόλεις κηρύσσοντες καθίστανον τὰς ἀπαρχὰς αὐτῶν, δοκιμάσαντες τῷ πνεύματι, εἰς ἐπισκόπους καὶ διακόνους τῶν μελλόντων πιστεύειν.—*Epist. ad Cor.* § 42, p. 57.

[46] Ἁμαρτία γὰρ οὐ μικρὰ ἡμῖν ἔσται, ἐὰν τοὺς ἀμέμπτως καὶ ὁσίως προσενέγκοντας τὰ δῶρα τῆς ἐπισκοπῆς ἀποβάλωμεν. Μακάριοι οἱ προοδοιπορήσαντες πρεσβύτεροι, οἵτινες ἔγκαρπον καὶ τελείαν ἔσχον τὴν ἀνάλυσιν.—*Epist. ad Cor.* § 44, p. 58.

[47] Christ. Riddle, Antiq. p. 5. Comp. Waddington's Church Hist. p. 35. Campbell's Lectures, p. 72.

the fourth century. This valuable relic of antiquity, the date of which is usually assigned to the year 140, harmonizes in a remarkable degree with that of Clement in recognizing but two orders of the clergy.[48] The first it denominates *presbyters*. Bishops are not once named in all the epistle. These presbyters are the inspectors and rulers of the church, having authority to administer its discipline and to exercise all the functions of its highest officers.

The conclusion, therefore, is inevitable that bishop and presbyter were still used interchangeably, and that both Paul and Polycarp speak of the same class of officers. Clement and Polycarp were contemporaries and survivors of the apostles. They resided, the one at Rome, the other in Asia Minor. They represent distinct portions of the Christian church, remote from each other, and widely different in language, in government and in national peculiarities.

It is also particularly noticeable that Polycarp specifies the qualifications necessary both for deacons [49] and for presbyters ;[50] and, like Paul the Apostle on a similar occasion, Tit. i. 5–9, makes no mention of what is proper in the conduct and character of a bishop.

A letter of Pius of Rome, A. D. 142–157, if received as genuine, is perhaps the earliest recognition of bishops as a distinct order, but they have still no official superiority. "Let the elders and deacons respect you, *not as a superior*, but as a servant of Christ."[51]

Justin Martyr, the Christian philosopher, who suffered martyrdom A. D. 165, two years before the death of Poly-

---

[48] Διὸ δέον ἀπέχεσθαι ἀπὸ πάντων τούτων ὑποτασσομένους τοῖς πρεσβυτέροις καὶ διακόνοις ὡς Θεῷ καὶ Χριστῷ.—*Ad. Phil.* c. 6.

[49] Ep. c. 5. [50] Ep. c. 6.

[51] Presbyteri et diaconi, non ut majorem, sed ut ministrum Christi observent. Cited by Killen.

carp, offers further confirmation of these views of the subject. In his description of public worship, after mentioning prayers and the fraternal salutation, he says: "There is brought to him who presides over the brethren, τῷ προεστῶτι τῶν ἀδελφῶν, bread and a cup of water, and wine; and he, taking them, offers up praise and glory to the Father of the universe, through the name of the Son and the Holy Ghost, and renders thanks for these his gifts. At the close of his petition and thanksgivings, all the people present say Amen; which, in the Hebrew language, signifies *so may it be*. And he who presides having given thanks, and the whole assembly having expressed their assent, they who are called among us deacons, διάκονοι, distribute the bread and the wine and water to each of those who are present, to partake of that which has been blessed. Also they carry to those who are not present."[52]

His testimony in the passage above cited is that two orders only officiated in their public worship and in their celebration of the eucharist. Soon after this he again describes their mode of public worship and of communion, and specifies the same officiating officers, the *president* of the brethren, and the *deacons*.[53] Nothing indicates any

---

[52] Ἀδελφοὶ κοινὰς εὐχὰς ποιησόμενοι ὑπέρ τε ἑαυτῶν καὶ τοῦ φωτισθέντος καὶ ἄλλων πανταχοῦ πάντων εὐτόνως. — — ἀλλήλους φιλήματι ἀσπαζόμεθα παυσάμενοι τῶν εὐχῶν. ἔπειτα προσφέρεται τῷ προεστῶτι τῶν ἀδελφῶν ἄρτος καὶ ποτήριον ὕδατος καὶ κράματος, καὶ οὗτος λαβὼν, αἶνον καὶ δόξαν τῷ πατρὶ τῶν ὅλων, διὰ τοῦ ὀνόματος τοῦ υἱοῦ καὶ τοῦ πνεύματος τοῦ ἁγίου, ἀναπέμπει καὶ εὐχαριστίαν ὑπὲρ τοῦ κατηξιῶσθαι τούτων παρ᾿ αὐτοῦ ἐπὶ πολὺ ποιεῖται. οὗ συντελέσαντος τὰς εὐχὰς καὶ τὴν εὐχαριστίαν, πᾶς ὁ παρὼν λαὸς ἐπευφημεῖ λέγων, Ἀμήν.—εὐχαριστήσαντος δὲ τοῦ προεστῶτος, καὶ ἐπευφημήσαντος παντὸς τοῦ λαοῦ, οἱ καλούμενοι παρ᾿ ἡμῖν διάκονοι, διδόασιν ἑκάστῳ τῶν παρόντων μεταλαβεῖν.—Apol. 1, c. 65, p. 82. Comp. Semisch's Justin Martyr. Trans. Edinburgh, 1843. Vol. I. pp. 28, 29.

[53] Apol. 1, c. 67, p. 83.

EQUALITY OF BISHOPS AND PRESBYTERS. 157

higher order or office than that of the officiating presbyter who conducted their worship and administered the sacrament; or if you call him bishop, he is still of the same order, distinguished clearly from the deacons, but differing in no wise from the order of presbyters.[54]

The authority of Irenaeus is claimed on both sides. He lived in the transition period, toward the close of the second century, and represents the office in a confused, transition state. He speaks of Hyginus, the eighth in the episcopal succession in Rome, and of bishops appointed by the apostles. But he makes only a relative distinction between bishops and presbyters; recognizes the succession of presbyters in the same sense as of bishops, and calls the bishops of Rome presbyters, implying no clear distinction between bishops and presbyters as separate officers. The passages are given in the margin.[55]

Irenaeus, a Greek of Asia Minor, was in his youth a hearer of the venerable Polycarp, the disciple of John. He spent his advanced life in Gaul, at Lyons, and died about the commencement of the third century, probably A. D. 202. Speaking of Marcion, Valentinus, Cerinthus, and other heretics, he says: "When we refer them to that apostolic tradition, which is preserved in the churches, through the succession of their *presbyters*, these men oppose

---

[54] Respecting this office of the προεστώς τῶν ἀδελφῶν, compare Milton's Prelatical Episcopacy, Prose Works, Vol. I. p. 76.

[55] Cum autem ad eam iterum traditionem, quae est ab Apostolis, quae per successiones *Presbyterorum* in ecclesiis custoditur, provocamus eos: adversantur traditioni, dicentes, se non solum *Presbyteris*, sed etiam *Apostolis* existentes sapientiores, sinceram invenisse veritatem.—*Irenaeus, Adv. Haer.* L. 3, c. 2, § 2, p. 175.

Traditionem itaque Apostolorum in toto mundo manifestatam in omni ecclesia adest respicere omnibus, qui vera velint videre; et habemus annumerare eos, qui ab Apostolis instituti sunt *Episcopi* in ecclesiis.—*Irenaeus*, c. 3, § 1, p. 175, et § 2, ibid.

the tradition." The author, in the next section, again styles these same presbyters, *bishops*. "We can enumerate those who were constituted by the apostles, *bishops* in the churches; their successors, also, even down to our time."

But the very same traditions and successions, which are here ascribed to the bishops, are just above assigned also to *the presbyters.*

Again, he speaks in a similar connection, of Polycarp, as a *bishop;* but, in another place, he styles him that *blessed and apostolic presbyter,* ἐκεῖνος ὁ μακάριος καὶ ἀποστολικὸς πρεσβύτερος.[56]

Again, "We ought to obey those *presbyters* in the church, who have succession, as we have shown, from the apostles; who, with the succession of the *episcopate,* received the certain gift of truth, according to the good pleasure of the Father."[57]

We cannot fail to observe that the terms *bishop* and *presbyter* are used by this ancient father as perfectly convertible

[56] Euseb. Eccl. Hist. Lib. 5, c. 20.

[57] Quapropter eis, qui in ecclesiis sunt, *Presbyteris* obaudire oportet, his, qui successionem habent ab Apostolis, sicut ostendimus; qui cum *Episcopatus* successione charisma veritatis certum secundum placitum Patris acceperunt, etc. After this: Qui vero crediti quidem sunt a multis esse *Presbyteri*, serviunt autem suis voluptatibus, et non praeponunt timorem Dei in cordibus suis, sed contumeliis agunt reliquos, et *principalis consessionis* tumore elati sunt et in absconsis agunt mala, et dicunt, *nemo nos videt*, redarguentur a verbo, etc.—Ab omnibus igitur talibus absistere oportet, adhaerere vero his, qui et Apostolorum, sicut praediximus, doctrinam custodiunt, et cum *Presbyterii* ordine sermonem sanum et conversationem sine offensa praestant, ad confirmationem et correptionem ceterorum. Finally, Τοιούτους Π ρ ε σ β υ τ έ ρ ο υ ς ἀνατρέφει ἡ ἐκκλησία. περὶ ὧν καὶ ὁ προφήτης φησίν δώσω τοὺς ἄρχοντάς σου ἐν εἰρήνῃ καὶ τοὺς ἐ π ι σ κ ό π ο υ ς ἐν δικαιοσύνῃ.—*Irenaeus*, L. 4, c. 26, § 2, 3, 4, p. 262; § 5, 263.

Qui ergo relinquunt praeconium ecclesiae imperitiam sanctorum *presbyterorum* arguunt, non contemplantes quanto pluris sit idiota re-

terms. Bishops he denominates presbyters; and presbyters, bishops, and ascribes the *episcopate* to presbyters.

We are not ignorant of the gloss that is given to these passages from Irenaeus, in the endeavor to defend the theory of an original distinction between bishops and presbyters. But the consideration of the episcopal argument is foreign to our purpose. The authorities are before the reader; and of their obvious meaning, any one is competent to form an independent, unaided judgment.

Titus Flavius Clemens, commonly known as Clement of Alexandria, lived at the close of the second and the beginning of the third century. He was at the head of the celebrated school at Alexandria, the preceptor of Origen, and the most learned man of his age. He speaks indeed of presbyters, bishops and deacons. After citing from the epistles various practical precepts, he proceeds to say that " numerous other precepts also, directed to select characters, have been written in the sacred books, some to *presbyters*, some to *bishops*, some to deacons, and others to widows."[58] In this enumeration he appears to have followed the order of the apostle in Tit. i. 5-7, mentioning presbyters first. He repeatedly shows, however, that there were at that time but two *orders—deacons* and *presbyters.*[59]

In his treatise, " What rich man can be saved?" Clement relates that John the apostle observing a young man of singular beauty, turning *to the bishop who presided over all,* commended him to his care in the presence of the church, and "*this presbyter,*" taking home the young man

---

ligiosus a blasphemo et impudente sophista, L. 5, c. 20, § 2. In the preceding section, he says, Omnes enim valde posteriores sunt quam *episcopi* quibus apostoli tradiderunt ecclesias. § 1.

[58] Paedag. Lib. 3, p. 264. Comp. also Strom. Lib. 6, p. 667.

[59] Ὁμοίως δὲ καὶ κατὰ τὴν ἐκκλησίαν, τὴν μὲν βελτιοτικὴν οἱ πρεσβύτεροι σώζο σιν, εἰκόνα τὴν ὑπερτικὴν οἱ διάκονοι.—*Strom.* Lib. 7, p. 700.

that had been committed to his care, nourished, educated and lost him. Thus Clement uses interchangeably the terms, bishop and presbyter, to designate the same person, and makes John address, as *bishop,* one who was, notwithstanding, a mere *presbyter.* "In this author we find a presbytery and deacons only, which is as forcible an exclusion of a third order, whether superior or intermediate, as can be reasonably expected from a writer who had no knowledge of a third." [60]

The account of Tertullian again, contemporary with Clement, both having died the same year, A. D. 220, harmonizes in a remarkable manner with that of Justin Martyr, as exhibited above. In describing the worship of Christian assemblies, he observes: "Certain approved elders, seniores, preside." [61] Aged men never presided by virtue of their age in ancient Christian assemblies. Besides, the passage indicates that these presidents were *chosen* to their office. The president is also denominated in the same chapter, *antistes,* a term exactly corresponding to that of προεστώς in Justin.

Tertullian represents the church of Africa, in which the episcopal government was earliest developed; but even in these churches the apostolical order had not yet been fully superseded by the hierarchy. The sum of his testimony, as well as of that of all who have gone before him, is, that there was but one order in the church superior to that of deacons. Tertullian stands "on the boundary between two different epochs in the development of the church." Henceforth the bishop assumes more prominence, but as yet he

---

[60] Chap. 42, pp. 667, 669, vol. 7, Sanct. Pat. Op. Polemica.
[61] Praesident probati quique seniores honorem istum non pretio, sed testimonio adepti; neque enim pretio ulla res Dei constat.—*Apol.* c. 39.

has not begun to be acknowledged as of an order superior to presbyters.

What if Tertullian, Clement, Irenaeus and others tell us of bishops? "It remains yet to be evinced out of this and the like places, which will never be, that the word bishop is otherwise taken than in the language of St. Paul and the Acts for an order above presbyters. We grant them bishops, we grant them worthy men, we grant them placed in several churches by the apostles, we grant that Irenaeus and Tertullian affirm this; but that they were placed in a superior order above the presbytery, show from all these words why we should grant. It is not enough to say that the apostle left this man bishop in Rome and that other in Ephesus, but to show when they altered their own decree set down by St. Paul, and made all the presbyters underlings to one bishop."[62]

To sum up all that has been said on the patristic identity of presbyters and bishops: they are known by the same names, they are required to possess the same qualifications, they discharge the same duties; they are therefore equal and identical in rank, office and duties—in all respects one and the same. This course of argumentation is precisely similar to that by which orthodoxy defends the supreme divinity of our Lord Jesus Christ and his equality with the Father. And none perhaps more readily admit the validity of this mode of argument, when applied to this cardinal principle in the Christian system, than the members of the

---

[62] Milton's Prelatical Episcopacy, Prose Works, Vol. I. p. 85. Constituit evangelista Marcus una cum Hakania patriarcha duodecim presbyteros qui nempe cum patriarcha manerent adeo ut cum vacaret patriarchates, unum ex duodecim presbyteris eligerent, cujus capiti reliqui undecim *manus imponentes* ipsi benedicerent et patriarcham crearent.—Eutychii Patriarchae Alexandr. Annal. interpr. Poverbio. Oxon. 1658, I. p. 331.

Episcopal communion. He is called by the names, He possesses the attributes, He receives the honors and performs the works of the Father, and therefore is one with Him. If, then, this course of reasoning commands our assent in these profound mysteries, why not much more in the case under consideration? We confidently rest in the conclusion of the learned Dr. Wilson, that "whatever misconstructions of the presbyterial office may have obtained, it is and always will be the highest ordinary office in the Christian church; and no presbyter, who is officially such, can be less than a bishop, and authorized to instruct, govern and administer, and ordain at least in conjunction with his co-presbyters of the same presbytery and council."

3. Bishops themselves, in their ministerial character, exercised only the jurisdiction and performed merely the offices of presbyters in the primitive church.

Ignatius speaks of bishops, presbyters and deacons, and, in strains almost of profane adulation, exalts the authority both of bishops and presbyters. But the learned need not be reminded that suspicion rests upon all the epistles of Ignatius. Many, both in this country and in Europe, most competent to decide upon their merits, have pronounced them undoubted forgeries. No reliance can be placed upon them as historical authority. The most probable opinion, and generally received, is, that they are filled with interpolations from various hands and of different dates, and are wholly unreliable. Such is Dr. Neander's opinion, as stated to the writer in conversation upon them.[63]

But let us admit the genuineness and authenticity of the epistles of Ignatius; his bishops are nothing more than the pastors each of a single congregation—merely parish minis-

---

[63] Comp. Milton's Prelatical Episcopacy, Prose Works, Vol. I. pp. 79, 80.

ters, *parochial bishops*. Though bearing the name of bishop, they are as unlike a modern diocesan as can well be imagined. This fact deserves a careful consideration. Let us not deceive ourselves with a name, a title. We are not inquiring after names, but things. The name determines nothing in regard to the official rank and duties of a primitive bishop. Give to a Congregational or Presbyterian minister this title, and you have made him truly a primitive bishop. These ancient dignitaries down to the third century, and in many instances even later, exercised no wider jurisdiction and performed no higher offices than a modern presbyter or any pastor of a single parish or congregation.

In support of the foregoing representation we have to offer the following considerations:

(*a*) By all primitive writers, the bishop's charge is denominated invariably a *church*, a *congregation;* never in the plural, *churches* or *congregations*.

(*b*) The Christians under the charge of one of these ancient bishops were all accustomed to meet in one place, like the people of a modern parish or congregation.

(*c*) All under his charge were, in many instances, as familiarly known to the bishop himself as are the people of a parish to their pastor.

(*d*) So many bishops were found in a single territory, of limited extent, that no one could have exercised a jurisdiction beyond the bounds of a single parish.

(*e*) The charge of a primitive bishop is known, in many instances, not to have equaled that of a modern presbyter or pastor.

(*a*) By all primitive writers the bishop's charge is denominated invariably a *church*, a *congregation;* never in the plural, *churches* or *congregations*.

As the epistles of Paul the Apostle are addressed to the church at Rome, at Corinth, at Ephesus, etc., so those of the apostolical fathers, Clement, Polycarp and Ignatius, are addressed, in like manner, to a single church—to the church at Corinth, at Philippi, at Ephesus, at Smyrna, etc. Neither is the word *church* ever used by the early fathers in a generic sense, for a national or provincial church, as we speak of the Church of England or of Scotland. This fact is worthy of particular attention as illustrative of the nature of a bishop's office. It presents his duties and his office in total contrast with those which are assigned to him by prelacy. It reveals to us the primitive bishop as merely a parish minister. "The epistles of the Apostle Paul give the clearest evidence that all the Christians *of one city*, from the beginning and ever after, formed one whole church." Such is the explicit declaration of Neander. "A council of elders was everywhere set over the churches to conduct their affairs."

In the sense above stated, the word in question is said to be used at least six hundred times in the writings of Eusebius alone.[64]

"As for the word diocese, by which the bishop's flock is now expressed, I do not remember that ever I found it used in this sense by any of the ancients. But there is another word still retained by us, by which they frequently denominated the bishop's cure, and that is *parish*."[65]

Instead, therefore, of presiding over thousands of his fellow-men with an authority which even princes might envy, this ancient bishop was nothing more than an humble parish minister, having the charge of some little flock, over

---

[64] Comp. Campbell's Lectures, pp. 106, 107, and Davidson's Ecclesiastical Polity, p. 75.

[65] King's Primitive Church, p. 15.

whom he had been duly appointed an overseer in the service of the chief Shepherd.

(*b*) The Christians, under the charge of these ancient bishops, were accustomed to meet in one place, like the people of a modern parish or congregation.

This is most clearly evident from the fathers of the second, and even of the third century, such as Ignatius,[66] Justin Martyr, Irenaeus, Tertullian and Cyprian. From the writings of these fathers it is evident that the whole flock assembled in the same place, ἐπὶ τὸ αὐτό.

This position has been indisputably established by Clarkson, and may be assumed as another illustration of the parochial episcopacy, which, in the ancient church, restricted the labors of the minister of Christ to a single church and congregation.[67]

(*c*) All under the bishop's charge were, in some instances, as familiarly known to him as are the people of a parish to their pastor.

Polycarp, for example, bishop of Smyrna, is exhorted by Ignatius to know all of his church by name, even the men-servants and maid-servants; to take care of the widows within his diocese; to take cognizance personally of all marriages; and to suffer nothing to escape his notice.[68]

All this requires of the bishop a personal acquaintance with the people of his charge, even more familiar, and a

---

[66] For the present purpose we may safely appeal to Ignatius; for though his works may be reasonably suspected of having been interpolated to aggrandize the episcopal order, they have never been suspected of any interpolation with a view to lessen it.

[67] D. Clarkson's Works. No Evidence for Diocesan Churches. Diocesan Churches not yet Discovered in the Primitive Churches. Comp. Campbell's Lectures, p. 109.

[68] Ἐξ ὀνόματος πάντας ζήτει. Δούλους καὶ δούλας μὴ ὑπερηφάνει. Χῆραι μὴ ἀμελείσθωσαν.—*Ignatius ad Polycarp*, c. 4.

personal supervision over them more minute, than that of the pastor of a single parish in any of our cities. Even the diocese of the bishop of Tyre was so small that he had a personal knowledge of every Christian within it.[69] Carthage, again, was one of the largest cities in the world; and yet Cyprian, the bishop of that city, made it a duty to preserve a familiar acquaintance with all his people, and to provide for the needy and destitute among them.[70] To such primitive episcopacy who can object?

(*d*) The bishops, in a single territory of limited extent, were so numerous that no one could have exercised jurisdiction beyond the bounds of a single parish.

Take, for example, a single province, that of Africa; and in doing this, we avail ourselves of the inquiries of another. "The testimony of Du Pin on this point, himself a prelatist, is invaluable. He describes, in the first place, the ancient province of Africa, as nearly commensurate with the modern Barbary States, and then proceeds to remark as follows:

"'In these parts it was customary to appoint bishops not only in great cities, but in villages, or villas, and in small cities (*in vicis aut villis et in modicis civitatibus*); which was guarded against by the 57th canon of the Council of Laodicea, and the 6th canon of that of Sardica. But that rule obtained, not in Africa, where it is on record that bishops were ordained not only in great cities, but in all the towns

---

[69] Schoene, Geschichtsforschungen, Bd. III. S. 336.

[70] Cumque ego vos pro me vicarios miserim ut expungeretis necessitates fratrum nostrorum sumptibus, si qui vellent suas artes exercere, additamento quantum satis esset desideria eorum juvaretis, simul etiam et aetates eorum et conditiones et merita discerneretis; ut etiam nunc ego, *cui cura incumbit omnes optimè nosse* et dignos quosque, et humiles et mites ad ecclesiasticae administrationis officia promoverem. —*Ep.* 38, p. 51.

(*in cunctis oppidis*), and not unfrequently in villages and military stations (*in vicis et castellis*); which multitude of bishops' sees, that had sprung up even from the very first rise of the African churches, was increased by the emulation of the Catholics and Donatists.'[71]

"Du Pin adds, 'We have drawn out of ancient documents the names of *six hundred and ninety bishoprics* in Africa.'[72] He annexes a catalogue of names, and refers in every instance to the document or documents where they are found. With reason, therefore, he says, 'there is not one of these that has not at some time a bishop, as may be gathered from ecclesiastical documents.'"

(*e*) The charge of a primitive bishop is known in many

---

[71] Du Pin's Sacred Geography of Africa, prefixed to his edition of "The Seven Books of St. Optatus, bishop of Mileve in Africa," on the schism of the Donatists, published at Paris, A. D. 1700, p. 57. Comp. Bingham's Antiq. of Christ. Church, B. 2, c. 12, § 3.

[72] Georg. Sac. Africae, p. 59. Schoene says, Geschichtsforschungen, Bd. III. 335, that in the time of Augustine there were *nine hundred* bishops in Africa.

Of the Donatists, 279 were present, many more than 120 were absent, and many of their bishoprics were vacant.—*Opera*, Vol. IX. p. 374, F. 375, 376, A. Antwerp, 1700.

Augustine also states that the Maximinianists were condemned by a council of 310 of the Donatists. Contra Parmeniam, Lib. 1, Tom. 8, c. 18, p. 15, B. Contra Crescon. Don. Lib. 3, c. 52, p. 315, E. Lib. 4, c. 7, p. 331, D. The Donatists, moreover, themselves boasted that they had more than 400 bishops in Africa. Post. Coll. c. 24, p. 411, D. In addition to all these, the Maximinianists afford another legion of bishops in this same province, 100 or more of whom condemned Priminianus. Contra Crescon. Don. Lib. 4, c. 6, p. 331, D., Post. Coll. c. 30. We are now prepared to make up the roll of African bishops: Catholics, 426; Donatists, 400; Maximinianists, 100. Total, 926—to say nothing of vacant sees. In such astonishing profusion are these dioceses, these episcopal sees, scattered broadcast over the single province of Africa.

instances not to have equaled that of a modern presbyter or pastor.

Bishops were found in small villages and military stations in Africa. Ischyrus was made bishop of a very small village, containing but few inhabitants.[73] Paul, one of the famous council of Nice, was only bishop of a fort, φρούριον, near the river Euphrates.[74] Eulogius and Barses, monks of Edessa, had each no city, but only a monastery for a diocese; or rather their title was merely honorary, an empty name, with which no charge was connected.[75] Others again were bishops of cities where there were no Christians whatever, and but few in the country round about.[76]

An ancient canon provides that "if there should be a place having a few faithful men in it to the extent of *twelve*, they shall write to the churches round about for their chosen men to come and examine him who is thought worthy of the bishop's degree." Another canon directs him to ordain two or three presbyters.[77] Thus our bishop becomes the minister of a church of *twelve* members.

The council of Sardica, c. 6, and of Laodicea, c. 57, in the fourth century, denounced the custom of ordaining bishops "in villages and small cities, lest the authority of a bishop should be brought into contempt." But a hundred years later, the custom still prevailed to a considerable extent. Even Gregory Nazianzen, one of the most learned and eloquent men of his age, worthy to have been "a professor of eloquence," after having studied in Caesarea, in

[73] Κώμη βραχυτάτη, καὶ ὀλίγων ἀνθρώπων.—*Athans. Apol.* 2, Vol. I. p. 200.

[74] Theodoret, Eccl. Hist. Lib. 1, c. 6.

[75] Οἳ καὶ ἐπισκόπω ἀμφω ὕστερον ἐγενέθην, οὐ πόλεως τινὸς ἀλλὰ τιμῆς ἕνεκεν. . . . χειροτονηθέντες ἐν τοῖς ἰδίοις μοναστηρίοις.—*Sozomen, Eccl. Hist.* Lib. 6, c. 34, p. 691.

[76] Schoene, Geschichtsforschungen, Bd. III. S. 336.

[77] Bunsen's Hippolytus, II. 305, III. 35, 36.

EQUALITY OF BISHOPS AND PRESBYTERS. 169

Alexandria, and in Athens, was bishop, in the last half of the fourth century, first of Zazime, "a dismal" place, and afterward of Nazianzus, πόλεως εὐτελοῦς, *vilis oppidi*, an inferior place.[78] Even in the middle of the fifth century diocesan episcopacy was but partially established. In some countries "there were bishops over many cities," but in others they were still "consecrated in villages," κώμαις.[79]

But we need not enlarge. If any one wishes for further information on this point, he has only to refer to Clarkson on Primitive Episcopacy, evincing a remarkable familiarity with the records of antiquity, in which facts almost innumerable have been brought together, all tending to show that the bishop of the primitive church had a charge no greater than a curate, or presbyter, or parish minister.

Grant, then, to prelacy all her claims. Run back her "unbroken succession" to these days of primitive simplicity, and it leads you up, not to an episcopal palace, but to the cottage, the cell, it may be, of an obscure curate. The modern bishop has only deceived himself with a name. While he reads of ancient bishops, he idly dreams of episcopal powers and prerogatives that were unknown in the church until the days of Constantine the Great. But on examination the delusion vanishes. The far-spreading domains of the diocesan shrink into a little hamlet; the proud episcopal palace becomes a poor parsonage, and the lofty prelate a humble presbyter, the pastor of a little flock.

The relations of the foregoing view to the exclusive validity of episcopal ordination are forcibly presented in the following passage from Clarkson in his Primitive Episcopacy:

"Hereby some mistakes about episcopal *ordinations*, of ill consequence, may be rectified. A bishop, in the best

---
[78] Socrates, Eccl. Hist. Lib. 4, c. 26, p. 242.
[79] Sozomen, Eccl. Hist. Lib. 7, c. 19, p. 734.

ages of Christianity, was no other than the pastor of a single church. A pastor of a single congregation is now as truly a bishop. They were duly ordained in those ages who were set apart for the work of the ministry by the pastor of a single church, with the concurrence of some assistants. Why they should not be esteemed to be duly ordained who are accordingly set apart by a pastor of a single church now, I can discern no reason, after I have looked every way for it. Let something be assigned which will make an essential difference herein; otherwise they that judge such *ordinations* here and in other reformed churches to be nullities, will hereby declare all the ordinations in the ancient church for three or four hundred years to be null and void, and must own the dismal consequences that ensue thereof. They that will have no ordinations but such as are performed by one who has many churches under him, maintain a novelty never known nor dreamt of in the ancient churches while their state was tolerable. They may as well say the ancient church had never a bishop (if their interest did not hinder, all the reason they make use of in this case would lead them to it), as deny that a reformed pastor has no power to ordain because he is not a bishop. He has episcopal ordination, even such as the canons require, being set apart by two or three pastors at least, who are as truly diocesans as the ancient bishops, for some whole ages."[80]

The original equality of bishops and presbyters continued to be acknowledged from the rise of the episcopal hierarchy down to the time of the Reformation.

The claims of prelatical episcopacy were attacked in the fifth century with great spirit by Jerome, who denied the superiority of bishops. Several passages from this author

[80] Primitive Episcopacy, pp. 182, 183. London, 1688. — *Works*, p. 241.

EQUALITY OF BISHOPS AND PRESBYTERS. 171

have already been given under another head, to which we subjoin the following in his commentary on Titus i. 5:[81]

(a) JEROME expressly denies the superiority of bishops to presbyters, by *divine right*. To prove his assertion on this head, he goes directly to the Scriptures; and argues as the advocates of parity do, from the interchangeable

---

[81] Idem est ergo Presbyter, qui et episcopus, et antequam *diaboli instinctu*, studia in religione fierent, et diceretur in populis: "Ego sum Pauli, ego Apollo, ego autem Cephae:" *communi Presbyterorum consilio* ecclesiae gubernabantur. Postquam vero unusquisque eos, quos baptizaverat, suos putabat esse, non Christi: *in toto orbe decretum est, ut unus de Presbyteris electus superponeretur caeteris ad quem omnis ecclesiae cura pertineret*, et schismatum semina tollerentur. Putet aliquis non scripturarum, sed nostram, esse sententiam Episcopum et Presbyterum unum esse; et aliud aetatis, aliud esse nomen officii; relegat Apostoli ad Philipenses verba dicentis; Paulus et Timotheus servi Jesu Christi, omnibus sanctis in Christo Jesu, qui sunt Philippis, cum Episcopis et Diaconis, gratia vobis et pax, et reliqua. Philippi *una* est urbs Macedoniae, et certe in una civitate *plures* ut nuncupantur, *Episcopi esse non poterant*. Sed quia *eosdem Episcopos illo tempore* quos et *Presbyteros* apellabant, propterea indifferentur de Episcopis quasi de Presbyteris est locutus. Adhuc hoc alicui videatur ambiguum, nisi altero testimonio comprobetur. In Actibus Apostolorum scriptum est, quod cum venisset Apostolus Miletum miserit Ephesum, et vocaverit Presbyteros ecclesiae ejusdem, quibus postea inter caetera sit locutus; *attendite vobis et omni gregi in quo vos Spiritus Sanctus posuit Episcopos, pascere Ecclesiam Domini, quam acquisivit per sanguinem suum*. Et hoc diligentius observate, quo modo *unius civitatis* Ephesi *Presbyteros* vocans, postea eosdem *Episcopos* dixerit.—Haec propterea, ut ostenderemus *apud veteres* eosdem fuisse Presbyteros et Episcopos. *Paulatim* vero, ut dissentionum plantaria evellerentur, ad *unum omnem solicitudinem esse delatam*.—Sicut ergo Presbyteri *sciunt se ex ecclesiae consuetudine* ei, qui sibi propositus fuerit, esse subjectos, ita Episcopi noverint se *magis consuetudine quam dispositionis dominicae veritate*, Presbyteris esse majores.—HIERONYMI *Com. in Tit.* I. 1, *Opp.* Vol. IV. p. 413, ed. Paris. 1093–1706. The same may be found in Rothe, S. 209. Comp. Mason's Works, Vol. III. pp. 225–228.

titles of bishop and presbyter;[82] from the *directions* given to them without the least intimation of difference in their authority; and from the *powers* of presbyters, undisputed in his day.

(*b*) JEROME states it as a *historical fact*, that this government of the churches *by presbyters alone*, continued until—to avoid scandalous quarrels and schisms, arising from the instigation of Satan—it was thought expedient to *alter* it;

(*c*) That this change in the government of the church, this creation of a superior order of ministers, took place, not at once, but *by degrees*—"*Paulatim*, by little and little;"

(*d*) That the elevation of one presbyter over the others was a *human contrivance;* was not *imposed* by authority, but *by the custom of the church;* and that the presbyters of his day *knew* this very well;

(*e*) That the first bishops were made by the *presbyters themselves*, and consequently they could neither have, nor communicate, any authority above that of presbyters. "*Afterward*, to prevent schism, one was *elected* to preside over the rest." Elected, commissioned by the *presbyters;* for he immediately gives you a broad fact, which it is impossible to explain away, that "at Alexandria, from the evangelist Mark to the bishops Heraclas and Dionysius, until about the middle of the third century, the presbyters *always chose* one of their number *as a president*, and gave him the title of bishop."[83]

The testimony of Jerome affords an authentic record of the *change* that was introduced into the government of the church, and the causes that led to this change, by which the original constitution was wholly subverted. It was in

---

[82] Apud veteres iidem episcopi et presbyteri fuerint; quia illud nomen dignitatis, est; hoc, aetatis.—*Ep. ad Oceanum*, Vol. IV. p. 648.

[83] Comp. Mason's Works, Vol. III. pp. 233-251, and Jewel, Defence of his Apology, pp. 122, 123.

his day a known and acknowledged fact, that prelacy had no authority from Christ or his apostles—no divine right to sustain its high pretensions. "The presbyters know that they are subject to their bishops," not by divine right or apostolical succession, but "*by the custom of the church.*"[84] And to the same effect is the admission of Augustine.

The most distinguished of the Greek fathers also concur with those of the Latin church in regard to the identity of bishops and presbyters. Chrysostom, A. D. 407, in commenting upon the apostle's salutation of the bishops of Philippi, exclaims: "How is this? Were there many bishops in one city? By no means; but he calls the presbyters by this name; for at that time both were so called. Wherefore, as I said, presbyters were anciently called bishops and stewards of Christ, and bishops were called presbyters. For this reason, even now, many bishops speak of their *fellow-presbyter,* and *fellow-minister;* and finally the name of *bishop and presbyter is given to each indiscriminately.*"[85]

Theodoret, also, who lived only a few years later than Chrysostom, exhibits substantially the same sentiments.

---

[84] Quanquam secundum honorum vocabula quae *jam* ecclesiae usus obtinuit, episcopatus presbyterio major sit.—*Ep. et Hier.*, 19, alias 82, § 33, Op. Vol. II. col. 153.

[85] Σὺν ἐπισκόποις καὶ διακόνοις, τί τοῦτο; μιᾶς πόλεως πολλοὶ ἐπίσκοποι ἦσαν; Οὐδαμῶς· ἀλλὰ τοὺς πρεσβυτέρους οὕτως ἐκάλεσε· τότε γὰρ τέως ἐκοινώνουν τοῖς ὀνόμασι, καὶ διάκονος ὁ ἐπίσκοπος ἐλέγετο. Διὰ τοῦτο γράφων καὶ Τιμοθέῳ ἔλεγε· τὴν διακονίαν σου πληροφόρησον, ἐπισκόπῳ ὄντι. ὅτι γὰρ ἐπίσκοπος ἦν, φησὶ πρὸς αὐτὸν χεῖρας ταχέως μηδενὶ ἐπιτίθει· καὶ πάλιν· ὃ ἐδόθη σοι μετὰ ἐπιθέσεως τῶν χειρῶν τοῦ πρεσβυτερίου· οὐκ ἂν δὲ πρεσβύτεροι ἐπίσκοπον ἐχειροτόνησαν. Καὶ πάλιν πρὸς Τίτον γράφων φησί· τούτου χάριν κατέλιπόν σε ἐν Κρήτῃ, ἵνα καταστήσῃς κατὰ πόλιν πρεσβυτέρους, ὡς ἐγώ σοι διεταξάμην· εἴ τις ἀνέγκλητος, μιᾶς γυναικὸς ἀνήρ· ἃ περὶ τοῦ ἐπισκόπου φησί. Καὶ εἰπὼν ταῦτα εὐθέως ἐπήγαγε· δεῖ γὰρ τὸν ἐπίσκοπον ἀνέγκλητον εἶναι, ὡς Θεοῦ οἰκονόμον, μὴ αὐθάδη. Ὅπερ οὖν ἔφην, καὶ οἱ πρεσβύτεροι τὸ παλαιὸν ἐκαλοῦντο ἐπίσκοποι καὶ διάκονοι τοῦ Χρισ-

In relation to the salutation of Paul to the Philippians, c. i. 1, he says, "the apostle calls the presbyters bishops; for they had at that time the same names, as we learn from the the history of the Acts of the Apostles (Acts xx. 17), *so that it is evident that he denominates the presbyters, bishops.*"[86] This sentiment he repeats in commenting on 2 Tim.[87]

The commentary of a Greek scholiast, of a later date, τοῦ, καὶ οἱ ἐπίσκοποι πρεσβύτεροι. ὅθεν καὶ νῦν πολλοὶ συμπρεσβυτέρῳ ἐπίσκοποι γράφουσι, καὶ συνδιακόνῳ· λοιπὸν δὲ τὸ ἰδιάζον ἑκάστῳ ἀπονενέμηται ὄνομα, ὁ ἐπίσκοπος καὶ ὁ πρεσβύτερος.—*Chrysostom, Ep. ad Phil.* Vol. XI. p. 194.

Διαλεγόμενος περὶ ἐπίσκοπον καὶ χαρακτηρίσας αὐτοὺς, καὶ εἰπὼν τίνα μὲν ἔχειν, τίνων δὲ ἀπέχεσθαι χρὴ, καὶ τὸ τῶν πρεσβυτέρων τάγμα ἀφεὶς, εἰς τοὺς διακόνους μετεπήδησε. Τί δήποτε; ὅτι οὐ πολὺ μέσον αὐτῶν καὶ τῶν ἐπισκόπων. Καὶ γὰρ καὶ αὐτοὶ διδασκαλίαν εἰσὶν ἀναδεδεγμένοι καὶ προστασίαν τῆς ἐκκλησίας· καὶ ἃ περὶ ἐπισκόπων εἶπε, ταῦτα καὶ πόεσβυτέροις ἁρμόττει· τῇ γὰρ χειροτονίᾳ μόνῃ ὑπερβεβήκασι καὶ τούτῳ μόνον δοκοῦσι πλεονεκτεῖν τοὺς πρεσβυτέρους.—*Ibid., Ep. ad Tim.* 1, Vol. XI. p. 604.

[86] Πᾶσι τὰ κατ' αὐτὸν ἐπιστέλλει, τοῖς δὲ τῆς ἱερωσύνης ἠξιωμένοις καὶ τοῖς ἀπὸ τούτων ποιμαινομένοις. ἁγίοις γὰρ τοὺς τοῦ βαπτίσματος ἀξιωθέντας ὠνόμασεν, ἐπισκόπους δὲ τοὺς πρεσβυτέρους καλεῖ, ἀμφότερα γὰρ εἶχον κατ' ἐκεῖνον τὸν καιρὸν τὰ ὀνόματα. Καὶ τοῦτο ἡμᾶς καὶ ἡ τῶν Πράξεων ἱστορία διδάσκει. Εἰρηκὼς γὰρ ὁ μακάριος Λουκᾶς, ὡς εἰς τὴν Μίλητον τοὺς Ἐφεσίων μετεπέμψατο πρεσβυτέρους ὁ θεῖος ἀπόστολος, λέγει καὶ τὰ πρὸς αὐτοὺς εἰρημένα· προσέχετε γὰρ φησιν ἑαυτοῖς καὶ παντὶ ποιμνίῳ, ἐν ᾧ ὑμᾶς ἔθετο τὸ πνεῦμα τὸ ἅγιον ἐπισκόπους, ποιμαίνειν τὴν ἐκκλησίαν τοῦ Χριστοῦ· καὶ τοὺς αὐτοὺς καὶ πρεσβυτέρους καὶ ἐπισκόπους ὠνόμασεν. Οὕτω καὶ ἐν τῇ πρὸς τὸν μακάριον Τίτον ἐπιστολῇ· διὰ τοῦτο κατέλιπόν σε ἐν Κρήτῃ, ἵνα καταστήσῃς κατὰ πόλιν πρεσβυτέρους, ὡς ἐγώ σοι διεταξάμην. Καὶ εἰπὼν ὁποίους εἶναι χρὴ τοὺς χειροτονουμένους ἐπήγαγε· δεῖ γὰρ τὸν ἐπίσκοπον ἀνέγκλητον εἶναι, ὡς Θεοῦ οἰκονόμον. Καὶ ἐνταῦθα δὲ δῆλον τοῦτο πεποίηκε· τοῖς γὰρ ἐπισκόποις τοὺς διακόνους συνέζευξε, τῶν πρεσβυτέρων οὐ ποιησάμενος μνήμην ἄλλως τε οὐδὲ οἷόν τε ἦν πολλοὺς ἐπισκόπους μίαν πόλιν ποιμαίνειν· ὡς εἶναι δῆλον ὅτι τ ο ὺ ς μ ὲ ν π ρ ε σ β υ τ έ ρ ο υ ς ἐ π ι σ κ ό π ο υ ς ὠ ν ό μ α σ ε.—*Theodoret, Ep. ad Phil.* p. 445, seq. Vol. III. ed. Halens.

[87] Πολλὰ καὶ τούτου (Epaphroditus) κατορθώματα διεξῆλθεν (Paul-

shows that these views were still retained in the Eastern church.[88]

This scholiast has but hinted at the argument from these passages, to which he refers, but he has said enough to show that the doctrine of the ministerial parity of bishops and presbyters was still maintained during the middle ages, in the Eastern church, and justly defended on the authority of the Scriptures.

Elias, archbishop, of Crete, A.D. 787, asserts the identity of bishops and presbyters; and, in commenting upon Gregory Nazianzen, remarks that this bishop, in the fifth century, was accustomed to denominate presbyters, *bishops*, making no distinction between them—a circumstance which this scholiast has noticed in many passages from Gregory.[89]

us), οὐκ ἀδελφὸν μόνον, ἀλλὰ καὶ συνεργὸν καὶ συστρατιώτην ἀποκαλέσας. Ἀπόστολον δὲ αὐτὸν κέκληκεν αὐτῶν ὡς τὴν ἐπιμέλειαν αὐτῶν ἐμπεπιστευμένον· ὡς εἶναι δῆλον ὅτι ὑπὸ τούτον ἐτέλουν οἱ ἐν τῷ προοιμίῳ κ λ η θ έ ν τ ε ς   ἐ π ί σ κ ο π ο ι, τ ο ῦ   π ρ ε σ β υ τ ε ρ ί ο υ   δ η λ ο ν ό τ ι   τ ὴ ν   τ ά ξ ι ν   π λ η ρ ο ῦ ν τ ε ς.—*Ibid. Ep. ad Tim.*, p. 459, Vol. III.

Ἐ π ί σ κ ο π ο ν δ ὲ ἐ ν τ α ῦ θ α τ ὸ ν π ρ ε σ β ύ τ ε ρ ο ν λ έ γ ε ι, ὡς τὴν πρὸς Φιλιππησίους ἐπιστολὴν ἑρμηνεύοντες ἀπεδείξαμεν.—*Ibid.* p. 652.

[88] Ἐπειδὴ λανθάνει τοὺς πολλοὺς ἡ συνήθεια, μάλιστα τῆς καινῆς διαθήκης, τοὺς ἐπισκόπους πρεσβυτέρους ὀνομάζουσα καὶ τοὺς πρεσβυτέρους ἐπισκόπους, σημειωτέον τοῦτον ἐντεῦθεν καὶ ἐκ τῆς πρὸς Τίτον ἐπιστολῆς, ἔτι δὲ καὶ πρὸς Φιλιππησίους καὶ ἐκ τῆς πρὸς Τιμόθεον πρώτης. Ἐκ μὲν οὖν τῶν Πράξεων ἐντεῦθέν ἐστι πεισθῆναι περὶ τούτου, γέγραπται γάρ οὕτως· Ἐκ δὲ τῆς Μιλήτου πέμψας εἰς Ἔφεσον μετεκαλέσατο τοὺς πρεσβυτέρους τῆς ἐκκλησίας. Καὶ οὐκ εἴρηκε τοὺς ἐπισκόπους, εἶτα ἐπιφέρει· ἐν ᾧ ὑμᾶς τὸ πνεῦμα τὸ ἅγιον ἔθετο ἐπισκόπους, ποιμαίνειν τὴν ἐκκλησίαν. Ἐκ δὲ τῆς πρὸς Τίτον ἐπιστολῆς. Καταστήσεις κατὰ πόλιν πρεσβυτέρους, ὡς ἐγώ σοι διεταξάμην. Ἐκ δὲ τῆς πρὸς Φιλιππησίους· Τοῖς οὖσιν ἐν Φιλίπποις συνεπισκόποις καὶ διακόνοις. Οἶμαι δὲ, ὅτι ἐκ τῆς προτέρας πρὸς Τιμόθεον ἀναλογισάμενος τοῦτο ἐκλαβεῖν· εἰ τις γάρ, φησι, τῆς ἐπισκοπῆς ὀρέγεται, καλοῦ ἔργου ἐπιθυμεῖ· δεῖ οὖν τὸν ἐπίσκοπον ἀνεπίληπτον εἶναι.—Cited by Rothe from Salmasius, Episcop. et Presb. p. 13.

[89] Greg. Naz., Vol. II. p. 830, Ed. Colon. 1590. Also Ed. Basil. 1571, pp. 262, 264.

Isidorus Hispalensis, bishop of Seville, in Spain, in the seventh century, and one of the most learned men of that age, copies with approbation the authority of Jerome given above, as an expression of his own sentiments.

We subjoin the authority of Bernaldus Constantiensis, a learned monk of the eleventh century,[90] and of Pope Urban, his contemporary.[91]

Gratian, a Benedictine, eminent for his learning and talents, a century later;[92] Nicholas Tudeschus, archbishop of Panorma, about A. D. 1428,[93] and even the papal canonist, Jo. Paul Launcelot, A. D. 1570,[94] all concur in the same sentiment.

[90] Quum igitur presbyteri et episcopi antiquitus, idem fuisse legantur etiam eandem ligandi atque solvendi potestatem, et alia nunc episcopis specialia, habuisse non dubitantur. Postquam autem presbyteri ab episcopali excellentia cohibiti sunt, coepit eis non licere quod licuit, videlicet quo decclesiastica auctoritas solis pontificibus exequendum delegavit.—*De Presbyterorum officio tract.* in monumentorum res Allemannorum illustrant. S. Blas, 1792, 4to. Vol II. 384, seq.

[91] Sacros autem ordines ducimus diaconatum et presbyteratum. Hos siquidem solos primitiva legitur ecclesia habuisse; super his solum preceptum habemus apostoli.—*Conc. Benevent,* an. 1090, can. 1.

[92] (Dist. XCV. c. 5), Epist. ad Evangel. (Dist. XCIII. c. 24), and Isidori His. (Dist. XXI. c. 1).

[93] Super prima parte Primi, cap. 5, ed. Lugdun, 1543, fol. 1126. Olim presbyteri in commune regebant ecclesiam et ordinabant sacerdotes.

[94] Institut. juris Canon. Lib. 1, Tit. 21, § 3. Comp. especially *Petavii* de ecclesiastica hierarchia Lib. 5, and dissertatt. theologic. Lib. 1, in his theolog. dogmat. Tom. 4, p. 164. On the other side, *Walonis Messalini* (Claud. Salmasii), diss. de episcopis et presbyteris. Lugd. Bat. 1641, 8vo. *Dav. Blondelli* apologia pro sententia Hieronymi de episcopis et presbyteris. Amstelod. 1616, 4to. Against these, *Henr. Hammondus* dissertatt. IV. quibus episcopatus jura ex sacra scriptura et prima antiquitate adstruuntur. Lond. 1651. The controversy was long continued. On the side of the Episcopalians, *Jo. Pearson, Guil. Beveridge, Henr. Dodwell, Jos. Bingham, Jac. Usserius.* On that of

In view of the whole course of the argument, it appears that the episcopal claim of an original distinction between bishops and presbyters is a groundless assumption. The existence of such a distinction has been denied by prelates, bishops and learned controvertists and commentators, both in the Eastern and Western churches, of every age down to the sixteenth century. It was unknown to those early fathers who lived nearest to the apostolical age, and some of whom were the immediate successors of the apostles. It was wholly unauthorized by the apostles themselves. Must we believe that the presbyter is a mere subaltern of the bishop, to perform the humbler offices of the ministry and to supply the bishop's lack of service? Must we believe, moreover, that the bishop, this honored and most important dignitary of the church, is a nameless nondescript, known by no title, represented by no person or class of persons in the apostolic churches, and having no distinct, specific duties prescribed in the New Testament? All this may be asserted and reaffirmed, as a thousand times it has been, but it can never be proved. Verily this vaunting of high church episcopacy is an insult to reason, a complacent assumption, which makes "implicit faith the highest demonstration." If any asserter of these absurd pretensions finds himself disquieted at any time by the renewed remonstrances of Scripture, truth and reason, to repel such impertinent intruders and restore the equilibrium of his mind, he has only to "shake his head and tell them how superior, after all, is faith to logic!"

The foregoing chapters exhibit an outline of that eccle-

---

the Presbyterians, *Jo. Dallaeus, Camp. Vitringa;* also the Lutherans, *Joach. Hildebrand, Just. Henn. Boehmer, Jo. Franc. Buddeus, Christ. Math. Pfaff,* etc. Comp. *Jo. Phil. Gabler* de episcopis primae ecclesiae Christ. eorumque origine diss. Jenae, 1805, 4to.

siastical organization which the churches received from the hands of the apostles, and which was continued in the primitive church for some time after the apostolic age. The government may not be strictly either congregational or presbyterian, but it involves the principles of both; it is altogether popular. The sovereign authority is vested in the people. From them all the laws originate; by them they are administered. Each community is an independent sovereignty, whose members are subject to no foreign ecclesiastical jurisdiction. Their confessions, formularies and terms of communion are formed according to their own interpretation of the laws of God; and if the deportment of any one is subject to impeachment, the case is decided by the impartial verdict of his brethren. Their officers are few; and their ministers, equal in rank and power, are the servants, not the lords of the people. The entire polity of the apostolic and primitive churches was framed on the principles, not of a monarchical hierarchy, but of a popular and elective government. It was a republican government administered with republican simplicity.

CHAPTER VII.

APOSTOLICAL SUCCESSION.

THE ministerial parity and identity of bishops and presbyters, so far as indicated by their names in the New Testament, are generally admitted, we believe, by Episcopalians themselves. "The name [bishop] is there given to the middle order, or presbyters; and *all* that we read in the New Testament concerning 'bishops' (including, of course, the words 'overseers' and 'oversight,' which have the same derivation) is to be regarded as pertaining to that middle grade. It was after the apostolic age that the name 'bishop' was taken from the second order and appropriated to the first." This admission of Bishop Onderdonk may be received as a fair expression of the views of the denomination. The office of bishop, then, either is not a divine, but a human institution, established after the apostolic age, or it is an office, an institution, without a name in the Scriptures. It is an order, an office, on which not only the validity of all the ordinances of the church, but the very existence of the church, depends. Without a bishop there neither is nor can be any church, according to the episcopal theory. And yet this order, indispensable to the existence of the church, is never once named by the Great Head of this church nor by his apostles while going through the earth ordaining and setting in order the churches of every land! Nay, more; this confusion is worse confounded by applying to this high and sacred order all the names, offices and attributes of an inferior grade. Believe it who can, we cannot; we will not cast upon Holy Writ such an imputation as this confusion of words and orders involves.

But with those whose faith staggers not under such demands upon its credulity, the controversy turns, not upon the equality, the identity of bishops and presbyters, but upon the question whether the apostles themselves had a permanent or a temporary office and character—whether they had or could have successors to perpetuate their own peculiar, specific office in the church. Their office is as definite and distinct as that of bishop, by the episcopal theory, is indefinite and indistinct. They were to be witnesses for Christ—witnesses of his ministry, his life, his death and his resurrection. Peter declares this to have been the specific object of choosing Matthias—*to be a witness with us of his resurrection*, Acts i. 21, 22; comp. ii. 32; v. 32; x. 39–42. This was to be the test of Paul's apostleship. Christ revealed himself to him "*to be his witness unto all men,*" Acts xxii. 14, 15; xxiii. 11; xxvi. 16. "Am I not an apostle? Have I not seen Jesus Christ our Lord?" 1 Cor. ix. 1. The office of the apostles, by these limitations, ends with themselves. They can have no successors. See Neander, p. 20.

As the first ministers of the church of Christ, the first to ordain ministers in all the churches, they have their successors in the Episcopal and in every duly-organized church of whatever denomination. There is an apostolical succession in the Presbyterian as truly as in the Episcopal Church. But when they of this church claim that through their apostolical succession there is a mysterious "sacramental grace," an invisible, imperceptible *tertium quid*, which alone gives validity to ordination and to every ordinance of the church, we may call for the proof thereof. The burden of proof lies upon them. What is this grace transmitted through your apostolical succession? Who has seen or handled it or felt its presence? What are the evidences of its presence or tokens of its departure? It is a latent principle, for ever latent, inoperative, unknown. All else is known by its effects, the only means by which everything material or immaterial can be made known. Verily, to set up such claims for such grace, so mysterious, so incomprehensible, cognizable neither by sense, consciousness nor experience, is to put an end to all argument, to set at defiance all reason. We have no common ground, no first principles, neither definition, axiom nor postulate, left for logical discussion.[1]

In the dark ages of disorder, degeneracy and corruption, has no graceless hypocrite crept in unawares, and, stealing the livery of succession from sinister motives, laid unholy hands upon the bishops whom he received to holy orders? If so, then this "golden chain of the succession," of which we hear so much as connected with the personal ministry of Christ and fastened to the throne of God, becomes a rope of sand given to the winds. A slight error or informality vitiates the whole; but the chances are infinite that some fatal flaw or breach in the long chain of the succession may interrupt the line of this electrical grace; and the misfortune is, that it can never be known by any palpable signs whether or not the line has been broken; neither, if once broken, can it ever be repaired. But the historical fact is, that this chain has many a broken link, in bishops irregularly introduced into office, without consecration, by some caprice of the populace or the supremacy of inspired power. Ambrose, Martin of Tours, Chrysostom, Eraclius, are examples to this effect, broken links in this golden chain, any one of which sunders for ever this connection with the

---

[1] Comp. Edinburgh Rev., April, 1843, pp. 269, 270.

throne of God. Comp. pp. 65, 71. The irony of the British reviewer is but a fit expression of the absurdity of this delusion:

"What bishop can be sure that he and his predecessors in the same line have always been duly consecrated? or what presbyter, that he was ordained by a bishop who had a right to ordain him? Who will undertake to trace up his spiritual pedigree unbroken to the very age of the apostles, or give us a complete catalogue of his spiritual ancestry?"[2]

How marvelous that men of acuteness and culture, eru-

[2] "We can imagine the perplexity of a presbyter thus cast in doubt as to whether or not he has ever had the invaluable 'gift' of apostolical succession conferred upon him. As that 'gift' is neither tangible nor visible, the subject neither of experience nor consciousness;—as it cannot be known by any 'effects' produced by it (for that mysterious efficacy which attends the administration of rites at its possessor's hands, is, like the gift which qualifies him to administer them, also invisible and intangible), he may imagine, unhappy man! that he has been 'regenerating' infants by baptism, when he has been simply sprinkling them with water. 'What is the matter?' the spectator of his distractions might ask. 'What have you lost?' 'Lost!' would be the reply; 'I fear I have lost my apostolical succession; or rather my misery is, that I do not know and cannot tell whether I ever had it to lose!' It is of no use here to suggest the usual questions, 'When did you see it last? When were you last conscious of possessing it?' What a peculiar property is that, of which, though so invaluable—nay, on which the whole efficacy of the Christian ministry depends—a man has no positive evidence to show whether he ever had it or not! which, if ever conferred, was conferred without his knowledge; and which, if it could be taken away, would still leave him ignorant, not only when, where and how the theft was committed, but whether it had ever been committed or not! The sympathizing friend might probably remind him that, as he was not sure he had ever had it, so, *perhaps* he still had it without knowing it. '*Perhaps!*' he would reply; 'but it is certainty I want.' 'Well,' it might be said, 'Mr. Gladstone assures you that, on the most moderate computation, your

dition, integrity and piety, can deceive themselves with such a figment of fanaticism and prelatical pride which so outrages all common sense and Christian charity! But there are men in that communion who, like Archbishop Whately, contemptuously discard this incomprehensible dogma. With his deliverances relating to it we dismiss the subject:

"Now what is the degree of satisfactory assurance that is thus afforded to the scrupulous consciences of any members of an episcopal church? If a man consider it as highly *probable* that the *particular minister* at whose hands he receives the sacred ordinances is really thus apostolically descended, *this* is the very utmost point to which he can, with any semblance of reason, attain; and the more he reflects and inquires, the more cause for hesitation he will find. There is not a minister in all Christendom who is able to trace up, with any approach to certainty, his own spiritual pedigree. The sacramental virtue—for such it is that is implied, whether the term be used or not—in the principle I have been speaking of, dependent on the imposition of hands, with a due observance of apostolical usages by a bishop, himself duly consecrated, ... this sacramental virtue, if a single link of the chain be faulty, must, on the above principles, be utterly nullified ever after in respect of all the links that hang on that one; the poisonous taint of informality, if it once creep in undetected, will spread the infection of necessity to an indefinite and irremediable extent.

"And who can undertake to pronounce that, during that long period usually designated the Dark Ages, no such taint ever was introduced? Irregularities could not have chances are as eight thousand to one that you have it!' 'Pish!' the distracted man would exclaim; 'what does Mr. Gladstone know about the matter?' And, truly, to *that* query we know not well what answer the friend could make."—*Edinburgh Rev.*, p. 271.

been wholly excluded without a perpetual miracle; and that no such miraculous interference existed, we have even historical proof. . . . We read of bishops consecrated when mere children; of men officiating who barely knew their letters; of illiterate and profligate laymen and habitual drunkards admitted to holy orders; and, in short, of the prevalence of every kind of disorder and reckless disregard of the decency which the apostle enjoins.

"It is no wonder, therefore, that the advocates of this theory studiously disparage reasoning, deprecate all exercises of the mind in reflection, deny appeals to evidence, and lament that even the power of reading should be imparted to the people. It is not without cause that they dread and lament 'an age of too much light,' and wish to 'involve religion in a solemn and awful gloom.' It is not without cause that, having removed the Christian's confidence from a rock to base it on sand, they forbid all prying curiosity to examine their foundation."[3]

"*Successors in the apostolic office the apostles had none. As witnesses of the resurrection, as dispensers of miraculous gifts, as inspired oracles of divine revelation,* THEY HAVE NO SUCCESSORS. *But as members, as ministers, as governors of Christian communities, their successors are the regularly admitted members, the lawfully ordained ministers, the regular and recognized governors of a regularly subsisting Christian church.*"[4]

[3] Kingdom of Christ Delineated, Essay II. § 29.
[4] Essay II. § 40.

CHAPTER VIII.

PRESBYTERIAN ORDINATION.

PRESBYTERIANS, in common with Episcopalians and other denominations, have adopted from the Scriptures, and retained substantially, one form of ordination, by the laying on of hands. We are accordingly as truly in the line of ecclesiastical descent and apostolical succession as Episcopalians. *The succession began undeniably with presbyterian elders ordained in every church,* and, as has been shown above, continued in this line a hundred years through the age of the apostles and the apostolic fathers, Clement, Polycarp and Irenaeus. "When we appeal to that tradition from the apostles, which is preserved in the church *by the succession of the presbyters,* they oppose this tradition." We ought to obey *the presbyters* in the churches, those who have, as we have shown, their succession from the apostles, who, *with the succession of the episcopate,* have received, according to the good pleasure of the Father, the gift of truth. The passages from Irenaeus are given above. In other passages he speaks in similar terms of the succession of *the episcopate,* the presbyteriate and the episcopate being with him the same order. Let it be particularly noted, also, that the succession is only *in persons,* incumbents *in office* merely, without the least reference to *any consecrating gift* or *grace* transmitted through this apostolical succession.

That the elders, ordained in the churches by Paul and the other apostles, did ordain others to assist and to succeed them, and these again, in like manner, there can be no doubt; but the right and the authority to ordain over any particular church they *derived from that body itself, not from the apostles.* The clergy are the authorized agents of the church, and act as such in ordaining the pastors whom such church or society may have chosen. Their authority, therefore, is derived from the church. Their ministerial office depends on their having been duly ordained according to the rules and usages of the church as by them authorized, not upon any mysterious sacramental virtue, transmitted in succession from the apostles. This apostolical succession is of no account whatever in establishing the validity of any ordination.

The assertion has a thousand times been made and a thousand times repeated that Timothy was bishop of the church at Ephesus, but the assertion has never been proved, neither can be. Neither is the nature of the particular office which he sustained at Ephesus the material point in the argument. But it is of the utmost importance in this connection to note that Timothy—if you please, Bishop Timothy—was inducted into the ministry by *presbyterian ordination*—"*by the laying on of the hands of the presbytery.*" This was the ordaining act. This is the only clear case of ordination recorded in the New Testament. And this was not episcopal, but *presbyterian ordination.* It establishes, therefore, beyond contradiction the validity of presbyterian ordination. Both for the apostolical succession of the presbyteriate and the validity of ordination by presbyterian ministers, we have clearer, higher, fuller authority than prelacy with all her proud pretensions can adduce for episcopal ordination.

We are not ignorant of the embarrassment which this presbyterian ordination of Timothy, their bishop, occasioned to episcopalians, nor of their efforts to evade the force of this example, but we care not to renew the discussion in this place. They deny but can never disprove the fact that there stands recorded by the apostle one instance "of presbyterian ordination, in the case of Timothy, and this should be allowed to settle the question. As there is no other undisputed case of ordination referred to in the New Testament, and as we may presume that on an occasion of the kind here referred to, everything essential to a valid ordination would be observed, it demonstrates that *presbyters had and have the right to ordain.*" [1]

In ministerial parity presbyters and bishops are convertible terms. Grant the equality and identity of the two, and you concede to presbyters the right to ordain. Allow them to ordain, and you admit their equality with bishops. This equality, established in the foregoing chapter, is acknowledged by episcopalians as undeniable in the apostolical churches. The apostles teach the validity of presbyterian ordination. Their authority and usage establish no uniform mode of ordination; they concede indirectly to presbyters this right, while not the least authority is given by them for exclusive ordination by bishops.[2]

The seven deacons were inducted into their office by prayer and *the laying on of hands*. This may have been, and perhaps was, the usual mode of setting apart any one to a religious service. But was the imposition of hands exclusively ordination? It was a right familiar to the Jews; and denoted *either a benediction, or the communication of miraculous gifts*. Jacob, in blessing the sons of Joseph, laid his hands upon their heads. So Jesus took young children in his arms and blessed them, *laying his hands upon them*. So Paul and Barnabas were dismissed, to go on their missionary tour, with the blessing of *the brethren at*

[1] Barnes' Apostolic Church, p. 223.
[2] Comp. Gerhardi. Loci Theolog. Vol. XII. p. 159.

Antioch, by the laying on of hands, Acts xiii. 3. Whatever may have been the specific office of the prophets and teachers at Antioch, they were not apostles. On the supposition, therefore, that the laying on of hands was performed by them, no reason appears why the same might not be done with equal propriety by presbyters. But this was not an ordination of Paul and Barnabas; for they had long been engaged in ministerial duties; neither does it appear that Paul was ever formally ordained.

The imposition of hands appears also in some instances to have occurred more than once, as is the case of Timothy, upon whom this rite was performed by the presbytery, 1 Tim. iv. 14; and again, by the apostle Paul, 2 Tim. i. 6.[3] This fact forbids the supposition that the laying on of hands was the solemnizing act in the rite of ordination, which, according to all ecclesiastical usage, cannot be repeated. In the passage, Acts xiv. 23, the phrase χειροτονήσαντες, etc., has been already shown to relate, with great probability, not to the consecration, but to the *appointment* of the elders in every church.[4] Comp. pp. 58–60.

---

[3] Rothe, Anfänge der Christ. Kirch. S. 161.

[4] "Where, it may be asked, resides the *right*, or power, and in what consists the importance, of *ordination*? It is not the source of ministerial authority; for that, as it has been endeavored to show, does not, and cannot, rest on human foundation. It does not admit to the pastoral office; for even in the Episcopal Church, the title to office, which is an indispensable prerequisite, is derived from the nomination of the person who has the disposal of the case. It is not office, but official character, which episcopal ordination is supposed to convey, together with whatsoever the advocates of episcopacy may chose to understand by those solemn words used by the ordaining bishop (an application of them which nonconformists deem awfully inappropriate), 'Receive the Holy Ghost.' The Jewish ordination, on the contrary, although sometimes accompanied, when administered by the apostles, by the communication of miraculous gifts, was in itself no more than

The rite of the imposition of hands was used by Christ, and with great propriety has been retained in the Christian church. But with the apostles it was the customary mode of imparting the χαρίσματα, the miraculous gifts of that age. So the converts at Samaria received the Holy Ghost, Acts viii. 17, and in like manner, when Paul had laid his hands upon the Ephesian converts, the Holy Ghost came upon them, *and they spake with tongues and prophesied*, Acts xix. 6. In the same sense is to be understood the gift, χάρισμα, which was bestowed on Timothy by prophecy, with the laying on of the hands of the presbytery, 1 Tim. iv. 14. The meaning simply is, that by the imposition of hands that peculiar spiritual gift denominated *prophecy* was imparted

a significant form of benediction on admission to a specific appointment. Of this nature were the offices connected with the synagogue, in contradistinction from those of the priesthood. When Paul and Barnabas were sent out from the church at Antioch, they submitted to the same impressive ceremony: not surely that either authority, or power of any kind, or miraculous qualifications, devolved upon the apostle and his illustrious companion by virtue of the imposition of presbyterian hands! What then is ordination? *The answer is, a decent and becoming solemnity, adopted from the Jewish customs by the primitive church, significant of the separation of an individual to some specific appointment in the Christian ministry, and constituting both a recognition on the part of the officiating presbyters of the ministerial character of the person appointed, and a desirable sanction of the proceedings of the church.* It is, however, something more than a mere circumstance, the imposition of hands being designed to express that fervent benediction which accompanied the ceremony, and which constitutes the true spirit of the rite. To an occasion which, when the awful responsibility of the pastoral charge is adequately felt, imparts to the prayers and the affectionate aid of those who are fathers and brethren in the ministry a more especial value, the sign and solemn act of benediction must appear peculiarly appropriate. This venerable ceremony may also be regarded as a sort of bond of fellowship among the churches of Christ, a sign of unity, and an act of brotherhood."—*Conder's Protestant Nonconformity*, Vol. I. p. 242.

to Timothy.[5] Of the same import are 2 Tim. i. 6, and 1 Tim. v. 22. Both relate to the communication of spiritual gifts. If the rite of ordination was implied and included in it, then the same act must be expressive both of this induction into office, and of the communication of spiritual gifts. This is Neander's explanation of the transaction. "The consecration to offices in the church was conducted in the following manner: After those persons to whom its performance belonged, had laid their hands on the head of the candidate—a symbolic action borrowed from the Jewish סְמִיכָה—they besought the Lord that he would grant what this symbol denoted, the impartation of the gifts of his Spirit for carrying on the office thus undertaken in his name. If, as was presumed, the whole ceremony corresponded to its intent, and the requisite disposition existed in those for whom it was performed, there was reason for considering the communication of the spiritual gifts necessary for the office, as connected with the consecration performed in the name of Christ. And since Paul from this point of view designated the whole of the solemn proceeding (without separating it into its various elements), by that which was its external symbol (as, in scriptural phraseology, a single act of a transaction consisting of several parts, and sometimes that which was most striking to the senses, is often mentioned for the whole), he required of Timothy that he should seek to revive afresh the spiritual gifts that he had received by the laying on of hands."[6]

The question has been asked, but never yet answered, who ordained Apollos? See Acts xviii. 24–26; 1 Cor. iii. 5–7.

It remains to consider the case of Paul the Apostle. Of whom did he receive ordination? One Ananias, a disciple

---

[5] Rothe Anfänge, I. S. 161.

[6] Neander, Apost. Kirch. 1, 213. Trans. I. 180. Comp. pp. 88, 300.

and a devout man according to the law, having a good report of all the Jews that dwelt at Damascus—this man prayed and laid his hands upon Paul, and *straightway he preached Christ in the synagogue.* Soon after this he spent three years in Arabia; then, for a whole year he and Barnabas *assembled themselves with the church and taught much people* at Antioch, Acts xi. 26. After all this, he was sent forth by the Holy Ghost on his mission to the Gentiles. Preparatory to this mission he was recommended to the grace of God by fasting, prayer and the imposition of hands. Even this was not done by any of the apostles, but by certain prophets and teachers, such as Simeon, Lucius and Manaen. Even on the supposition, therefore, that these were the solemnities of Paul's ordination, he was not episcopally ordained. But, in truth, they had no reference whatever to his ordination. On the authority of his divine commission he had already been a preacher for several years. It was not a new appointment, but an appointment to a new work, which in no degree helps forward the cause of prelatical ordination.[7]

We have adopted from apostolic usage a significant, impressive and becoming rite, by which to induct one into the sacred office of the ministry. The rite ought always to be observed. But no direct precept, no uniform usage, gives to this rite the sanction of divine authority; above all, there is not in all the Scriptures the least authority for confining the administration of it exclusively to the bishop. The idea of a bishop's receiving the Holy Ghost in regular succession from the holy apostles, and transmitting the heavenly grace to others by the laying on of his hands, is a figment of prelatical pride and superstition unauthorized in Scripture and unknown in the earliest ages of the church. In the apos-

---

[7] Bowdler's Letters on Apostolical Succession, p. 22.

tolic age, ordination was performed by the laying on of the hands of the presbytery, not of the bishops.

In the age immediately subsequent to that of the apostles, episcopal ordination was equally unknown, both bishops and presbyters being still the same. Clement knows no distinction between bishops and presbyters. Polycarp knows nothing of bishops. Each specifies but two orders or grades of officers in the church, of which the deacons are one. Presbyters or bishops of necessity form the other order, and are one and the same. Justin Martyr, again, speaks of only two grades, of which deacons form one. Irenaeus, still later, accords the apostolic succession to *presbyters*, who, *with the succession of the episcopate*, have received the certain gift of truth according to the good pleasure of the Father.[8] Clement of Alexandria and Tertullian recognize no clear distinction between bishops and presbyters as different orders.

We have, however, direct proof that presbyters, in the primitive church did themselves ordain. This is found in the epistle of Firmilian from Asia Minor to Cyprian in Carthage, A. D. 256. In explanation of the ecclesiastical polity of these churches, he says: "All power and grace is vested in the church, where the *presbyters*, *majores natu*, preside, who have authority to baptize, to impose hands [in the reconciling of penitents], and *to ordain*."[9] Firmilian wrote in the Greek language from Asia; but we have a Latin translation of his epistle in the writings of Cyprian. No one who has any acquaintance with these languages can

---

[8] Qui successionem habent ab apostolis . . . qui cum episcopatus successione, charisma veritatis certum placitum Patris acceperunt.—Cont. Haer. IV. c. 26, § ii. 4.

[9] Omnis potestas et gratia in ecclesia constituta sit; ubi praesident *majores natu*, qui et baptizandi, et manum imponendi, et ordinandi, possident, potestatem.—*Cyprian, Epist.* 75, § 7, p. 145.

doubt that the *majores natu* of the Latin is a translation of πρεσβύτεροι in the original. Both the terms πρεσβύτεροι and *majores natu* mean the same thing; and each may, with equal propriety, be rendered *aged men, elders, presbyters*.[10] The episcopal hierarchy was not fully established in these Eastern churches so early as in the Western. Accordingly, we find the presbyters here in the full enjoyment still of their original right to ordain. No restrictions have yet been laid upon the presbyters in the administration of the ordinances. Whatever clerical grace is essential for the right administration of baptism, of consecration and of ordination is still retained by the presbyters.

This authority is in perfect harmony with that of Irenaeus given above, that the succession and the *episcopate* had come down to his day, the latter part of the second century, through a series of presbyters, who, with the episcopate, enjoyed the rights and exercised the prerogatives of bishops, ordination being of course included. "This passage," says Goode, "appears to me decisive as to Irenaeus' view of the matter."[11]

To the foregoing testimonies succeeds that of the author of the Commentaries on St. Paul's Epistles, attributed to Hilary the Deacon, A. D. 384. "The apostle calls Tim-

---

[10] Reeves, the translator of Justin, a churchman, who loses no opportunity of opposing sectarians, allows, in his notes on the passage προεστώς, etc., that this προεστώς of Justin, the *probati seniores* of Tertullian, the *majores natu* of Firmilian, and the προεστῶτες πρεσβύτεροι or presiding presbyters of St. Paul, 1 Tim. iv. 17, were all one and the same. Now Tertullian, Cyprian, or Firmilian, the celebrated bishop of Caesarea in Cappadocia, and St. Paul, all mean presbyters. Their language cannot be otherwise interpreted without violence. Presbyter, says Bishop Jewell, is expounded in Latin by *major natu.—Smyth's Presbyt. and Prelacy*, p. 367.

[11] Goode's Divine Rule, Vol. II. p. 66.

othy, created by him *a presbyter*,[12] a bishop (for the first presbyters were called bishops), that when he departed, *the one that came next might succeed him.*"

A *presbyter*, it is to be observed, becomes the successor of the apostle; and the apostolical succession comes down through him, as through a bishop, plainly establishing the validity of presbyterian ordination. "Every bishop is a presbyter, but not every presbyter a bishop. *For he is bishop who is chief among the presbyters.* Moreover, he notices that Timothy was ordained a presbyter, but *inasmuch as he had no other above him, he was a bishop.*" Hence he shows that Timothy, a *presbyter*, might ordain a *bishop*, because of his equality with him. "For it was neither lawful

---

[12] "Timothy is here said, we may observe, to have been ordained a *presbyter*. And I cannot but think that the passage, 1 Tim. iv. 14, is favorable to this view. For without adopting the translation which some have given of this passage, viz., 'with the laying on of hands for the office of a presbyter,' if we retain our own version, which appears to me more natural, who or what is '*the presbytery?*' Certainly not consisting altogether of the apostles, though it appears, from 2 Tim. i. 6, that ordination was received by Timothy partly from St. Paul. But if presbyters joined in that ordination, it could not be to a higher *sacerdotal* grade or order than that of the presbyterhood. Nor is this inconsistent with his being called elsewhere an apostle, which name might be given him as one appointed to be a superintendent of a church."—*Divine Rule*, Vol. II. p. 64.

Timotheum, presbyterum a se creatum, episcopum vocat, quia primi presbyteri episcopi appellabantur, ut recedente uno sequens ei succederet. Comment. in Eph. iv. 11, 12. Inter Op. Ambros., ed. Ben., Vol. II. app. col. 241, 242. The "*Council*" may be what Tertullian calls "*consessus ordinis.*"

The author of the "Questiones in Vet. et Nov. Test.," which have been ascribed to Augustine, but are probably not his, says: "In Alexandria, and through the whole of Egypt, if there is no bishop, a presbyter *consecrates.*" (In Alexandria et per totam Ægyptum si desit episcopus consecrat presbyter.) Where, however, one MS. reads, *confirms* (consignat). See Aug. Op., Vol. III. app., col. 77. On this

nor right for an inferior to ordain a superior, inasmuch as one cannot confer what he has not received." [13]

There is another passage in striking coincidence with the foregoing, probably from the same author, though found in an appendix to the works of Augustine: "That by presbyter is meant a bishop the Apostle Paul proves when he instructs Timothy, whom he had ordained a presbyter, respecting the character of one whom he would make a bishop. For what else is the bishop than the *first presbyter*, that is, the highest priest? For he [the bishop] calls them [the presbyters] by no other names than *fellow-presbyters* and *fellow-priests*. He therefore considers them of the same grade as himself." But he is careful by no means to do the same with regard to clerical persons of inferior rank. Not even with the deacons, for to place himself in the same category with them would be degrading his own rank.

subject, the 13th canon of the Council of Ancyra (in the code of the Universal Church) is also worth notice.—*Divine Rule*, ibid.

There are also indirect confirmatory proofs. Such, I think, is afforded by the account we have in Eusebius (vi. 29) of the appointment of Fabianus to the bishopric of Rome, for the assembly that met to elect a bishop having fixed upon him, *placed him at once on the episcopal throne* ('Αμελλήτως ἐπὶ τοῦ θρόνον τῆς ἐπισκοπῆς λαβόντας αὐτὸν ἐπιθεῖναι), which seems to me irreconcilable with the notion that episcopal consecration was essential to entitle him to the episcopal seat; for he was installed in it without any such consecration.

[13] Post Episcopum tamen Diaconi ordinationem subjicit. Quare? nisi quia Episcopi et Presbyteri una ordinatio est? Uterque enim sacerdos est, sed Episcopus primus est; ut omnis Episcopus Presbyter sit, non omnis Presbyter Episcopus; hic enim Episcopus est, qui inter Presbyteros primus est. Denique Timotheum Presbyterum ordinatum significat; sed quia ante se alterum non habebat, Episcopus erat. Unde et quemadmodum Episcopum ordinet ostendit. Neque enim fas erat aut licebat, ut inferior ordinaret majorem; nemo enim tribuit quod non accepit.—*Comment. in* 1 *Tim.* iii. 8, *inter Ambros. Op. Vol. II. app.* 295.

"Does the bishop call the *deacons* his *fellow-deacons?* Certainly not; because they are far inferior to him, and it were a disgrace to call the *judge a mere manager of a clerk's office.*" If any are disposed to call in question this interpretation of the phrase *judicem dicere primicerium,* I will only say that it was given to me by Prof. Rothe of Heidelberg, with whose name the reader has become familiar by frequent references to his learned work on the Origin of the Christian Church. The following is also his exposition of the passage: "Where there is a real difference of office and rank, the *higher officer* cannot include himself in the official designation of the *lower* without degrading himself. It would be a downright insult to address the president of a court as the head of his clerks. Just so it does not enter the mind of the bishop to call his deacons *fellow-deacons,* making himself thereby a deacon. Between these two officers there exists an actual difference in rank. On the other hand, he calls the presbyters his *fellow-presbyters,* because he sees no real difference between his office and theirs, but only a difference *in degree;* that is, he considers himself, in relation to the presbyters, as only *primus inter pares,* chief among equals. The offices of bishop and presbyter, therefore, are essentially one and the same; the very thing which Ambrosiaster wishes to prove. 'For in Alexandria and throughout all Egypt, upon the decease of the bishop, the presbyter confirms *(consignat).*' " [14]

Here the presbyter performs another of the episcopal

---

[14] Presbyterum autem intelligi Episcopum probat Paulus Apostolus, quando Timotheum, quem ordinavit Presbyterum instruit, qualem debeat creare Episcopum. Quid est enim Episcopus nisi primus Presbyter, hoc est summus sacerdos? Denique non aliter quam Compresbyteros, Condiaconos suos dicit Episcopus? Non utique, quia multo inferiores sunt, et turpe est, *judicem dicere primicerium.—Augustin. Op. Vol. III. app. p.* 77. *Quaestiones in Veteris et Nov. Test. ex utroqua mixtim, ed. Bened. Antwerp,* 1700–1703.

functions, administering the rite, not only of ordination, but of *confirmation*.[15]

The full sacerdotal power is possessed by every presbyter, according to the authority of the earliest fathers. They know no distinction between bishops and presbyters. The right to ordain still belongs to him; and the bishop, when selected to preside over his fellow-presbyters, receives no new consecration or ordination, but continues himself to ordain *as a presbyter*. Within the first hundred and fifty years of the Christian era not an instance occurs of exclusive ordination by a bishop.

We have next the authority of Jerome, who died A. D. 426. He was one of the most learned of the Latin fathers. Erasmus styles him "by far the most learned and most eloquent of all the Christians, and the prince of Christian divines." Jerome received his education at Rome, and was familiar with the Roman, Greek and Hebrew languages. He visited Egypt, and traveled extensively in France and the adjacent countries. He resided, in the course of his life, at Constantinople, at Antioch, at Jerusalem, and at Bethlehem. By his great learning, and his extensive acquaintance with all that related to the doctrines and usages both of the Eastern and of the Western churches, he was eminently qualified to explain the rights and prerogatives of the priesthood.

"What does a bishop, ordination excepted, that a pres-

---

[15] Whether the verb *consignare* expresses the confirmation of the baptized, or the imposition of hands upon those who were ordained, or on penitents, the work expressed by it was correctly accomplished by presbyters, in the absence of the bishop, whose precedence was founded only on custom and the canons of the church. But these could not have legalized such acts of the presbyter had not his authority been apostolical. He was therefore duly authorized to perform the functions of the episcopal office.

byter may not do?[16] This, however, is said of the relations of bishop and presbyter *as they then were*. This restriction of the right of ordaining to the bishops alone was a recent innovation, which had begun to distinguish them from the presbyters, and to subvert the original organization of the church. But it was an acknowledged fact, in his day, that the bishops had no authority from Christ or his apostles for their unwarrantable assumptions. "As the presbyters know that it is by the *custom of the church* that they are subject to him who is placed over them, so let the bishops know that they are above presbyters rather by the custom of the church than by the fact of our Lord's appointment, and that they (both bishops and presbyters) ought to rule the church in common, in imitation of the example of Moses."[17]

He reviews the same subject with great point in his famous epistle to Evagrius, or, more properly in modern editions, to Evangelus. He rebukes with great severity certain persons who had preferred deacons in honor "above *presbyters,* i. e., *bishops.*" Having thus asserted the identity of bishops and presbyters, he proves his position from Phil. i. 1; from Acts xx. 17, 28; from Titus i. 5; from 1 Tim. iv. 14; from 1 Pet. v. 1; from 2 John i. 1; and from 3 John i. 1.

"As to the fact that AFTERWARD one was ELECTED to preside over the rest, this was done as a remedy against schism; lest every one drawing his proselytes to himself

---

[16] Quid enim facit, excepta ordinatione, Episcopus, quod presbyter non faciat?—*Ep. ad Evang. Ep.* 101 alias 85. *Op. Ed. Paris*, 1693–1706, p. 803. The same sentiment is expressed by Chrysostom: Τὴν χειροτονίαν. μόνην πρεσβυτέρους ἀναβαίνειν; only in ordaining do bishops excel presbyters.

[17] Comment. in Epist. ad Titus, c. 1, v. 5. Op. Vol. IV. Paris, 1693–1706, p. 413. See Rheinwald, 25.

should rend the church of Christ. It had been the custom in the church at Alexandria, from the evangelist Mark to the bishops Heraclas and Dionysius, for the presbyters to choose one of their own number, make him president and call him bishop; in the same manner as if an army should MAKE an emperor; or the deacons should choose from among themselves one whom they knew to be particularly active, and should call him ARCH-DEACON. For, excepting ordination, what is done by a bishop which may not be done by a presbyter?"[18]

Here the presbyters themselves elect one of their number and make him a bishop, so that even the bishop is ordained by the presbyters, if indeed it can be called an *ordination;* if not, then he is only a presbyter still, having no other right to ordain than they themselves have. Such, Jerome assures us, is the usage "*in every country.*" There was but one ordination for bishops and presbyters in his time, though bishops had now begun exclusively to administer it. But it had been the custom of the church, from the beginning, for bishops and presbyters to receive the same ordination. This is another consideration of much importance, to

---

[18] Sicut ergo Presbyteri sciunt, se ex Ecclesiae consuetudine ei, qui sibi praepositus fuerit, esse subjectos, ita Episcopi noverint, se magis consuetudine quam dispositionis Dominicae veritate Presbyteris esse majores, et in commune debere Ecclesiam regere. . . . . Audio quendam in tantam erupisse vecordiam, ut Diaconos Presbyteris, id est Episcopis, anteferret. Quod autem postea unus electus est, qui ceteris praeponeretur, in schismatis remedium factum est, ne unusquisque ad se trahens Christi Ecclesiam rumperet. Nam Alexandriae a Marco Evangelista usque ad Heraclam et Dionysium Episcopos, Presbyteri semper unum ex se electum in excelsiori gradu collocatum Episcopum nominabant, quomodo si exercitus Imperatorem faciat, aut Diaconi eligant de se quem industrium noverint et Archidiaconum vocent. Quid enim facit excepta ordinatione Episcopus, quod Presbyter non faciat? Comment. in Epist. ad Tit.—*Ep. ad Evang.* 101, p. 803.

show that presbyters were entitled to ordain. Having themselves received episcopal ordination as truly as the bishops, they were equally qualified to administer the same.

That the right of ordination belonged to presbyters is evident from the authority of Eutychius of Alexandria, the most distinguished writer among the Arabian Christians of the tenth century.

"I am quite aware that very considerable learning has been employed in the attempt to explain away this passage, and the reader who wishes to see how a plain statement may thus be darkened, may refer to the works mentioned below." [19]

Gieseler remarks that "it is at least certain that the part which is contradictory to the usage of later times has not been interpolated; and so far it has an historical value." [20]

[19] The following is Selden's translation of the passage from the Arabic: "Constituit item Marcus Evangelista duodecim Presbyteros cum Hanania, qui nempe manerent cum Patriarcha, adeo ut cum vacaret Patriarchates, eligerent unum e duodecim Presbyteris cujus capiti reliqui undecim manus imponerent eumque benedicerent et Patriarcham eum crearent, et dein virum aliquem insignem eligerent eumque Presbyterum secum constituerent loco ejus qui sic factus est Patriarcha, ut ita semper extarent duodecim. Neque desiit Alexandriae institutum hoc de Presbyteris, ut scilicet Patriarchas crearent ex Presbyteris duodecim, usque ad tempora Alexandri Patriarchae Alexandrini qui fuit ex numero illo cccxviii. Is autem vetuit ne deinceps Patriarcham Presbyteri crearent. Et decrevit ut mortuo Patriarcha convenirent Episcopi qui Patriarcham ordinarent. Decrevit item ut, vacante Patriarchatu, eligerent sive ex quacunque regione, sive ex duodecim illis Presbyteris, sive aliis, ut res ferebat, virum aliquem eximium, eumque Patriarcham crearent. Atque ita evanuit institutum illud antiquius, quo creari solitus a Presbyteris Patriarcha, et successit in locum ejus decretum de Patriarcha ab Episcopis creando."
—*Eutch. Patr. Alex. Ecclesiae suae orig.* Ed. J. Selden. London, 1642. 4to., pp. 29-31. Comp. Abr. Echell. Eutychius Vindicatus, Morinus De Ordinat Renaudot. Hist. Patriarch Alex.

[20] Cited in the author's Christian Antiquities, p. 103. In addition

The right of presbyters to ordain, and the validity of presbyterian ordination, was never called in question, according to Planck, until the bishops began, about the middle of the third century, to assert the doctrine of the apostolical succession. "With the name it seemed desirable also to inherit the authority of the apostles. For this purpose they availed themselves of the right of ordination. The right of ordination of course devolved exclusively upon the bishops as alone competent rightly to administer it. As they had been duly constituted the successors of the apostles, so also had they alone the right to communicate the same in part or fully by the imposition of hands. From this time onward, to give the rite more effect, it was administered with more imposing solemnity." And in all probability it became customary at this early period to utter, in the laying on of hands, those words of prelatical arrogance and shocking irreverence, "Receive the Holy Ghost" for the office and work of a bishop.[21]

Dr. Neander has assured the writer, in conversation on this point, that beyond a doubt presbyters were accustomed to ordain in the ages immediately succeeding the apostles. The testimony of Firmilian, given above, is, according to Neander, explicit in confirmation of this fact, and the same sentiments are also expressed or implied in his works. If further evidence is needed on this point, it is given at length and with great ability by Blondell, who, after occupying one hundred quarto pages with the argument, sums up the result of the discussion in the following syllogism:

"To whom the usage of the church has assigned in reality the same functions, to them it has also from the beginning

---

to the authors mentioned above by Goode, are Le Quien and Petavius. Comp. also Neander, Allgem. Gesch. I. S. 325, 326, 2d edit., Note. J. F. Rehkopf, Vitae Patriarcharum Alexandr. fasc. I. and II.

[21] Planck, Gesell. Verfass. I. S. 158–161.

ascribed the same ministerial parity, and, of course, the same dignity.

"But the usage of the church has assigned to bishops and presbyters, in reality, the same functions in the right of confirmation, of dedication of churches, of taking the veil, of the reconciling of penitents, and in the ordination of presbyters, deacons, etc.

"Therefore it has from the beginning declared that bishops and presbyters are in all respects equal, and, of necessity, that they are the same in dignity or rank." [22]

Even the decrees of ecclesiastical councils, which restrict the right of ordination to the bishops alone, distinctly imply that from the beginning it was not so limited. Why deny to presbyters the right to ordain, by a formal decree, if they had never enjoyed that right? The prohibition is an evident restriction of their early prerogatives.

But we forbear; enough has been said to vindicate the right of presbyters to ordain and to perform all the functions of the ministerial office. How extraordinary the hardihood with which, in the face of authorities a thousand times collated and repeated, we are still told that "the idea of ordination by any but bishops was an unheard-of thing in the primitive church!" [23]

"Such is the result of the appeal to the early fathers. They are so far from giving even a semblance of support to the episcopal claim, that, like the Scriptures, they everywhere speak a language wholly inconsistent with it, and favorable only to the doctrine of ministerial parity. What,

---

[22] Apologia pro sententia Hieronomi de Episcopis et presbyteris. Amstelod. 1616, 4to.

[23] "So much for the idea of any but bishops ordaining in the primitive church. Never was this allowed before the Reformation, either in the church or by any sect, however wild!"—*Review of Coleman's Christian Antiquities*, by H. W. D., a presbyter in Philadelphia.

then, shall we say of the assertions so often and so confidently made, that the doctrine of a superior order of *bishops* has been maintained in the church 'from the earliest ages,' in 'the ages immediately succeeding the apostles,' and 'by all the fathers from the beginning?' What shall we say of the assertion that the Scriptures, *interpreted* by the writings of the *early fathers*, decidedly support the same doctrine?"[24]

We have even high episcopal authority for presbyterian ordination. Repugnant as is this view of ordination to the modern advocates of episcopacy, it accords with the sentiments of Archbishop Cranmer and the first Protestant bishops of the Church of England.[25]

A volume might be filled with authorities from the English church alone, in which both her most distinguished prelates and her most eminent scholars concede to presbyters a virtual equality with bishops and the right to ordain.

The Necessary Erudition of a Christian Man, drawn up with great care, approved by both houses of Parliament in 1543, and prefaced by an epistle from the king himself, declares that " priests [*presbyters*] and bishops are, by God's law, one and the same, and that the powers of *ordination* and excommunication belong equally to both." Under

[24] Miller's Letters, pp. 108, 109.

[25] See transcript of the original, which was subscribed with Cranmer's own hand, in Bishop Stillingfleet's *Irenicum*, Part II. c. 8, § 2. See also Burnet's *History of the Reformation*, P. I. pp. 318, 321. Cited from Conder's Nonconformity. Many other authorities from English writers are given in S. Mather's Apology for the Liberty of the Churches, chap. 2, p. 51. They have also been collected and collated with great industry and research by Rev. Dr. Smyth, in his Apostolical Succession and his Presbytery not Prelacy. So also in an article in the Christian Spectator, New Series, Vol. II. p. 720, from whence several of the authorities given below are taken.

Elizabeth it was enacted by Parliament "that the *ordination* of foreign churches should be held valid."

The learned Whittaker, of Cambridge, declares the doctrine of the Reformers to be that "presbyters, being by divine right the same as bishops, *they might warrantably set other presbyters over the churches.*"

Archbishop Usher, one of the brightest ornaments of the Episcopal Church, on being asked by Charles I., in the Isle of Wight, whether he found in antiquity that "*presbyters alone did ordain?*" answered, "*Yes,*" and that he would show his Majesty more—"even where *presbyters* alone successively ordained *bishops;*" and he brought as an instance of this, the presbyters of Alexandria choosing and making their own bishop from the days of Mark till Heraclas and Dionysius.

Bishop Stillingfleet says: "It is acknowledged by the stoutest champions of episcopacy, before these late unhappy divisions, that ordination performed by presbyters in case of necessity is valid."

Bishop Forbes: "Presbyters have by divine right the power of ordaining as well as of preaching and baptizing."

Sir Peter King, Lord Chancellor of England, after asserting the equality of bishops and presbyters, and showing at length that the latter had full authority to administer the ordinances, adds: "As for ordination, I find clearer proofs of presbyters *ordaining* than of their administering the Lord's Supper."

The doctrine of the *divine right* of bishops, from which that of the exclusive validity of their ordination proceeds, was promulgated in a sermon preached January 12, 1588, by Dr. Bancroft, at St. Paul's Cross, in the presence of a vast assembly of members of Parliament, the nobility and the court. He maintained that bishops are a distinct order from priests or presbyters, and have authority over them *jure divino*, and directly from God. This bold and novel assertion created a great sensation throughout the kingdom. It was a vast extension of the prerogatives of the bishops, by which the oppression of the Puritans was increased to an incalculable degree. "The greater part even of the prelatic party themselves were startled by the novelty of the doctrine; for none of the English Reformers had ever regarded the bishops as anything else but a human institution, appointed for the more orderly government of the church, and they were not prepared at once to condemn as heretical all churches where that institution did not exist. Whitgift himself, that furious, intolerant zealot, perceiving the use which might be made of such a tenet, said that the doctor's sermon had done much good—though, for his own part, he rather wished than believed it to be true."[26] The doctrine was reaffirmed half a century later by Laud and his party,[27] and from that time has been the favorite dogma of many in the Episcopal Church.

Even at the present time the validity of Presbyterian ordination is acknowledged by many in the Episcopal Church.

Goode, who has written with great ability against the Tractarians, says: "I admit that for the latter point [ordination by bishops alone, as successors of the apostles], there is not any Scripture proof; but we shall find here, as in other cases, that as the proof is not to be found in Scripture, so antiquity also is divided with respect to it; and moreover, that though it is the doctrine of our church, yet that it is held by her with an allowance for those who may differ from her on that point, and not as if the observance of it was requisite by divine command, and essential to the validity of all ordinations; though for the preservation of the full *ecclesiastical* regularity of her own orders, she has

---

[26] Hetherington's History of Westminster Assembly, pp. 49, 50.
[27] Hallam's Constitutional History, Vol. II. pp. 440, 441.

made it essential to the ministers of her own communion."[26] In support of this opinion he proceeds to enumerate many of the authorities of the fathers given above.

Finally, we add the following extract, not again from an "irreverent dissenter"—to use the flippant cant of one of the Tractarians—but from a devoted son of their own church, a distinguished layman of England, who has written with great ability and good effect against the doctrines of Puseyism and the high-church party.

"It is no part of my plan to trace the origin or course of departure from the system of church government in the apostolical times, as it lies before us in all its simplicity. I admit—indeed, as the lawyers say, it is a part of my case—that some change was unavoidable; and I see nothing in the present constitution of the church of England that is inconsistent with the *principles* of the apostles. But to say that they are identical, is a mere abuse of words. Still less is it to be heard say without some impatience, that there is safety in her communion only, as she has descended from the apostles, through all the changes and abominations that have intervened."

If, then, all this be so, there seems to be an end to the question; for, under whatever circumstances the privilege of ordaining was afterward committed to the bishop, he could of necessity receive no more than it was in their power to bestow from whom he received it, who were co-ordinate presbyters, not superiors. At whatever period, therefore, it was adopted, and with whatever uniformity it might be continued, and whatever of value or even authority it might hence acquire, still as an apostolical institution it has none; there is a gap which never can be filled, or rather, the link by which the whole must be sus-

[26] Divine Rule, Vol. II. pp. 57, 58.

pended is wanting and can never be supplied. There can be no apostolical succession of that which had no apostolical existence; whereas, the averment, to be of any avail, must be, not only that it existed in the time of the apostles, but was *so* appointed by them as that there can be no true church without it."

" I am aware that in St. Jerome's time there existed generally, though by no means universally, this difference between the bishop and the presbyters, viz., that to the former was then confided the power of ordination. It may be difficult to fix the period exactly when the episcopate was first recognized as a distinct *order* in the church, and when the consecration of bishops, as such, came into general use. Clearly not, I think, when St. Jerome wrote. Thus much at least is certain, that the government of each church, *including the ordination of the ministry*, was at first in the hands of the presbytery." [29]

The change was gradual, *paulatim*. " Power always passes slowly and silently, and without much notice, from the hands of the many to the few; and all history shows that ecclesiastical domination grows up by little and little." [30] Comp. p. 171, note.

REMARKS.

1. The primitive church was organized as a purely religious society.

It had for its object the promotion of the great interests of morality and religion. It interfered not with the secular or private pursuits of its members, except so far as they related to the great end for which the church was formed— the promotion of pure and undefiled religion.

---

[29] Bowdler's Letters, pp. 32, 33.
[30] Dr. Hawks, in Smyth's Eccl. Republicanism, p. 166.

2. It employed only *moral means* for the accomplishment of religious ends.

The apostles sought, by kind and tender entreaty, to reclaim the wandering. They taught the church to do the same, and to separate the unworthy from their communion. But they gave no countenance to the exercise of arbitrary authority.

3. The apostolical churches had no relations to any civil government.

But the church soon began to be assimilated to the form of the existing civil governments, and in the end a "hierarchy of bishops, metropolitans and patriarchs arose, corresponding to the graduated rank of the civil administration. Ere long the Roman bishop assumed pre-eminence above all others."[31] United with the civil authority in its interests, assimilated to that power in its form of government, and secularized in its spirit, the church, under Constantine and his successors, put off its high and sacred character, and became a part of the machinery of state government. It first truckled to the low arts of state policy, and afterward, with insatiable ambition, assumed the supreme control of all power, human and divine.

4. The primitive church was fitted to any form of civil government, and to any state of society.

Voluntary and simple in their organization, entirely removed from all connection with the civil government, with no confederate relations among themselves, and seeking only by the pure precepts of religion to persuade men in every condition to lead quiet and holy lives, these Christian societies were adapted to any state of society and any form of government. They commended themselves with equal facility to the rich and the poor, the learned and the un-

---

[31] Ranke's Hist. of the Popes, Eng. Trans., Vol. I. p. 29.

learned, the high and the low, to the soldier, the fisherman or the peasant. They gathered into their communion converts from every form of government, of every species of superstition, and of every condition in life, and by wholesome truths and simple rites trained them up for eternal life.

5. It subjected the clergy to salutary restraints by bringing them, in their official character, under the watch of the church.

The consciousness that their whole life was open to the judicial inspection of those to whom they ministered, and by whom they were most intimately known, could not fail to create in the clergy a salutary circumspection, the restraints of which an independent ministry under another system can never feel.

6. It served to guard them against the workings of an unholy ambition, a thirst for office and the love of power.

This thought is necessarily implied in the preceding, but it is of such importance that it deserves a distinct consideration. Those disgraceful contests for preferment, the recital of which crowds the page of history, belong to a later age and a different ecclesiastical polity, a prelatical organization.

7. It tended to guard the clergy against a mercenary spirit.

The vast wealth of a church establishment, and the princely revenues of its incumbents, offer an incentive to this sordid passion which Paul in his poverty could never have felt, and which none can ever feel, who are contented to receive only a humble competence, as a voluntary offering at the hands of those for whom they labor.

8. The system was well suited to guard the church from the evils of a sectarian spirit.

In the church of Christ were Jews, jealous for the law of their fathers. There were also Greeks, who, independent of the Mosaic economy, had received the gospel and become Christians, without being Jews in spirit. Had now the church assumed the form of a national establishment, with its prescribed articles of faith, its ritual, etc., it is difficult to conceive how the opposing views of these different parties could have been harmonized. The disturbing influence of a sectarian spirit was strongly manifested in all the churches, so that it required all the wisdom and influence of the apostles to unite their Christian converts in an organization so simple as that which they did establish.

9. It left the apostles and pastors free to pursue their great work without let or hindrance from ecclesiastical authority or partisan zeal.

An explanation, given and received in the spirit of mutual confidence, reconciled the brethren whose prejudice was excited by the preaching of Peter to the Gentiles. The unhappy division between Paul and Barnabas ended in the furtherance of the gospel, both being at liberty, notwithstanding this sinful infirmity, to prosecute their labors for the salvation of men without being arrested by the ban of a hierarchy or trammeled by ecclesiastical jealousy.

10. The order of the primitive church was calculated to preserve peace and harmony among the clergy.

One in rank and power, and holding the tenure of their office at the will of their people, they had few temptations, comparatively, to engage in strife one with another for preferment.

We know, indeed, that Jerome assigns the origin of episcopacy to the ambitious contentions of the clergy in the primitive church; as though this were an expedient to heal their divisions. If this be true, we have only to say that the remedy proved to be infinitely worse than the evil which it would cure. After the rise of diocesan episcopacy and the establishment of the various grades of the hierarchy, the spirit of faction rose high among the clergy. Insatiable ambition possessed all orders among the priesthood, raging like a pestilence through their several ranks. The age of Constantine and his successors, within which the system of prelacy was matured, was pre-eminently the age of clerical ambition.

"In the age we speak of, which seems too justly styled *ambitionis saeculum*, the age of ambition, though those whose designs agree with the humor of it have esteemed it most inimitable, scarce any in the church could keep their own that had any there greater than themselves; some bishops, and not only the presbyters, found it so, the *great* still encroaching upon those whose *lower* condition made them obnoxious to the ambition and usurpation of the more potent.

"In that unhappy time, what struggling was there in bishops of all sorts for more greatness and larger power! What tugging at councils and court for these purposes." [32]

Socrates, the ecclesiastical historian, A. D. 439, alleges that he has intermingled the history of the *wars* of those times *as a relief* to the reader, that he may not be continually detained with the ambitious contentions, φιλονικία, of the bishops and their plots and counterplots against each other.[33]

11. It was happily suited to ensure to the people a useful and efficient ministry.

Select a few from among their ministerial brethren, exalt them to the high places of episcopal power, encircle them with the mitre, the robe, and all the "paraphernalia of pontifical dignity," enthrone them securely in authority, settle them quietly in their palaces to enjoy the ample benefices of an irresponsible office; and, however gratifying may be the favors which you have bestowed, you have done little to advance their ministerial usefulness.

---

[32] Clarkson's Primitive Episcopacy, Works, p. 221.
[33] Introduction to Lib. 5.

Besides, the days of a bishop's activity and usefulness soon pass away, but his *office* still remains. When once made bishop, and when he has thus received the indelible, invisible mark of episcopal grace, he is absolutely shut up to the necessity of continuing in office, however unworthy or unfit he may prove or find himself to be.[34]

What an incumbrance to the ministrations of the truth as it is in Jesus, again, are the forms and rites and observances of the Episcopal service! Here are *thirty-six* festivals and *one hundred* fasts, as specified in the prayer book, annually claiming the attention of the preacher. Then there is the "holy catholic church," the mysteries of the sacraments, baptismal regeneration, and the awful presence in the elements of the eucharist; the holy order of bishops, "the ascending orders of the hierarchy," "the most excellent liturgy," the validity of episcopal ordination, "covenant mercies," etc., etc., all pressing their claims on the attention of the Episcopal minister and demanding a place in the ministrations of the pulpit.

Add to these the sublimer doctrines of prelacy. Let him begin to discourse about apostolic succession, divine right, postures, attitudes, "wax candles, altar-cloths, chaplets, crosses, crucifixes, and mummery of all kinds," and it is not difficult to conjecture what place the great doctrine of

---

[34] Constit. and Canons of Prot. Epis. Church, pp. 301, 303. "So far," says Dr. Hawks, "as our research has extended, this law is without a precedent in the history of the Christian church. We may be mistaken, but we believe that ours is the first church in Christendom that ever legislated for the express purpose of preventing episcopal resignations; for this canon prescribes so many restrictions that the obstacles render it almost impossible for a bishop to lay down his jurisdiction. The matter is one which the practice of the church has heretofore left to be settled between God and the conscience of the bishops, and it may well be questioned whether it be not best in all cases there to leave it."—*Cited from Smyth's Eccl. Republicanism*, p. 167.

Christ and him crucified must hold in his teachings, or what efficacy his ministry will have in winning souls to Christ by the preaching of the truth as it is in Jesus.

But how different from all this was the ministry of Christ and of the apostles! Armed with the panoply of heaven, the word of God alone, the sword of the Spirit, the first preachers of the Christian religion went forth conquering and to conquer. By the simple instrumentality of the word, mighty through God to the pulling down of strongholds, they quickly spread the triumphs of the cross through every land, and carried up their conquests to the very throne of the Caesars. Be ours a religion that creates and enjoys such a ministry.

12. This primitive system served to make an efficient laity.

Instead of excluding them from the concerns of the church, like some other forms of church government, and requiring of them chiefly to attend to their forms of worship and pay their taxes, this primitive system of ecclesiastical polity devolved upon the members of the church the duties of discipline and the care of the church. It trained them to live and to care for the interests of religion. It quickened their graces by calling them into habitual exercise. It gave an efficient practical character to their religion. Look at those churches in England and America which bear the closest resemblance to this primitive organization. Observe their members in the private walks of life. Look at their efficiency in missionary operations, their noble charities, and their generous labors in every department of Christian benevolence. They are not merely devout worshipers within the church and decent moralists without, but everywhere eminently intelligent, efficient and liberal. They *serve* God as well as worship him. Not content merely to cultivate the private virtues of the Christian, the laity gain a habit of counseling and acting for the church and for their fellow-men, which gives to their religion an enterprising, practical, business character.[35] But the general character of any people is moulded and formed by the government, civil and religious, under which they live.[36]

13. Such an ecclesiastical organization as that which we have been contemplating, harmonizes with and fosters our free institutions.

There is a mutual relation and adaptation between our free, republican government and a popular ecclesiastical organization like that of the apostolical and primitive church. Such a system harmonizes with our partialities and prejudices; it coincides with our national usages; it is congenial with all our civil institutions. This consideration is enough of itself to outweigh, a thousand-fold, all that has

---

[35] "Oh that we had the zeal of some other denominations of Christians, against whom we too often boast ourselves, but whose liberality puts our penuriousness to open shame! It is but a few days since a single firm in this city, consisting of three members, gave $15,000 to sustain the Presbyterian Theological Seminary of New York; yet Bishop McIlvaine, wanting little more than this same sum to relieve one of the noblest of the institutions of our church, has to beg from city to city, from rich to poor, and is at this moment in anxious suspense whether his mission may not fail because men are lovers of their own selves, instead of being constrained by the love of Christ to give freely of what they have so freely received. It may be stated as a humiliating fact, showing the low estate of our church, that no sum above $250 has yet been received from any one in aid of Kenyon College, though numbers reside in this city who could cancel the debt themselves, and never feel the loss of so trifling a sum. When shall we see men awakening to a sense of their responsibility and their stewardship to God? When shall we hear them exclaim, with Zaccheus, 'Lord, the half of my goods I give to the poor?'"—*Epis. Rec.* Oct. 21, 1843.

[36] Comp. Milton's Prose Works, Vol. I. p. 167.

ever been urged in favor of prelacy. Indeed, the spiritual despotism of that system, its absolute monarchical powers, constitute one strong objection to it. It is the religion of despots and tyrants. Such, in its papal form, it has always been; and such, we cannot doubt, is still one inherent characteristic of high, exclusive episcopacy, however it may be modified by circumstances. The Church of England, from the time of its establishment, says Macaulay, "continued to be, for more than one hundred and fifty years, the servile handmaid of monarchy, the steady enemy of public liberty."[37] James, the tyrant of that age, uniformly silenced every plea in behalf of the Puritans, with the significant exclamation, "No bishop, no king, and no king, no bishop." So indispensable is the hierarchy to a monarchy. But in a free republic it is a monstrous anomaly.

On the other hand, be it remembered, "the New Testament is emphatically a republican book. It sanctions no privileged orders; it gives no exclusive rights. All who imbibe its spirit and obey its precepts are recognized as equals; children of the same Father; brethren and sisters in Christ, and heirs to a common inheritance.

"The Puritans imbibed the same spirit, and derived their principles from the same pure source of light, of holiness and freedom. They modeled their churches after the primitive form, and founded them on the basis of entire independence and equality of rights. Twice in their native land had they saved the British constitution from being crushed by the usurpations of the Stuarts; and Hume, who was never backward to reproach both their character and their principles, is compelled to acknowledge that what of liberty breathes in that constitution is to be ascribed to the influence of the Puritans.[38] These were the men who settled

[37] Miscellanies, Boston ed. I. p. 249.
[38] "So absolute, indeed, was the authority of the crown, that the

New England. They came here bearing in their bosoms the sacred love of liberty and religion; and ere they left the little bark that had borne them across the ocean, they formed themselves 'into a civil body politic,' having for its basis this fundamental principle, that they *should be ruled by the majority.* Here is brought out the grand idea of a free, elective government.[39]

"Many more graceful and more winning forms of human nature there have been, and are, and shall be; many men, many races there are, and have been, and shall be, of more genial dispositions, more tasteful accomplishments, a quicker eye for the beautiful of art and nature, less disagreeably absorbed, less gloomily careful and troubled about the mighty interests of the spiritual being or of the commonwealth. . . . . But where, in the long series of ages that furnish the matter of history, was there ever one—*where one*, better fitted by the possession of the highest traits of man, to do the noblest work of man; better fitted to consummate and establish the Reformation—to save the English constitution, at its last gasp, from the fate of other European constitutions, and prepare, on the granite and iced mountain summits of the New World, a still better rest for a still better liberty?"[40]

In conclusion, we would acknowledge, with devout gratitude to God, the rich inheritance which we have received

precious spark of liberty had been kindled and was preserved by the Puritans; and it was to this sect, whose principles appear so frivolous, and habits so ridiculous, that the English owe the whole freedom of their constitution." Again, "It was only during the next generation that the noble principles of liberty took root, and spreading themselves under the shelter of Puritanical absurdities, became fashionable among the people."—*Hume's Eng.* Vol. V. pp. 183, 469.

[39] Hawes' Tribute to the Memory of the Pilgrims, pp. 61-63, 83, 84.
[40] Speech of Hon. Rufus Choate before N. Eng. Soc. N. York, Dec. 25, 1843.

from our Puritan forefathers, in the religious institutions which they have transmitted to us.

They have given us a religion, more nearly allied, both in spirit and in form, to scriptural Christianity, than any other that has ever risen upon the world—a religion, more abundant in blessings, and more highly to be prized than any other; a religion, from which the whole American system, with all its institutions, social, civil and religious, has arisen. Our pilgrim fathers, while at anchor off our coast, and before they set foot upon these shores, after solemn prayer to the God of nations, entered mutually into a solemn compact, on board the Mayflower, to establish a government here "for the glory of God and the advancement of the Christian faith." With this intent they landed and entered upon their great work, as if conscious of their high destiny, reared up by God to establish and extend those principles of civil and religious freedom which they had so nobly defended in their fatherland. There they had suffered the loss of all things and shed their blood freely in their inflexible adherence to these principles. Harassed and wearied, but not dismayed, by their continual bonds, imprisonments and persecutions at home, and by their exile abroad, they resolved to seek an asylum in the wilderness of the New World, where, in peaceful seclusion, they might establish a government "for the glory of God and the advancement of the Christian faith." The Bible was their statute-book; and their religion, that primitive Christianity which God gave to the world through the medium of our Lord and his apostles. In fulfillment of their design, their first care was to set up the tabernacle of the Lord in this wilderness. They erected the church, and fast by this the school-house; then the court-house, the academy, the college, while yet they were of one faith and one name. No other form of religion was known, in this land of the pilgrims, until the great principles of the American system were developed and established here by our Puritan forefathers.

They were no ordinary men. They lived for no ordinary purpose. They were men the most remarkable that the world has ever produced. They lived for a nobler end, for a higher destiny than any others that have ever lived. These are the men to whom our country owes her religion, with all the blessings, social, civil and literary, that follow in its train. These are the venerable men whose blood still flows in our veins, and into whose inheritance we have entered. Peace to their silent shades. Fragrant as the breath of morning be their memory. The winds of two centuries have swept over their graves. The effacing hand of time has wellnigh worn away the perishable monuments which may have marked the spot where sleeps their honored dust. But they still live. They live in the immortal principles which they taught;—in the enduring institutions which they established. They live in the remembrance of a grateful posterity; and they will live on, through all time, in the gratitude of unborn generations, who, in long succession, shall rise up and call them blessed. And shall we, "who keep the graves, and bear the names, and boast the blood" of these men, disown their church, or cast out as evil and revile their religion? No; by the memory of these noble men; by their holy lives, their heavenly principles, their sacred institutions; by the sustaining strength which they themselves are still giving to our own freedom, and to the great cause of civil and religious liberty throughout the earth—let us never give up the religion of our fathers. No, never, never!

CHAPTER IX.

THE RISE OF EPISCOPACY.

THE rise of the episcopate is perhaps the most difficult problem in ecclesiastical history. This change in the organization of the apostolical churches begins about the middle of the second century, within one hundred years of the apostles, and half a century from St. John the Evangelist. It is introduced without controversy, discussion or objection "before the apostles are cold in their graves."

Episcopacy asserts and challenges an explanation. We accept the challenge, acknowledging the difficulty.

But the theory of episcopacy involves difficulties, on the other hand, still greater. It claims that *from the first* there was an order of ministers in the church superior to that of presbyters; that this order is indispensable to the organization and government of the church, the administration of its ordinances and the consecration of its officers. All clerical authority and grace centres in this order, so that without it there is, there can be, no church on earth. And yet this superior order—the life and power of the church—not only had, for many years, no distinctive name of its own, but was by the apostles mingled indiscriminately and interchangeably with an inferior order, so that both orders had two names in common with each other. That is, the apostles themselves, in setting in order the churches, make an entire distinction in these *offices*, but an entire confusion in their *names*. The two offices, entirely distinct, totally unlike, have each two names in common; or, to reverse the statement, these *two* names are applied indiscriminately by divine appointment and by inspiration to two offices which are entirely different! Such confusion on subjects so momentous, and from such a source, verily transcends all belief! It makes the Bible the most deceptive, unintelligible book that was ever written.

This change in the polity of the church, again, is offset by other ecclesiastical changes, the history of which is equally unknown—the general adoption of the sign of the cross; the change from adult to infant baptism, or the contrary; the use of the chrism in baptism; standing at the Lord's supper at one time, kneeling at another; the multiplication of offices in the church: lectors, acolytes, sub-deacons. What authentic contemporary history records these changes?

The appointment and ecclesiastical ascendancy so readily acquired by the bishop, when attentively considered, admits a reasonable explanation. Various causes may have favored the ascendancy. The parochial system, as in history it is denominated, may have favored his promotion.

The church of the metropolis became, in the quaint style of church history, the mother-church to smaller, dependent fraternities in the country; and the clerical head of this church, the principal man among his brethren, the presiding officer of their assemblies and councils. This accidental ascendancy of the central church, and of its clergy, led on the rapid development of the episcopal system; and, finally, ended in the overthrow of the popular government of the primitive church.

The gospel was first preached in large cities and towns, such as Jerusalem, Antioch, Ephesus and Corinth. These churches then became central points of effort and of influence for the extension of Christianity in the region roundabout.

The early Christians were often dispersed abroad, also, by persecution; and, like the first Christians, Acts viii. 4, "went everywhere preaching the word."

Strangers and visitors in the principal cities, where the gospel was preached, frequently became converts to Christ, and returned home to make known his gospel, as they might have opportunity and ability, in the places where they resided.

When it became expedient for Christian converts in the country to have separate places of worship, these new organizations took the form of the parent church, and still looked to that for instruction and support as they might need. This dependence gave rise to a gradual connection and coalition between the churches in the country and the central church in the city. That dependence and the consequent coalition was the result of various natural causes and local circumstances which claim a more specific enumeration.

1. The churches in the country were only branches of the parent stock, and owned a filial relation to the mother-church.

2. They received their first spiritual teachers and pastors from this church; and these would naturally retain their attachment to the church from which they came.

3. The connection between the country and the city, in the ordinary course of business, had its influence in bringing the churches in the country into connection with that in the city.

4. The persecution, and consequent distress which came upon the churches, brought them into closer connection one with another.

5. The city was the centre of political influence and power for the government and protection of the country. This consideration had its influence in promoting a similar

relation between the churches in the city and those in the country.

6. An ancient custom obtained, of attributing to those churches which had been founded by the apostles a superior degree of honor and a more exalted dignity. On which account it was usual, when any dispute arose respecting principles or tenets, for the opinion of these churches to be asked. In cases of doubt and controversy the Christians of the West had recourse to the church of Rome; those of Africa, to that of Alexandria; and those of Asia, to that of Antioch for counsel.[1]

7. The city church was comparatively rich and powerful; and could administer to the wants of the feeble churches as they might need.

8. Protection and aid from the civil authority was chiefly to be sought through the same medium. The minister of the city could apply in their behalf to the Roman governors who resided there.

Thus, in various ways, the churches in the large cities, in process of time, gathered about them several smaller churches in the vicinity, over which they extended their guardianship and care.

The above representations exhibit the rise of the diocesan form of government, not as based on any "theory of the church," but as an expedient for the peace of the church, and the result of the mutual relations of the churches in the country to that in the city. The church of the metropolis gradually spread itself out as an extensive parish over the adjacent territory. And the presiding presbyter of this city became, virtually, the bishop over the same extent of country. "Was it not natural and according to the ordinary course of things to make a distinction between the

---

[1] Comp. Mosheim, De Rebus Christ. Saec. II. § 21.

bishop of the city and the other clergy? Would not they themselves cheerfully make the distinction, and give him special tokens of their consideration? Would they not accost him with peculiar respect, and by silent consent give him the pre-eminence? And would he not, on the other hand, requite all this by his manifold services?"[2]

Throughout the second and third centuries there was no established law or rule binding the smaller churches in a coalition with the greater, or bringing them into subjection to it. But that which at first was conceded voluntarily was afterward claimed as a right. Conventional usage became established law; the controlling influence of the bishop an official prerogative; and thus, in the end, the diocesan form of government was settled upon the church.

This view of the subject is not new, nor is it put forth as original with the writer. It has the sanction of many authors, from whom the above particulars have been derived. Of these it is sufficient to mention Spittler,[3] Pertsch,[4] Mosheim,[5] Planck,[6] Neander,[7] Guerike,[8] Siegel,[9] Schoene,[10] W. Böhmer,[11] D'Aubigné.[12]

---

[2] Gesellschafts-Verfass., I. S. 82, 83. Comp. also 546–562, respecting this system at a later period.

[3] Can. Rechts. § 4–10.

[4] Ib. § 17–23, und Kirchen Hist., Sec. II.

[5] De Rebus Christ. Saec., II. § 37, note 3.

Gesell. Verfass. S. 18–83, 546–572.

[7] Allgem. Kirchen Gesch. 1, 2d ed. S. 314–316. Tr. pp. 184–186. Comp. his Apost. Gesch. 1, 50, 198, seq., 406. Allgem. Kirch. 1, 327, 328, 2d ed. Tr. pp. 191, 192.

[8] Ib. S. 95–97.

[9] Kirchliche Verfass. 2, S. 454–473; 4, S. 378.

[10] Geschichtsforschungen, Vol. 3, S. 336–340. See also Conc. Carthag. c. 31; Bracar. c. 1; Àgath. c. 53; Tarracon. c. 8.

[11] Alterthumswissenschaft. 1, S. 230–236.

[12] Hist. of Reformation, Vol. I. p. 18. N. Y. 1843.

The care of the churches was entrusted, not to one man, but to several, who constituted a *college of presbyters*, and divided the duties of their office among themselves. Various circumstances early gave rise to a distinction among the elders, and, finally, to their permanent division into bishops and presbyters.

1. The appointment of a *presiding elder* over the college of presbyters in the churches. A plurality of elders represents the church at Jerusalem, at Ephesus, Acts xx. 17–28; at Philippi, Phil. i. 1, and in the cities in Crete. In such a college of elders it would be convenient, if not indispensable, for one of their number to act as the moderator or president of their assemblies. Such a designation, however, would confer on the presiding elder no *official* superiority over his fellow-presbyters; but, coupled with age and talents and spiritual gifts, it might give him a controlling influence in the government of the church. This control, and his official rank as the προεστώς, the presiding elder, which was first conceded to him by his fellow-presbyters only *as to a fellow-presbyter*, a *primus inter pares*, he began in time to claim as his official prerogative. This assumption of authority gave rise to the gradual distinction between bishop and presbyter, and in the course of the second and third centuries resulted in the division of the clergy into two distinct orders, bishops and presbyters.

This exposition of the origin of the episcopal office has the sanction of the most approved authorities, particularly of the distinguished historian whose works we have so often cited,[13]

---

[13] Apost. Kirch. 1, 39, seq., 3d ed. 50, 198, seq., 406. Allgem. Gesch. 1, 324, seq., 2d ed. "In the Acts, a plurality of presbyters always appears next in rank to the apostles, as representatives of the church at Jerusalem. If any one is disposed to maintain that each one of these presbyters presided over a smaller part of its special meetings, still it must be thereby established that, notwithstanding these

THE RISE OF EPISCOPACY. 225

to whom we may add Gieseler,[14] Guerike,[15] Gabler,[16] Mosheim,[17] Pertsch,[18] and many others.

2. The duties and responsibilities of the bishop in times of persecution had their influence in exalting this officer, and separating him further both from the presbyters and the people. The bishop of the metropolis became the counselor and guardian of the churches.

3. The rage and vengeance of their persecutors fell oftenest upon him; and, while it excited for him the sympathy and veneration of the churches, prepared them more readily to acquiesce in his authority.[19]

4. As the church increased in number, the intercourse between each member individually and the bishop became less, and a corresponding separation between him and his people of necessity ensued.

5. Many of the bishops were the successors of the apostles, or were bishops of apostolical churches, and this circumstance gave them additional influence.[20] The bishops of

divided meetings, the church formed a whole, over which this deliberative college of presbyters presided, and therefore the form of government was still of a popular character."—*Neander, Apost. Kirch.* I, c. 2, 3d ed. "This plurality of ministers over the same church continued, even to the fourth century, to be the order of the churches."—*Planck, Gesell. Verfass.* 1, 551.

[14] Lehrbuch der Kirchengesch. 3, Aufl. 1, 118.
[15] Kirch. Geschichte, I. S. 89-93, 2d ed.
[16] De Epis. primae eccl. Eorumque origine.
[17] Hist. Eccl. 3, p. 108, seq., and Kirchenrecht, by Ernst, S. 52.
[18] Can. Recht. S. 42. Kirch. Hist., Saec. II. c. 5, § 8-15. Compare, especially, Ziegler's Versuch der Gesch. der Kirch. Verfass. S. 34-61.
[19] Spittler's Can. Recht. c. 1, § 5.
[20] Comp. Tertull., De Praescript. Advers. Haeret. c. 20, 26, 36. Peter de Marca, de Concord. Sacerd. et Im. Lib. 5, c. 20. Lib. 7, c. 4, § 6, seq.

Rome,[21] of Carthage, of Jerusalem,[22] and others, derived importance from this consideration.[23]

6. The distinction between the *clergy* and *laity*, which began about this time, is worthy of particular notice. In the apostolical churches the office of teaching was not restricted to any particular class of persons. All Christians accounted themselves the priests of God; and between the church and their spiritual leaders very little distinction was known. This fact is so universally acknowledged that it were needless to multiply authorities in proof of it. But it forcibly indicates the nature of the original constitution of the church.[24] The distinction, accordingly, of pastors and people into two distinct orders, the *clergy* and the *laity*, distinctly marks the workings of that spirit which was fast obliterating the features of its early organization. Tertullian, †218, is the first to mention this distinction.[25] The people have now become an inferior order, the distinction between them and the higher order of the clergy widens fast, and the government of the church which has hitherto

---

[21] Irenaeus Advers. Haer. Lib. 3, c. 2; 4, c. 26; 5, c. 20, 44.

[22] Firmil. ap. Cyp. Epist. 75.

[23] Mosheim, De Rebus Christ., Saec. II. § 21. In this section and the accompanying note is given a full and interesting illustration of the canonical authorities of such churches. Comp. also Gieseler, Lehrbuch, S. 160–163. Note.

[24] Nonne et laici sacerdotes sumus? Differentiam inter ordinem et plebem constituit *ecclesiae auctoritas;* adeo ubi ecclesiastici ordinis non est consessus et offers, et tingis et sacerdos tibi es solus.—*De Exhortat. Castit.* c. 7, p. 522. Primum omnes docebant et omnes baptizabant; ut cresceret plebs et multiplicaretur omnibus inter initia concessus est et evangelizare et baptizare et scripturas explorare.—*Hilary,* cited by *Neander, Allgem. Gesch.* I. S. 311. Vol. I. Tr. p. 182. Comp. S. 324, seq., especially 335–337, 2d ed. Comp. Cyprian, Ep. 76. Suicer, Thesaurus, art. κλῆρος, Guerike, Kirch. Gesch. Vol. 93, 94, and J. H. Böhmer, De Differentia inter Ordinem Ecclesiast., etc.

[25] De Monogamia, c. 12, p. 533.

been vested in the people passes rapidly into the hands of the bishop.

7. The clergy begin to claim authority from the analogy between their office and that of the Jewish priesthood. They are no longer incumbents in office at the pleasure of the people and dependent upon them, but divinely constituted the priests of God, and divinely appointed by him to instruct and to rule over the church. "When once the idea of a Mosaic priesthood had been adopted in the Christian church, the clergy soon began to assume a superiority over the laity. The customary form of consecration was now supposed to have a certain mystic influence, and henceforth they stand in the position of persons appointed by God to be the medium of communication between him and the Christian world." [26]

8. From this it was but a slight modification to assert the divine right of episcopacy and the apostolical succession in the line of the bishops. Sentiments to this effect are of frequent occurrence in the writings of Cyprian, †258. The bishops also assumed new titles, such as *sacerdotes*,[27] *priests*, *high-priests*, rulers of the church, etc.[28]

Finally, these arrogant assumptions ended in the claim of guidance and wisdom from on high by the communications of the Spirit of God. This was also the false and flat-

---

[26] Gieseler, Cunningham's Trans. I. p. 156. Comp. Münscher, Handbuch der Christ. Dog. 3, p. 15. Conder's Protestant Nonconformity, Vol. I. p. 224. Comp. Planck, Gesell. Verfass. I. S. 163. Mosheim de Rebus. Saec., II. § 24.

[27] Comp. Cyp. Ep. 3, 4, 59. Spitler's Can. Recht. c. 1. § 11. Henke, Allgem. Gesch. der Christ. Kirch. 1, p. 120. Mosheim, De Rebus, Saec. III. § 24.

[28] Origen, Hom. 2, in Jer. Adv. Cels. Lib. 3. In Math. Tract. 31, 32.

tering dream of Cyprian,[29] and has been the favorite dogma of prelacy from his time to the present day.

The following comprehensive summary offers a fit conclusion to the preceding remarks: "In process of time the bishops found means to abridge the rights of the presbyters, the deacons and the people. Such is the course of the world. They who are honored with the respect and entrusted with the affairs of society, agreeably to the natural love which every man has for pre-eminence, seek for greater distinction, and the people favor the desire. Strife and contention are the necessary consequences of dividing offices of trust among many, and these struggles usually end in the advancement of him who is highest in office. Even Cyprian, who acknowledged the authority of the church over the bishop, and his duty in all things to act in concert with the clergy, had still the address so to exalt the power of the bishop as to overthrow the rights both of the clergy and the people. He affirmed that God made the bishops; that they were the vicegerents of Christ, and responsible to none but to God. He was the father of this dogma; and the bishops continued to claim this prerogative until the ninth century, when the pope appropriated it exclusively to himself.[30]

The bishops rose in rank and power, not by any sudden and violent assumption of diocesan authority, but by the silent concession and approbation, at first, of both the presbyters and the people.

The most competent and reliable authority on the subject of the rise of episcopacy is Jerome, of the fourth century, one of the most learned and candid of the fathers. He

[29] Placuit nobis sancto spiritu suggerente et Domino per visiones multas et manifestas admonente.—*Cyprian*, *Epist.* 54, p. 79. Conc. Car. A. D. 252.

[30] Kirchenrecht, by Ernst. S. 61-63.

asserts the original equality and identity of presbyters and bishops. In proof of this identity he appeals to the use interchangeably of presbyters and bishops as different names of one and the same office. But a change was introduced gradually, "*paulatim,*" by which the bishop was distinguished from presbyters as the moderator of their presbytery, himself being only a presbyter, *primus inter pares.* This appointment of a bishop by the presbyters as their presiding officer was an expedient to suppress the schisms that had arisen in the churches by the instigation of Satan. Once invested with authority to act efficiently in his oversight of the churches, he might, it was presumed, more successfully heal their divisions. Bishop and presbyter being still the same, the one term became descriptive of age; the other, of office.[31] By enlarging the powers of this office, committing the care of the churches into the hands of an efficient overseer, their disorders might be healed and peace promoted. Their ablest and most influential men being selected for this office, became the centre of authority and

---

[31] Aliud aetatis, aliud esse nomen officii. Comment in Epist. ad Tit. Illud nomen dignitatis est; hoc aetatis Epist. 83 ad Oceanum presbyterum. Presbyter et episcopus, aliud aetatis, aliud dignitatis est nomen.—*Epist.* 85 *ad Evagrium.*—*Ad Evangelum.*

Idem est ergo presbyter qui et episcopus; et antequam Diaboli instinctu, studia in religione fierent, et disceretur in populis. Ego sum Pauli; ego Apollo; ego autem Cephae, communi presbyterorum consilio ecclesiae gubernantur. Postquam vero unusquisque eos quos baptizaverat suos putabat esse non Christi, in toto orbe decretum est ut unus de presbyteris electus superponeretur caeteris, ad quem omnis ecclesiae cura pertineret, et schismatum semina tollerentur.—*Comment in Epist. ad Tit.*

Audi et aliud testimonium in quo manifestissime comprobatur eundem esse episcopum atque presbyterum. . . . Quod autem postea unus electus est qui caeteris praeponeretur, in schismatis remedium factum est.—*Epist.* 85 *ad Evagrium.*—*Ad Evangelum.*

power, and gradually arrogated to themselves the principal share in the government of the churches.

The testimony of Hilary, a learned contemporary of Jerome, fully sustains his authority respecting the rise of the episcopate. At first, all were accustomed to teach and to baptize; but after the general establishment of the churches, a different order prevailed. The deacons were not permitted to preach, nor the clergy or the laity to baptize. Bishops and presbyters were the same, but when presbyters were found unworthy of their prerogatives, a change was made in the mode of appointing a chairman of the eldership, not by seniority, but by election—according to merit rather than age.[32]

This theory of Jerome and Hilary respecting the rise of episcopacy is adopted by Neander in the following paragraph:

"Since the presbyters constituted a deliberative assem-

[32] Primum enim omnes docebant et omnes baptizabant quibuscunque diebus vel temporibus fuisset occasio. . . . Ut ergo cresceret plebs et multiplicaretur, omnibus inter initia concessum est et evangelizare, et baptizare et scripturas in ecclesia explanare. At ubi omnia loca circumplexa est ecclesia, conventicula constituta sunt, et rectores, et cetera officia in ecclesiis sunt ordinata; ut nullus de clero auderet, qui ordinatus non esset, praesumere officium quod sciret non sibi creditum vel concessum; et coepit alio ordine et providentia gubernari ecclesia; quia si omnes eadem possent, irrationabile esset, et vulgaris res, et vilissima videretur. Hinc ergo est unde nunc neque diaconi in populo praedicant, nec clerici vel laici baptizant, neque quocunque die credentes tinguntur nisi aegri. Ideo non per omnia conveniunt scripta Apostoli ordinationi quae nunc in ecclesia est, quia haec inter ipsa primordia sunt scripta; nam et Timotheus (presbyterum à se creatum) episcopum vocat; quia primum presbyteri episcopi appellabantur, ut recedente uno sequens ei succederet. Denique apud Ægyptum presbyteri consignant, si praesens non sit episcopus. Sed quia coeperunt sequentes presbyteri indigni inveniri ad primatus tenendos, immatuta est ratio, prospiciente Concilio ut non ordo sed meritum crearet

bly, it would of course soon become the practice for one of their number to preside over the rest. . . . Soon after the apostolic age, the standing office of president of the presbytery must have been formed; which president, as having pre-eminently the *oversight* over all, was designated by the special name of Ἐπίσκοπος, and was thus distinguished from the other presbyters. Thus the name came at length to be applied exclusively to this presbyter, while the name presbyter continued at first to be common to all; for the bishops, as presiding presbyters, had no official character other than that of the presbyters generally. They were only *primi inter pares*. The aristocratic constitution will ever find it easy, by various gradual changes, to pass over to the monarchical; and circumstances, when the need becomes felt of guidance by the energy and authority of an individual, will have an influence above all things else to bring about such a change."[33]

It may be profitable, in this connection, to consider the exposition of this origin of episcopacy by a learned and liberal English bishop: "After these [the apostles] were deceased, and the main power left in the presbyteries, the several presbyters enjoying an equal power among themselves, especially being many in one city, thereby great occasion to many schisms, partly by the bandying of the presbyters one against another, partly by the sidings of the people with some against the rest, partly by the too common use of the power of ordination in presbyters, by which they were more able to increase their own party by ordaining those who would join with them, and by this means to perpetuate schisms in the church;—upon this, when the

---

episcopum multorum sacerdotum judicio constitutum; ne indignus temere usurparet, et esset multis scandalum.—*Comment in Eph.* 4. Comp. p. 195.

[33] Hist. Vol. I. 190, 191. Trans.

wiser and graver sort considered the abuses following the promiscuous use of this power of ordination; and, withal, having in their minds the excellent frame of the government of the church under the apostles and their deputies, and for preventing of further schisms and divisions among themselves, they unanimously agreed to choose one out of their number who was best qualified for the management of so great a trust, and to devolve the exercise of the power of ordination and jurisdiction to him; yet so as that he act nothing of importance without the consent and concurrence of the presbyters, who were still to be as the common council to the bishop. This I take to be the true and just account of the original episcopacy in the primitive church, according to Jerome; which model of government, thus contrived and framed, sets forth to us a most lively character of that great wisdom and moderation which then ruled the heads and hearts of the primitive Christians."[34]

The history of the rise of episcopacy in this country illustrates the centralization of power by gradual and silent concession.

It is well known that the introduction of episcopacy into this country gave rise to long and bitter controversy. The objection, made from within the Episcopal churches as well as from without, was, that its form of government is anti-republican, and opposed to the spirit of our free institutions. The House of Burgesses, in Virginia, composed chiefly of Episcopalians, declared their abhorrence of bishops, unless at the distance of three thousand miles, and denounced "the plan of introducing them, in the most unexceptionable form, on this side of the Atlantic, as a pernicious project."

When, at last, episcopacy was introduced, it was only by a compromise—the Episcopalian churches consenting to

Stillingfleet's Irenicum, P. II. chap. VI.

submit to diocesan episcopacy, only in a form greatly modified and divested of its most obnoxious features. To the exclusion of the laity from a free and full participation in the affairs of the government they would not for a moment submit. Such, according to Bishop White, was the prejudice of Episcopalians "against the name, and much more against the office of a bishop, that, but for the introduction of the laity into the government of the church, no general organization would probably have been formed." Accordingly, the people were allowed freely to choose their own pastors, and to have a full representation in all their courts. This American episcopacy was so modified, and the prelatical powers of the bishop so restricted by the checks and balances of republican principles, that the English prelates, on the other hand, were reluctant to confer the episcopate upon Bishop White, alleging that he "entertained a design to set up episcopacy on the ground of *presbyterial and lay authority.*"

Such was American episcopacy, at first—qualified as much as possible, by the infusion of popular principles to restrain the arbitrary powers of the bishop. But what now has this same episcopacy become? What now the powers of the bishop, compared with what they then were? He possesses power almost as arbitrary as that of an Eastern despot; and assumes to rule by an authority independent of the will of his subjects. The bishops are permanent and irresponsible monarchs, restrained by no judicial tribunal. The house of bishops admit no order of the inferior clergy to their general convention. They ordain, depose and restore to the ministry, at pleasure, whom they will; "so that a Puseyite bishop may fill the church with impenitent and unconverted men." He can prevent any congregation from settling the minister of their choice, or displace one at his will, and may, "*upon probable cause,*" forbid any clergyman from another diocese to officiate in his own. Such is the fearful nature of those powers which are now entrusted to this spiritual despot in our free republic.[35]

All this is in total contrast to the organization of the primitive church. In this, "all the members, as organs of the whole and of the one spirit which gave it life, were to co-operate, each in his appropriate place, for the common end; and some of the members acted in this organization of parts as the pre-eminently guiding ones. But it could hardly work itself out in a natural way, from the essence of the Christian life and Christian fellowship, that this guidance should be placed in the hands of only one individual. *The monarchical form of government was not suited to the Christian community of spirit.*"[36]

---

[35] These facts and principles, with the original authorities for them, are disclosed more at length in the writings of Dr. Smyth, to whom we are chiefly indebted for the above abstract of them. Compare, especially, Apost. Succession, pp. 507–509, and Ecclesiastical Republicanism, pp. 153–172.

[36] Neander, Hist. Vol. I. p. 183. Trans.

CHAPTER X.

THE PROGRESS OF EPISCOPACY.

THE diocesan, metropolitan, patriarchal and papal government was gradually matured, and settled upon the churches in the several provinces at different times. The third century may be regarded as the period in which it was chiefly consolidated and established.

The means of its development were:

1. The formal organization of the diocesan government was chiefly effected by means of provincial synods and councils.

The consideration of these councils belongs to another work.[1] But whatever may have been their origin, such ecclesiastical assemblies were regularly held in Asia Minor in the third century, and were frequently convened in other provinces, for the transaction of business relating to the interests of the church.[2] The bishops, having once acquired the power of giving laws to the church, instead of legislating for the churches in their name and as their *representatives*, assumed the right of giving laws to the church by virtue of their *episcopal office;* and for this assumption they claimed, as has been already mentioned, the sanction

---

[1] Ancient Christianity Exemplified, chap. xxiii. pp. 475-488.

[2] Necessario, says Firmilian, A. D. 257, apud nos fit, ut per singulos annos seniores et praepositi in unum conveniamus, ad disponenda ea quae curae nostrae commissa sunt.—*Cyp. Ep.* 75, p. 143.

of divine authority, *jure divino*, as the ministers of God and under the guidance of his Spirit.[3]

The above representation is only an epitome of the sentiments of Planck,[4] Mosheim and many others.[5] Mosheim remarks that "these councils were productive of so great an alteration in the general state of the church as nearly to effect the entire subversion of its ancient constitution. For, in the first place, the primitive rights of the people, in consequence of this new arrangement of things, experienced a considerable diminution, inasmuch as thenceforward none but affairs of comparatively trifling importance were ever made the subject of popular deliberation and adjustment, the councils of the associated churches assuming to themselves the right of discussing and regulating everything of moment or importance, as well as of determining all questions to which any sort of weight was attached. In the next place, the dignity and authority of the bishops were very much augmented and enlarged. They at length took it upon them to assert that they were the legitimate successors of the apostles themselves, and might, consequently, by their own proper authority, dictate to the Christian flock. To what extent the inconveniences and evils arising out of these preposterous pretensions reached in after times is too well known to require any particular notice in this place."[6]

[3] *Placet! Visum est!* is the style not unfrequently in which the summary decisions of their councils are given; or if the decision relates to an article of faith, *credit catholica ecclesia!* Athanasius, De Synodo. Arimin. et Seluciae, Ferdin. de Mendoza, De Confirmatione Conc., Ill. Lib. 2, c. 2, cited by Spittler.

[4] Gesellschafts-Verfass. I. S. 90–100.

[5] Compare also Henke and Vater, Allgemein. Kirchen Gesch. I. S. 120, seq. Eichhorn, Can. Recht. I. S. 20. Riddle's Chron. pp. 32, 33.

[6] De Rebus Christ., Saec. II. § 23; comp. Saec. II. § 22; Saec. III. § 24. Also, Kirch. Recht. S. 65, 66.

2. The doctrine of the *unity* of the church had an influence in consolidating the churches under an episcopal government.

This notion was early developed. It occurs in the epistle of the church of Smyrna concerning the martyrdom of Polycarp.[7] It was more distinctly advanced by Irenaeus and Tertullian in the second century, and, in the third, became the favorite dogma of Cyprian,[8] and, after him, of many others.[9] It contributed to the establishment of uniform laws and regulations under an episcopal hierarchy.[10] This idea of a holy catholic church, one and indivisible, extending through all lands and binding together in one communion the faithful of every kindred and people, was a conception totally unlike the apostolical idea of union in love and fellowship in spirit.

3. The correspondence and intercourse between the bishops of different provinces had much influence in establishing their diocesan authority.

By mutual understanding they acted unitedly and in concert, and aided each other in the promotion of their common ends.[11]

4. The *Disciplina Arcani*, the sacred mysteries of the church, while they shed an air of awful sanctity over its solemnities, were well suited to inspire the people with a profound veneration for the bishop, who was the high-

---

[7] Euseb. Eccl. Hist. Lib. 4, c. 15, § 1. A. D. 167.

[8] Pro corpore totius ecclesiae cujus per varias quasque provincias membra digesta sunt.—*Ep.* 30, p. 41.

[9] Planck, Gesell. Verfass. I. S. 100, seq. Rothe, Anf. Christ. Kirch. I. S. 576-589.

[10] Neander, Allgem. Gesch. I. S. 355, 371, 2d ed. Tr. I. pp. 207-217. D'Aubigné's Hist. of the Reformation. N. Y. 1843. Vol. I. pp. 20-22.

[11] Siegel, Handbuch. 1, art. Briefwechsel, Rheinwald's Arch. § 4, p. 99.

priest of these rites and the chief agent in administering them.[12]

5. The catechetical instructions and discipline preparatory to admission into the church had a powerful influence in giving authority to the doings of the church and preparing the mind for a passive submission to her jurisdiction.

The candidates for admission were divided into various classes; and, ascending by slow gradations through these, with manifold solemnities, finally approached the sacred shrine of the church. The details of the system belong to another work.[13] "These new regulations were the surest and strongest means man could have devised to give greater importance to the church in the eyes of the new members; and to inspire them with a sense of the importance of the privilege bestowed in receiving them into its communion, which again would revert to the interests of the church."[14]

6. To the same effect, also, was all that system of penance which was matured in connection with the foregoing regulations.

This was wholly unknown in the early period of the church. It was developed in connection with the catechetical discipline which has already been mentioned, and was indeed a part of the same system.[15] It was administered by the bishop, who alone had authority to inflict or to remove these penances.[16] Thus it became a scourge in his

[12] Comp. the author's Ancient Christianity, pp. 276–284.
[13] Comp. Ibid. pp. 118, 302, 399.
[14] Planck, Gesell. Verfass. I. S. 132.
[15] Planck, Gesell. Verfass. I. S. 131–141.
[16] The councils of Nice, A. D. 325, c. 5, and of Antioch, A. D. 341, c. 20, make some provision against the flagrant injustice which one might suffer in this way from the bishop. But the council of Elliberis, A. D. 305, and of Sardica, A. D. 347, give to the bishop unlimited authority in this matter. Osius, episcopus dixit. Hoc quoque omnibus placeat, ut sive diaconus, sive presbyter, sive quis clericorum

hand which he could at any time apply to those who might become the objects of his displeasure.

II. Results of the diocesan organization.

1. It established the pre-eminence of the bishop in the city over the neighboring churches.

2. It was a virtual disfranchisement of the laity.

It removed the checks and guards of a popular government against the exercise of arbitrary power. It invested the bishops with prerogatives, which can never be entrusted with safety to any man or body of men. "To revive Christ's church is to expel the Antichrist of the priesthood, which, as it was foretold of him, *as God, sitteth in the temple of God, showing himself that he is God*, and to restore its disfranchised members, the laity, to the discharge of their proper duties in it, and to the consciousness of their paramount importance." [17]

3. The government was oppressive to the laity. It entrusted to the bishop exclusively the right of ecclesiastical censure.

ab episcopo suo communione fuerit privatus, et ad alterum perrexerit episcopum, et scierit ille ad quem confugit, eum ab episcopo suo fuisse abjectum, non oportet ut ei communionem indulgeat. Quod si fecerit, sciat se convocatis episcopis causas esse dicturum. Universi dixerunt: Hoc statutum et pacem servabit, et concordiam custodiet.—c. 13 (16). This was one of the most celebrated councils of the age. It was composed of one hundred and sixty-six bishops convened both from the Eastern and Western churches, at the head of whom was the venerable Hosius, who, it would seem, proposed it as an expedient to preserve peace and harmony among the bishops.—Εἴ τις κληρικὸς ἢ λαικὸς ἀφωρισμένος ἤτοι ἄδεκτος, ἀπελθὼν ἐν ἑτέρᾳ πόλει, δεχθῇ ἄνευ γραμμάτων συστατικῶν, ἀφωριζέσθω καὶ ὁ δεξάμενος καὶ ὁ δεχθείς· εἰ δὲ ἀφωρισμένος εἴη, ἐπιτεινέσθω αὐτῷ ὁ ἀφορισμός, ὡς ψευσαμένῳ καὶ ἀπατήσαντι τὴν ἐκκλησίαν τοῦ θεοῦ.—*Can. Apost.* 12 (13), p. 2. Comp. the author's Ancient Christianity, pp. 451–471.

[17] Christian Life, by Arnold, p. 52.

This gave the bishops a dangerous control over the private members of the church. Under censure they had no redress, however unjustly it might have been inflicted, and could only be restored at the pleasure of their own diocesan.[18]

4. It destroyed the independence of the clergy under the diocesan.

The bishops soon found means to effect the complete subjection of the clergy to their control. They allowed them, in no instance, to travel into a neighboring province without a passport from the bishop. Much less could a presbyter or deacon transfer himself from one church to another without the bishop's consent. If any one should presume so to do, or if another should receive him who came without the bishop's consent, the consequence was expulsion from office.[19]

5. It entrusted the bishop with a dangerous prerogative, by giving him the control of the revenues of the church.

The goods and property of the church, its revenues and receipts of every kind, were submitted to the disposal of the bishop.[20]

---

[18] Smyth's Eccl. Republicanism, pp. 81, 82.

[19] Εἰ τις πρεσβύτερος ἢ διάκονος ἢ ὅλως τοῦ καταλόγου τῶν κληρικῶν ἀπολείψας τὴν ἑαυτοῦ παροικίαν εἰς ἑτέραν ἀπέλθῃ, καὶ παντελῶς μεταστὰς διατρίβῃ ἐν ἄλλῃ παροικίᾳ παρὰ γνώμην τοῦ ἰδίου ἐπισκόπου· τοῦτον κελεύομεν μηκέτι λειτουργεῖν, μάλιστα εἰ προσκαλουμένου αὐτὸν τοῦ ἐπισπου αὐτοῦ ἐπανελθεῖν οὐχ ὑπήκουσεν ἐπιμένων τῇ ἀταξίᾳ· ὡς λαϊκὸς μέντοι ἐκεῖσε κοινωνείτω.—*Apost. Can.*, 14 (15), *Bruns*, p. 3. Comp. also, Conc. Antioch, c. 3. Laodic. c. 42. Arelat. I. c. 21. Chalced. c. 20. Nice, c. 16. Carthag. 1, c. 5. Sardic. 16, 18, etc., etc. Siegel, 11, S. 462.

[20] Πάντων τῶν ἐκκλησιαστικῶν πραγμάτων ὁ ἐπίσκοπος ἐχέτω τὴν φροντίδα καὶ διοικείτω αὐτά, ὡς θεοῦ ἐφορῶντος· μὴ ἐξεῖναι δὲ αὐτῷ σφετερίζεσθαι τι ἐξ αὐτῶν ἢ συγγένεσιν ἰδίοις τὰ τοῦ θεοῦ χαρίζεσθαι· εἰ δὲ πένητες εἶεν, ἐπιχορηγείτω ὡς πένησιν, ἀλλὰ μὴ προφάσει τούτου τὰ τῆς ἐκκλησίας ἀπεμπλείτω. Προστάττομεν ἐπίσκοπον ἐξουσίαν ἔχειν τῶν τῆς ἐκκλησίας

The council of Antioch, A. D. 341, gave the bishops entire control over all the property of the church; and the synod of Gangra, A. D. 362-370, pronounced their solemn anathema upon any one who should either give or receive any of the goods of the church without authority from the bishop.[21] The oppressive results of this system are clearly and concisely stated by Siegel,[22] and more at length by Planck.[23] Without the guidance of another, however, they must be obvious to any one.

6. It gave the bishop unjust power over the clergy, by allowing him to inflict upon them ecclesiastical censure.

It gave the bishop, who inflicted the penalty, the sole right of removing it at pleasure. This crafty policy had more influence than any other in completing the subjugation of the clergy, and settling upon the churches the government of an oppressive ecclesiastical aristocracy. The

πραγμάτων· εἰ γὰρ τὰς τιμίας τῶν ἀνθρώπων ψυχὰς αὐτῷ πιστευτέον, πολλῷ ἂν μᾶλλον δέοι ἐπὶ τῶν χρημάτων ἐντέλλεσθαι, ὥστε κατὰ τὴν αὑτοῦ ἐξουσίαν πάντα διοικεῖσθαι, καὶ τοῖς δεομένοις διὰ τῶν πρεσβυτέρων καὶ διακόνων ἐπιχορηγεῖσθαι μετὰ φόβου τοῦ θεοῦ καὶ πάσης εὐλαβείας· μεταλαμβάνειν δὲ καὶ αὐτὸν τῶν δεόντων (εἴγε δέοιτο) εἰς τὰς ἀναγκαίας αὑτῷ χρείας καὶ τῶν ἐπιξενουμένων ἀδελφῶν, ὡς κατὰ μηδένα τρόπον αὐτοὺς ὑστερεῖσθαι· ὁ γὰρ νόμος τοῦ θεοῦ διετάξατο, τοὺς τῷ θυσιαστηρίῳ ὑπηρετοῦντας ἐκ τοῦ θυσιαστηρίου τρέφεσθαι· ἐπείπερ οὐδὲ στρατιῶταί ποτε ἰδίοις ὀψωνίοις ὅπλα κατὰ πολεμίων ἐπιφέρονται.—*Apost. Can.* 37 (39), 40 (41), *Bruns,* pp. 6, 7. First claimed by Cyprian; resisted by presbyters. See Apost. Const. p. 369-69.

[21] Εἴ τις καρποφορίας ἐκκλησιαστικὰς ἐθέλοι λαμβάνειν ἢ διδόναι ἔξω τῆς ἐκκλησίας παρὰ γνώμην τοῦ ἐπισκόπου ἢ τοῦ ἐγκεχειρισμένου τὰ τοιαῦτα, καὶ μὴ μετὰ γνώμης αὐτοῦ ἐθέλοι πράττειν, ἀνάθεμα ἔστω. Εἴ τις διδοῖ ἢ λαμβάνοι καρποφορίαν παρεκτὸς τοῦ ἐπισκόπου ἢ τοῦ ἐπιτεταγμένου εἰς οἰκονομίαν εὐποιίας, καὶ ὁ διδοὺς καὶ ὁ λαμβάνων ἀνάθεμα ἔστω.—*Conc. Gang.* 7, 8, *Bruns,* p. 108. Comp. Conc. Aurel. 1, c. 14, 15.

[22] Handbuch, 11, S. 463.

[23] Gesell. Verfass. I. S. 381-402. Comp. Locke, etc. p. 280.

right of appeal to the civil authority was also strictly denied.[24]

7. It was the occasion, in a great degree, of breaking down the good order and discipline of the church, which had hitherto prevailed.

"The bishops claimed to have the highest authority, and acted accordingly in the government of the church. The presbyters refused to acknowledge this claim, and strove to make themselves independent of the bishops. This strife between the presbyterian and episcopal systems is of the utmost importance in developing the moral and religious state of the church in the third century. Many presbyters made use of their influence to disturb the order and discipline of the church. This strife was, in every way, injurious to its order and discipline."[25]

THE METROPOLITAN GOVERNMENT.

This was not the production of a day, but the result of a gradual modification of the diocesan government, by a further concentration of episcopal power, and the extension of its influence over a wider range of territory. These modifications were not altogether the same in every country, nor were they simultaneously effected. The metropolitan government was developed in the Eastern church as early as the first half of the fourth century. The Council of Nice, A. D. 325, c. 4, ordered that the "bishops should in the provinces be subject to the metropolitan;" and again, c. 6, it ordered "that the bishop of Alexandria should rule over those of the adjacent provinces in conformity to established usage, and that no one should be appointed bishop

---

[24] Conc. Antioch, Can. 11.
[25] Neander, Allgem. Kirch. Gesch. I. S. 329, 330, 2d ed.

without the consent of the metropolitan." The Council of Antioch, A. D. 341, c. 9, defined and established fully the rights of the metropolitan.

The establishment of a hierarchy in the West followed at a period somewhat later.

The capital of the province was not, of necessity, the seat of the metropolitan see, nor did the limits of a metropolitan jurisdiction uniformly coincide with those of a province. This distinction was conferred upon Jerusalem, Antioch, Caesarea, Alexandria, Ephesus, Corinth, Rome, Carthage, Lyons and others. Thus in time the metropolitan government, in place of the diocesan, was settled upon the whole Christian church.

I. Means of its establishment.

The supremacy which the bishops had already acquired, together with the rapid extension of Christianity, soon introduced this organization as a new form of the hierarchy. It was the prerogative of the metropolitan to summon the meetings of the synod, to make the introductory address, to preside over their deliberations and to publish the results of their council. The provincial bishops soon became emulous of receiving consecration at the hands of the metropolitan; and, accordingly, he began, as opportunity presented, to assume to himself the exclusive right of ordaining. It early became a canonical rule that the metropolitan should ratify the ordinary acts of the provincial bishops, which gave him power to reject all who were obnoxious to him.[26] About the beginning of the fourth century, the prerogatives of the metropolitan began to be the subject of statute regulations.[27]

[26] Com. Ziegler's Versuch. S. 69–71.

[27] The development of the metropolitan system is briefly stated by Siegel, Handbuch. 11, S. 264, seq.: and more at length, by Planck, Gesell. Verfass. I. S. 572–598, and by Ziegler, S. 61–164.

We have now reached that period in the history of the church, in which its government appears in almost total contrast with that of its apostolical and primitive organization. The supreme authority is no longer vested in the church collectively, under a popular administration, but in an ecclesiastical aristocracy; and the government of the church is thus entrusted to a clerical hierarchy, who both make and administer the laws, without the intervention of the people. This, then, is a proper point at which to pause and contemplate the practical results of the system of ecclesiastical polity which has taken the place of that which the church originally received at the hands of the apostles.

II. Results of this system may be contemplated in their relations to the laity, to the clergy and to the general interests of religion.

1. In regard to the laity.

a) It destroyed the sovereignty of the church as a collective body, by denying to them the right to enact their own laws.

"The idea that the church meant the clergy—the hierarchy exclusively—constituted the first, the fundamental apostasy."[28] The law-making power was entirely in the hands of the bishops, who gave laws to the people under the pretended sanction of divine authority, and executed them at ther own pleasure. "From the spirit of most of the ordinances which these new law-givers made for the laity, this much, at least, is apparent in the execution of them, that they were directly designed or adapted to bring the people yet more under the yoke of the clergy, or to give them opportunity more frequently and firmly to exercise their power."[29]

[28] Coleridge, Aids to Reflection. Comp. Bunsen's Hippolitus, Vol. II. p. 11–13; III. p. 246, 1st edition Planck Gesell. I. S. 285.
[29] Gesell. Verfass. I. S. 452, 453.

(*b*) It exposed the laity to unjust exactions by uniting the *legislative* and *executive* branches of government.

The clergy enjoyed many privileges, by which, on the one hand, they were in a measure shielded from the operation of the law, and, on the other, were entrusted with civil and judicial authority over the laity. Three particulars are stated by Planck:

1. In certain civil cases they exercised a direct jurisdiction over the laity.

2. The state submitted entirely to them the adjudication of all offences of the laity of a religious nature.

3. Certain other cases, styled ecclesiastical, *causae ecclesiasticae*, were tried before them exclusively.

The practical influences of this arrangement, and its effects upon the clergy and the laity, are detailed by the same author, to whom we must refer the reader.[30]

(*c*) The laity were separated injuriously from the control of the revenues which they contributed for the maintenance of the government of the church and for charitable purposes.

All measures of this nature, instead of originating with the people, as in all popular governments, began and ended with the priesthood.[31] The wealth of the laity was now made to flow in streams into the church. New expedients were devised to draw money from them.[32] Constantine himself also contributed large sums to enrich the coffers of

---

[30] Gesell. Verfass. I. S. 308, seq.

[31] Conc. Gan. Can. 7, 8. Bracar. 11, c. 7. The above canons clearly indicate the unjust and oppressive operation of this system.

[32] It was a law of the church in the fourth century that the laity should every Sabbath partake of the sacrament; the effect of which law was to augment the revenues of the church, each communicant being required to bring his *offering* to the altar. Afterward, when this custom was discontinued, the offering was still claimed.—*Cong. Agath.* A. D. 585, c. 4.

the church, which he also authorized, A. D. 321, to inherit property by will.[33] This permission opened new sources of wealth to the clergy, while it presented equal incentives to their cupidity. With what address they employed their newly-acquired rights is apparent from the fact stated by Planck, "that in the space of ten years every man, at his decease, left a legacy to the church; and within fifty years the clergy in the several provinces, under the color of the church, held in their possession one *tenth part* of the entire property of the province. By the end of the fourth century the emperors themselves were obliged to interpose to check the accumulation of these immense revenues: a measure which Jerome said he could not regret, but he could only regret that his brethren had made it necessary."[34]

(*d*) The system in question was a violation of the rights of the laity to choose their religious teachers.

The clergy were appointed by the bishop, and the bishop, again, was elected by the clergy. The intervention of the people was often a mere form, and even the form itself was finally discontinued.

(*e*) The tendency of this form of government was to render the laity indifferent to the religious interests of the church.

It left them no part in administering the concerns of the church, and they would do little for the promotion of its purity. If scandals abounded, it belonged not to them to remove them. If a case of discipline occurred, its management began and ended with the clergy.

(*f*) The tendency of the system was to sunder the private members of the church from each other and to interfere with their mutual fellowship and watchfulness.

---

[33] Cod. Theod. 4, 16; Tit. 2, c. 4; Euseb. Lib. 10, 6; Sozomen, Lib. 1, c. 8; Lib. 5, 5.

[34] Gesell. Verfass. I. S. 281. Comp. Pertsch, Kirch. Hist. sec. 11, c. 9.

They were received by the clergy to the *ordinances* of the church, rather than to the fellowship, the confidence and affection of brethren, one with them in heart, in sympathy and Christian love.

This mutual estrangement and the general neglect of Christian watchfulness and discipline which dishonored the church at this time are forcibly exhibited by Eusebius, who lived in the age now under consideration. He says: "After Christianity, through too much liberty, was changed into laxness and sloth, then began men to envy and revile one another, and to wound one another as if with arms and spears in actual warfare. Then bishop arose against bishop and church against church. Great tumult prevailed, and hypocrisy and dissimulation were carried to the highest pitch. And then began the divine vengeance, as is usual, to visit us; and such was the condition of the church that the most part came not freely together." [35]

"As things now are," says Chrysostom, "all is corrupted and lost. The church is little else than a stall for cattle or a fold for camels and asses; and when I go out in search of sheep I find none. All are rampant and refractory as herds of horses and wild asses; everything is filled with their abounding corruptions." [36] Similar sentiments occur abundantly in the writers of the third and fourth centuries and in the ages following.

(*g*) This system was a gross infringement on the right of private judgment in religion.

It was a law strictly enforced that every layman should believe blindly, without inquiry, without evidence, all that the church, represented by the bishops in synod, should prescribe. The evidence he was not competent to examine. Here is the origin of that papal policy which denies the

[35] Eccl. Hist. 8, c. 1.
[36] Chrysostom, Hom. 89, in Math. Vol. VII. p. 830.

Bible to the laity, and the pattern of that *"prudent reserve"* which Puseyism inculcates in preaching the gospel to the common people. The exercise of one's private judgment, leading him to dissent from the prescribed articles, was not only regarded as a heinous sin, but as a violation of the law of the state, punishable with severe penalties.[37]

"In endeavoring by the secular arm to compel all the Christians to entertain the same speculative opinions on the questions then debated, the sovereigns at once turned free discussions into controversy and strife. They inflamed instead of extinguishing party spirit. They formally divided the church into sects. They entailed the disputes of their own times as an inheritance of sorrow to posterity, and wrote INTOLERANCE over the portal of the house of God."[38]

2. Results of the metropolitan government upon the clergy.

The clergy, under this system, appear in many respects in strong contrast with the ministry of the apostolic and primitive churches.

(a) The increase of the churches would, of necessity, require a corresponding increase in the number of its ministers. Even in the second century there were Christian churches which had twenty or thirty presbyters, and sometimes as many deacons.[39] But we have now several entirely new classes of officers in the church, *sub-deacons, acolytes, readers, exorcists, door-keepers*, etc. To these were subsequently added many others, *advocates, σύνδικοι, apocrisiarii, cimeliarchs, custodes, mansionarii, notarii, oiconomoi, syncelli*, etc., etc. The specific duties of these several officers are

---

[37] Sozomen, Eccl. Hist. Lib. 7, c. 9. Codex Theodosian, L. 16, tit. 3, 1. 2. Justinian Novell, 6, 42. Arnold, Wahre Abbildung, c. 8.

[38] Rev. Thomas Hardy, cited in Dr. Brown's Law of Christ respecting Civil Obedience, p. 512.

[39] The author's Ancient Christianity, Art. Deacons, p. 163.

briefly stated in the author's Ancient Christianity,[40] and more at length in the larger works of Bingham, Augusti, Siegel and Böhmer.

(*b*) The distinctions between the different orders of the clergy are drawn with great care, and cautiously guarded.

The councils of the period abound with canons defining the boundaries of the several grades of the clergy. Gregory Nazianzen, A. D. 360, in view of these ambitious contentions, exclaims, "How I wish there had been no precedence, no priority of place, no authoritative dictatorship, that we might be distinguished by virtue alone. But now this right hand, and left hand, and middle, and higher and lower, this going before and going in company, have produced to us much unprofitable affliction—brought many into a snare, and thrust them out among the herd of the goats; and these, not only of the inferior order, but even of the shepherds, who, though masters in Israel, have not known these things."[41] "I am worn out with contending against the envy of the holy bishops; disturbing the public peace by their contentions, and subordinating the Christian faith to their own private interests." .... "If I must write the whole truth, I am determined to absent myself from all assemblies of the bishops; for I have never seen a happy result of any councils, nor any that did not occasion an increase of evils, rather than a reformation of them, by reason of these pertinacious contentions, and this vehement thirst for power, such as no words can express."

(*c*) The clergy manifest a strong party feeling.

They have become one party, and the church another; each with their separate interests. And these, too often, are contrary, the one to the other. This spirit manifested itself particularly in their synods, where the bishops sought

---

[40] Chapter IX. pp. 179–190.
[41] Orat. 28, Vol. I. p. 484.

to depress as much as possible the other orders of the clergy. For proof of this, reference may be had to the councils of Elvira, Neocaesarea and Nice.

"They (the bishops) had the means of carrying any measure for their own advantage; and while they continued united, it was not easy for a whole church, even, and much less for a single individual of the clergy, or of the laity, to oppose them. Even if a whole church came into collision with their bishop, they must submit to the decision of the provincial synod, of the metropolitan, and also of his fellow-bishops. The danger was, that these all, and even the churches of the province, would agree in a coalition against the party who began the prosecution; so that, in the end, they would be excluded from the bonds of Christian fellowship. Who can suppose that the bishops could be men, and not act, in such circumstances, for the interests of their order."[42]

(d) Strong temptations were presented to the lower orders of the clergy to become the sycophants of the higher for the promotion of their own interests.

"They flatter the rulers, they affectionately salute the influential, they carefully wait upon the rich; the glory of God they disregard; his worship they defile, religion they profane, Christian love they destroy. Their ambition is insatiable; they are ever striving after honor and fame. They aspire to be high in office; and, to accomplish this end, spare not to excite the worst of enmities among the best of friends."[43] This is said by a Roman bishop, of his own

---

[42] Planck, Gesell. Verfass. I. S. 179. Comp. p. 129. Ziegler's. Versuch. etc. S. 56, 57. Ep. Philagrio, 65, al. 59, p. 823, and Ep. Procopio, 55, al. 42, p. 814. Conc. Antioch. c. 1, Synod. Gangr. c. 7, 8. Conc. Chalcedon, c. 8. Conc. Const. c. 6. Comp. Conc. Laodic. c. 20, 42, 56.

[43] Leo VII. Epist. ad Episc. Bavar. ap. Aventinum et in Catal. Test. Vet. p. 209. Cited in Arnold's Wahre Abbildung, S. 919. Euseb. VIII. 1.

clergy; and Gregory Nazianzen, at an earlier period, charges them with flattering the great and crouching to them in every way. "But when they had others in their power, then were they more savage than lions."[44] At another time he describes them as "seducing flatterers, flexible as a bough, savage as a lion to the weak, cringing as a dog to the powerful; who knock at the doors, not of the learned, but of the great, and value highest, not what is useful, but what is pleasing to others."[45]

"Wherever," says Robert Hall, "religion is established by law, with splendid emoluments and dignities annexed to its profession, the clergy, who are candidates for these distinctions, will ever be prone to exalt the prerogative, not only in order to strengthen the arm on which they lean, but that they may the more successfully ingratiate themselves in the favor of the prince, by flattering those ambitious views and passions which are too readily entertained by persons possessed of supreme power. The boasted alliance between church and state, on which so many encomiums have been lavished, seems to have been little more than a compact between the priest and the magistrate to betray the liberties of mankind, both civil and religious. To this the clergy on their part, at least, have continued steady, shunning inquiry, fearful of change, blind to the corruptions of government, skillful to *discern the signs of the times*, and eager to improve every opportunity and to employ all their art and eloquence to extend the prerogative and smoothe the approaches of arbitrary power."

(*e*) The clergy were entrusted with the exercise of both ecclesiastical and civil powers.

Constantine gave to the bishops the right of deciding in

[44] Objurgat. in Cler. Cited in Wahre Abbildung, S. 918.

[45] De Episcopis, p. 1031. Ed. Basil. 1571. Ed. Colon. 1590. Vol. II. p. 304.

secular matters, making them the highest court of judicature, and ordering that their judgment should be final and decisive as that of the emperor himself,[46] whose officers were accordingly required to execute these decisions.[47]

With this union of church and state under Constantine, the way was opened for the exercise of clerical influence in many ways over the secular interests of both. Siegel has mentioned one crafty device, which sufficiently discovers the aspirations of prelatical ambition after political power. This was the rule which required "the subordinate clergy to obtain permission from the metropolitan to pay their visits to the emperor." The design of this expedient was to overrule the appeals of the inferior clergy to Caesar, by hindering them in their approaches to him. In short, the policy of the bishops was to embarrass others as much as possible in making appeal to the civil authority, while they themselves employed it to accomplish their own party purposes.

"Hundreds of cases to this effect occur in the history of the fourth and fifth centuries. And all this, as any one must see, was entirely natural, according to the ordinary course of things. When so often availing themselves of this right of appeal to the emperors as they did, could the bishops fail to remember that they could in this way not only serve the church, but promote also their own convenience and the furtherance of their designs?"[48]

(*f*) A secular and mercenary spirit dishonored the clergy.

So prevalent was this spirit among the clergy that the council of Eliberis, A. D. 305, saw reason to rebuke and

[46] Κρείτω τῆσ τῶν ἄλλων δικαστῶν ὡσανεὶ παρὰ τοῦ βασιλέως ἐξενεχθεῖσαν.

[47] Siegel, Handbuch, I. p. 247. Socrat. E. Hist. b. 7, 7. Com. Valesius, in Euseb. De Vit. Const. Lib. 4, c. 27.

[48] Planck, Gesell. Verfass. I. S. 269–271. Comp. S. 453, 454. Conc. Antioch, c. 11, 12.

restrain it by requiring them, if they must engage in trade, to confine their operations to their own province.[49]

"The church that before by insensible degrees welked and impaired, now with large steps went down hill decaying; at this time Antichrist began first to put forth his horn, and that saying was common, that former times had wooden chalices and golden priests; but they, golden chalices and wooden priests. 'Formerly,' says Sulpitius, speaking of these times, 'martyrdom by glorious death was sought more greedily than now bishoprics by vile ambition are hunted after;' and in another place: 'they gape after possessions, they tend lands and livings, they hoard up their gold, they buy and sell; and if there be any that neither possess money nor traffic, what is worse, they sit still and accept gifts, and prostitute every endowment of grace, every holy thing, to venal purposes.' Thus he concludes: 'All things went to rack by the faction, willfulness and avarice of the bishops; and by this means God's people and every good man were held in scorn and derision.'"[50]

(g) The bishops learned to torture and pervert the language of Scripture to give importance to their order.

From their reference to the Jewish priesthood sprang the

---

[49] Conc. Eliberis, c. 19. Comp. Conc. Aurel. 3, c. 27. Basil the Great complains that some of the bishops administered ordination for hire, making even this "grace" an article of merchandise. A practice which he justly condemns.—*Ep.* 53, Vol. III. p. 147.

The bishop of Bangor, in Wales, has been reminded of his episcopal duty by a petition from fifty of the clergy of his diocese, who are shocked at the state of things there. It seems from their address that numbers of the clergy live entirely at their ease, do nothing, and get well paid for it. Others, again, neglect their own parishes to serve as curates to other rectors, and thus add to their income. Some of the best-endowed benefices absolutely neglect the people; while, in many cases, the services are held at hours when nobody can attend.

[50] Milton's Prose Works, Vol. I. p. 22.

conceit of the divine right of episcopacy, of the apostolical succession, and of the validity and necessity of episcopal ordination. On this topic another shall speak, who has written on the constitution of the church more at length and with greater ability than any other historian. After adverting to their reference to the Jewish priesthood, to the transfer of the names of that priesthood to the clergy of the Christian church, and to the analogies which were sought out between the chief priests of the temple and the bishops of the church, Planck proceeds to say: "It is easy to see, and was foreseen, what advantages they might gain if they could once bring this notion into circulation—that the bishops and presbyters were set apart not by the church, *but by God himself;*[51] that they held their office and the rights of their office from God, and not from the church; that they were not the servants of the church, but ordained of God to be its overseers, and appointed by him to be the guardians of its sanctity; that the service of the ministry for this new religion must be performed altogether by them and by their body; and, therefore, that they must of necessity constitute themselves a distinct order and form a separate caste in the church; all this was clearly manifest to their minds, and accordingly they sought out with all diligence the analogies from which all these consequences could so easily be drawn.

"In view of the obvious advantages which the bishops would gain from the prevalence of such sentiments, one is not surprised that Cyprian sought so much to propagate them in his day. Having, therefore, so much interest in the promulgation of these sentiments, from which proceeded, as a necessary consequence, the *divine right* of their office, the bishops found means more fully to establish them by

[51] It was a favorite sentiment of Cyprian that God makes the priests. Deus qui sacerdotes facit —*Epist.* 69, 52.

claiming to be *the successors of the apostles*. They accordingly began now for the first time to promulgate, with a specific intent, this doctrine of the apostolical succession. The bishops had, indeed, from the beginning of the second century,[52] appropriated to themselves the title of the successors of the apostles, but it occurred to no one, and least of all to them, that they had of right inherited the authority of the apostles and were instated in all their rights. These claims, however, were not only put forth before the middle of the third century as an acknowledged right, but the bishops carefully availed themselves of the advantages resulting from an inheritance of the apostolical succession.

"One of the advantages claimed was the exclusive right of ordination. This favorite doctrine has ever since held a conspicuous place among their rights in the church. Indeed, it has been the ruling sentiment of the episcopal hierarchy, the foundation of this entire theory of an ecclesiastical ministry. The church was taught to believe that the right in question was borrowed from the ancient Jews, and that the apostles, by means of it, had originally inducted bishops and presbyters into office.[53] It was instructed that the laying on of hands was not merely a symbolical rite, but that it must be regarded as a religious act, having in itself a certain efficacy by which the individual upon whom it had been rightly performed was not only invested with

---

[52] This author supposes the distinction between bishop and presbyter to have prevailed from the beginning—a distinction, however, appropriately implying no official superiority. "The bishop perhaps regarded himself as somewhat different from a presbyter, but not at all superior to him. He thought himself more than a presbyter only inasmuch as he had more to do than a presbyter."—*Gesell. Verfass.* Bd. I. S. 31.

[53] Potestas Apostolis data est ... et episcopis, qui eis vicaria ordinatione successerunt.—*Cyprian*, Ep. 75.

all the rights of the office, but was also rendered competent to impart to others the same clerical grace. In a word, a mysterious and supernatural power was ascribed to this laying on of hands, by which the Holy Spirit was transmitted to the person who received ordination from them; just as the apostles, by the laying on of their hands, communicated the gift of working miracles, Acts viii. 17; x. 47.

"When once the bishops had come to be regarded as the *successors* of the apostles, they could easily lay claim also to the prerogatives and gifts of the apostles. Hence the doctrine that none but the bishops could administer a valid ordination; for they, by being constituted the successors of the apostles, had alone the power, by the laying on of the hands, to impart a similar gift, with ability to transmit it unimpaired to others. In order more deeply to impress the new doctrine upon the minds of the people, or to inspire them with a firmer belief in it, they took care also to administer the rite of ordination with the appearance of greater formality and solemnity. This, in all probability, was the true reason for the custom of saying, in the laying on of the hands, *Accipe Sanctum Spiritum*, Receive the Holy Ghost!

"In the same connection came also the suggestion that it was important, not merely for the bishops, but for the presbyters and deacons also, to receive ordination.[54] They were accordingly ordained; and the great end designed by all these things would be accomplished—*that of impressing more deeply upon the minds of the people that the clergy are a pecu-*

---

[54] Cyprian at least admonished the deacons to remember that God appointed the apostles, *i. e.*, the *bishops*, but the deacons were constituted the ministers of the church by the apostles. Apostolos, id est episcopos Dominus elegit; diaconos autem apostoli sibi constituerunt ministros.—*Ep.* 9.

liar class of persons, set apart by God himself as a distinct order in the church." [55]

(*h*) The clergy manifested an intolerant, persecuting spirit.

It is the legitimate effect of such pretensions as have been specified in the foregoing article. Dissent from their doctrines becomes a denial of God's truth; disobedience to their authority, rebellion against God; and heresy, the most heinous of sins. Accordingly, the great strife now is to guard against the spread of heretical opinions. Many, according to Epiphanius, were expelled from the church for a single word or two, which might seem to be contrary to the faith.[56] The charges were frequently groundless, often contemptible; and so multifarious withal, that it might be difficult to say what in human conduct or belief has not been branded as heresy. For a priest to appear in worship without his surplice was heresy.[57] To fast on Saturday or Sunday, "heresy, and a damnable thing." [58] This zeal against heretics was quickened, also, by that avarice which seized upon their houses, their lands, their property of every description, and confiscated them for the benefit, ostensibly, of the church, but really as a gratuity to the pious zeal of their clerical persecutors.[59]

---

[55] Gesell. Verfass. I. S. 157–163.

[56] Epist. ad Johan. Hieros. Vol. II. Op. p. 314. The least deviation from the prescribed formularies and creeds of the church was heresy, according to the famous law of Arcadius, A. D. 395. Haeritici sunt qui vel levi argumento a judicio catholicae religionis et tramite detecti fuerint deviare.—*Cod. Theodos.* L. 16, tit. V. de Haeret. 6, 28.

Under Elizabeth, ministers and women of high culture were thrust "into dangerous and loathsome jails, among the most facinorous and vile persons," for not praying by the book.

[57] Apoph. Pat. apud Cotelerium, T. 1, Mon. Graec. p. 684.

[58] Nomo Canon, Gr. apud eundem, c. 129.

[59] Cod. Theodos. L. 16, tit. 5, 6, 43, 52, 57. A full statement of

And yet, under this treatment, as might have been foreseen, heresies came up into the church like the frogs of Egypt. Epiphanius, who, in the fourth century, wrote several books against heresies, announces no less than *eighty distinct kinds of heresy.* But the most obnoxious feature of this rage against heresy is, that it often became only a persecuting intolerance of the pious, whose religious life rebuked the godless ministry that was over them. "One may see," says Jerome, "in most of the cities, bishops and presbyters, who, when they perceive the laity to seek the society of the pious, and hospitably to entertain them, immediately become jealous, and murmur against them, lay them under bans, and thrust them out of the church; so that one can do no more than what the bishop or overseer does. But to live a virtuous life is sure to provoke the displeasure of these priests; so unmerciful are they toward these poor men, and seize them by the neck, as if they would draw them away from all that is good, and harass them with all manner of persecutions." [60]

"It was a thing, of course, that all would strive for admission into that order which was in the enjoyment of such wealth, and power, and distinction." [61] This was the great evil of this whole system of church-government. *Hinc illi prima mali labes*—hence, the source and fountain of that tide of corruption which came in upon the church like an overwhelming flood. [62] The instances that have already been mentioned, clearly indicate the degeneracy of the clergy, which appears more fully in the following particulars:

these persecutions is given in Vol. VI. p. 118. Leipsic, 1743. Socrat. Eccl. Hist. Lib. 7, c. 7; c. 29. Comp. Jerom. Comment in Ep. I. ad Tit. Lib. 2 in Ezech. c. 34, Vol. III. p. 943.

[60] Comment. in Epist. 1 ad Tit.
[61] Gesell. Verfass. I. 332.
[62] Comp. Mosheim, De Rebus Christ., Saec. III. § 25.

THE PROGRESS OF EPISCOPACY. 259

(*a*) Their pride, their haughty, supercilious and ostentatious bearing.

Every effort was made to exalt the dignity of the bishops. They assumed the titles of priests, high-priests, apostles, successors of the apostles; their highness, their excellence, their worthiness, their reverence, the enthroned, the height of the highest dignity, the culminating point of pontifical glory;—these were the terms of base adulation employed to set forth the dignity of these ministers of Christ,[63] supported by presbyters on either hand, while the deacons stood lightly dressed and girded high as nimble servitors to do the bishop's bidding.[64] They had separate seats and *princely thrones* in the church. All rose to do them reverence as they came in, and stood until the bishops were seated, and often the people were required to *stand* in the presence of the bishops.[65] They were decked out in gorgeous apparel, and

---

[63] Pertsch, Can. Recht. 49. More at length, in his Kirch. Hist. Saec. II. c. 3, § 15, 16, 18.

[64] Apost. Const. II. c. 57.

[65] The following canon of the Council of Maçon, A. D. 581, dictated, as they gravely tell us, by the Holy Spirit, is sufficient to illustrate the artifices of this kind to secure the respect of the people: Et quia ordinationi sacerdotum annuente deo congruit de omnibus disponere et causis singulis honestum terminum dare; ut per hos reverentissimos canones et praeteritorum canonum viror ac florida germina maturis fructibus enitescant, statuimus ut si quis saecularium quempiam clericorum honoratorum in itinere obviam habuerit, usque ad inferiorem gradum honoris veneranter sicut condecet Christianum illi colla subdat, per cujus officia et obsequia fidelissima christianitatis jura promeruit. Et si quidem ille saecularis equo vehitur clericusque similiter, saecularum galerum de capite auferat et clerico sincerae salutationis munus adhibeat. Si vero clericus pedes graditur et saecularis vehitur equo sublimis, illico ad terram defluat et debitum honorem praedicto clerico sincerae caritatis exhibeat, ut deus, qui vera caritas est, in utrisque laetetur, et dilectioni suae utrumque adsciscat. Qui vero haec quae *spiritu sancto dictante* sancita sunt transgredi voluerit,

even suspended sacred relics from their shoulders, to impress the multitude with a more profound reverence for their order.[66] Even Origen, A. D. 253, complains that there are, especially in the larger cities, overseers of the people of God, who seek to outdo the pomp of heathen potentates, surrounding themselves, like the emperors, with a body-guard and making themselves terrible and inaccessible to the poor.

(*b*) Their ignorance and incompetence rightly to discharge the duties of their office.

By favoritism, intrigue and cunning many found their way into office who were wholly unqualified for it; and the church was afflicted with an incompetent and unworthy ministry.[67] While mere boys, they were sometimes invested with the clerical office, so that the fourth council of Toletum, A. D. 633, by solemn enactment, provides for their education and training for their duties.[68] "No physician," says Gregory Nazianzen, A. D. 370, "finds employment until he has acquainted himself with the nature of diseases; no painter until he has learned to mix colors, and acquired skill in the use of the pencil. But a bishop is easily found. No preparation is requisite for his office. In a single day we make one a priest, and exhort him to be wise and learned, while he knows nothing; and brings no needful qualification for his office but a desire to be a bishop."[69]

ab ecclesiae quam in suis ministris dehonorat, quamdiu episcopus illius ecclesiae voluerit suspendatur.—C. 15, *Bruns*, Vol. II. p. 254. The gradations of rank which were observed with so much precision were made subservient to the same end, and indicate the same spirit. Comp. Planck, I. p. 358–368.

[66] Conc. Bracar. 3, c. 5.   [67] Conc. Tol. 4, c. 19.

[68] Nos, et divinae legis, et conciliorum praecepti immemores infantes et pueros, levitas facimus ante legitimam aetatam ante experientiam vitae.—*Conc. Tol.* 4, c. 20. Comp. Conc. Narbon. c. 11.

[69] Orat. 20, De Basil. Ed. Colon. 1590, p. 335.

They are teachers, while yet they have to learn the rudiments of religion. Yesterday, impenitent, irreligious; and to-day, priests; old in vice; in knowledge young."[70] "They are, in their ministry, dull; in evil-speaking, active; in study, much at leisure; in seductions, busy; in love, cold; in factions, powerful; in hatred and enmity, constant; in doctrine, wavering. They profess to govern the church, but have need themselves to be governed by others."[71]

(c) The total neglect of Christian discipline, and the general corruption of the church, were the necessary consequences of a secular ministry.

"Formerly, the church of Christ was distinguished from the world by her piety. Then, the walk of all or of most Christians was holy, unlike that of the irreligious. But now are Christians as base, and, if possible, even worse than heretics and heathens."[72] "How unlike themselves are Christians now!" says Salvianus, A. D. 460. "How fallen from what they once were! when we might rejoice, and account the church as quite pure, if it had only as many good as bad men in it. But it is hard and sad to say, that the church, which ought, in all things, to be well pleasing to God, does little else than provoke his displeasures."[73] This is but a faint sketch of his complaint. Much more to the same effect is said by this writer, and confirmed by others, which we gladly pass in silence. Enough of this sad tale of the degeneracy of the church, of which the half has not been told. "No language," says Chrysostom, "can describe

---

[70] Orat. 21. In Laud. Anthanas. p. 378.

[71] Sidonius Apollinaris, A. D. 486, Lib. 7, Ep. 9. Biblioth. Vet. Pat. VI. p, 1112. Comp. Mosheim, De Rebus Christ., Saec. III. § 26.

[72] Comp. Chrysostom Hom. 32, § 7, in Math. 36, § 5, on 1 Cor.

[73] Lib. 6, De Gub. Dei in Biblioth. Pat. Vet. Vol. VIII. p. 362, seq.

the angry contentions of Christians, and the corruption of morals that prevailed, from the time of Constantine to that of Theodosius."[74]

Of grosser enormities we forbear to speak. Much that is recorded both of the clergy and the people, in the period now under consideration, cannot with propriety be transferred to these pages. Suffice it to say, there is evidence sufficient to show that a shocking degeneracy of morals pervaded all classes of society. It began, confessedly, with the clergy—in their worldliness and irreligion, their neglect of duty, their departure from the faith, and corrupt example.[75] From the time of Constantine, the tide of corruption, which had begun to set in upon the church, became deep and strong, and continued to rise and swell until it wellnigh overwhelmed her. There were still examples, indeed, of men high in office in the church, who nobly strove to turn back this flood of iniquity; but they too frequently strove in vain, as their lamentations over her degeneracy plainly show.

Wearied, however, with the oppressive hand of prelatical power that was upon her, and sickened at the sight of the ungodliness which had come up into the church, and sat enthroned in her high places, the pure spirit of piety withdrew, in silent sadness, to the cloistered cell, drew the curtains and reposed in her secret recesses through the long night of darkness that settled upon the world.

The object of the Christian emperors was to bring all their subjects to embrace Christianity by making a professed faith in Christ the passport to favor and to power. The consequence was, that multitudes pressed up to the

[74] Hom. 49, in Math. p. 202. Opus imperfectum.

[75] Chrysostom expressly says, that they were the cause of this degeneracy of the laity. In Math. 23. Comp. also, Catal. Test. Verit. p. 77.

altar of the Lord, eager to be invested with the robes and the office of the Christian ministry, who had nothing of its spirit.[76]

Such was the wayward policy, the fatal mistake of the first Christian emperors. Such were its disastrous results. My kingdom, saith Christ, is not of this world. Christianity, though mingling freely in the affairs of men, like its great Author, works its miracles of mercy and of grace by powers that are hidden and divine. It stoops to no carnal policy, no state chicanery, no corrupt alliances; while, like an angel of mercy, it goes through the earth, for the healing of the nations. To borrow the profound thoughts and beautiful language of Robert Hall: "Christianity will civilize, it is true; but it is only when it is allowed to develop the energies by which it sanctifies. Christianity will inconceivably ameliorate the condition of being. Who doubts it? Its universal prevalence, not in name, but in reality, will convert this world into a semi-paradisaical state; but it is only while it is permitted to prepare its inhabitants for a better. Let her be urged to forget her celestial origin and destiny—to forget that she came from God, and returns to God; and, whether employed by the artful and enterprising as the instrument of establishing a spiritual empire and dominion over mankind, or by the philanthropist as the means of promoting their civilization and improvement—she resents the foul indignity, claps her wings and takes her flight, leaving nothing but a base and sanctimonious hypocrisy in her room."[77]

[76] Comp. Sermon by Thomas Hardy, D.D. Cited in Dr. Brown's Law of Christ, pp. 511, 512.

[77] Address to Eustace Carey.

THE PATRIARCHAL GOVERNMENT.

This was only a farther concentration of ecclesiastical power, another stage in the process of centralization, which was fast bringing the church under the absolute despotism of the papacy. Man naturally aspires to the exercise of arbitrary power; or, if he must divide his authority with others, he seeks to make that number as small as possible.[78]

In the course of the period from the fourth to the sixth century, arose four great ecclesiastical divisions, whose primates bore the title of patriarch. These were Rome, Constantinople, Alexandria and Antioch. Few topics of antiquity have been the subject of so much controversy as that relating to the patriarchal system, as may be seen in the works of Salmasius, Petavius, Sismondi, Scheelstrate, Richter and others. Suffice it to say, however, that the Council of Chalcedon, A. D. 451, established five patriarchates. The Council of Nice, A. D. 325, c. 6, 7, of Constantinople I, A. D. 381, c. 2, 5, and of Ephesus, A. D. 431, act. 7, had already conferred the distinction without the title. The incumbents of these episcopal sees were already invested with civil powers. Theodosius the Great conferred upon Constantinople the second rank, a measure greatly displeasing to Rome, and against which Alexandria and Antioch uniformly protested. Jerusalem had the honor and dignity of a patriarchate, but not the rights and privileges.[79]

[78] Comp. Planck, Gesell. Verfass. I. S. 598-624. Ziegler's Versuch. etc. 164-365.

[79] Hence the Romans were accustomed to say, Patriarchae in ecclesia primitus fuere, tres per se et ex natura sua—Romanus, Alexandrinus et Antiochenus; duo per accidens, Constantinopolitanus et Hierosolymitanus. Comp. Justinia. Nov. Constit. 123. Schroeckh, Kirch. Gesch. Thl. 17, S. 45, 46. Comp. Art. Patriarch, in the works of Augusti, Siegel, Rheinwald, W. Böhmer, etc.

The aspirations of prelatical ambition after sole and supreme power are sufficiently manifest in that bitter contest, which was so long maintained by the primates of Rome and Constantinople, for the title of universal patriarch or head of the church universal.[80] Great political events finally decided this controversy in the course of the fifth and sixth centuries in the West, and in the East in the seventh century, in favor of the church of Rome. This decision resulted in the supremacy of the pope and the establishment of the papal system.

THE PAPAL GOVERNMENT.

This was the last refinement of cunning and self-aggrandizement; the culminating point of ecclesiastical usurpation, toward which the government of the church under the episcopal hierarchy had been for several centuries approaching. It was an ecclesiastical monarchy, a spiritual despotism, which completed the overthrow of the authority of individual churches as sovereign and independent bodies.

The bishop of Rome began his splendid career with the overthrow of the emperor's authority in Italy. The decline of the Eastern empire, the famous war respecting image-worship and other events, political and ecclesiastical, favored the designs of the Pope of Rome until he proudly proclaimed himself "the successor of St. Peter, set up by God to govern not only the church, but the whole world." So that he as God sitteth in the temple of God, showing himself that he is God.

Thus, as we have seen, ecclesiastical history introduces first to our notice single independent churches; then, churches having several dependent branches; then, diocesan

---

[80] Πατριάρχος τῆς οἰκουμένης, episcopus occumenicus, universalis ecclesiae papa, etc.

churches; then, metropolitan or provincial churches; and then, national churches attempered to the civil power. In the end, we behold two great divisions of ecclesiastical empire, the Eastern and the Western, now darkly intriguing, now fearfully struggling with each other for the mastery, until the doctrine of the *unity* of the church is consummated in the assumed sovereignty of the Pope of Rome, who sits enthroned in power, claiming to be the head of the church on earth. The government of the church was at first a democracy, allowing to all its constituents the most enlarged freedom of a voluntary religious association. It became an absolute and iron despotism. The gradations of ecclesiastical organization through which it passed were, from congregational to parochial—parochial to diocesan—diocesan to metropolitan—metropolitan to patriarchal—patriarchal to papal.

The corruptions and abominations of the church through that long night of darkness which succeeded the triumph of the Pope of Rome were inexpressibly horrible. The record of them may more fitly lie shrouded in a dead language than be disclosed to the light in the living speech of men. The successors of St. Peter, as they call themselves, were frequently nominated to the chair of "his holiness" by women of infamous and abandoned lives. Not a few of them were shamefully immoral, and some, monsters of wickedness. Several were heretics, and others were deposed as usurpers. And yet this church of Rome, "with such ministers and so appointed—a church corrupt in every part and every particular, individually and collectively, in doctrine, in discipline, in practice"—this church prelacy recognizes as the only representative of the Lord Jesus Christ, in the period now under consideration, invested with all his authority, and exercising divine powers on earth! She boasts her ordinances, her sacraments, transmitted for a thousand years unimpaired and uncontaminated through such hands! High-church episcopacy proudly draws her own apostolical succession through this pit of pollution, and then the followers of Christ, who care not to receive such grace from such hands, she calmly delivers over to God's "uncovenanted mercies!" Nay, more; multitudes of that communion are now engaged in the strange work of "unprotestantizing the churches" which have washed themselves from these defilements.[81] The strife is, with a proud array of talents, of learning, and of episcopal power, to bury all spiritual religion again in the grave of forms, to shroud the light of truth in the gloom of popish tradition, and to sink the church of God once more into that abyss of deep and dreadful darkness from which she emerged at the dawn of the Reformation. In the beautiful and expressive language of Milton, their strife is to "reinvolve us in that pitchy cloud of infernal darkness, where we shall never more see the sun of truth again, never hope for the cheerful dawn, never more hear the bird of morning sing."

[81] Some of these unprotestantizing efforts are sketched by Lord J. Russell as follows: "There is a danger, however, which alarms me much more than any aggressions of a foreign sovereign. Clergymen, of our own Church, who have subscribed the Thirty-nine Articles, and acknowledged in explicit terms the Queen's supremacy, have been the most forward in leading their flocks, 'step by step, to the very verge of the precipice.' The honor paid to saints, the claim of infallibility for the Church, the superstitious use of the sign of the cross, the muttering of the liturgy so as to disguise the language in which it is written, the recommendation of auricular confession, and the administration of penance and absolution—all these things are pointed out by clergymen of the Church of England as worthy of adoption, and are now openly reprehended by the bishop of London in his charge to the clergy of his diocese."

REMARKS.

In connection with the view which we have taken of the rise and progress of the episcopal system in the ancient church, we offer a few remarks upon its present characteristics and practical influence.

1. We object to prelacy as a departure from the order of the apostolical and primitive churches.

Nothing is plainer than that the government of the church, in the beginning, was not episcopal. And though we are not bound by any divine authority to an exact conformity with the primitive model, yet we cannot doubt that the apostles were guided by wisdom from above in giving to the churches a different organization, popular in principle, simple in form, and better suited to the exigencies of the church in every condition of society.

While, therefore, with so much gravity and self-complacency, episcopacy talks of her "adherence to the Holy Scriptures and to apostolical usage," we must be permitted to object to her whole ecclesiastical polity as an innovation upon the scriptural system and a total departure from the usage of the apostles without any good reason or beneficial results.

2. Prelacy removes the laity from a just participation in the government and discipline of the church.

Such is prelacy—a government administered *for* the people, the great expedient of despotism in every form. The government of the primitive church was administered *by* the people, the great safeguard of popular freedom, whether civil or religious.

Discipline is also administered *for* the church by the clergy. But the laity are the safest and best guardians of the purity of the church. In transferring this duty from the laity to the clergy, episcopacy does great injustice to the private members of the church, and equal injury to the cause of pure and undefiled religion.

3. Prelacy creates unjust distinctions among the clergy, whose character and profession is the same.

The Scriptures authorize no distinction in the duties, privileges or prerogatives of bishops and priests, or presbyters. The distinction is arbitrary and unjust. It denies to a portion of the clergy the performance of certain duties for which they are duly qualified, and to which they are fully entitled in common with the bishops. It hinders the inferior clergy in the performance of their proper ministerial duties, and degrades them in the estimation of the people.

4. Prelacy is intolerant and exclusive.

This is one of its most obnoxious characteristics. That this single church should assume to be the only true church, and its clergy the only authorized ministers; that the only valid ordinances and sacraments are administered in their communion; that they alone, of all to whom salvation by grace is so freely published, are received into covenant mercy,—all this is nothing else than a proud and sanctimonious self-righteousness. There is an atrocity of character in this spirit which can unchurch the saints of God of every age, in every Christian communion, save one, and consign them, if not to perdition, to God's uncovenanted mercy—an atrocity which in other days has found its just expression in the fires of Smithfield and in the slow torture of the *auto-da-fé*.

A profound expositor of the constitutional history of England has sketched the origin of these high pretensions in the English Church. Bancroft, the chaplain of Archbishop Whitgift, broached these doctrines, but Archbishop Laud has the credit of reaffirming and establishing them. "Laud and his party began, about the end of Elizabeth's reign, by preaching the divine right, as it is called, or absolute indispensability of episcopacy, a doctrine of which the first traces, as I apprehend, are found about the end of Elizabeth's reign. They insisted on the necessity of episcopal succession, regularly derived from the apostles. They drew an inference from this tenet, that ordinations by presbyters were, in all cases, null." Of Lutherans and Calvinists they began now to speak "as aliens, to whom they were not at all related, and schismatics, with whom they held no communion; nay, as wanting the very essence of Christian society. This again brought them nearer, by irresistible consequence, to the disciples of Rome, whom, with becoming charity, but against the received creed of the Puritans, and perhaps against their own articles, they all acknowledged to be a part of the catholic church." [82]

5. Prelacy is monarchical and anti-republican.

It is monarchical in form, monarchical in spirit, and, until transplanted to these States, has been, always and everywhere, the handmaid of monarchy. Here it is a mere exotic, altogether uncongenial with our own republican soil. Its monarchical tendencies and sympathies are clearly exhibited by Hallam, whose work on the Constitutional History of England, Macaulay characterizes as "the most impartial book that he ever read." "The doctrine of passive obedience episcopacy taught in the reign of Elizabeth even in her homilies. To withstand the Catholics, the reliance of Parliament was upon the 'stern, intrepid and uncompromising spirit of Puritanism.' Of the conforming churchmen in general they might well be doubtful." [83]

The doctrine of the king's absolute authority was inculcated by the Episcopal clergy. "Especially with the high-church party it had become current." [84]

[82] Hallam's Constitutional History, Vol. I. pp. 540, 541.
[83] Ibid. pp. 262, 263. [84] Ibid. pp. 437, 438.

Under Charles I. "they studiously inculcated that resistance to the commands of rulers was, *in every conceivable instance*, a heinous sin. It was taught in their homilies."[85] "It was laid down in the canons of convocation, 1606."[86]

James considered episcopacy essential to the existence of monarchy, uniformly embodying this sentiment in his favorite aphorism, "No bishop, no king."[87]

Elizabeth and her successors, says Macaulay, "by considering conformity and loyalty as identical, at length made them so."

"Charles himself says in his letters that he looks on episcopacy as a stronger support of monarchical power than even an army. From causes which we have already considered, the Established Church had been, since the Reformation, the great bulwark of the prerogative."[88] She was, according to the same eloquent writer, for more than one hundred and fifty years, "the servile handmaid of monarchy, the steady enemy of public liberty. The divine right of kings and the duty of passively obeying all their commands were her favorite tenets. She held them firmly, through times of oppression, persecution and licentiousness; while law was trampled down; while judgment was perverted; while the people were eaten as though they were bread."[89]

6. A monarchy in spiritual things does not harmonize with the spirit of Christianity.[90]

Our fathers came here to establish "a state without king or nobles, and a church without a bishop." They sought to establish themselves here as "a people governed by laws

---

[85] Hallam's Const. Hist. Vol. I. p. 264.   [86] Ibid. pp. 567–570.
[87] Neal's History of the Puritans, Vol. II. pp. 43, 44.
[88] Macaulay's Miscellanies, Vol. I. p. 293. Boston ed.
[89] Ibid. p. 249.
[90] Neander Hist. Vol. I. p. 183. Trans.

of their own making and by rulers of their own choosing." And here, in peaceful seclusion from the oppression of every dynasty, whether spiritual or temporal, they became an independent and prosperous commonwealth. But what affinity, what sympathy has its government, civil or religious, with that of episcopacy? the one republican, the other monarchical; in sympathy, in principle, in form, they are directly opposed to each other. We doubt not that most of the members of that communion are friends to our republican government; but we must regard their religion as a strange, unseemly anomaly here—a religious government, arbitrary and despotic, in the midst of the highest political freedom; a spiritual despotism in the heart of a free republic!

7. Prelacy is a corrupt compromise with paganism.

The entire order of the church, after the union of church and state under the Christian emperors, became, by its conformity to paganism, a paganized ecclesiasticism. Many of the festivals of the church were adopted from pagan feasts. Ash Wednesday, Palm Sunday, Easter, St. John's Day, All Soul's, Candlemas and Christmas, all have a strong analogy to the festivals of heathen nations; and impure orgies of the Lupercalia and Saturnalia, all have a fit representation in the grotesque fooleries, revelry and licentiousness of the Carnival. The ministry of the gospel is changed to a sacrificial priesthood; the communion-table, to an altar, and the Lord's Supper, into the sacrifice of the mass. The secret mysteries of the heathen—their holy water,[91] their ritualistic forms, their prayers from a book in

---

[91] Occupat Aeneas aditum; corpusque recenti spargit aqua. Aen. VI. 635. Ovid. Pont. 3, 2, 73.

"Every person who came to the solemn sacrifices was purified by water. To which end, at the entrance of the temples, there was com-

an exact form of words and in a barbarous and unknown language, the attendant notifying the progress of the ceremonials, all are transferred to the church with little or no change in form, save that the acolyte in the church has substituted the *bell* for the trumpet of the pagan ritual.[92] The images and sacred relics of the pagans, their *lares*, their *penates* and their deified heroes, all have their representatives in the relics—saints and martyrs of the Catholic Church. Their purgatory is only a slight modification of the remedial penalties of the dead according to pagan superstition.[93] From the worship of Diana, Juno, or Venus, the pagan readily turned to that of the Virgin in the church. Prayers for the repose of the dead were offered by pagans, as by Christians in the papal church, and the public assemblies of both were dismissed in precisely the same terms—"Ite, missa est."[94] In walking the streets of Rome, by turning a corner, you pass out of *Minerva* street into *Jesus* street. By a turn as short, as easy, the passage is made from Paganism to Romanism. The Pantheon, with-

monly a vessel full of holy water."—Potter's Antiq. of Greece, Vol. II. p. 260. Comp. Prideaux's Connections, Part II. Book IV.

When Julian, in Gaul, was entering a temple to offer incense, "the priests, in accordance with the pagan custom, sprinkled holy water upon them with the branch of a tree. A drop of water fell upon the robe of Valentinian, who was a Christian, and he rebuked the priest with great severity. It is even said that he tore off, in the presence of the emperor, the part of the garment on which the water had fallen, and flung it from him."—*Sozomen*, Eccl. Hist. Lib. 6, c. 6. Potter's Antiquities of Greece, Vol. I. p. 286.

[92] Vidimus .... alium custodem dari qui attendat, alium vero praeponi, qui faveri linguis jubeat; *tibicinem, canere*.

[93] Non tamen omne malum miseris, nec funditus omnes
Corporeae excedunt pestes,
Ergo exercentur poenis, veterumque malorum
Supplicia expendunt.—Aen. VI. 736–739.

[94] Bib. Sac. May, 1844, p. 402, Note.

out change, becomes a Catholic church, and a statue of the Sybil is worshiped as the Virgin Mary. The statue of Jupiter Capitolinus passes from the Capitoline Hill into St. Peter's church, the image of that patron saint. No Catholic passes without kissing its toes, of which three of the nails have been worn away by the lips of the devotees. On a certain day the cardinals are seen sweeping up the nave of St. Peter's, in their scarlet robes, to perform the same devotions. Such is the strange mixture of Paganism with Romanism. Roman polytheism blended with Christianity has debased our holy religion to a baptized Paganism.

This holy catholic church, one and indivisible, deriving divine rights by regular succession from the apostles—what is it? what its unity, its purity? Who this house of Aaron, that have kept all the while the sacred fire of the altar, borne up and defended the tabernacle of the Lord, and guarded from all profane intrusion the ark of the covenant? Has no hypocritical intruder crept in among the Lord's anointed, and with unholy hands essayed these awful mysteries, vainly assuming to transmit, by uncanonized rites, this heavenly grace? Has no link been broken in this mysterious chain, stretching on from the distant age of the apostles to the present? Has no irregularity disturbed the succession, no taint of heresy marred the purity of its descent in this church, which can embrace within its ample folds the superstitions, idolatries and pollutions of paganism, blended with a debased Christianity? What form of error, what delusion, what schism, what creature of sin, has not at some time found a place within this holy immaculate church, as a component part of this strange catholic unity—a unity only of chaos, corruption and infinite confusion?

PART SECOND.

INFORMAL IN ITS WORSHIP.

CHAPTER XI.

PRAYERS OF THE PRIMITIVE CHURCH.

THE religious worship of the primitive Christians was conducted in the same simplicity and freedom which characterized all their ecclesiastical polity. They came together for the worship of God, in the confidence of mutual love, and prayed, and sung, and spoke in the fullness of their hearts. A liturgy and a prescribed form of prayer were alike unknown, and inconsistent with the spirit of their worship.

In this chapter, it will be my object to establish the following propositions:

I. That the use of forms of prayer is opposed to the spirit of the Christian dispensation.

II. That it is opposed to the *example* of Christ and of his apostles.

III. That it is unauthorized by the *instructions* of Christ and the apostles.

IV. That it is contrary to the simplicity and freedom of primitive worship.

V. That it was unknown in the primitive church.

I. The use of forms of prayer is opposed to the spirit of the Christian dispensation.

"The truth shall make you free." One part of this freedom was exemption from the burdensome rites and formalities of the Jewish religion. "The Lord's free man" was no longer bound to wear that yoke of bondage. According to the perfect law of liberty, James i. 25; ii. 12. Paul reproved Peter and others for their needless subjection to the bondage of the Jewish ritual, which imposed unauthorized burdens upon Christians, Gal. ii. 4, seq.; iii. 1, seq.; iv. 9, seq.; Rom. x. 4, seq.; xiv. 5, 6; Col. ii. 16–20. This perfect law of liberty, which the religion of Christ gave to his followers, imposed upon them no cumbersome rites; it required no prescribed forms, with the exception of the simple ordinances of baptism and the Lord's Supper.

Indications of irregularity and disorder are, indeed, apparent in some of the churches whom Paul addresses; particularly among the Corinthians, 1 Cor. xiv. 1, seq. These irregularities he severely rebukes, assuring them that God is not the author of confusion, but of peace, verse 33: of harmony in sentiment and in action. He ends his rebuke by exhorting them to let all things be done decently, and in order; declaring, at the same time, that the things which he writes on this subject *are the commandments of God*, verse 37. He commends the Colossians, on the other hand, for the good order and propriety which they observed; "joying and beholding their *order*, and the steadfastness of their faith," Col. ii. 5.

We will not assert that the spirit of prayer is incompatible with the use of a prescribed form; but we must feel that the warm and gushing emotions of a pious heart flow not forth in one unvaried channel. Who, in his favored moments of rapt communion, when with unusual fervor of devotion he draws near to God, and leaning on the bosom of the Father, with all the simplicity of a little child, seeks to give utterance to the prayer of his heart—who, under such circumstances, breathes to heaven his warm desires through the cold formalities of a prayer-book? When praying in the Holy Ghost, the Spirit itself helping our infirmities and making intercession for us with groanings that cannot be uttered, must we, can we, employ any prescribed form of words to express these unutterable things?[1] "Prayer by book," says Bishop Wilkins in his Gift of Prayer, "is commonly of itself something *flat and dead;* floating for the most part in generalities, and not particular enough for each several occasion. There is not that life and vigor in it to engage the affections as when it proceedeth immediately from the soul itself, and is the natural expression of those particulars whereof we are most sensible. It is not easy to express what a vast difference a man may find in respect to inward comfort and satisfaction between those private prayers that are rendered from the affections and those prescribed forms that we say by rote or read out of a book." So prayed not our Lord. Such were not the prayers of his disciples. This proposition introduces our second topic of remark.

II. The use of forms of prayer is opposed to the example of Christ and the apostles.

Several of our Lord's prayers are left on record, all of which plainly arose out of the occasion on which they were offered, and were strictly *extemporaneous.* So far as his example may be said to bear upon the subject, it is against the use of forms of prayer.

The prayers of the apostles were likewise occasional and *extemporaneous.* Such was the prayer of the disciples at the election of Matthias, Acts i. 24; of the church at the release of Peter and John, iv. 24–31; of Peter at the raising to life of Tabitha, ix. 40; of the church for the release of Peter under the persecution of Herod; and of Paul at his final interview with the elders of Ephesus, xx. 36; he

[1] Comp. Bishop Hall, in Porter's Homiletics, p. 294.

kneeled down upon the beach and prayed as the struggling emotions of his heart allowed him utterance.

It is particularly worthy of remark, that in all the examples of prayer in the New Testament, several of which are recorded apparently entire, there is no *similarity of form or of expression, nor any repetition of a form*, with the single exception of the response, Amen, Peace be with you, etc. Even our Lord's Prayer is never repeated on such occasions; nor is there, in all the New Testament, the slightest indication of its use either by the apostles or by the churches which they established.

Paul often requests the prayers of the churches to whom he writes, in regard to particulars so various and so minute as to forbid the supposition that they could have been expressed in a liturgy. The same may be said in regard to his exhortations to prayer, some of which, at least, are generally admitted to have relation particularly to *public prayer*, 1 Tim. ii. 1, seq. Who, on reading these various exhortations, without any previous opinions or partialities, would ever have been directed, by all that the apostle has written, to the use of any form of prayer?

Our Lord's Prayer itself is recorded with variations so great as to forbid the supposition that it was designed to be used as a prescribed form, as the reader must see by a comparison of the parallel passages in the margin.[2]

[2] In Matt. vi. 9-13.

ΠΑ'ΤΕΡ ἡμῶν ὁ ἐν τοῖς οὐρανοῖς· ἁγιασθήτω τὸ ὄνομά σου.

Ἐλθέτω ἡ βασιλεία σου· γενηθήτω τὸ θέλημά σου, ὡς ἐν οὐρανῷ, καὶ ἐπὶ τῆς γῆς.

Τὸν ἄρτον ἡμῶν τὸν ἐπιούσιον δὸς ἡμῖν σήμερον.

Καὶ ἄφες ἡμῖν τὰ ὀφειλήματα ἡμῶν,

In Luke xi. 2-4.

ΠΑ'ΤΕΡ, ἁγιασθήτω τὸ ὄνομά σου· ἐλθέτω ἡ βασιλεία σου.

Τὸν ἄρτον ἡμῶν τὸν ἐπιούσιον δίδου ἡμῖν τὸ καθ' ἡμέραν.

Καὶ ἄφες ἡμῖν τὰς ἁμαρτίας ἡμῶν

So great is the variation in these two forms that many have supposed they ought to be regarded as two distinct prayers. Such was the opinion of Origen. He notices the different occasions on which the two prayers were offered, and concludes that the resemblance is only such as might be expected from the nature of the subject.[3]

III. The use of forms of prayer is unauthorized by the instructions of Christ and the apostles.

If any instructions to this effect were given by Christ, they were in connection with the prayer which he taught his disciples. We have therefore to examine somewhat in detail the nature and design of the Lord's Prayer. The views of the learned respecting the nature of our Lord's Prayer and the ends designed by it are arranged by Augusti under three classes:

1. Those who maintain that Christ offered no prescribed form of prayer either for his immediate disciples or for believers in any age, but that he gave this as an example of the filial and reverential spirit in which we should offer our prayers to God, and of the simplicity and brevity which ought to characterize our supplications, in opposition to the vain repetitions of the heathen and the ostentatious formal-

ὡς καὶ ἡμεῖς ἀφίεμεν τοῖς ὀφειλέταις ἡμῶν.

Καὶ μὴ εἰσενέγκῃς ἡμᾶς εἰς πειρασμὸν, ἀλλὰ ῥῦσαι ἡμᾶς ἀπὸ τοῦ πονηροῦ.

καὶ γὰρ αὐτοὶ ἀφίεμεν παντὶ ὀφείλοντι ἡμῖν·

καὶ μὴ εἰσενέγκῃς ἡμᾶς εἰς πειρασμόν.

The doxology is generally supposed to be spurious; but without noticing the omission of this in Luke, the prayers are as various as they might be expected to be, if delivered extemporaneously on two different occasions, without any intention of offering either as a prescribed form of prayer.

[3] Βελτίον ἢ διαφόρους νομίζεσθαι τὰς προσευχὰς κοινά τινα ἐχοίσας μέρη. Περὶ εὐχῆς.—Vol. I. p. 227.

ities of the Pharisees. It is worthy of remark that this was originally given immediately after rebuking such hypocritical devotions, Matt. vi. 5. Augustine, A. D. 400, expressly declares that Christ did not teach his disciples what *words* they should use in prayer, but what *things they should pray for,* when engaged *in silent, mental prayer.*[4]

2. Those who contend that it is a specific and invariable form, to be used by Christians in all ages, like the baptismal formula in Matt. xxviii. 19, 20, though not to the exclusion of other forms of prayer.

3. Others incline to the opinion that the prayer is an epitome of the Jewish forms of prayer which were then in use, and that it comprised, in its several parts, the very words with which their prayers began, and which were embodied in one, as a substitute for so many long and unmeaning forms of prayer.

Whatever be the true view of this subject, it is remarkable that our Lord's Prayer was not in use in the age of the apostles. Not the remotest allusion to it occurs either in the history of the acts of the apostles or in their epistles. The supposition that, in all cases of prayer by the disciples and early Christians, the use of this form must be presumed, like that of the baptismal formula, is altogether gratuitous and groundless.

In the apostolical fathers, also, no trace is found of this prayer. Neither Clement, nor Polycarp, nor any father, makes allusion to it, antecedent to Justin Martyr, A. D. 148. And he informs us that in Christian assemblies, the presiding minister offered up prayer and thanksgiving, *as he was able,* ὅση δύναμις αὐτῷ, and that thereupon the people answered Amen! This expression, as we shall show in an-

---

[4] Non enim *verba,* sed *res ipsas* eos verbis docuit, quibus et seipsi commonefacerent a quo, et quid esset orandum cum in penetralibus, ut dictum est, mentis orarent.—*De Magistro,* c. 1, Vol. I. p. 402.

other place, means—*as well as he could, or to the best of his ability.* It shows that public prayers were not confined to any precomposed forms. The Lord's Prayer may have been used in connection with these extemporary addresses of the minister; but there is no evidence of such a usage. In describing the ceremony of baptism, Justin speaks of the use which is made of "the name of the universal Father," τὸ τοῦ Πατρὸς τῶν ὅλων, which is supposed by some to be an allusion to the expression, "our Father which art in heaven."

Lucian, A. D. 180, in his Philopatris, speaks of *the prayer which begins with the Father*, εὐχὴ ἀπὸ Πατρὸς ἀρξάμενη, which may possiby be a similar allusion to our Lord's Prayer.

Nothing much more explicit occurs in Irenaeus. He says, however, "*Christ has taught us to say in prayer, 'And forgive us our debts;' for he is our Father, whose debtors we are, having transgressed his precepts.*"[5] This passage only shows his acquaintance with the prayer, but proves nothing in relation to the liturgical use of it. The same may be said of Clement of Alexandria, who makes evident allusion to the Lord's Prayer in several passages.[6]

The Apostolical Constitutions belong to a later age, and cannot, therefore, be introduced as evidence in the question under consideration.

Tertullian, at the close of the second century and beginning of the third, together with Origen and Cyprian, who lived a few years later, gives more authentic notices of the Lord's Prayer.

Tertullian not only quotes the Lord's Prayer in various parts of his writings, but he has left a treatise "On Prayer," which consists of an exposition of it, with some remarks appended, concerning the customs observed in prayer. In

[5] Adv. Haeres. Lib. 5, c. 17.
[6] Especially Paedag. Lib. 3.

this treatise, which he is supposed to have written before he went over to Montanism, A. D. 200, Tertullian represents this prayer, not merely as an exemplar, or pattern of Christian petitions, but as the quintessence and ground of all prayer; and as a summary of the gospel.[7] He strongly recommends, however, other prayers, and enumerates the several parts of prayer, such as supplication, entreaty, confession of sin, and then proceeds to show that we may offer other petitions, according to our circumstances and desires, having premised this legitimate and ordinary prayer, which is the foundation of all.[8]

Cyprian, † A. D. 258, repeats the sentiments of Tertullian, whom he recognizes, to a great extent, as his guide in all points of doctrine. He wrote a treatise on the Lord's Prayer, on nearly the same plan as that of Tertullian. He has less spirit, but is more full than his predecessor; and often explains his obscurities. Cyprian says that our Lord, among other important precepts and instructions, gave us a form of prayer and taught us for what we should pray. He also styles the prayer, our public and common prayer;[9] and urges the use of it by considerations drawn from the nature of prayer, without asserting its liturgical authority or established use.

Origen, contemporary with Cyprian, has a treatise on prayer, in the latter part of which he comments at length upon the Lord's Prayer. His remarks are extremly dis-

[7] De Oratione, c. 1, pp. 129, 130.

[8] Quoniam tamen Dominus, prospector humanarum necessitatum, seorsum post traditam orandi disciplinam, "petite," inquit "et accipietis;" et sunt, quae petantur pro circumstantia cujusque, *praemissa legitima et ordinaria, oratione quasi fundamento; accidentium jus est desideriorum jus est superstruendi extrinsicus petitiones.*—De Orat. c. 10.

[9] Inter cetera sua salutaria monita et praecepta divina, ... etiam orandi ipse formam dedit, ... publica est nobis et communis oratio. —De Oratione, pp. 204-206.

cursive, and chiefly of a moral and practical character; so that we derive no satisfactory information from him respecting the liturgical use of this prayer, or of these prayers rather as he regards them. He, however, warns his readers against *vain repetitions and improper requests*, charging them not *to battologize* in their prayers;—an error which they could have been in no danger of committing, had they been guided by the dictation of a prayer-book. The explanation which he gives implies the use of extemporaneous prayer.[10]

It appears from the foregoing authorities, that our Lord's Prayer was never regularly used by the apostles themselves, nor by the churches which they founded until the close of the second century and beginning of the third. From this time it began to be used, and in the fifth and sixth centuries was a part of the public liturgies of the church.

With reference to the Lord's Prayer we subjoin the following remarks:

1. *It is questionable whether the words of this prayer were indited by our Lord himself.* If we adopt the theory of many, that it is a compend of the customary prayers in the religious service of the Jews, how can it with propriety be affirmed that our Lord gave to his disciples any *form of prayer* whatever as his own?

2. *This appears not to have been given to the disciples as a form of public prayer*, but as a specimen of that spirituality and simplicity which should appear in their devotions, in opposition to the "vain repetitions of the heathen" and the heartless formalities of the Pharisees. It merely enforces a holy importunity, sincerity and simplicity in *private prayer*. It was a prayer to be offered *in secret*, as the context in both instances indicates, Matt. vi. 3–14; Luke xi. 1–13.

3. Our Lord expressly enjoined upon his disciples to offer other petitions, of the highest importance, for which no form

[10] De Oratione, c. 21, p. 230.

is given. The gifts of the Holy Spirit are offered to those who shall ask, while yet no prescribed formula is given in which to make known our requests for this blessing. We have, therefore, the same authority, even from Christ himself, for extemporaneous as for precomposed prayer. Our Lord had no intention of prescribing an exact model of prayer, while at the same time he taught us to pray, without any form, for the highest blessing which we can receive.

4. A strict adherence to this form is incompatible with a suitable recognition of Christ as our Mediator and Intercessor with the Father. "Hitherto," said our Lord in his last interview with his disciples before he suffered, "ye have asked nothing *in my name.*" But a new and peculiar dispensation was opening to them, by which they might have "boldness to enter into the holiest by the blood of Jesus." The petitions of that prayer might, indeed, be suitable to the Christian in every age, and in all stages of his spiritual progress; but they are appropriate rather to those under the law than to those under grace.

5. This prayer belongs rather to the economy of the Old than to that of the New Testament. Christ was not yet glorified. The Spirit was not given; neither was the law of ordinances abolished. However useful or important it may have been in the worship of God under the Old Testament, is it of necessity imposed upon us under that better covenant which God has given, and by which he gives us nearness of access to his throne, without any of the formalities of the ancient Jewish ritual, only requiring us to worship him in spirit and in truth?

6. The variations of phraseology in the forms given by the evangelists are so great as to forbid the supposition that it is a specific and prescribed form of prayer. The only form of prayer that can be found in the Scriptures is recorded on two occasions, with such variations as to ex-

clude the possibility of deriving from either any authorized and unchangeable form. They have that general resemblance, united with circumstantial variations, which might be expected in the prayers of one who was careful only to utter the *same sentiments* without any studied phraseology or set form of words. They are as various as two extemporaneous prayers might be expected to be, if uttered upon two similar occasions with reference to the same subject.[11]

IV. The use of forms of prayer is contrary to the simplicity and freedom of primitive worship.

All the early records of antiquity relating to the ecclesiastical polity of the primitive Christians and to their rites of religious worship concur in the representation that they were conducted with the utmost simplicity, in total contrast both with the formalities of the ancient Mosaic ritual and with the various forms of episcopal worship and government which were subsequently introduced.[12] The men of those days accounted themselves the priests of God; and each, according to his ability, claimed the liberty not only to teach and to exhort, but even to administer the ordinances. All this is explicitly asserted in the commentary upon Eph. iv. 11, ascribed to Hilary of Rome, about A. D. 360: "After churches were everywhere established and ecclesiastical orders settled, the policy pursued was different from that which at first prevailed. *For, at first, all were accustomed to teach and to baptize, each on every day alike, as he had occasion.* Philip sought no particular day or occasion in which to baptize the eunuch, neither did he interpose any season of fasting. Neither did Paul and Silas delay the baptism of the jailer and all his house. Peter had the assistance of

[11] On this whole subject, comp. Augusti, Denkwürdigkeiten, Vol. V. S. 88-134.

[12] Comp. Schoene, Geschichtsforschungen, I. S. 91-132.

no deacons, nor did he seek for any particular day in which to baptize Cornelius and his household. He did not even administer the baptism himself, but entrusted this duty to *the brethren* who had come with him from Joppa; as yet there were no *deacons,* save the seven who had been appointed at Jerusalem. That the disciples might increase and multiply, all, in the beginning, were permitted to preach, to baptize and to expound the Scriptures. But when Christianity became widely extended, small assemblies were formed, pastors and presidents were appointed, and other offices instituted in the church. No one presumed without ordination to assume the office of the clergy. The writings of the apostles do not in all respects accord with the existing state of things in the church, *because these things were written at the time of the first organization of the church.*" [13]

There is a passage in Tertullian, also, indicative of the same absence of prescribed form and regularity: "After the reading of the Scriptures, psalms are sung, or addresses are made, or prayers are offered." [14] All is unsettled. The exercises are freely varied, according to circumstances. This absence of all established forms, and the universal enjoyment of religious liberty and equality, were, indeed, sometimes misunderstood and abused, even by the churches to whom the apostle writes; but they were far from offering any encouragement to the disorders and extravagancies of fanaticism. Observe, for example, the following upbraidings of such irregularities by Tertullian: "I must not fail to describe in this place the religious deportment of these heretics: how unseemly, how earthly, how carnal; without gravity, without respect, without discipline; how inconsist-

---

[13] Comment. ad Eph. iv. 11. Ambros. Opera, Vol. III. Comp. p. 230.

[14] Jam vero prout Scripturae leguntur, aut psalmi canuntur, aut adlocutiones proferuntur, aut petitiones delegantur.—*De Anima,* c. 9.

ent with their religious belief! Especially, it is wholly uncertain who may be a catechumen, who a Christian professor. They all assemble and sit promiscuously as hearers, and pray indiscriminately. How impudent are the women of these heretics, who presume to teach, to dispute, to exorcise, to practice magic arts upon the sick, and perhaps even to baptize! Their elections to offices in the church are hasty, inconsiderate and irregular. At one time they elect neophytes; at another, men of the world; and then apostates from us, that they may, at least, gain such by honor, if not by the truth. Nowhere is promotion easier than in the camps of rebels, where one's presence is a sure passport to preferment. Accordingly one is bishop to-day; to-morrow, another; to-day a deacon, to-morrow a reader; and he who is now a presbyter, to-morrow will be again a layman."[15]

In relation to this passage, which Neander quotes at length, he offers the following remarks, which we commend to the attentive consideration of the reader: "We here see the operations of two conflicting parties, one of which regards the original organization of the apostolical churches as a divine institution and an abiding ordinance in the church, essential to the spread of a pure Christianity. The other, which contends for an unrestrained freedom in all external matters, opposes these views as foreign to the freedom and simplicity which the spirit of the gospel encourages. It denies that the kingdom of God, itself inward, unseen, can need any outward organization for the support and spread of that kingdom. It contends that all Christians belong to the priesthood; and this it would practically exemplify by allowing no established distinction between the clergy and the laity, but permitting all in common to teach and to administer the sacraments—*two parties which*

---

[15] De Praescriptionibus Haeret. c. 41.

we often see opposed to each other in the subsequent history of the church. One of them lays great stress upon the outward organization of the visible church, by not suitably distinguishing between what may be a divine institution and what a human ordinance; the other holds the doctrine of an invisible kingdom; but overlooking the necessities of weak minds, which are incapable of forming conceptions of objects so spiritual, rejects with abhorrence all such ordinances." [16]

This same conflict of parties was transferred from the synagogue to the church. In the former, one party contended for a strict conformity to the Jewish ritual; the other insisted that no ritualistic forms should restrain the utterances of the soul in prayer, but each should pray according to the promptings of his own heart.[17]

V. The use of forms of prayer was unknown in the primitive church.

The apostolical fathers Clement and Polycarp give us no information concerning their modes of worship in the age immediately succeeding that of the apostles. The circumstances of their meeting in secresy and under cover of the latest hours of the night, together with other inconveniences, must be very unfavorable to the use of a liturgy, or any form of prayer. Tertullian and Eusebius represent the primitive Christians, of whom Pliny speaks, to have come together *ad canendum Christo, to sing praise to Christ.*

We are left, then, to the conclusion, that the apostolical churches neither used any forms of prayer, nor is such use authorized by divine authority. In this conclusion we are sustained by various considerations, drawn from the foregoing views of the simplicity of primitive worship.

---

[16] Antagonisticus, pp. 340, 341. 1825.
[17] Leyrer. in Hertzog's Encycl. 15, p. 307, supported by Jost. II. p. 45.

1. The supposition of a form of prayer is opposed to that simplicity, freedom of speech and absence of all formalities which characterized the worship of these early Christians.

In nothing, perhaps, was the worship of the Christian religion more strikingly opposed to that of the Jewish than in these particulars. The one was encumbered with a burdensome ritual, and celebrated, with many imposing formalities, by a priesthood divinely constituted, whose rank, and grades of office, and duties were defined with great minuteness, and observed with cautious precision. The other prescribed no ritual; designated no unchanging order of the priesthood; but, simply directing that all things should be done decently and in order, permitted all to join in the worship of God with unrestrained freedom, simplicity and singleness of heart. The one requires the worshiper to come with awful reverence, and, standing afar off, to present his offering to the appointed priest, who alone is permitted to bring it near to God. The other invites the humble worshiper to draw near in the full assurance of faith, and, leaning on the bosom of the Father with the confiding spirit of a little child, to utter his whole heart in the ear of parental love and tenderness. Is it not contrary, then, to the economy of this gracious dispensation to trammel the spirit of this little child with a studied form of speech; to chill the fervor of his soul by the cold dictations of another; and require him to give utterance to the struggling emotions of his heart in language, to him, uncongenial? Does it comport with the genius of primitive Christianity to lay upon the suppliant, in audience with his Father in heaven, the restraints of courtly formalities and the studied proprieties of premeditated prayer? The artlessness and simplicity of primitive worship afford a strong presumption in favor of free, extemporaneous prayer.

2. This presumption is strengthened by the example of

Christ and his apostles, all of whose prayers, so far as they are recorded or the circumstances related under which they were offered, were strictly extemporaneous.

This argument has been already duly considered, and may be dismissed without further expansion in this place.

3. We conclude that no forms of prayer were authorized or required in the apostolical churches, because no instructions to this effect are given either by Christ or the apostles.

The Lord's Prayer was not a prescribed form of prayer, neither was it in use in the apostolical churches; nor are any intimations given in the New Testament of any form of prayer, prayer-book, or ritual of any kind, unless the response, to which allusion is made in 1 Cor. xiv. 16, be considered as such. Here, then, is a clear omission, manifestly designed to show that God did not purpose to give any instructions respecting the manner in which we are to offer to him our prayers. This argument from the *omissions* of Scripture is presented with great force by Archbishop Whately in support of the opinion which we here offer, and we shall accordingly adopt his language to express it.

After asserting that the sacred writers were supernaturally withheld from recording some things, he adds: "On no supposition, whatever, can we account for the omission, by all of them, of many points which they do omit, and of their scanty and slight mention of others, except by considering them as withheld by the express design and will (whether *communicated* to each of them or not) of their heavenly Master, restraining them from committing to writing many things which, naturally, some or other of them, at least, would not have failed so to record.

"We seek in vain there for many things which, humanly speaking, we should have most surely calculated on finding. 'No such thing is to be found in our Scriptures as a catechism, or regular *elementary introduction* to the Christian religion; neither do they furnish us with anything of the nature of a systematic creed, set of articles, confession of faith, or by whatever other name one may designate a regular, complete compendium of Christian doctrines: *nor again do they supply us with a liturgy for ordinary public worship, or with forms for administering the sacraments, or for conferring holy orders;* nor do they even give any precise *directions* as to these and other ecclesiastical matters;—anything that at all corresponds to a rubric, or set of canons.'

"Now these omissions present a complete moral demonstration that the apostles and their followers must have been *supernaturally withheld* from recording a great part of the institutions and regulations which must, in point of fact, have proceeded from them;—withheld, *on purpose* that other churches, in other ages and regions, might not be led to consider themselves bound to adhere to several formularies, customs and rules that were of local and temporary appointment; but might be left to their own discretion in matters in which it seemed best to divine wisdom that they should be so left."[18]

4. No form of prayer, liturgy or ritual was recorded or preserved by the contemporaries, inspired or uninspired, of the apostles, or by their immediate successors.

This consideration is nearly allied to the former, and is so forcibly urged by Archbishop Whately that we shall again present the argument in his own words: "It was, indeed, not at all to be expected that the Gospels, the Acts and those Epistles which have come down to us, should have been, considering the circumstances in which they were written, anything different from what they are; but the question still recurs, why should not the apostles or their followers have also committed to paper what, we are sure, must have been perpetually in their mouths, regular in-

[18] Kingdom of Christ, pp. 82, 83.

structions to catechumens, articles of faith, prayers and directions as to public worship and administration of the sacraments? Why did none of them record any of the prayers, of which they must have heard so many from an apostle's mouth, both in the ordinary devotional assemblies, in the administration of the sacraments, and in the 'laying on of hands,' by which they themselves have been ordained?"[19]

The superstitious reverence of the early Christians for productions from the apostles and their contemporaries is apparent in the numerous forgeries of epistles, liturgies, etc., which were published under their name. Had any *genuine* liturgies of the apostolical churches been written, it is inconceivable that they should all have been lost, and such miserable forgeries as those of James, Peter, Andrew and Mark have been substituted in their place. Some discovery must have been made of these among other religious books and sacred things of the Christians, which in times of persecution were diligently sought out and burned. Strict inquiry was made after such; and their sacred books, their sacramental utensils, their cups, lamps, torches, vestments and other apparatus of the church were often delivered up, and burnt or destroyed. But there is no instance on record of any form of prayer, liturgy or book of divine service having been discovered in the early persecutions of the church. This fact is so extraordinary, that Bingham, who earnestly contends for the use of liturgies from the beginning, is constrained to admit that they could not have been committed to writing in the early periods of the church, but must have been preserved by oral tradition, and used "*by memory*, and made familiar by known and constant practice."[20] The reader has his alternative, between this

---

[19] Kingdom of Christ, pp. 252, 253.
[20] Antiq. Book 13, c. 5.

supposition, and that of no liturgy or prescribed form of prayer in those days of primitive simplicity. Constantine took special care to have fifty copies of the Bible prepared for the use of the churches of Constantinople, and, by a royal commission, entrusted Eusebius, the historian, with the duty of procuring them.[21] How is it, that the service-book was entirely omitted in this provision for the worship of God? Plainly, because they then used none.

5. The earliest fathers, in defending the usages of the church and deciding controversies, make no appeal to liturgies, but only to *tradition*.

"For these and other rites of a like character," says Tertullian, in speaking of the ceremonies of baptism and of the Lord's Supper—"for these, if you seek the authority of Scripture, you will find none. Tradition is your authority, confirmed by custom and faithfully observed."[22] But these should have a place in a liturgy. Cyprian advocates the mingling of water with wine at the Lord's Supper, by an appeal to tradition, without any reference to the liturgy of James.[23]

Firmilian, his contemporary, admits that the church at Rome did not strictly observe all things which may have been delivered at the beginning, "so that it was vain even to allege the authority of the apostles."[24]

Basil, A. D. 378, is even more explicit. After mentioning several things which are practised in the church without scriptural authority, such as the sign of the cross, praying toward the East, and the form of invocation in the consecration of the elements, he proceeds to say: "We do

[21] Euseb. Vit. Constant. Lib. 4, 36.

[22] Harum et aliarum hujusmodi disciplinarum si legem expostules scripturarum, nullam invenies. Traditio tibi praetenditur autrix, consuetudo confirmatrix, fides observatrix.—*De Corona Mil.* c. 4.

[23] Ep. 63, c. 2, ad Caecil.

[24] Ep. ad Cyprian, inter Ep. Cyp. 75, p. 144.

not content ourselves with what the apostle or the Gospel may have carefully recorded; with these we are not satisfied; but we have much to say before and after the ordinance, derived *from instructions which have never been written*, as having great efficacy in these mysteries." Among these unwritten and unauthorized rites, he enumerates afterward the consecration of the baptismal water. "From what writings, ἀπὸ ποίων ἐγγράφων," he asks, "comes this formulary? They have none; nothing but silent and secret tradition." [25]

From the fact that the appeal is only to tradition, we conclude, with Du Pin and others, that the apostles neither authorized nor left behind them any prescribed form of worship or liturgy.

6. That simplicity in worship which continued for some time after the age of the apostles forbids the supposition of the use of liturgical forms.

We return now to the second and third centuries, and, from the testimonies, particularly of Justin Martyr and Tertullian, we learn that the worship of the Christian church at this period continued to be conducted in primitive simplicity, without agenda, liturgy or forms of prayer.

Justin Martyr, in his Apology in behalf of the Christian religion, which he presented to the Roman emperor, Antoninus Pius, about A. D. 138 or 139,[26] gives a detailed account of the prevailing mode of celebrating the ordinances of baptism and the Lord's Supper in the Christian church, in which he repeatedly mentions the *prayers* which are offered in these solemnities: "After baptizing the believer and making him one with us, we conduct him to the brethren, as they are called, where they are assembled, fervently to offer their common supplications for themselves, for him

---

[25] De Spiritu Sancto, c. 27.
[26] Justin Martyr, by C. Semisch, Vol. I. p. 72. Trans. Ed. 1843.

who has been illuminated and for all men everywhere; that we may live worthy of the truth which we have learned, and be found to have kept the commandments, so that we may be saved with an everlasting salvation. After prayer, we salute one another with a kiss. After this, bread and a cup of wine and water are brought to the president, which he takes, and offers up praise and glory to the Father of all things, through the name of the Son and of the Holy Spirit, and gives thanks that we are accounted worthy of these things. When he has ended the prayers and the thanksgiving, all the people present respond Amen! which, in Hebrew, signifies *So may it be.*"

The description above given relates to the celebration of the Lord's Supper when baptism was administered. In the following extract Justin describes the ordinary celebration of the supper on the Lord's day: "On the day called Sunday we all assemble together, both those who reside in the country and they who dwell in the city, and the commentaries of the apostles and the writings of the prophets are read as long as time permits. When the reader has ended, the president, in an address, makes an application, and enforces an imitation of the excellent things which have been read. *Then we all stand up together and offer up our prayers.* After our prayers, as I have said, bread and wine and water are brought, and the president, in like manner, offers prayers and thanksgivings *according to his ability, ὅση δύναμις αὐτῷ,* and the people respond, saying Amen!"[27]

Justin, according to Eusebius,[28] wrote his Apologies at Rome. He was personally acquainted with most of the principal churches in every land. Whether we regard this as descriptive of the usage of the church at Rome or of the churches generally, it is gratifying to learn, from a witness

[27] Apol. 1, 61, 65, 67, pp. 71, 82, 83. See above, 168.
[28] Hist. Eccl. Lib. 4, c. 11.

so unexceptionable, that the church in his time continued still to worship God in all the simplicity of the primitive disciples. They meet as brethren in Christ; they exchange still the apostolical salutation, the kiss of charity; the Scriptures are read, and the president or pastor makes a familiar address, enforcing the practical duties which have been presented in the reading; a prayer is offered in the consecration of the sacred elements, in which the suppliant prays *according to his ability*, following only the suggestions of his own heart, without any form; after this, they receive the bread and the wine in remembrance of Christ. All is done in the affectionate confidence, the simplicity and singleness of heart of the primitive disciples.[29]

The testimony of Justin, however, is claimed on both sides. The whole controversy hinges on that vexed passage, ὅση δύναμις αὐτῷ. The congregation all stood up, and the president prayed, ὅση δύναμις αὐτῷ, *according to his ability*. Some understand by this phrase, that he *prayed with as loud a voice as he could;* the very mention of which interpretation is its sufficient refutation: *cujus mentio est ejus refutatio.* Others translate it, *with all the ardor and fervency of his soul.*

Such are the interpretations of those who contend for the use of a liturgy in the primitive church. On the other hand, Justin is understood to say that the president prayed *as well as he could*, to the best of his ability, or, as Tertullian says, "*ex proprio ingenio.*" If this be the true meaning, it leads to the conclusion that the prayers offered on this occasion were strictly extemporaneous. This is the interpretation not only of non-conformists generally, but of some churchmen. It is the only fair interpretation of the phrase, according to the *usus loquendi* of this author.

[29] Comp. Schoene, Geschichtsforschungen der Kirch. Gebräuche, I. S. 102, 103.

The same expression occurs in other passages of our author, which may serve to illustrate his meaning in this equivocal phrase:

"We who worship the Ruler of the universe are not atheists. We affirm, as we are taught, that he has no need of blood, libations and incense. But, with supplication and thanksgivings, we praise him according to our ability, ὅση δύναμις, *for all which we enjoy*, ἐφ' οἷς προσφερόμεθα πᾶσιν, having learned that worthily to honor him is not to consume in fire by sacrifice what he has provided for our sustenance, but to bestow it upon ourselves and upon the needy, to show ourselves thankful to him by invocations and hymns for our birth, our health and all that he has made, and for the vicissitudes of the season."[30]

The Catholic and Episcopal rendering of this passage makes the author say, that in *all our offerings*, ἐφ' οἷς προσφερόμεθα πᾶσιν, we praise him, ὅση δύναμις, with the *utmost fervency of devotion*. This, however, is a mistaken rendering of the verb, προσφέρομαι, which, in the *middle voice*, means not to offer in sacrifice or to worship, but to *participate, to enjoy*. So it is rendered by Scapula, Hedericus, Bretschneider, Passow, etc. The passage relates, not to an act of sacrifice, nor of *public worship*, as the connection shows, but to deeds of piety toward God and of benevolence to men, done according to their ability; by which means they offered the best refutation of the groundless calumnies of their enemies, who had charged them with an atheistical neglect of the gods. The declaration is, that for all their blessings they express, *according to their ability*, thanksgivings to God, and testify their gratitude by deeds of charity to their fellow-men.

"Having, therefore, exhorted you, ὅση δύναμις, *according to our ability*, both by reason and a visible sign or figure, we

---

[30] Apol. 1, c. 13, pp. 50, 51.

know that we shall henceforth be blameless if you do not believe, for *we have done what we could for your conversion.*"[31] He had done what he could; by various efforts of argument and exhortation and by visible signs he had labored, according to his ability, to bring them to receive the truth. The exhortation was the free expression of his heart's desire for their conversion. Can there be any doubt that the phrase denotes the same freedom of expression in prayer?[32]

If one desires further satisfaction on this point, he has only to turn to the works of Origen, in which this and similar forms of expression are continually occurring, to denote the invention, ability and powers of the mind. Origen, in his reply to the calumnies of Celsus, proposes to refute them "according to his ability."[33] In his preface, he has apologized for the Christians "as well as he could."[34] These Christians sought, "as much as possible," to preserve the purity of the church.[35] They strove to discover the hidden meaning of God's word, "according to the best of their abilities."[36] In these instances the reference is not to the fervor of the spirits, the ardor of the mind, but to the exercise of the mental powers. The act performed is done

[31] Apol. 1, c. 55, p. 77.
[32] Comp. King, in the author's Ancient Christianity, 274, 309.
[33] Ὅση δύναμις, Lib. 6, § 1, Vol. I. p. 694; so also, κατὰ τὸ δύνατον, § 12, p. 638.
[34] Κατὰ τὴν παροῦσαν δύναμιν, Praef. Lib. contr. Cel.
[35] Ὅση δύναμις, Contr. Cel. Lib. 3, Vol. I. p. 482.
[36] Lib. 6, § 2, p. 630. Comp. also in Comment. in Matt. ὅση δύναμις, Tom. 17, Vol. III. p. 809; κατὰ τὸ δύνατον, Tom. 16, Vol. III. p. 735; κατὰ δύναμιν, Tom. 17, Vol. III. p. 779, also Vol. IV. p. 6; κατὰ τὴν παροῦσαν δύναμιν, Tom. 17, Vol. III. p. 794.

In Clarkson's Discourse on Liturgies many other passages are given from Justin, Origen, Chrysostom, Basil, etc., all illustrating the same use of the phrase. Select Works, London, 1846, p. 294, seq.

according to the ingenuity, the talents of the agents in each case.

Basil, in giving instructions how to pray, advises to make choice of scriptural forms of thanksgiving, and when you have praised him thus, *according to your ability,* ὡς δύνασαι, exactly equivalent to δύναμις—then he advises the suppliant to proceed to petitions.[37] The Greeks and the Romans pray each in their own language, according to Origen, and each praises God *as he is able.*[38] But enough has been said upon this point, and the reader may safely be left to his own conclusions.

We come next to Tertullian. " We Christians pray with eyes uplifted, with hands outspread, with head uncovered; and, ... *without a monitor, because from the heart.*"[39] Can this be the manner of one praying from a prayer-book? Clarkson has shown, with his usual clearness, that the heathen worshiped by ritual, ... and rehearsed their prayers from a book; and that Tertullian says this to contrast the Christian mode of worship with these heartless forms. The ancient fire-worshipers " read the daily offices of their liturgy" before their sacred fire. The Pagan liturgy of the old Romans was read in a language obsolete and almost unintelligible, like the present Romish liturgy. The Lacedemonians were strict liturgists.[40] But these warm-hearted Christians needed no such promptings to give utterance to their devotions. Out of the abundance of the heart the mouth speaketh.

[37] Basil, De Ascet., Vol. II. p. 536.
[38] ὡς δύναται, Origen Contra Cels. Lib. 8, c. 37, p. 769.
[39] Illuc sursum suspicientes Christiani manibus expansis, quia innocuis, capite nudo, quia non erubescimus; denique sine monitore, quia de *pectore oramus.*—*Apol.* c. 30.
[40] Clarkson, Liturgies. Prideaux, Connections, Part I. Book IV. Potter's Antiq. of Greece, I. p. 281-288.

Again, "When the sacramental supper is ended, and we have washed our hands, and the candles are lighted, every one is invited to sing unto God, as he is able; either in psalms collected from the Holy Scriptures or composed by himself, *de proprio ingenio*. And as we began, so we conclude all with prayer."[41]

From Tertullian we have the earliest information respecting the religious ordinances of the churches in Africa. The reader will not fail to notice that this church also retains still the simplicity of the apostolical churches mingled with some Roman customs. Their religious worship opens with prayer, after which the Scriptures are read and familiar remarks are offered upon them. Then follows the sacramental supper, or more properly the love-feast of the primitive church, which they begin with prayer. After the supper, any one is invited to offer a sacred song, either from the Scriptures, or indited by himself. And the whole ends with prayer. The entire narrative indicates a free, informal mode of worship, as far removed from that which is directed by the agenda and rituals of liturgical worship as can well be conceived.

In the same connection, Tertullian also forcibly illustrates the sincerity and purity of this primitive worship. Speaking of the subjects of their prayers, he says: "These blessings I cannot persuade myself to ask of any but of Him from whom alone I know that I can obtain them. For he only can bestow them. And to me he is covenanted to grant them. For I am his servant, and him only do I serve. For this service I stand exposed to death, while I offer to him the noblest and best sacrifice which he requires—*prayer proceeding from a chaste body, an innocent soul and a sancti-*

---

[41] Apol. c. 39. This *implies* extempore prayer, though does not exclude a devout use of a form, *memoriter*.

fied spirit."[42] Beautiful exemplification of the words of our Lord to the woman of Samaria: " Believe me, the hour cometh when ye shall neither in this mountain, nor yet at Jerusalem, worship the Father. God is a spirit, and they that worship him must worship him in spirit and in truth.' John iv. 21, 24.

The authority of Tertullian is against the supposition that the primitive churches used forms of prayer. " We pray *without a monitor, because from the heart,"* sine monitore quia de pectore. This passage is conclusive evidence that their prayers were informal, extempore, in contrast with those of the heathen, whose custom was to rehearse their prayers from a prescribed form, repeating the words *after a monitor* reading from the prayer-book the exact form of words. We Christians have no form, no monitor; because we pray from the heart, and out of the abundance of the heart the mouth speaketh. The custom is affirmed and examples given in the notes.

Alexander the Great, on the eve of battle, calls Aristander, his monitor, his priest, to rehearse his prayers in order to propitiate his gods. Decius the Roman consul, and Claudius the emperor, prayed in like manner under similar circumstances.[43]

---

[42] Apol. c. 30. Comp. De Orat. 29.

[43] Vidimus certis praecationibus, obsecrasse summos magistratus: et, ne quid verborum praetereatur, aut praepesterum dicatur, de scripto praeire aliquem; . . . . cujus sacri praecationem, qua solet praeire quindecimvirûm collegii magister si quis legat, etc.,—*Pliny.* Nat. Hist. B. XXVIII. 2. Alexander, non alias magis territus, ad vota et preces Aristandrum vocari jubet. Ille in candida veste, verbenas in manu praeferens, capite velato *praeibat preces regi* Jovem, Minervam, victoriamque propitianti.—*Q. Curtius*, Lib. IV. c. 13. In hac tripidatione, Decius consul M. Vabrium, magna voce inclamat! Deorum inquit, ope, Valeri, opus est, Agedum, pontifex publicus populi Romani, praei verba, quibus me pro legionibus devoveam. Then

The manner was, at the beginning of the third century, to repeat the Lord's Prayer as the basis and pattern of all appropriate prayer to God, and then to enlarge in free, unpremeditated supplications, according to the circumstances and desires of the suppliant.

Another circumstance mentioned above by Tertullian shows how far the worship of the primitive Christians was at this time from being confined to the prescribed and unvarying formalities of a ritual. It appears that in their social worship each was invited to sing praises to God either from the Holy Scriptures or "*de proprio ingenio,*" *of his own composing.* Grant, if you please, that these sacred songs may have been previously composed by each. They are still his own, and have to the hearer all the novelty and variety of a strictly extemporaneous effusion. So he who leads in prayer, like the one who sings his song, may offer a free prayer which he has previously meditated. But, in the opinion of many, such songs may have been offered *impromptu*, like the songs of Moses and Miriam, and Deborah, Simeon and Anna. Augustine speaks of such songs, and ascribes to divine inspiration the ability to indite them. The improvisatori of the present age are an example of the extent to which such gifts may be cultivated without any supernatural aid."[44] If, therefore, such freedom was allowed in their psalmody, much more might it be expected in their prayers.

7. The *attitude* of the primitive Christians in prayer is

---

he prays to Janus, Jupiter, Mars, Quirinus, Bellona, etc., the pontifex maximus directing the form.—Liv. Lib. VIII. c. 9. Claudius made a rule that, dira avi in urbe aut in Capitolio visa, obsecratio haberetur, eamque ipse, jure Maximi Pontificis, commonito pro rostris, populo, *praeiret.*—*Sueton.* Claudius, c. 22.

[44] Comp. Walch. De. Hymn. Eccl. Apost. § 20. Münter, Metr. Offenbar. Pref.

against the supposition that they used a prayer-book. It was with arms raised toward heaven and hands outspread,[45] or it was kneeling and prostrate, with the eyes closed, to shut out from view every object that might divert the mind from its devotions, or, as Origen expresses it, "*closing the eyes of his senses, but erecting those of his mind.*" Few facts in ancient history are better attested than this. The coins that were struck in honor of Constantine represent him in the attitude of prayer. But how? Not with prayer-book in hand, but *with hands extended* and *eyes upturned, as if looking toward heaven, ὡς ἄνω βλέπειν δοκεῖν ἀνατεταμένος.*[46]

"His portrait also at full length was placed over the entrance gates of the palaces in some cities, the eyes upraised to heaven, and the hands outspread as if in prayer."

We raise the head and lift the hands to heaven.[47]

Now all this, if not absolutely incompatible with the use of a liturgy, must be allowed to have been a very inconvenient posture, upon the supposition that a liturgy was employed.

8. We have yet to add that the manner in which preconceived prayers began to be used is decisive against any divine authority for their use. That in the earliest stages of the episcopal system there was no settled and invariable form of prayer is an acknowledged historical fact. All that was required was that the prayers should not be unpremeditated, but previously composed and committed to writing. Still they were *occasional*, and may have had all the variety

---

[45] Illuc sursum suspicientes Christiani manibus expansis, etc. Tertul. Apol. c 30. Comp. De Orat. c. 14. Non tollimis tantum sed expandimus [manus]. Οὕτως αὐτάς εἰς εὐχὴν ανατείνωσιν.—*Chrysost. in Homil.* 57.

[46] Euseb. Vit. Const. Lib. IV. c. 15.

[47] Προσεντείνομεν τὴν κιφαλὴν καὶ τὰς χεῖρας εἰς οὐρανὸν αἴρομεν.— *Clemen. Alex. Strom.* Lib. 7.

and adaptation of extempore prayers. This fact strikingly exhibits an intermediate state in the transition of the church from that freedom and absence of forms which characterized her earliest and simplest worship to the imposing formalities of a later date. But it precludes the supposition that an authorized liturgy could have previously existed.

9. If it were necessary to multiply arguments on this point, we might mention the secret discipline of the church as evidence against the use of a liturgy. This of itself is regarded by Schöne and others as conclusive on this subject, a written and prescribed liturgy being quite incompatible with these mysteries. Basil refused to give explanations in writing to Miletus, but referred him to Theophrast for verbal information, that so the mysteries might not be divulged by what he would have occasion to write. "Mysteries," said Origen also, with reference to the same point, "must not be committed to writing." The sacramental prayers and baptismal rites, which should have a place in a liturgy, were among these profound mysteries. How they could have been kept veiled in such mystery if recorded in a prayer-book, is past our comprehension.

Basil, of the fourth century, informs us that he pronounced the doxology with varied phraseology—that the baptismal formulary was unrecorded, and that the church had not even a written creed or confession.[48] Clarkson has shown by a multitude of citations that the same is true of every part of religious worship which a liturgy prescribes. He has also given many instances of occasional prayers, which are inconsistent with the supposition that they were rehearsed from a prayer-book.[49]

Finally, the origin of these ancient liturgies and the oc-

---

[48] Αὐτὴν δὲ ὁμολογίαν τῆς πίστεως εἰς πατέρα καὶ υἱὸν καὶ ἅγιον πνεῦμα ἐκ ποίων γραμμάτων ἔχομεν.—*De Spiritu Sancto*, c. 27, p. 57; comp. p. 55.

[49] Discourse on Liturgies.

casion on which they were prepared is no recommendation of them.

They were adopted from pagan rituals, and had their origin in an ignorant and degenerate age. Palmer ascribes the four original liturgies, in which all others have originated, to the *fifth century.* He thinks, however, that some expressions in one may perhaps be traced to the fourth. The utmost that even the credulity of the Oxford Tractarians pretends to claim in favor of their antiquity is, that "one, that of Basil, may be traced with tolerable certainty to the fourth century, and three others to the middle of the fifth."[50] Ambrose, Augustine, Gregory, Basil and Chrysostom, those great luminaries of the church, had passed away, and an age of ignorance and superstition had succeeded. Riddle of Oxford, the faithful chronicler of the church, gives the following sketch of the degeneracy of this age, the close of the fourth century:

"*Superstitious veneration of martyrs* and their relics, credulous reliance upon their reputed powers of intercession, reports of miracles and visions at their tombs, and other follies of this kind, form a prominent feature in the religion of the age.

"*New Festivals during this century.*—Christmas-day, Ascension-day, Whitsunday (in the modern sense).

"*Baptismal Rites, Ceremonies,* etc.—1. Wax tapers in the hands of the candidates; 2. Use of salt, milk, wine and honey; 3. Baptisteries; 4. Easter and Whitsuntide, times of baptism; 5. Twofold anointing, before and after baptism; 6. Dominica in Albis.

"*The Lord's Supper,* 1, was now commonly called Missa by the Latins; 2. Tables had come into use, and were now called *altars;* 3. *Liturgies used at the celebration of the rite;*

---

[50] Tract, No. 63, Vol. I. p. 439.

4. Elements still administered in both kinds as before;
5. No private masses.

"*Rapid progress of church oligarchy, and formation of the patriarchate.*"

Again, A. D. 439: "*Christian morality declines.*—Two distinct codes of morals gradually formed, one for perfect Christians, and another for the more common class of believers; the former consisting of mysticism and ascetic or overstrained virtue, *the latter in the performance of outward ceremonies and ritual observances.* The distinction itself unsound and mischievous; the morality, to a great extent, perverted or fictitious.

"History now records fewer examples of high Christian character than before. Complaints of the fathers and decrees of councils lead us to fear that *impiety and disorderly conduct* prevailed within the borders of the church to a melancholy extent. *Superstition makes rapid progress.*"[51]

Out of this age, when nothing was introduced "but corruptions and the issues thereof, no change made in the current usages but for the worse, no motions from its primitive posture but downward into degeneracy"—out of this age proceeded the first liturgy, the offspring of ignorance and superstition!

The clergy had become notoriously ignorant and corrupt, unable suitably to guide the devotions of public worship; and to assist them in their ignorance and incompetence, liturgies were provided for their use.[52] "When, in process of time, the distinguished fathers of the church had passed

---

[51] Riddle's Chronology, A. D. 400, A. D. 439.

[52] The reader will find abundant evidence of this ignorance in the councils of this age and in Blondell, Apologia Hieron., pp. 500, 501, Clarkson, Discourse on Liturgies, Works, 364–374, and Witsius, Exercitat. De Oratione, § 30, 31, p. 85. In the council of Ephesus, in the fifth century, Elias signs his name by the hand of another, *because*

away, and others of an inferior standing arose in their places with less learning and talents for public speaking—as barbarism and ignorance continued to overspread the Roman empire, and after the secret mysteries of Christianity had been done away, or, at least, had assumed another form of manifestation—then the clergy, not being competent themselves to conduct the exercises of religious worship to the edification of the people, saw the necessity of providing themselves with written formulas for their assistance. For this purpose men were readily found to indite and transcribe them. In this manner arose its formularies, which are known under the name of liturgies and missals, and which afterward, in order to give greater authority to them, were ascribed to distinguished men, and even to the apostles themselves, as their authors." [53]

Shall, then, superstition, ignorance and barbarism, rather than God's own word, teach us how we may most acceptably pray unto him? Shall we forsake the example of Christ and the apostles to imitate ignorant men, who first made use of a liturgy because they were unable, without it, decently to conduct the worship of God?

How forcibly does the formality of such liturgical services contrast with the simplicity and moral efficacy of primitive

---

he could not write his name; eo quod nesciam literas. So, also, Cajumas: *propterea quod literas ignorem.*

The ignorance of the English clergy was equally notorious. Alfred the Great declares that he did not know a single priest south of the Thames who was able to read prayers.—*Spelman's Life of Alfred.*

The books of homilies, even as late as the reigns of Edward VI. and of Queen Elizabeth, were prepared for the use of the clergy, because they were too ignorant to prepare original discourses for themselves. "Had there been men enough who could preach, there would have been never a homily devised."

[53] Sechöne, Geschichtsforschungen, der Kirch. Gebräuche, II. S. 120, 121.

worship! Christianity ascends the throne, and, in connection with the secular power, gives laws to the state. The government has a monarch at its head; and the church, bishops in close alliance with him. The simple rites of religion, impressive and touching by their simplicity, have given place to an imposing and princely parade in religious worship. Splendid churches are erected. The clergy are decked out with gorgeous vestments, assisted by a numerous train of attendants, and proceed in the worship of God with all the formalities of a prescribed and complicated ritual. Age after age these liturgical forms continue to increase with the superstition and degeneracy of the church, until her service becomes encumbered with an inconceivable mass of missals, breviaries, rituals, pontificals, graduals, antiphonals, psalteries, etc., alike unintelligible and unmeaning.

But the simplicity of primitive Christianity gives it power. It has no cumbersome rites to embarrass the truth of God. Nothing to dazzle the eye, to amuse and occupy the mind that is feeling after God, if haply it may find him. All its solemn rites are in harmony with the simplicity of that system of gospel truth which is at once the wisdom of God and the power of God in the conversion of men.

REMARKS.

1. To the people of the congregation forms of prayer are inappropriate.

How variable the infinite play of the passions in the heart, and how preposterous the attempt to give utterance to them in one unvarying tone! As if the harp of David were always strung to the same key and sounded one unchanging note! First stereotype the mind and heart of man, and then is he prepared to express his devotions in the unvarying letter of a liturgy.

Amid all the ills that man is heir to, new and unforeseen calamities are ever and anon met with, which bring men to the throne of grace with supplications and entreaties of a special character, whereof the liturgy takes no account.

2. Liturgical forms become wearisome by constant repetition.

The love of change is inherent in the breast of man. We must have variety. Without it, even our refined pleasures lose their charm in a dull and dead monotony. So a liturgy, however excellent in diction or noble in sentiment, loses its interest by perpetual repetition. The continual recurrence even of the best possible form, that of the Lord's Prayer, injures its effect upon our own mind. We have heard it at the table in our daily meals; at morning and evening prayer, and in some instances it has been the only prayer offered in our hearing on such occasions; at funerals, at marriages, in baptism, in confirmation, at the sacrament of the Lord's Supper, and in every public service, not once merely, but twice or thrice, and even more than this; as if no religious act could be rightly done without the introduction somewhere of the Lord's Prayer. Such ceaseless repetition only creates a weariness of spirit which earnestly craves a freer and more informal mode of worship. "How often have I been grieved to observe coldness and comparative indifference in the *reading-desk*, but warmth and animation in the pulpit! In how many different places have I been obliged to conclude, This man preaches in earnest, but prays with indifference! I have asked myself, I have asked others, what is the reason of such conduct."[54] The case so embarrassing to our churchman is easily explained. At the reading-desk the Episcopal preacher utters the cold dictations of another; in the pulpit he expresses the warm

[54] Churchman, in Christian Observer, 1804, p. 271.

suggestions of his own heart. Here, accordingly, his utterance is instinct with life and spirit; there, it is changed by perpetual repetition into chilling indifference, a monotonous dead letter.

3. A liturgy is often not in harmony with the subject of discourse.

The preceding remarks relate to the disadvantages of the liturgy to the people; the present, and some that follow, have reference to the inconvenience experienced by the clergymen from the same source. Every preacher knows the importance of harmony in his services. And if permitted, in the freedom of primitive worship, to direct them accordingly, he studiously seeks to make the impression from the prayers, the psalmody and the reading of the Scriptures coincident with the subject of his sermon; so that all may conspire to produce a single impression upon the hearer. The final result upon the audience is ascribable in a great degree to the harmony which pervades the entire service. But here the liturgy interposes its unyielding forms to break up this harmony of the service and sadly to impair the effect of it upon the audience.

4. The liturgy is not a suitable preparation for the impression of the sermon.

Much of the practical *effect* of the preacher's discourse depends upon the previous preparation of the mind for it. This preparation results, in a great degree, from a happy adaptation of the preliminary services to this end. But the preliminaries of the liturgy move on with unvarying formality, carrying the mind, it may be, directly away from the subject of the discourse that is to follow, or leaving the audience uninterested and unprepared for any quickened impression from the preacher. All has been done with cold and decent formality, but the profiting of the hearer is not apparent. How much of the inefficacy of the pulpit in the Episcopal Church is ascribable to this cause, we leave the reader to judge.

5. A liturgy curtails unreasonably the time allotted to the sermon.

A sermon may be, and often is, too long; it may also be too short. Following the protracted recitals of the liturgy, it is necessarily crowded into a narrow space at the conclusion of a service which has already unfitted the audience for a calm, sustained attention to the preacher. What he has to say must be quickly said; he therefore hurries through a brief and superficial exposition of his subject and dismisses it with a hasty application, before it has had time to assume in the hearer's mind that importance which belongs to its momentous truths. The final result is that it falls powerless upon the consciences of the audience.

6. The liturgy exalts the inventions of man above the truth of God.

The liturgy is ever prominently before the audience, claiming the first attention, the highest place in all the acts of worship. The tendency of the whole arrangement is to keep back the word of God, to hold in check its power as the means of salvation, and to substitute in its place a system of mere formalism.

In this connection the profound remarks of Archbishop Whately, respecting undue reliance on human authority, are worthy of serious consideration. He exposes with great force the disposition of men to "obtrude into the place of Scripture, creeds, catechisms and liturgies, and other such compositions, set forth by any church." The disposition he ascribes to deep-seated principles of our nature. He supposes that nothing but a miraculous providence could have so directed the apostles and primitive Christians that they left no such formulary of religious worship or compend of the Christian faith. "Such a systematic course of instruction, carrying with it divine authority, would have superseded the framing of any *other*—nay, would have made even the alteration of a single word, of what would on this supposition have been Scripture, appear an impious presumption. . . . . So that there would have been an almost inevitable danger that such an authoritative list of credenda would have been regarded, by a large proportion of Christians with a blind, unthinking reverence, which would have exerted no influence on the character. They would have had a form of godliness; but, denying the power therof, the form itself would have remained with them only the corpse of departed religion."[55]

The Romans were ritualists of the severest order. A deviation in a single word from their liturgical forms was an ill omen, vitiating the efficacy of their prayer. To prevent this, a prompter was required to rehearse the prayer, word for word, for the devotee at his devotions. The introduction of new liturgical forms was a grievous offence against the state. In the time of the first Punic war there was a crowd of women who neither sacrificed nor prayed according to the established form. This first gave great umbrage to good men, then it was reported to the Senate, who severely reprimanded the aediles and triumvirs—answering to our grand jury—because they had not prevented it, and ordered the praetor—the mayor of the city—to suppress the evil. This he accomplished by ordering all who had in their possession forms of prayer, or written rubrics, to deliver them to him before the first of April.[56]

Thus history repeats itself from age to age. The ritualists of to-day, in enacting again these heathenish superstitions

---

[55] Errors of Romanism, pp. 49-61.

[56] Edixit ut quicunque libros vaticinos, praecationesve, aut artem sacrificandi conscriptam haberet eos libros omnes literasque ad se ante calendas Apriles deferret.—*Liv.*, lib. XXV. c. 1.

of the Romans, forcibly illustrate the foregoing profound remarks of Archbishop Whately, while they suggest an urgent reason for confining the ceremonials of religion within the strictest limits. But this continual recital of creeds and confessions, this perpetual profession of faith in the "holy catholic church," these rites of the ritual ever recurring and foremost in importance, to which everything else gives place in public worship,—who can doubt the practical influence of all this? It casts into shade and distance God's own word. It brings forward the dictations of canonized tradition as the rule of faith and of worship; and spiritual truth is forgotten in this parading of the ceremonials of religion.

7. The book of Common Prayer dishonors the holy Sabbath.

We have sought in vain for any clear expression of the divine authority of the Lord's day. It is specified in the calendar among many other holy days of the holy church, some of which seem to be regarded with equal reverence. The specifications respecting it all serve to direct the mind to it as merely an ordinance of the church. They bring it down from its lofty place as a divine institution, and blend it unworthily with a multitude of saints' days, which a blind superstition first established and still venerates. When the true doctrine of the sacred Sabbath was first promulgated, it encountered for half a century the furious opposition of the established church on this very principle, that it was derogatory to the authority of the church, and to the reverence due to its festivals and fasts. Its advocates were suspended from their ministerial duties, deposed and imprisoned for daring to assert that this holy Sabbath depended on higher authority than the usage and decrees of the church. Whatever may be the sentiments of Episcopalians at present respecting this day, we cannot resist the conviction that it has in the prayer-book no higher place than the other holy days of the church.

8. We object to the popish origin and tendencies of the English liturgy.

It is a translation and compend of the popish ritual, and still savors strongly of its origin. Must we, in this nineteenth century, go back to the dark ages of popery to learn from its traditions, its superstitions, how we may best worship God in spirit and in truth? But this "pathetic litany," "this noble liturgy," it is said, "is it not admirable?"

Let us examine a little. What change has the liturgy undergone in passing over from the Romish to the English Church. The chief points of distinction, according to Hallam, are the following:

1. The liturgy was translated into the vernacular language of the people. Formerly it had been in an unknown tongue.

2. Its acts of idolatrous worship to saints and images were expunged.

3. Auricular confession was done away; or rather it was left to every man's discretion, and went into neglect.

4. "The doctrine of transubstantiation, or the change, at the moment of consecration, of the substances of bread and wine into those of Christ's body and blood," was discarded.

5. The celibacy of the clergy was abolished.[57]

With these modifications the religion of Rome became that of the Church of England. And to this day her ritual, crudely formed in the infancy of Protestantism, which Milton denominates "an extract of the mass translated,"* continues, with little variation, to be the liturgy of the whole Episcopal Church in England and America.

[57] Constitutional History, Vol. I. pp, 116–126.
* See the Appendix.

Miles Coverdale objected to it that it was "reformed *Pope-wise.*" To which Whitehead, one of the commission under Elizabeth to reform the service, replied that they were "under her strait behest to purge the liturgy of all that might give scandal or offence to the papists." Thus it was "patched together out of the popish matins, even-song and mass-books." Many of the Catholics continued in office under the establishment, considering that "there was nothing in the service of the English Church which was repugnant to that of Rome." As the ancient church condescended to a debasing compromise with Paganism, so the English Church studiously sought alliance with Romanism.

For similar reasons the Puritans refused the ceremonies and vestments of the Established Church. It was "receiving papistical habits into the church. We refuse not to wear such apparel as shall be thought, to the godly and prudent magistrates, most decent to our vocation, and to discern us from men of other callings, *so that we may even keep ourselves pure from the defiled robes of Antichrist.*" These dissenters were called PURITANS, " as men that did profess a greater *purity* in the worship of God, and a greater detestation of the ceremonies and corruptions of Rome, than the rest of their brethren."[58]

Even the book of homilies was drawn up at the same time "to supply the defect of preaching, which few of the clergy at that time were capable of performing."[59]

The liturgy had at first, and still retains, many popish affinities. These are seen in the canonizing of saints and celebration of saints' days; in the absolution by the priests,

---

[58] Long and earnest discussions on these topics are detailed in Hopkins' Puritans, Vol. I. Chaps. VIII., IX., XII., XIII., and in authorities there cited. Comp. Stillingfleet, Irenicum, p. 149, Am. ed.

[59] Neal's History of Puritans, I. p. 90. Hetherington's History of Westminster Divines, p. 21.

modified so as to unite the Protestant idea of forgiveness of sin by God alone with the popish absolution by the priest; in the endless reiterations of the Lord's Prayer; in the inordinate prominence that is given to liturgical forms; in the qualified and cautious phraseology of the communion service, and the special care that *all the consecrated bread and wine* shall be eaten and drunk, so that none of it shall be carried out of the church,—a point upon which the papists are ridiculously superstitious.[60] These popish tenets are seen particularly in the baptismal regeneration of the liturgy, by which the child becomes "regenerate and grafted into the body of Christ's church. . . . . We yield thee hearty thanks, most merciful Father, that it hath pleased thee to regenerate this infant with thy Holy Spirit, to receive him for thine own child by adoption."

The practical effect of this baptismal regeneration is illustrated by the following anecdote from the British Quarterly. One had fallen from his horse in hunting. His physician, perceiving his case to be desperate, endeavored in vain to direct his patient to Christ. The next morning he was calm and hopeful, saying: "Ah, doctor, you yesterday told me many things, but you did not tell me of what I have been reminded this morning—that in baptism I was made a member of Christ, a child of God, an inheritor of the kingdom of heaven." He died quietly, resting on this hope.[61]

The order of confirmation is so conducted as to confirm one in the delusion that he has become "regenerate by

---

[60] In the amendment of the liturgy, under Elizabeth, "the words used in distributing the elements were so contrived as neither to offend the Popish, or Lutheran, or Zuinglian communicant."—*Hallam's Const. Hist.* Vol. I. p. 150, note. Very catholic and accommodating!

[61] British Quarterly, Jan., 1868, p. 22.

water and the Holy Ghost," *through the instrumentality of this rite*, rather than by that grace which is the gift of God. The burial service, also, is exceedingly objectionable: "Forasmuch as it hath pleased Almighty God, of his great mercy, to take *unto himself* the soul of our deceased brother here departed, we therefore commit his body to the ground; earth to earth, ashes to ashes, dust to dust, *in sure and certain hope of the resurrection to eternal life* through our Lord Jesus Christ." This is said of every one alike, however profligate his life, however hopeless his death. In the American service, instead of this, at the grave is said or sung, "I heard a voice from heaven saying unto me, 'Write, From henceforth blessed are the dead who die in the Lord; even so, saith the Spirit, for they rest from their labors.'" Rev. xiv. 13. The practical influence of the burial service is apparent from the following remark of Archbishop Whately: "I have known a person, in speaking of a deceased neighbor, whose character had been irreligious and profligate, remark how great a comfort it was to hear the words of the funeral service read over her, 'because, poor woman, she had been such a bad liver.'"[62]

The London Quarterly, January, 1868, relates that when the burial service was read over a poor prostitute at her grave, one of her companions was heard to say to another, with an oath, "Nan, there is no fear, then, for us, for she was a precious deal worse than we are."

In ordination the bishop, according to the ritualistic theory and the natural import of the terms, does not merely pray for the gift of the Holy Spirit in these words, *horrendi carminis*—Receive the Holy Spirit—but as a minister of grace actually communicates the gift of the Holy Ghost; and in the absolution the priest, by divine authority committed to him, assumes to absolve the penitent from sin, all

[62] Errors of Romanism, p. 55.

which is a close assimilation, a near approach to the blasphemies of popery, and a severe impeachment of the Episcopal prayer-book.

A numerous and influential party of the Episcopal Church in this country have recently published a manifesto, in which they "say that the essential principle of High Church tendencies is an entire subversion of the Protestant and evangelical character of our Reformed Church. It transforms the ministry of the gospel into a priesthood; baptism into a magical rite; the Lord's Supper into the sacrifice of the mass; evangelical liberty into bondage to manifold observances and ceremonies; and the one church of Christ, "the blessed company of all faithful people," into the body of those who recognize and conform to a mere sacerdotal system. They believe, also, that the present crisis of Protestantism demands a higher degree of sympathy and co-operation among the various evangelical bodies into which they are divided."

A devoted churchman has recently published an able pamphlet on the "Romanizing germs" in the prayer-book: "Certain seminal doctrines, which, being planted and taking root, in due time spring up and bear Romanism as their fruit. It may be modified by the soil which nourishes it, and by the circumstances of its growth. It is Romanism still."

Three principal germs or seeds of Romanism in the prayer-book are indicated by the author:

1. The Bible is not the sole rule of faith.

2. The ministry is an exclusive priesthood, with supernatural powers.

3. The sacraments, when administered by this priesthood, are of singular efficacy.

"In view of these facts, we are forced to regard the prayer-book *as the fountain* whence flows that stream of

Romanizing influence which is rapidly growing into a mighty river, and with its many branches penetrating our whole church. Thus our author writes in sympathy with others of the clergy who 'regard with alarm the influence of the prayer-book upon many of the souls committed to their charge.'"

However many of the Episcopal Church may repudiate the semi-popish delusion of Puseyism, which has come up over the length and breadth of the land, it is indirectly supported, if not plainly taught, in her ritual. The prayer-book was a sinful compromise with the corruptions of the Church of Rome. "The scheme was merely to rob the Babylonian enchantress of her ornaments; to transfer the full cup of her sorceries to other hands, spilling as little as possible by the way. The Catholic doctrines and rites were to be retained in the Church of England." [63]

The high ritualists of England recently boasted before the Royal Commission that they are "a large and increasing, if not actually the largest, party in the church, the only true and conscientious members of the English Church;" "that they are in perfect harmony with the prayer-book and the practice of the earlier church; that they are endeavoring to assimilate both the doctrines and the practice of the English Church to that of Rome by catholicizing the church, and by every means pushing on this great catholic revival to reunite this severed branch again with the true Catholic Church." Their assimilation to the Church of Rome is apparent in the following particulars:

1. In restoring the ancient vestments of the bishops and the other clergy.

2. The two lights on the altar.

3. The incense.

[63] Macaulay's Review of Hallam's Constitutional History. See in the Appendix a further illustration of this.

4. The mixed chalice.

5. The eastward position, in front of the altar, of the priest and his assistants in the celebration of the communion.

6. The use of the wafer-bread.

7. The presence of the faithful for what is styled "spiritual communion."

8. The elevation of the consecrated elements for the purpose of adoration.

"Then, rising, the celebrant should at once elevate it with the first finger and thumb of both hands for the worship of the faithful while he is saying, Do this in remembrance of me."[64]

The celebrated Dr. Wiseman expresses in the liveliest terms his gratification at "the movement" of the Oxford Tractarians "toward Catholic ideas and Catholic feelings." He has "watched its progress with growing interest," because he "saw in it the *surest guarantee* and *principle of success*. The course which we (papists) ought to pursue seems simple and clear: *to admire* and *bless*, and, at the same time, to *second* and *favor*, as far as human means can, the *course* which God's providence has opened and is pursuing, but *to be careful how we thwart it*. It seems to me impossible to read the works of the Oxford divines, and especially to follow them chronologically, without discovering a daily approach toward our holy church, both in doctrine and affectionate feeling. Our saints, our popes, our rites and ceremonies, offices, nay, our very rubrics are precious in their eyes, far, alas! beyond what many of us consider them."[65]

---

[64] London Quarterly, Jan., 1868. Methodist London Quarterly, Oct., 1867.

[65] Cited in Rev. H. H. Beamish's Letter to Dr. Pusey, p. 9.

CHAPTER XII.

PSALMODY OF THE PRIMITIVE CHURCH.

The singing of spiritual songs constituted, from the beginning, an interesting and important part of religious worship in the primitive church. The course of our remarks on this subject will lead us to consider:

I. The argument for Christian psalmody as a part of religious worship.
II. The mode of singing in the ancient church.
III. The changes in the psalmody of the church.

I. Argument for the psalmody of the primitive church.
1. From reason.
Praise is the appropriate language of devotion. A fervent spirit of devotion instinctively seeks to express itself in song. In the strains of poetry, joined with the melody of music, it finds an easy and natural utterance of its elevated emotions. Can it be doubted, then, that that Spirit which was shed abroad upon the disciples after our Lord's ascension would direct them to the continued use of the sacred psalmody of their own Scriptures, indited by the inspiration of the same Spirit? Is it unreasonable to suppose that the glad spirit with which they continued praising God might direct them to indite other spiritual songs to the praise of their Lord, whose wondrous life and death so employed their contemplations and whose love so inspired their hearts? The opinion has been expressed by Grotius,

and is supported by many others, that we have, in Acts iv. 24–30, an epitome of such an early Christian hymn to Christ.[1]

2. From analogy.

The singing of songs constituted a great part of the religious worship of all ancient nations. In all their religious festivals and in their temples those pagan nations sung to the praise of their idol gods.[2] The worship of the Jews, not only in the temple, but in their synagogues and in their private dwellings, was celebrated with sacred hymns to God. Many of the loftiest, sweetest strains of Hebrew poetry were sung by their sacred minstrels on such occasions. Christ himself, in his final interview with his disciples before his crucifixion, sung with them the customary paschal songs at the institution of the sacrament,[3] and by his example sanctified the use of sacred songs in the Christian church. All analogy drawn from other forms of religious worship, pagan and Jewish, requires us to ascribe to the primitive Christians the use of spiritual songs in their public devotions.

3. From Scripture.

The same is clearly indicated in the writings of the New Testament.

---

[1] Comp. Augusti, Denkwürdigkeiten, Vol. V. p. 248.

[2] Semper id est cordi musis, semperque poetis
  Ut divos celebrent, laudes celebrentque virorum
  Ὑμνεῖν ἀθανάτους, ὑμνεῖν ἀγαθῶν κλέα ἀν'ρῶν.
      Theocritus, cited by Gerbert, Musica Sacra, T. 1. Pref. Comp. 61, § 5, in which are many references of a similar kind.

[3] The collect for such occasions is comprised in Psalms cxiii.–cxviii., the first two before the paschal supper, and the remainder after it. The theory has been advanced, but without reason, that Christ himself indited the hymn on this occasion. Neither is it necessary to suppose that all the hymns above-mentioned were sung by him and the disciples at this time.

Without doubt, in the opinion of Münter,[4] the gift of the Holy Spirit on the day of Pentecost was accompanied with poetic inspiration, to which the disciples gave utterance in the rhapsodies of spiritual songs, Acts ii. 4, 13, 47. The opinion of Grotius and others with reference to Acts iv. 24–30 has already been mentioned. But there are other passages which clearly indicate the use of religious songs in the worship of God. Paul and Silas, lacerated by the cruel scourging which they had received, and in close confinement in the inner prison, prayed and sang praises to God at midnight, Acts xvi. 25. The use of psalms and hymns and spiritual songs, moreover, is directly enjoined upon the churches by the apostle as an essential part of religious devotions, Col. iii. 16; Eph. v 14, 19. The latter epistle was a circular letter to the Gentile churches of Asia;[5] and, therefore, in connection with that to the church at Colosse, is explicit authority for the use of Christian psalmody in the religious worship of the apostolical churches.[6]

The use of such psalmody was not restricted merely to the *public* worship of God. In connection with the passage from Ephesians, the apostle warns those whom he addresses against the use of wine and the excesses to which it leads, with reference to those abuses which dishonored their sacramental supper and love-feasts. In opposition to the vain songs which, in such excesses, they might be disposed to sing, they are urged to the sober, religious use of psalms and hymns and spiritual songs.

The phraseology indicates that they were not restricted to the use of the psalms of David merely, as in the Jewish

[4] Com. Münter, Metrisch. Uebersetz. der Offenbar. Johann. Vorrede, S. 17.

[5] Neander's Apost. Kirch. I. 450, 3d ed.

[6] All this is shown at length by J. G. Walch, De Hymnis Ecclesiae Apostolicae.

worship, but were at liberty to employ others of appropriate religious character in their devotions. The Corinthians were accustomed to make use of songs composed for the occasion, 1 Cor. xiv. 26. And though the apostle had occasion to correct their disorderly proceedings, it does not appear that he forbade the use of such songs. On the contrary, there is the highest probability that the apostolic churches did not restrict themselves simply to the use of the Jewish Psalter.

Grotius and others have supposed that some fragments of these early hymns are contained not only, as above mentioned, in Acts, but perhaps also in 1 Tim. iii. 16. Something like poetic antithesis they have imagined to be contained in James i. 17; 1 Tim. i. 1; 2 Tim. ii. 11–13. The expression in Revelation, "I am Alpha and Omega, the first and the last," has been ascribed to the same origin, as has also Rev. iv. 8, together with the song of Moses and the Lamb, Rev. xv. 3, and the songs of the elders and the beasts, Rev. v. 9–14. Certain parts of the book itself have been supposed to be strictly poetical, and may have been used as such in Christian worship, such as Rev. i. 4–8; xi. 15–19; xv. 3, 4; xxi. 1–8; xxii. 10–18. But the argument is not conclusive; and all the learned criticism, the talent and the taste that have been employed on this point leave us little else than uncertain conjecture on which to build an hypothesis.

4. From history.

The earliest authentic record on this subject is the celebrated letter from Pliny to Trajan, just at the close of the apostolic age, A. D. 103, 104. In the investigations which he instituted against the Christians of his period, he discovered, among other things, that they were accustomed to meet before day to offer praise to Christ as God, or as *a*

God, as some contend that it should be rendered.[7] The expression is somewhat equivocal, and might be used with reference to the ascription of praise in prayer or in song. But it appears that these Christians rehearsed their *carmen invicem alternately*, as if in responsive songs, according to the ancient custom of singing in the Jewish worship. Tertullian, only a century later, evidently understood the passage to be descriptive of this mode of worshiping God and Christ, for he says that Pliny intended to express nothing else than assemblies before the dawn of the morning, for singing praise to Christ and to God, *coetus antelucanos, ad canendum Christo et Deo*.[8] Eusebius also gives the passage a similar interpretation, saying that Pliny could find nothing against them save that, arising at the dawn of the morning, they sang hymns to Christ as God, Πλὴν τό γε ἅμα τῇ ἕω διεγειρομένους τὸν Χριστὸν Θεοῦ δίκην ὑμνεῖν.[9] Viewed in this light, it becomes evidence of the use of Christian psalmody among the Christians immediately subsequent to the age of the apostles.[10] Tertullian himself also distinctly testifies to the use of songs to the praise of God by the primitive Christians. Every one, he says, was invited in their public worship to sing unto God, according to his ability, either from the Scriptures or *de proprio ingenio, one indited by himself*, according to the interpretation of Münter. Whatever may be the meaning of this phrase, the passage clearly asserts the use of Christian psalmody in their religious worship. Again, he speaks of singing in connection with the reading of the Scriptures, exhortations and prayer in public worship.[11]

---

[7] Carmen Christo quasi Deo dicere secum invicem.—*Epist.* Lib. 10, 97.

[8] Apolog. c. 2.   [9] Eccl. Hist. Lib. 3, 32.

[10] Münter, Metrisch. Offenbar. S. 25.

[11] De Anima, c. 9.

Justin Martyr also mentions the songs and hymns of the Ephesian Christians. "We manifest our gratitude to him by worshiping him in spiritual songs and hymns, praising him for our birth, for our health, for the vicissitudes of the seasons and for the hopes of immortality."[12]

Eusebius also has left on record the important testimony of an ancient historian at the close of the second century: "Who knows not the writings of Irenaeus, Melito and others which exhibit Christ as God and man? And how many songs and odes of the brethren there are, written from the beginning, ἀπ' ἀρχῆς, by believers, which offer praise to Christ as the Word of God, ascribing divinity to him!"[13] This passage not only presents a new and independent testimony to the use of spiritual songs in the Christian church from the remotest antiquity to the praise of Christ as divine, but it shows that these in great numbers had been committed to writing, as it appears, for continued use. So that we here have evidence of the existence of a Christian hymn-book from the beginning.

The testimony of Origen, A. D. 254, again, of the church of Alexandria, is to the same effect. In answer to the charge of Celsus, that the Christians worshiped the great God and sang hymns also to the sun and to Minerva, he says, "We know the contrary, for these hymns are to him

---

[12] Apol. c. 13. Justin Martyr wrote, as is supposed, also a work on Christian psalmody, the loss of which we have deeply to deplore. Living within half a century of the age of the apostles, it would be particularly interesting to receive from him a treatise on this interesting subject. The references are from Semisch, Euseb. Eccl. Hist. Lib. 4, c. 18, and Phot. Bibl. Cod. Vol. I. p. 95, ὁ ἐπιγραφόμενος ψάλτης. Comp. Fabric. Bibliothec. Graec. ed Harl. VII. p. 67.

[13] Ψαλμοὶ δὲ ὅσοι καὶ ᾠδαὶ ἀδελφῶν ἀπ' ἀρχῆς ὑπὸ πιστῶν γραφεῖσαι, τὸν λόγον τοῦ Θεοῦ τὸν Χριστὸν ὑμνοῦσι θεολογοῦντες.—Eccl. Hist. Lib. 5, 28.

who alone is called God over all, and to his only-begotten [Son]."[14]

Christ, the only-begotten of the Father, is the burden of these primitive songs and hymns. Here is he set forth *doctrinally*, θεολογικῶς, *as the incarnate Word of God*, as God and man. His mediatorial character was the subject of the songs of these apostolical and primitive saints. This sacred theme inspired the earliest anthems of the Christian church; and as it has ever been the subject of her sweetest melodies and loftiest strains, so doubtless will it continue to be until the last of her ransomed sons shall end the songs of the redeemed on earth, and wake his harp to nobler, sweeter strains in heaven.[15]

One hymn of the primitive church has come down to us entire. It is found in the Paedagogue of Clement of Alexandria, a work bearing date about one hundred and fifty years from the time of the apostles; but it is ascribed to another, and assigned to an earlier origin. It is wanting in some of the manuscripts of Clement. It contains figurative language and forms of expression which were familiar to the church at an earlier date; and, for various reasons, is regarded by Münter and Bull[16] as a venerable relic of the early church,

---

[14] Against Celsum, Lib. 8, c. 67, p. 792, ed. Runei: ὕμνους γὰρ εἰς μόνον τὸν ἐπὶ πᾶσι λεγόμενον θεὸν, καὶ τὸν μονογενῆ αὐτοῦ.

[15] Whatever may be the doctrinal truth in regard to the character of Christ, it is abundantly evident that he was worshiped as divine in the prayers and psalmody of the primitive church. See the author's Ancient Christianity, p. 328. This truth, again, is confirmed by the fact mentioned by Neander, that, "In the controversy with the Unitarians, at the close of the second and beginning of the third century, their opponents appealed to those hymns in which, aforetime, Christ had been worshiped as God."—*Allgem. Kirch. Hist.*, I. 523, 2d ed. Tr. I. p. 304.

[16] Metrisch. Offenbar., S. 32. Bull's Defensio Fidei Nicaenae, § 111, c. 2, p. 316, cited by Münter.

which has escaped the ravages of time, and still remains a solitary remnant of the Christian psalmody of that early age. It is certainly very ancient, and the earliest that has been preserved and transmitted to us. It is a hymn to Christ, and shows what was the strain of these devotions. We see in it the heart of primitive piety laboring to give utterance to its emotions of wonder, love and gratitude, in view of the offices and character of the great Redeemer.[17]

The songs of the primitive Christians were not restricted to their public devotions. In their social circles and around their domestic altars they worshiped God in the sacred song; and in their daily occupations they were wont to relieve their toil and refresh their spirits by renewing their favorite songs to Zion. Persecuted and afflicted —in solitary cells of the prison, in the more dismal abodes of the mines to which they were doomed, or as wandering exiles in foreign countries—they forgot not to sing the Lord's song in the prison or the mine, or the strange lands to which they were driven.[18]

II. Mode of singing in the ancient church.

Both the Jews in their temple-service and the Greeks in their idol-worship were accustomed to sing with the accompaniment of instrumental music. The converts to Christianity accordingly must have been familiar with this mode

---

[17] The reader will find this hymn in the author's Ancient Christianity, pp. 334, 335. It is an anapaestic ode, with occasional interchanges of spondees and dactyls, which this measure admits. It is supposed also to consist of parts, which may have been sung in responses. The divisions are as follows: lines, 1–10, 11–28, 29–45, 46–63.

[18] Comp. Jamison, cited in Christian Antiquities, p. 375. It would not be difficult to adduce original authorities to this effect, but we must confine ourselves more particularly to the devotional psalmody of their public worship.

of singing. The word, ψαλλεῖν, which the apostle uses in Eph. v. 19, is supposed by critics to indicate that they sang with such accompaniments. The same is supposed by some to be intimated by the golden harps which John, in the Apocalypse, put into the hands of the four-and-twenty elders. But it is generally admitted that the primitive Christians employed no instrumental music in their religious worship. Neither Ambrose, nor Basil, nor Chrysostom,[19] in the noble encomiums which they severally pronounce upon music, make any mention of instrumental music. Basil condemns it as ministering only to the depraved passions of men.[20]

It seems from the epistle of Pliny that the Christians, of whom he speaks, sang *alternately, in responses*. The ancient hymn from Clement, above mentioned, seems to be constructed with reference to this method of singing. There is, also, an ancient but groundless tradition extant in Socrates[21] that Ignatius was the first to introduce this style of music in the church at Antioch. It was familiar to the Jews, who often sang responsively in the worship of the temple. In some instances the same style of singing may have been practiced in the primitive church. But responsive singing is generally allowed not to have been in common use during the first three hundred years of the Christian era. This mode of singing was common in the theatres and temples of the Gentiles, and for this reason was generally discarded by the primitive Christians.[22] It was first practiced in the Syrian churches; it was introduced into the

[19] Ambrose, in Ps. 1, Praef. p. 740. Basil, in Ps. 1, Vol. II. p. 713. Chrysostom, in Ps. 41, Vol. V. p. 131.

[20] Hom. 4, Vol. I. p. 33.

[21] Eccl. Hist. Lib. 6, c. 8.

[22] Theodorus Mopsnes, quoted by Nicetas Momin. Thesaur. Orthodox. Lib. 5, c. 30, in Biblioth. Vet. Pat. XXV. p. 161.—*Augusti, Denkwürdigkeiten,* Vol. V. p. 278.

Eastern churches by Flavian and Diodorus in the middle of the fourth century;[23] from them it was transferred by Ambrose, A. D. 370, to those of the West, and it soon came into general use in these churches under the name of the Ambrosian style of music.[24]

Sacred music must, at this time, have consisted only of a few simple airs which could easily be learned, and which, by frequent repetition, became familiar to all. An ornate and complicated style of music would have been alike incompatible with the circumstances of these Christian worshipers and uncongenial with the simplicity of their primitive forms.[25]

In their songs of Zion, both old and young, men and women, bore a part. Their psalmody was the joint act of the whole assembly in unison. Such is the testimony of Hilary, A. D. 355.[26] Ambrose remarks that the injunction of the apostle, forbidding women to speak in public, relates not to singing, "for this is delightful in every age and suited to every sex."[27] The authority of Chrysostom is also to the same effect. "It was the ancient custom, as it is still with us, for all to come together, and unitedly to join in singing. The young and the old, rich and poor, male and female, bond and free, all join in one song. . . . . All worldly distinctions here cease, and the whole congregation form one general chorus."[28]

Each was invited, at pleasure, and according to his ability,

[23] Theodoret, Eccl. Hist. Lib. 2, c. 19, p. 622.
[24] August. Confess. 9, c. 7. Paulini, Vet. Ambros. p. 4. Comp Augusti, Denkwürdigkeiten, Vol. V. p. 300.
[25] Augusti, Denkwürdigkeiten, Vol. V. p. 288.
[26] Comment. in Ps. 65, p. 174.
[27] In Ps. 1, Praef. 741. Comp. Hexaemeron, Lib. 3, c. 5, p. 42.
[28] Hom. 11, Vol. XII. p. 349. Hom. 36, in 1 Cor. Vol. X. p. 340. Comp. Gerbert, Musica Sacra, Lib. 1, § 11, who has collected many other authorities to the same effect.

to lead their devotions in a sacred song indited by himself. Such was the custom in the Corinthian church. Such was still the custom in the age of Tertullian, to which reference has already been made. Augustine also refers to the same usage, and ascribes to divine inspiration[29] the talent which they manifested in this extemporaneous psalmody.

Such was the psalmody of the early church. It consisted in part of the psalms of David, and in part of hymns composed for the purpose, and expressive of love and praise to God and to Christ.[30] Few in number, and sung in rude and simple airs, they yet had wonderful power over those primitive saints. The sacred song inspired their devotions both in the public and private worship of God. At their family board it quickened their gratitude to God, who gave them their daily bread. It enlivened their domestic and social intercourse, it relieved the weariness of their daily labor, it cheered them in solitude, comforted them in affliction and supported them under persecution. "Go where you will," says Jerome, "the ploughman at his plough sings his joyful hallelujahs, the busy mower regales himself with his psalms, and the vine-dresser is singing one of the songs of David. Such are our songs—our love-songs as they are called—the solace of the shepherd in his solitude, and of the husbandman in his toil."[31] Fearless of reproach, of persecution and of death, they continued, in the face of their enemies, to sing their sacred songs in the streets and market-places and at the martyr's stake. Eusebius declares himself an eye-witness to the fact that, under their persecutions in Thebais, "they continued to their latest breath to sing psalms and hymns and thanksgivings to the God of

[29] Cited by Münter, Metrisch. Offenbar. The sentiments of Grotius also are to the same effect.
[30] Neander, Allgem. Kirch. Hist. I. S. 523, 2d ed. Tr. I. p. 304.
[31] Ep. 17, ad Marcellam. Cited in Arnold's Abbildung, S. 174.

heaven."[32] And the same is related of many others among the early martyrs. We are informed by Chrysostom that it was an ancient custom to sing the 140th psalm every evening, and that the Christians continued through life the constant singing of this psalm.[33] The song of Zion was a sacred fountain, which, like living waters in a desert, sustained in this barren wilderness the growth and vigor of primitive piety, and overspread with perpetual verdure the vineyard of the Lord. On this point the sentiments of Herder are peculiarly interesting, and no one can speak with more authority respecting the psalmody of the ancient church. After remarking that the earliest hymns of the Latin church exhibit little poetic talent or classic taste, he adds: "But who can deny their influence and power over the soul? These sacred hymns of many hundred years' standing, and yet at every repetition still new and unimpaired in interest, what a blessing have they been to poor human nature! They go with the solitary into his cell, and attend the afflicted in distress, in want and to the grave. While singing these one forgets his toil, and his fainting, sorrowful spirit soars in heavenly joys to another world. Back to earth he comes to labor, to toil, to suffer in silence and to conquer. How rich the boon, how great the power of these hymns!"[34] He proceeds to say that there is in these an efficacy and power which lighter songs, which philosophy itself, can never have—a power which is not

---

[32] Eccl. Hist. 8, c. 9.

[33] Chrysost. in Ps. 140, Tom. 5, p. 427.

[34] Augustine gives the following account of the power of this music over him on the occasion of his baptism: "Oh how freely was I made to weep by these hymns and spiritual songs, transported by the voices of the congregation sweetly singing! The melody of their voices filled my ear, and divine truth was poured into my heart. Then burned the sacred flame of devotion in my soul, and gushing tears flowed from my eyes, as well they might."—*Confess.* Lib. 9, c. 6, p. 118.

ascribable to anything new or striking in sentiment or powerful in expression. And then rises the question, "Whence, then, have they this mighty power? What is it that so moves us?" To which he replies, *Simplicity and truth.* "Embodying the great and simple truths of religion, they speak the sentiment of a universal creed—they are the expression of one heart and one faith. The greater part are suitable to be sung on all occasions and daily to be repeated. Others are adapted to certain festivals; and as these return in endless succession, so the sacred song perpetually repeats the Christian faith. Though rude and void of refined taste, they all speak to the heart, and, by ceaseless repetition, sink deep the impress of truth. Like these, the sacred song should ever be the simple offering of nature, an incense of sweet odors, perpetually recurring with a fragrance that suffers no abatement."[35] Such is the simple power of truth wrought into the soul by the hallowed devotions of the sanctuary. Striking the deepest principles of our nature, stirring the strongest passions of the heart, and mingling with our most tender recollections and dearest hopes, is it strange that the simple truths and rude airs of the sacred songs should deeply move us? So presented, they only grow in interest by continued repetition. And in the lapse of years these time-hallowed associations do but sink the deeper in the soul:

> "Time but the impression stronger makes,
> As streams their channels deeper wear."

III. Changes in the psalmody of the church.

In the course of a few centuries from the fourth onward, several variations were introduced in the mode of performing this part of public worship, the effect of which was to

---

[35] Briefe zur Beförderung der Humanitat. 7, Samml. S. 28, seq. Cited by Augusti, Denkwürdigkeiten, Vol. V. p. 296, 297.

withdraw the people from any direct participation in it, and to destroy in a great degree its moral power.

1. The first of these changes has been already mentioned, singing alternately by responses. This was introduced into the Syrian churches, afterward into the Eastern church, and finally into the Western by Ambrose. In this the congregation still bore some part, all uniting in the chorus and singing the responses.

2. The appointment of *singers* as a distinct class of officers in the church, for this part of religious worship marks another alteration in the psalmody of the church. These were first appointed in the fourth century. But the people continued, for a century or more, to enjoy their ancient privilege of all singing together.

3. Various restrictions were from time to time laid upon the use of hymns *of human composition* in distinction from the inspired psalms of David. Heretics of every name had their sacred hymns, suited to their own religious belief, which had great effect in propagating their errors. To resist their encroachments, the Established Church was driven to the necessity either of cultivating and improving its own psalmody, or of opposing its authority to stay the progress of this evil. The former was the expedient of Ambrose, Hilary, Gregory Nazianzen, Chrysostom, Augustine, etc. But the other alternative in turn was also attempted. The churches by ecclesiastical authority were restricted to the use of the Psalter and other canonical songs of the Scriptures. All hymns of merely human composition were prohibited as of a dangerous tendency and unsuitable to the purposes of public worship. The synod of Laodicea, A. D. 344–346, c. 59, passed a decree to that effect. The decree was not, however, fully enforced. But this and similar efforts on the part of the clergy had the effect to discourage the use of such religious songs. The Arians of that age

also opposed these ancient sacred hymns for a different reason, and cultivated a higher style of sacred music.

4. The introduction of instrumental music. The tendency of this was *to secularize* the music of the church, and to encourage singing by a choir. Such musical accompaniments were gradually introduced, but they can hardly be assigned to a period earlier than the fifth and sixth centuries. Organs were unknown in church until the eighth or ninth century. Previous to this they had their place in the theatre, rather than in the church. They were never regarded with favor in the Eastern church, and were vehemently opposed in many places in the West. In Scotland no organ is allowed to this day, except in a few Episcopal churches. "In the English convocation, held A. D. 1562, in Queen Elizabeth's time, for settling of the liturgy, the retaining of organs was carried only *by a casting vote*."

5. The introduction of *profane, secular music into the church* was one of the principal means of corrupting the psalmody of the church. An artificial, theatrical style of music, having no affinity to the worship of God, began to take the place of those solemn airs which before had inspired the devotions of his people. The music of the theatre was transferred to the church; which, accordingly, became the scene of theatrical pomp and display, rather than the house of prayer and of praise, to inspire, by its appropriate and solemn rites, the spiritual worship of God. The consequences of indulging this depraved taste for secular music in the church are exhibited by Neander in the following extract: "We have to regret that, both in the Eastern and the Western church, their sacred music had already assumed an artificial and theatrical character, and was so far removed from its original simplicity that even in the fourth century the Abbot Pambo of Egypt complained that heathen melodies [accompanied as it seems with the

action of the hands and the feet] had been introduced into their church psalmody."[36] Isidorus of Pelusium also complained of the theatrical singing, especially that of the women, which, instead of inducing penitence for sin, tended much more to awaken sinful desires.[37] Jerome, also, in remarking upon Eph. v. 19, says: "May all hear it whose business it is to sing in the church. Not with the voice, but with the *heart*, we sing praises to God. Not like the comedians should they raise their sweet and liquid notes to entertain the assembly with theatrical songs and melodies in the church; but the fear of God, piety and the knowledge of the Scriptures should inspire our songs. Then would not the voice of the singers, but the utterance of divine word, expel the evil spirit from those who, like Saul, are possessed with it. But instead of this, that same spirit is invited rather to the possession of those who have converted the house of God into a pagan theatre."[38]

The assembly continued to bear some part in the psalmody of the church even after this had become a cultivated theatrical art, for the practice of which *the singers* were appointed and trained as a distinct order in the church. The congregation may have continued for a time to join in the chorus or in responses. But is it conceivable that a promiscuous assembly could unite in such theatrical music as is here the subject of complaint? Music, executed in this manner, was an art which must require in its performers a degree of skill altogether superior to that which all the members of a congregation could be expected to possess.

---

[36] Μελῳδοῖσιν ἀσματα καὶ ῥυθμίζουσιν ἠχοῖς σείουσι χεῖρας καὶ μεταβαίνουσι (βάλλουσι?) πόδας.—Scriptores Ecclesiastici, De Musica, T. 1, 1784, p. 3.

[37] Isidor. Pelus. C. 1, Ep. 90, Biblioth. Vet. Pat. Vol. VII. p. 543.

[38] Comment. in Ep. Eph. Lib. 3, c. 5, T. 4, p. 387, ed. Martianay. Cited in Allgem. Kirch. Gesch. II. S. 681, 2d ed.

6. The practice of sacred music, as an ornamental, cultivated art, took it yet more completely from the people. It became an art which only a few could learn. The many, instead of uniting their hearts and their voices in the songs of Zion, could only sit coldly by as spectators. They might, indeed, unite in some simple chorus, and are generally understood not to have been entirely excluded from all participation in the psalmody of the church until the sixth or seventh century. Gregory the Great was instrumental in bringing singing schools into repute, and after him Charlemagne. Organs came about this time into use. But in the early periods of the Christian church instrumental music was not in use in religious worship.

7. The clergy eventually claimed the right of performing the sacred music as a privilege *exclusively their own.* This expedient shut out the people from any participation in this delightful part of public worship.

Finally, the more effectually to exclude the people, the singing was in Latin. Where that was not the vernacular tongue, this rule was of necessity an effectual bar to the participation of the people in this part of public worship. Besides, the doctrine was industriously propagated that the Latin was the appropriate language of devotion, which became not the profane lips of the laity in these religious solemnities; but only those of the clergy, who had been consecrated to the service of the sanctuary. The Reformation again restored to the people their ancient and inestimable right. But in the Roman Catholic Church it is still divided between the chants of the priests and the theatrical performances of the choir, which effectually pervert the devotional ends of sacred music.

REMARKS.

1. To accomplish, in the happiest manner, the devotional ends of sacred music the congregation should unitedly join in it.

In advancing an opinion so much opposed to the taste of the age, the writer has no expectation that it will be received with the consideration which, in his opinion, its importance demands. For he cannot resist the conviction that, in separating the congregation generally from a participation in this delightful part of public worship, we have taken the most effectual measure, as did the Catholic clergy in the period which has passed under review, to destroy the *devotional* influence of sacred music. What, may we ask, was the secret of the magic charm of sacred music in the early Christian church? Whence its mighty influence over those primitive saints? It was that the great truths of religion were embodied in their psalmody, and set to such simple airs that all could blend their voices and their hearts in the sacred song; and, though they may have exhibited little of what is denominated musical taste, or of the symphonies of a modern oratorio, they offered unto God the melody of the heart, by far the noblest praise. Their sacred songs became, as we have seen, the *ballads* of the people,[39] sung at all times and upon every occasion. Religious truth became inwrought into the very soul of these Christians by their sacred songs. It entered not only into their public devotions, but into their family worship, their domestic pleasures and their social entertainments. Thus religious truth addressed itself to the hearts of the people in a manner

---

[39] One has wisely said: "Let me make the ballads of the people, and I care not who makes their laws." But connected with religion their power is immensely increased.

the most persuasive possible. It became associated, both with the most endearing recollections of the heart and its most hallowed associations. Will the music of our churches, however skillfully played upon the organ, or sweetly sung by a few select voices, ever so move the heart and mould the character of the whole society? No; like the cold coruscations of the Northern Lights, it does but amuse and delight the spectator for a while and then passes away, leaving the bosom dark and cheerless as before. But when the music of the church is let down from the orchestra to the congregation below, and runs with its quickening influence from man to man, until all feel their souls ascending in the song which they unitedly raise to God, then it is that the

> "Heart grows warm with holy fire,
> And kindles with a pure desire."

No one can witness the worship of the churches in Germany without being struck with the devotional influence of their psalmody. They are a nation of singers. Rarely is one seen in the church, whether old or young, who does not join in the song;[40] and with an evident interest which

[40] The singing is the most devotional part of the religious worship of the Lutheran and Evangelical churches of Germany, and in proportion to the other parts of worship is extended to an inordinate length. For example, on one occasion in the ordinary services of the Sabbath, the singing before sermon was observed, by the writer, to occupy *fifty minutes*. In the course of this time two prayers were offered, neither of which occupied the space of *three minutes*, and two portions of Scripture were read, which did not occupy more than five minutes. All the prayers, including the litany, did not exceed ten minutes in length; while the singing employed near an hour. The prayers are liturgical forms to a great extent, briefly rehearsed at different times by the clergyman, in which the congregation seem not to be deeply interested. The singing is the act of the congregation unitedly, with which they are never weary—with which, I had almost said, they never appear to be satisfied.

it has not been the good fortune of the writer often to witness or to experience in the churches of America. In our country this subject is encompassed with intrinsic difficulties which we pass without remark. But were it possible ever to make the modification under consideration in our church-music, even at the expense of the musical skill and talent which are now displayed, we must believe that much would be gained to the devotional influence of our sacred music. What though, in humbler strains and more simple airs, the churches raise to God their sacred songs of praise? What if some discordant notes occasionally disturb the harmony of the music? if still they do but fulfill the apostolical injunction, singing and making melody in their *hearts* to the Lord, the noblest, the best, the only true end of sacred music is accomplished. Such are the strains which He who inspires the songs of heaven delights most to hear:

> "Compared with these, Italian trills are tame;
> The tickled ears no heartfelt raptures raise."

We subjoin the remarks of Prof. B. B. Edwards upon the sacred psalmody of the Germans: "In this delightful exercise the whole congregation, without exception, unite. Those who might have been wearied with the sermon were awakened in the hymn with the whole heart. The writer can never forget a spectacle of this kind which he saw in one of the old churches in Nuremberg. The great edifice was crowded, one-half of the audience, at least, standing. The sermon had been delivered in a fervent manner, and had apparently much interested the feelings of the audience. Immediately a powerful and well-toned organ sent its peals through all the corners and recesses of the cathedral, and in a moment every adult and child in the vast throng broke forth in praise to the Redeemer in one of those old hymns, mellowed by time, and which breathe not of earth, but of heaven. The effect, at least upon a stranger, was overpowering. Nothing like it can be produced by a small choir, however scientifically trained. The performance of the latter must be comparatively dead, because, being so artistic or scientific, or so modern, or it has been subject to so many mutations, that few could join in it if they were permitted so to do. The music for a popular audience must be simple; and then, especially if a great multitude unite, it will often be affecting and sublime. The singing in German churches sometimes occupies an hour, or more than an hour."

2. Christian psalmody was one of the principal means of promoting the devotions of the primitive church.

Enough remains on record in relation to this subject to show what interest these venerable saints and martyrs had in their sacred songs—enough to show what power their psalmody possessed to confirm their faith, to inspire their devotions, to bring them nigh to God and to arm them with more than mortal courage for the fiery conflict to which they were summoned in defence of their faith. Has this most interesting and important part of religious worship its just influence with us? Is its quickening power shed abroad over our assemblies like the spirit of heavenly grace, warming the cold heart into spiritual life and reviving its languid affections, as if with a fresh anointing from on high?

3. Christian psalmody affords the happiest means of enforcing the doctrinal truths of religion.

Reason with man, and you do but address his understanding; you gain, it may be, his cold convictions. Embody the truth in a creed or confession of faith; to this he may also yield assent, and remain as unmoved as before. But express it in the sacred song. Let it mingle with his devotions in the sanctuary and in the family; let his most endeared associations cluster around it as the central point, not only of his faith, but of his hopes, his joys; and what before was a speculative belief, has become his living sentiment—the governing principle both of the understanding and the heart. The single book of psalms and hymns, therefore, does unspeakably more to form the doctrinal sentiments of men than all the formularies, creeds and confessions of polemics and divines. "The one," says Augusti, " is chiefly for the minister; the other is in the hands of the people, and is, as you may say, his *daily creed.*"[41] The heart, in religion, as in everything else, governs the understanding. The sacred song that wins the one fails not also to convince and to control the other. With great propriety, therefore, has the hymn-book long been styled the *Layman's Bible.*[42]

Every religious denomination, accordingly, has its hymn-book; and in ancient times the same was true of every religious sect. The spiritual songs of the primitive Christians were almost exclusively of a doctrinal character. " In fact, almost all the prayers, doxologies and hymns of the ancient church are nothing else than prayers and supplications to the triune God or to Jesus Christ. They were generally altogether doctrinal. The prayers and psalms, of merely a moral character, which the modern church has in great

---

[41] Denkwürdigkeiten, V. S. 411.

[42] Augusti, Denkwürdigkeiten, V. S. 411; also, 277. Augustine recognizes the same sentiment, as follows: Cum reminiscor lachrymas meas quas fudi ad cantus ecclesiae tuae in primordiis recuperatae fidei meae, et nunc, ipso quod moveor, non cantu, sed rebus quae cantantur, cum liquida voce et convenientissima modulatione cantantur, magnam instituti hujus utilitatem rusus agnosco. Tamen cum mihi accidit ut me amplius *cantus* quam res quae canitur moveat, poenaliter me peccare confiteor, et tunc mallem non audire cantantem.—*Confess.* L. 10, c. 33, Vol. I. p. 141.

abundance, in the ancient were altogether unknown."[43] And yet modern Christians have not been inattentive to this mode of defending their faith. Their different collections of psalms and hymns abound with those that are expressive merely of points of doctrine at the expense, often, of all poetical imagery or expression.[44]

4. Christian psalmody is one of the most efficient means of promulgating a religious system among a people.

This was one of the earliest and most successful expedients for spreading the ancient heresies of the church. Bardasanes, the famous Syrian Gnostic, in the latter part of the second century, made this the principal means of propagating his sentiments. He composed songs expressive of the tenets which he would inculcate, and adapted them to music to be sung by the people. His son, Harmonius, followed the example of his father; and such "was the influence of their efforts that the Syrian church was well nigh overrun with their errors."[45] And not only the Gnostics, but the Manicheans, the Donatists, and almost every heretical sect, employed, with surprising success, the same means of promulgating their tenets. Taught by their example, the orthodox finally sought, in the same manner, to

[43] Augusti, Denkwürdigkeiten, Vol. V. p. 417.

[44] For example, the successive stanzas of one of the hymns in the Lutheran collection, begin, each, with one of the terms at the beginning of the creed: 1. I believe in God the Father, etc. 2. I believe in God the Son, etc. 3. I believe in God the Holy Ghost, etc.

[45] Composuit carmina et ea modulationibus aptabit, finxit psalmos induxitque metra, et mensuris ponderibusque distribuit voces. Ita propinavit simplicibus venenum dulcedine temperatum; aegroti quippe cibum recusabant salubrem. Davidem imitatus est, ut ejus pulchritudine ornaretur ejusque similitudine commendaretur. Centum et quinquaginta composuit hic quoque psalmos.—*Ephraem Syrus*, in Hymn 53, p. 553. Comp. Sozomen, h. e. 3, c. 16. Theodor. Lib. 4, c. 29; also, I. c. 22. Denkwürdigkeiten, Vol. V. S. 272, 273.

resist the progress of their errors. Such were the efforts of Ephraem the Syrian, Hilary, Augustine, and others.[46]

Luther well understood this method of propagating truth and refuting error, and employed it with a skillful hand. For his great work he possessed remarkable qualifications, seldom united in one man. Among his varied accomplishments, not the least important were his poetical and musical talents. He was taught music with the first rudiments of his native language; and when, as a wandering minstrel, he earned his daily bread by exercising his musical powers in singing before the doors of the rich in the streets of Magdeburg and Eisenach, he was as truly preparing for the future Reformer as when, a retired monk in the cloister at Erfurt, he was storing his mind with the truths of revelation, with which to refute the errors and expose the delusions of papacy. One of his earliest efforts at reform was the publication of a psalm-book, A. D. 1524, composed and set to music chiefly by himself.[47] The songs of Luther confirmed the Christian's faith and soothed the sufferings of the martyr at the stake. One of his earliest hymns he consecrated to commemorate the martyrs of Brussels; and the whole Reformed church felt the sustaining influence of this

---

[46] Augusti, Denkwürdigkeiten, Vol. V. S. 275, 276, 414, 415. For further information on this point, see J. Andr. Schmidt, De modo propagandi religionem par carmina. Helmst. 1720. 4to.

[47] This psalm-book is usually ascribed to Luther, though it bears not his name. It contained eight psalms, of which, however, but one bears his name. But he published, in 1525, two editions, the first containing sixteen, and the other forty. In the collection of sacred music in use by the Lutheran churches in Germany, consisting of two hundred and fifty-three tunes, *twenty-five* are ascribed to Luther, either as the author of them, or as having been revised by him and adapted to the use of the church. The authorship of a few is doubtful, though they are assigned to that age.

single song which we give in the margin.⁴⁸ His associate, Hans Sach, co-operated with him by publishing, in 1523, the "*Nightingale of Wittenberg.*" His efforts at an earlier period at Nuremberg had great influence in promoting the work of the Reformation. "From a humble workshop, situated at one of the gates of the imperial city of Nuremberg, proceeded sounds that resounded through all Germany, preparing the minds of men for a new era, and everywhere endearing to the people the great revolution that was then in progress. The spiritual songs of Hans Sachs, his Bible in verse, powerfully assisted this work. It would perhaps, be difficult to say to which it was most indebted, the Prince, Elector of Saxony, administrator of the empire, or the shoemaker of Nuremberg!"

The psalms of the church in the time of the Reformation were wholly of a doctrinal character. "Hymns merely inculcating moral truths, which are so abundant in modern collections, were unknown at this early period. As now in

[48] Flung on the heedless winds
   Or on the waters cast,
Their ashes shall be watched
   And gathered be at last.
And from that scattered dust,
   Around us and abroad,
Shall spring a plenteous seed
   Of witnesses for God.

Jesus hath now received
   Their latest living breath,—
Yet vain is Satan's boast
   Of victory in their death.
Still—still—though dead they speak,
   And trumpet-tongued proclaim
To many a waking land,
   The one availing Name.
                    —*Cited from D'Aubigné.*

symbols and catechisms we have an abstract of the Christian faith, so then was the substance of the fundamental doctrines of the Christian faith embodied in their divine songs." [49] Weapons so simple were employed with surprising effect by the great Reformer. Even his enemies acknowledged their hated power. "These hymns, many of which are manufactured in Luther's own laboratory and sung in the vernacular tongue of the people, it is wonderful what power they have in propagating the doctrines of Luther? Some of them doctrinal in their character, others imitating devotional psalms, they repeat and blazon abroad the faults of the Catholic Church, whether real or imaginary." [50] Such is the mighty power of sacred psalmody in propagating the Christian faith:

"These weapons of our holy war,
Of what almighty force they are!"

Have our missionaries employed with due diligence and

[49] Augusti, Denkwürdigkeiten, Vol. V. S. 287.
[50] Cantilenae vernaculo idiomate, quarum plurimae ex ipsius Lutheri officina sunt profectae, mirum est, quam promoveant rem Lutheranam. Quaedam dogmaticae, aliae aemulantur psalmos pios;—recitant exagitantque Christianorum vitia sive vera, sive ficta. *Thomas de Jesu* (Didacus Davila), *Thesaur. sapient. divinae*, T. 2, p. 541. Luther inserted in the title-page of his hymn-book, published at Wittenberg, in 1543, the following stanza:

"Viel falscher Meister jetzt Lieder dichten,
Siehe dich für, und lern' sie recht richten.
Wo Gott hin bauet sein' Kirch' und sein Wort,
Da will der Teufel seyn mit Trug und Mord."
—*Augusti, Denkwürdigkeiten*, Vol. V. S. 287.

"*Now* many false guides with their songs would o'erreach us;
Beware of their arts, which should forcibly teach us:
Where God is advancing his Church and his Word,
There will Satan be with his cunning and sword."

The influence of congregational singing in England at an early pe-

skill this mode of warfare and applied these weapons with sufficient success to their assaults upon the strongholds of Satan?

5. The influence of sacred music is too much overlooked as a means of *moral discipline* in our efforts to educate the young and to reform the vicious.

Has it the place which its great importance demands in our primary schools and higher seminaries of learning? In Germany the child is universally taught to sing in the primary school. Singing is as much a part of the instruction in these schools as arithmetic or grammar. This is one of the blessings which they owe to their great Reformer. "Next to theology," said Luther, "it is to *music* that I give the highest place and the greatest honor.[51] A schoolmaster ought to know how to sing; without this qualification I would have nothing to do with him." Can a more amiable provision be made for the future happiness of the child than to train his heart and ear for the delights of music by teaching his infant lips to sing the praises of his God and Saviour?

riod in the Reformation is noticed by Bishop Jewell: "A change now appears visible among the people, which nothing promotes more than inviting them to sing psalms. This was begun in one church in London, and did quickly spread itself, not only through the city, but in neighboring places. Sometimes at Paul's Cross there will be six thousand singing together." By the Act of Uniformity, 1548, the practice of using any psalm openly "in churches, chapels, oratorios and other places" was authorized. At length, after being popular for a while in France and Germany, among both Roman Catholics and Protestants, as psalmody came to be discountenanced by the former as an open declaration of Lutheranism, so in England psalm-singing was soon abandoned to the Puritans, and became almost a peculiarity of Nonconformity."—*Conder's View of all Religions*, p. 321. Note.

[51] Ich gebe nach der Theologia, der Musica den nähesten Locum und höchste Ehre. Opp. W. 22, S. 2253.—*Cited by D'Aubigné.*

In our admirable system of prison discipline has it its proper place among the reforming influences which are employed to quicken the conscience of the hardened transgressor and turn him from the error of his ways?[52] Has the power of sacred music been sufficiently employed to restore the insane? We know the magic power of David's harp to tame the ferocious and frenzied spirit of Saul; will not the same means have a similar effect to soothe and to tranquilize the poor maniac's bewildered soul and to restore him to his right mind? We submit these inquiries respectfully to the careful consideration of the reader, and leave the subject for the discussion of abler pens. The classic poets beautifully illustrate the power of music by making the harp of Orpheus stay the rivers in their course and the winds in their flight, leading the listening oaks along, taming savage beasts and more savage men.[53]

Finally: This subject suggests the importance of simplicity in church psalmody.

Let our sacred songs be simple in their poetry. Such is the poetry of nature, of devotion, of the Scriptures. If we would have the songs of Zion come from the heart, the off-

---

[52] "I always keep these little rogues singing at their work," said a distinguished overseer of an institution for juvenile offenders in Germany—"I always keep them singing; for while the children sing, the devil cannot come among them at all; he can only sit out doors there and growl; but if they stop singing, in comes the devil."—*Prof. Stowe on Com. Schools*, p. 26.

[53] Fluminum lapsus celeresque ventos
    Blandum et auritas fidibus canoris
        Ducere quercus.—*Hor. Car.* 1, 12, 10.

Silvestres homines sacer interpresque deorum
Coedibus et victu foedo deterruit Orpheus
Dictus ob hoc lenire tigres rabidosque leones.
                                    —*Ad Pisones*, 391.

spring of pure and deep emotion—if we would have them stir the souls of the whole assembly for heartfelt, sympathetic worship—they must be indited in the simplicity of pure devotion. And let the notes of sacred music have the same delightful simplicity. Let them be adapted to congregational singing. Let all be trained to sing as early and as universally as they are taught to read; and if we would have the soul ascending in the song, let the whole assembly join in the solemn hymn which they raise to God. The primitive church knew nothing of a choir set apart and withdrawn from the congregation for the exclusive performance of this delightful part of public worship. "The Bible knows nothing of a worship conducted by a few in behalf of a silent multitude, but calls upon everything that hath breath to join in this divine employ." Have we done well, then, in substituting for the voice of all the people in the praise of God the voice of a few in a choir? For the sweet simplicity of ancient melodies, hallowed by a thousand sacred associations, have we wisely introduced the musical display of modern airs? Have we done well in substituting, even for the rude simplicity of our fathers, if such you please to call it, the profane and secular airs of some modern harmonies? After admiring those noble portraits of the great and revered Reformer which adorn the galleries of his native country, clad in the easy, simple and appropriate costume of his age, who would endure the sight of that venerable form dressed out in the modern style, so trim and sleek, of a fashionable fop? With the same wretched taste do we mar, in attempting to mend the music of the great masters of another age by conforming it to the style of the present.

It is gratifying to observe in the public journals and current literature of the day the return of the public mind to a better taste in sacred music, and to notice that several of the ablest masters in the country have entered in earnest upon the work of reform. Heaven speed their work and hasten on the day when, with sweet accord of hearts and voices attuned to the worship of God, all shall join in singing to his praise in the great congregation.

CHAPTER XIII.

HOMILIES IN THE PRIMITIVE CHURCH.

UNDER this head we shall direct our attention,

I. To the discourses of Christ and of the apostles.
II. To the homilies of the fathers in the Greek church.
III. To those of the fathers in the Latin church.

I. The discourses of Christ and of the apostles.

The reading of the Scriptures, in connection with remarks and exhortations, constituted a part of the social worship of the primitive church. The apostles, wherever they went, frequented the synagogues of the Jews, where, after the reading of the Scriptures, an invitation was given to any one to remark upon what had been read. In this way they took occasion to speak of Christ and his doctrines to their brethren. Their addresses were occasional and apposite; varied according to the circumstances of the hearer, and addressed, with great directness and pungency, to the understanding and the heart.

In the Acts we have brief notices of several of the addresses of Peter and of Paul, and of one from Stephen, from which we may gather a distinct impression of their style of address. The first from Peter was before the disciples, who, to the number of one hundred and twenty, were assembled to elect a substitute in the place of the traitor Judas, Acts i. 15. It is calculated to soothe the minds of his hearers, oppressed by the melancholy end of this apostate, by showing that all had transpired according to the prediction of God's word, and to fulfill the counsel of his will.

The second was delivered on the occasion of the shedding abroad of the Holy Spirit on the day of Pentecost, Acts ii. 14. After refuting the malicious charge of having drunk to excess, he proceeds to show from the Scriptures that all which the multitude saw was only the fulfillment of ancient prophecy; he charges them with having crucified the Lord Jesus Christ, whom God had exalted as a Prince and a Saviour to give repentance unto Israel and remission of sins. Such was the force of his cutting reproof that three thousand were brought to believe in Christ crucified.

His third address, on the occasion of healing the lame man in the temple, Acts iii., was of the same character and attended with a similar result. His fourth and fifth were delivered before the Sanhedrim, in defence of himself and the apostles, Acts iv. 7; v. 29. Of these we only know that the subject was the same as the preceding—Christ wickedly crucified and slain by the Jews, and raised from the dead for the salvation of men. Before Cornelius the centurion, Acts vi. 34, after explaining the miraculous manner in which his Jewish prejudices had been overruled, and how he had been led to see the comprehensive nature of the gospel system, he gives an outline of its great truths, attested by the Scriptures, relating to Christ, to the resurrection and the final judgment. All these discourses manifest the same boldness and fervency of spirit, and are directed to produce the same result—repentance for sin and faith in Christ.

Stephen, in his defence before the Sanhedrim, Acts vii., traces the history of God's dispensations to the Jews, and of their treatment of his servants the prophets, whom they had rejected and slain, and charges them with having finally consummated their guilt by becoming the betrayers and murderers of the Holy and Just One. Paul, in his address at Antioch, pursues the same style; showing how, from age to age, God had been unfolding his purpose to give salvation to men by Jesus Christ, and finally bringing the whole to bear with tremenduous force in its application to his hearers. "Beware, therefore, lest that come upon you which is spoken in the prophecy: Behold, ye despisers, and wonder and perish; for I work a work in your day, a work which ye shall in no wise believe, though a man declare it unto you," Acts xiii. 40, 41. Time would fail us to follow the apostle in his masterly address before the Areopagus at Athens, Acts xvii. 22—his affecting interview with the elders of Ephesus at Miletus, Acts xx. 18—his admirable defence before the Jews, and before Festus and Agrippa, the king, Acts xxii., xxiii., xxvi. With the Greeks he reasoned as a Greek, making no reference to the Jewish Scriptures; but, from their own poets and the natural principles of philosophy and of religion, convincing them of the vanity of their superstitions. With the Jews he reasoned as a Jew out of their own sacred books, and testified to all, both Jew and Greek, the great doctrines of repentance and faith in Christ, the resurrection of the dead and the general judgment.

The addresses of the apostles are remarkable at once for their simplicity and their power. None ever preached with such effect as they. Wherever they went converts were multiplied and churches reared up, in defiance of all opposition, and in the face of every conceivable discouragement. Strong in faith and mighty in the Scriptures, these few men, in a few short years, made greater conquests over the kingdom of Satan and won more souls to Christ than all the missionaries of all Christendom have gained in half a century. Whence, then, this mighty power? Without venturing far into this interesting field of inquiry, we may offer a few suggestions in relation to the characteristics of the apostles' preaching.

1. They insisted chiefly on a few cardinal points, comprising the great truths of the Christian religion.

Christ, and him crucified; repentance; faith in Christ and the remission of sins; the resurrection; and the general judgment;—these are the great points to which all their addresses are directed. The simplicity of these truths gave a like simplicity to their preaching. Beaming full on their own minds, and occupying their whole soul, these momentous truths fell from their lips with tremendous power upon the hearts and consciences of their hearers. No power of oratory or strength of argument could equal the awful conception which they had of what they preached. They could, therefore, speak in the fullness of their hearts, and with earnestness and simplicity, what they had heard, and seen and felt. The word thus spoken was quick and powerful; it cut to the heart; it converted the soul.

2. Their full conviction of the truths which they preached gave directness and pungency to their addresses.

Honest in their sacred cause, and much impressed with what they said, and anxious only to fasten the same impression in the minds of their hearers, they spoke with honest earnestness the convictions of their inmost soul. These strong convictions gave them the noblest eloquence, the eloquence of truth and of nature. *Pietas est quod disertum facit*, says the great Roman orator. Piety inspires true eloquence. This was the secret of their eloquence. They felt the high importance of what they said; and, springing from the heart, their exhortations touched the hearts of those to whom they spake.

3. Their preaching was wholly *scriptural*—based on the

Scriptures and restricted to the single purpose of making manifest the truths of God's word.

They preached Jesus Christ, in the very character in which he is revealed in the word of God, and to which all the prophets have given testimony. Standing thus in the counsel of the Lord, they had strong ground of defence, and holy boldness in declaring what God had said. Their preaching was, accordingly, in the demonstration of the Spirit and of power. Armed with this energy divine, is it wonderful that the word spoken had this quickening power?

4. The contradiction and persecution which they continually experienced gave peculiar earnestness and power to their ministrations.

One who, like Paul, could say, "None of these things move me, neither count I my life dear unto myself, so that I might finish my course with joy and the ministry which I have received of the Lord Jesus, to testify the gospel of the grace of God," Acts xx. 24—such a man only waxes bolder in the truth by all the conflicts to which he is called, and summons up unwonted powers in proclaiming the gospel which he preaches at the peril of his life. Standing in jeopardy every hour, with an eye fixed on eternity and fearless of every foe, is it surprising that with surpassing energy and power the apostles declared the gospel of the grace of God to their fellow-men?

5. They preached in God's name, and were sustained by the undoubted assurance of his support.

They were ambassadors for God, and, supported by his authority, had great boldness in declaring the messages of his grace. If God be for us, who can be against us? Strong in the Lord and in the power of his might, fearless of danger and of death, they gave themselves up to the guidance of his Spirit, speaking as the Holy Ghost gave them utterance; and, like their Lord, teaching as one having authority, and not as the Scribes.

After those fragments of the public addresses of Christ and the apostles which are recorded in the Scriptures, no example of a similar discourse in the primitive church remains, until we come down to Origen in the third century. It is, however, generally admitted that such familiar remarks, in connection with the reading of the Scriptures, continued uniformly to constitute a part of the social and public worship of the primitive Christians. Such instructions were expected particularly from the presbyters, Acts xx. 28; 1 Pet. v. 2, but the privilege of public speaking was not restricted to them. The freedom of primitive worship permitted any one, with the exception of the female sex, to speak in religious assemblies. This was not originally the exclusive or principal duty of the presbyter.[1] Hilary's testimony to this effect has already been given.[2] Origen, again, was invited by the bishops of Caesarea and the vicinity to preach in public, though he had never been ordained as a presbyter.[3]

Tertullian and Justin Martyr each say enough to show that the churches of Africa and Asia respectively still conducted their religious worship in the freedom and simplicity of earlier days. "We meet together to read the Holy Scriptures, and, when circumstances permit, to admonish one another. In such sacred discourse we establish our faith, we encourage our hope, we confirm our trust, and quicken our obedience to the word by a renewed application of its

---

[1] Apost. Kirch. 1, c. 5. Comp. J. H. Böhmer, Dissertat. 7. De Dif. inter ordinem ecclesiast., etc., § 39. Eschenberg, Versuch Religionsvorträge, S. 85. Rothe, Anfänge, Vol. I. S. 155–160.

[2] Chap. 7, p. 257.

[3] Euseb. Eccl. Hist. 6, c. 19. Comp. Lib. 5, c. 10; Lib. 6, 19.

truths."[4] The whole account indicates that "the brethren" sought, by familiar remarks and mutual exhortations, to enforce a practical application of the portion of the Scriptures which had been read, and to encourage one another in their religious hopes and duties.

The account from Justin, which has already been given (p. 295), corresponds with that of Tertullian, with the single exception that the addresses were from the presiding presbyter, who conducted the worship of the assembly. In both instances it was a *biblical exercise*, designed to enforce a practical application of the truths which had been presented in the reading. Not a single text, but the entire passage from the Scriptures which had been read, was the subject of remark. This style of expository preaching continued apparently into the third century; before the close of which, a rhetorical, theatrical mode of address was introduced.[5]

The taste of the present age is against this style of preaching; and, by common consent of pastor and people, it has fallen into neglect. But it has certain peculiar advantages, which deservedly recommend it to the consideration of every minister of Christ.

1. It is recommended by apostolical precedent.

The apostles were directed by wisdom from on high, to adopt, or, if you please, to continue this mode of address in the Christian church. They were content simply to commend the truth to their hearers as God had revealed it. They strove, as the only and ultimate end of all their preaching, to lay open the heart and conscience to the naked truth of God. So presented and applied, that truth became quick and powerful in producing the end of all preaching,—the conviction and conversion of men.

2. This style of preaching is recommended by its practical efficacy.

[4] Tertullian, Apol. 39.
[5] Rheinwald, Archaeol. p. 279. Comp. Euseb. Orat. pro Const. etc.

Never, elsewhere, has the ministry of man been attended with results so interesting and momentous as were those which followed the ministrations of the holy men in the first ages of the church, who knew no other style of address than the one we are considering, and who simply sought to give a plain exposition of Scripture, with a direct and pungent application to the hearer.

3. Expository preaching gives variety to the ministrations of the pulpit.

The preacher, by continually offering the hasty suggestions of his own mind, is in danger of falling into a regular train of thought and illustration; and this, by frequent recurrence, may give sameness to his ministrations, and render them as monotonous, almost, as the regular tone of his voice. His sermons, thrown off in quick succession from a mind jaded by the ceaseless recurrence of the same duties, may not unfrequently exhibit to the hearer only the separate lineaments of the same features. But in the various portions of the sacred volume there is a variety, a richness and fertility which no uninspired intellect ever possessed; and these, if successively introduced, may be an exhaustless theme of discourse, ever new, gratefully diversified, and yet alike interesting and edifying in their turn. All Scripture is given by inspiration of God, and is profitable for doctrine, for reproof, for correction, for instruction in righteousness, that the man of God may be perfect, thoroughly furnished unto all good works, 2 Tim. iii. 16. Why for ever set this aside to inflict upon our auditory what is too often the production of a barren mind, or a wearied intellect and a cold heart.

4. Expository addresses afford the happiest means of applying religious instruction to all classes and conditions of men.

In a consecutive exposition of the Scriptures a vast variety of topics arises, which, discreetly handled, may be made the means of enforcing duties that otherwise would never be embraced within the teachings of the ministry. A single epistle of Paul, or one of the evangelists, thus expounded, will in a few months lead the preacher to remark upon many subjects which otherwise, in the whole course of his ministry, might never find a place in his public discourses.

5. The preparation of such discourses affords the preacher the happiest opportunity of enriching his own mind with varied and profitable learning.

Many a sermon is written without the addition of a single valuable thought, or of a new fact to the acquisitions of the preacher. But how varied the inquiries which arise in the attempt to elucidate a portion of Scripture! Geography, history, philology, philosophy, theology, doctrinal and practical, all are put in requisition, and bring their varied contributions to elucidate the sacred page and to enrich his own mind. His lexicons are recalled from the neglected shelf. His Bible in the original tongue is resumed. He drinks at the sacred fountain, refreshing alike to the heart and the mind, and returns to his people with fresh acquisitions that make him both a wiser man and a better preacher.

Finally, this mode of address, above all others, gives the preacher opportunity to bring the truth of God, with its living, life-giving power, to bear upon the minds of his people.

That which the preacher speaks is now no longer his own. It is Jehovah's awful voice calling upon the hearer to listen obediently to his high commands. The audience may cavil at the preacher or sit by in cold indifference, but they have a solemn interest in these messages of God to them. Opposition is silenced, and the ear is opened to attend while Jehovah speaks. What would have fallen powerless from the preacher's lips now comes with divine authority and power to convince and convert the soul. Multitudes on earth and in heaven can attest the mighty power of divine truth thus plainly set forth from the word of God in bringing them to repentance. Let the minister observe the moral efficacy of his various ministrations, and he will find that when he has withdrawn *himself* most from the notice of his hearers, and brought forward the word of God to unfold to them its tremendous truths, then has he seen the happiest fruits of his labors. Let him return after a long absence to the former scene of his labors, and he will find that while his hearers have forgotten his most elaborate sermons, they still remember his faithful expositions of the word of God in the evening lecture.

II. Homilies in the Greek church.[6]

From the third century the homilies of the Greek and Roman fathers are so different that it will be most convenient to consider them separately, confining our attention to that period which extends in the Greek church from Origen, A. D. 230, to Chrysostom, A. D. 400, and in the Roman from Cyprian, A. D. 258, to Augustine, A. D. 430.

With Origen a new style of public address began in the Greek church, which had, indeed, some advantages, but was attended by many and still greater faults. The following brief outline of the characteristics of the style of preaching now under consideration, and of the circumstances which led to its adoption, is given chiefly from Eschenberg, who is admitted to have written on this subject with candor and discrimination.

[6] The writers of the period now under consideration are Origen, A. D. 230; Gregory of Neocaesarea, A. D. 240; Athanasius, A. D. 325; Basil the Great, A. D. 370; Gregory of Nyssa, A. D. 370; Gregory Nazianzen, 379. Among others of less note may be classed Methodius, A. D. 290; Macarius, A. D. 373; Ephraem the Syrian, A. D. 370; Amphiloginus, A. D. 370–375, and Nectarius, A. D. 381.

1. Origen introduced that allegorical mode of interpreting the Scriptures which, while it affected to illustrate, continued for a long time to darken the sacred page. Not content with a plain and natural elucidation of the historical sense of the text, it sought for some hidden meaning, darkly shadowed forth in allegorical, mystical terms. Great as was Origen in talent, industry and learning, he showed still greater weakness in the childish fancies in which he indulged as an interpreter of Scripture. The great respect in which he was held gave currency to his mode of preaching, so that he became the father of all that allegorical nonsense which for a long time continued to dishonor the public preaching of the ancient church.

2. The sermons of the period under consideration were occupied with profitless polemical discussions and speculative theories.

The question with the preacher seems too often to have been, not what will produce the fruits of holy living and prepare the hearer for eternity, but how the opinions of another can best be controverted—worthless dogmas, it may be, deserving no serious consideration. Whether those who adopted them would be made wiser and better was a question not often asked. Doctrinal points, rather than moral truths, were taught from the Scriptures; and often were sentiments condemned which were truly just, while others were extolled which were wholly worthless.

3. The preachers of this period claimed most undeserved respect for their own authority.

Flattered by the great consideration in which they were held and the confidence in which the people waited on them for instruction, they converted the pulpit into a stage for the exhibition of their own pertinacity, ignorance and folly. They manifested an angry impatience at the errors of others, persecuted them for following their own convictions, and condemned them for refusing assent to arbitrary forms prescribed by the priesthood as conditions of salvation. With all their self-conceit, they manifested a time-serving spirit. As the opinions of the court and of the principal men in the nation favored one religious party or another, so were they more or less reserved in exposing the errors of the same. The polemic discourses from the pulpit changed with every change of administration; and what a short time before had been advanced as wholesome truth, under a change of circumstances was denounced as damnable heresy.

4. The sermons of this period were as faulty in style as they were exceptionable in the other characteristics which have been mentioned.

Not only was the simplicity which characterized the teachings of Christ and of the apostles in a great measure lost in absurd and puerile expositions of Scripture, and corrupted by the substitution of vain speculations derived especially from the Platonic philosophy, but the style of the pulpit was in other respects vitiated and corrupted. Philosophical terms and rhetorical flourishes, forms of expression extravagant and far-fetched, biblical expressions unintelligible to the people, unmeaning comparisons, absurd antitheses, spiritless interrogations, senseless exclamations and bombast disfigure the sermons of the period now under consideration.

Causes which contributed to form the style above described:

1. The prevalence of pagan philosophy.

The preacher was compelled to acquaint himself with the philosophical speculations of the day, to expose their subtleties, and he unconsciously fell into a similar mode of philosophizing.

2. The conversion of many philosophers to Christianity, especially at the beginning of this period, had an influence in corrupting the simplicity of the Christian system, both in doctrine and in discourse.

They sought to incorporate their philosophical principles with the doctrines of Christianity, and to introduce their rhetoric and sophistries into the discourses of the clergy. Every discussion gave occasion for the introduction of various forms of expression unknown in Scripture. But to give greater authority to such discussions, certain phrases were selected from the Scriptures to which a meaning was attached similar to the philosophical terms in use, and out of this strange combination a new dialect was formed for the pulpit. In this way the few and simple doctrines of Christianity received from an impure philosophy many additions from time to time, and by continual controversy were darkened the more, and gradually almost excluded from the instructions of the pulpit.

3. The evil in question was aggravated by the want of suitable preparation for the ministry.

Some betook themselves to the schools of the Platonic philosophy, and became practiced in the arts of the orators and sophists of the day. Others sought, in deserts and in cloisters, to prepare themselves for the sacred office. Here they brooded over what they had previously read and heard. Removed from intercourse with men, they only learned to be visionary, perverse, self-willed and immoral. The consequence was that their instructions abounded with false, distorted views of virtue and doctrine, and of the means of moral improvement.

4. Ignorance of just principles of interpretation contributed to the same result.

Philo, Plato and others were read instead of the evangelists and Paul and the other apostles. The Hebrew was little cultivated, and the true principles of interpretation were unknown.

5. A blind self-conceit had much influence in setting aside the great truths and duties of religion.

Forgetful of the religious edification of his people, the preacher was occupied with speculations upon trifling and unmeaning things. These, accordingly, were the topics of his public discourses whenever he was not employed in the endeavor to expose some heretical dogma.

6. The religious controversy of the day gave an unprofitable direction to the instructions of the pulpit.

The preacher had constantly the attitude of a polemic, watching with a vigilant eye any defection from the truth, and hastening to oppose the outbreak of some destructive heresy.

7. The increasing influence of the bishop.

This was itself a new source of polemical discussion. The bishops at the head of their churches, and, in the larger cities, already having great authority over the presbyters and deacons, would not receive from these the least contradiction. Not content merely to be honored, the bishops would be implicitly obeyed. To this demand some one perhaps ventured to dissent. If he had the courage or inconsideration to advance an opposite opinion concerning a doctrine of Scripture, or a sentiment avowed in a public address, he was, if possible, ejected from office by the bishop, and for what he had said or written was condemned as a heretic.

8. The increasing formalities of public worship had no small influence in diverting the mind from the true object of public religious instruction.

These forms, of which Christianity in its original simplicity had so few, were generally multiplied; great attention was paid to the adorning of the churches; festivals became numerous; rites and ceremonies were multiplied; the effect of all which was to turn off the mind from the essential truths and duties of religion and fasten attention upon other things, which have not the least influence in promoting the spiritual improvement of man. The preacher sought to adapt his addresses to these forms and festivals,[7] and often fell into extravagances and fanaticisms. Monks, ascetics and recluses were extolled as saints and commended as examples of piety.

Finally, the effeminacy, the tendency to gloom and melancholy, and the love of the marvelous which have ever characterized the Eastern nations, became to some extent infused into the religious discourses of their preachers.

III. Homilies in the Latin church.

The writers of this same period, from A. D. 250 to 400,

[7] "Of this depraved state of the public mind we have a striking example from Socrates. In relating the endless discords of the churches in regard to their rites and festivals, he refers to the decision of the apostolical council, Acts xv. 23-30, to show that the apostles gave no instructions touching these forms, but insisted only on moral duties, and proceeds to say: 'Some, however, regardless of these practical injunctions, treat with indifference *every species of licentiousness*, but contend as if for their lives for the *days when a festival should be held.*'"—*Eccl. Hist.* Lib. 5, c. 22. The same degeneracy characterized the church before the Reformation. "In proportion as a higher value was attached to outward rites, the sanctification of the heart had become less and less an object of concern; dead ordinances had everywhere usurped the place of a Christian life; and by a revolting yet natural alliance, the most scandalous debauchery had been combined with the most superstitious devotion. Instances are on record of theft committed at the altar, seduction practiced in the confessional, poison mingled with the Eucharist, adultery perpetrated at the foot of the cross."—*D'Aubigné's Ref.* Vol. III. p. 348. This is one of the evils of prelacy. It encourages a debasing superstition which, by corrupting the doctrines of religion, vitiates the morals of the people,

to whom reference is had in the following remarks, are Cyprian, Zeno and Ambrose. The characteristic distinctions between these and the Greek fathers, whose public discourses have been considered, are given by our author in the following summary:

1. The Latins were inferior to the Greeks in their exegesis of the Scriptures. They accumulated a multitude of passages without just discrimination or due regard to their application to the people.

2. They interested themselves less with speculative and polemic theology than the Greeks.

3. They insisted upon moral duties more than the Greeks, but were equally unfortunate in their mode of treating these topics, by reason of the undue importance which they attached to the forms and ceremonies of religion; hence their reverence for saints and relics, their vigils, fasts, penances and austerities of every kind.

4. In method and style the homilies of the Latin fathers are greatly inferior to those of the Greeks.

Causes productive of these characteristics.

1. The lack of suitable means of education.

They neither had schools of theology like the Greeks, nor were they as familiar with the literature and oratory of their own people. Ambrose was promoted to the office of bishop with scarcely any preparation for its duties.

2. Ignorance of the original languages of the Bible.

Of the Hebrew they knew nothing; of the original of the New Testament they knew little; and still less of all that is essential to its right interpretation. When they resorted to the Scriptures, it was too frequently to oppose heresy by an indiscriminate accumulation of texts. When they attempted to explain, it was by perpetual allegories.

3. The want of suitable examples and a just standard of public speaking.

Basil, Ephraem the Syrian and the two Gregories were contemporaries, and were mutual helps and incentives to one another. Others looked to them as patterns for public preaching. But such advantages were unknown in the Latin church. The earlier classic authors of Greece and Rome were discarded from bigotry; or, through ignorance, so much neglected that their influence was little felt.

4. The unsettled state of the Western churches should be mentioned in this connection.

Persecuted and in exile at one time, at another engaged in fierce and bloody contests among themselves,[8] the preachers of the day had little opportunity to prepare for their appropriate duties. Literature was neglected. Under Constantine, Rome herself ceased to be the seat of the fine arts, and barbarism began its disastrous encroachments upon the provinces of the Western church.

5. The increasing importance of the bishop's office.

The pride of the bishops and their neglect of their duty as preachers kept pace with their advancement in authority. As in the Greek church, so also in the Latin, this sense of their own importance gave a polemic character to their preaching. But in the latter church they became careful to assert and defend their own dignity; indolent and pleasure-loving, as their incomes increased. They sought, in every possible way, to promote their own power and self-aggrandizement. They created new and needless offices, better suited to assist them in commanding, in governing and in maintaining their dignity than to promote the instruction and edification of the people.

---

[8] The contests for the election of bishops often ran so high as to end in bloodshed and murder, of which an example is given in Walch's History of the Popes, p. 87. Ammianus Marcellinus, Lib. 27, c. 3.

Others sought, by the appearance of great sanctity, by celibacy and seclusion, by fasting and the like, to maintain and to augment their importance. In the practice of these austerities they wasted so much time that little remained to be employed in preparation for public speaking.

6. The increase of the ceremonies and forms of public worship.

The effect of all these was to give importance to the bishop; and, in his zeal for the introduction and general adoption of them, the essential points of the Christian religion were forgotten. Need we relate with what zeal Victor, the Roman bishop, engaged in the controversies respecting Easter and the ceremonies connected with it? What complicated rites were involved with the simple ordinance of baptism, and the abuses with which they were connected; what importance, what sanctity was ascribed to their fasts, and what controversies arose between the Latin and the Greek church from the reluctance of the latter to adopt the rites of the former? What incredible effects were ascribed to the sign of the cross?[9] Where indeed would the enumeration end if we should attempt a specification of all the ceremonies, with their various abuses, which were introduced during the period under consideration? Thus ancient episcopacy touched with its withering blight the ministrations of the pulpit, both in the churches of the East and of the West.[10]

To the foregoing view we subjoin one or two remarks:

1. Episcopacy is an encumbrance to the faithful minister in the discharge of his appropriate duties.

---

[9] Cyprian, Lib. 2, Testimon. adv. Indaeos, c. 21, 22. Lactant. Instit. Lib. 4, c. 27, 28, Vol. I. p. 594, ed. Bünemann.

[10] Many other particulars in relation to the homilies of the ancient church are given in the author's Christian Antiquities, c. 12, pp. 237–252; Ancient Christianity, pp. 348, 349.

HOMILIES IN THE PRIMITIVE CHURCH. 369

The reader has noticed what obstacles these ancient prelatists of the church encountered in their ministry. So much attention was requisite to guard the episcopal prerogatives, such vigilance to root out the heresies that were perpetually shooting up in rank luxuriance within the church; so much time was wasted in useless discussions about rites and forms, festivals and feasts and all the ceremonials of their religion, as sadly to divert their attention from their appropriate work of winning souls to Christ.

All this is only the natural result of an exclusive and formal religion. Such a religion addresses itself powerfully to strong, original principles of our nature. And the results are as distinctly manifest in modern as they were in ancient prelacy. Undue importance is given to the externals of religion, which have little or no place in the ministrations of the pulpit. In the perpetual lauding of the church, her rites and her liturgy; in the conscious reliance upon her ordinances; in the sanctimonious exclusiveness, which boasts of apostolical succession and divine right; in the sleepless vigilance to guard against any imaginable departure from the rubric,—in all these we see the influences still at work which wrought such mischief in the ministry of ancient prelacy; still, as then, embarrassing the faithful preaching of Christ and him crucified. The charges of the bishops and the sermons of the clergy show distinctly the strong bias which the mind receives from a religion surcharged with ceremonials and boasting its exclusive prerogatives. These unconsciously assume undue importance in the preacher's mind. His Bible furnishes him with a text; but too frequently his rubric suggests his subject.[11] Such is the natural course of the human mind.

---

[11] Even the Christian Observer, for May, 1804, has an article from a churchman, gravely inquiring, not after the best means for the conversion of men and their continuance in the Christian faith, but for

It fastens strongly upon what is outward and sensual; forgetful of that which is inward and spiritual. "The Divine Founder of Christianity, as if in wise jealousy of a tendency which may be so easily abused, confined the ceremonials of his religion within the strictest limits."

According to the canons of the church, which were

> the "most effectual means which a faithful clergyman can take during his life, *in order to prevent his flock from becoming Dissenters after his death !*" As though the highest ends of a faithful Episcopal minister were, not to save the souls of his people, but to save them from becoming *Dissenters.* In the foregoing remarks allusion has hardly been made to the Puseyite party in that church; and yet a late writer claims, on that side, *nine* of the thirteen charges which have been delivered by English bishops within a short time past; and even of the remaining four, only one was decidedly against the party. One of this class, instead of being absorbed in the great doctrines of the gospel, is intent, with almost a mystic monomania, upon the arrangement of the merest trifles—clerical costume and pulpit etiquette, chaplets, crosses, crucifixes, wax candles, flowers, "red," "white" and "intermingled."
>
> "Nescio quid meditans nugarum et totus in illis."
>
> Notice, for example, the solemn fatuity of these instructions from the Directorium Anglicanum for the ordination of deacons: "The bishop will enter the cathedral church, vested in purple cassock, rochet, chimera, episcopal ring, zucchetto and birretta. If he do not vest in the sacristy, he will remove his vestments from the altar. . . . . On reaching the faldstool, the bishop will remove his birretta and deliver it to the deacon, who, in his turn, will deliver it to an acolyte. He will wear the zucchetto till the assumption of the mitre. The gloves will be carried on a salver. . . . . The bishop, on being vested with the dalmatis, sits down; and the deacon removes the episcopal ring and hands it to the sub-deacon to place on a salver held by an acolyte for that function. The gloves are then presented on a salver, and should be so arranged that the right may lie at the side of the deacon and the left at that of the sub-deacon. In putting on the gloves, the deacon assists at the right and the sub-deacon at the left," pp. 223, 224.—*London Quarterly,* Jan., 1867.

adopted in 1603, "whosoever shall affirm that the rites and ceremonies of that church are 'wicked, antichristian or *superstitious*' shall be excommunicated, *ipso facto*, and not restored until he repent and publicly revoke his wicked errors," Can. 6. The seventy-fourth canon directs that archbishops and bishops shall wear the accustomed apparel of their degrees, and that the subordinate orders shall "wear gowns with standing sleeves, straight at the hands; or wide sleeves, with hoods or tippets of silk or sarcanet, and square caps." They are not to wear "wrought night-caps, but only plain night-caps of black silk, satin or velvet." At home they may wear "any comely or scholar-like apparel, provided it be not cut or pinkt; and that in public they go not in their doublet and hose, without coats or cassocks; and that they wear not any light-colored stockings." All this is gravely entered in the canons of the church, and "ratified by letters-patent from the king, under the great seal of England, after having been diligently read with great contentment and comfort."

2. As a conservative principle, to preserve the unity of the church, episcopacy is entirely inadequate.

If the unity of the church consists in *a name* merely, and in *forms*—in the use of a prayer-book and surplice—then may episcopacy be said to preserve this unity; but in what else have they of this communion ever been united? how else have they kept the unity of the faith? In the ancient church what was the success of the episcopal expedient to preserve the unity of the church. Let Milton reply: "Heresy begat heresy with a certain monstrous haste of pregnancy in her birth, at once born and bringing forth. Contentions, before brotherly, were now hostile. Men went to choose their bishop as they went to a pitched field, and the day of his election was like the sacking of a city, sometimes ending in the blood of thousands; .... so that, instead of finding prelacy an impeacher of schisms and faction, the more I search the more I grow into all persuasion to think rather that faction and she, as with a spousal ring, are wedded together, never to be divorced."[12]

What idea does the profession of episcopacy at present give of one's religious faith? Is he Calvinistic, Arminian, or Unitarian; high-church or low-church; Puseyitish, semi-popish, or what? "The religion of the Church of England," says Macaulay, "is so far from exhibiting that unity of doctrine which Mr. Gladstone represents as her distinguishing glory, that it is, in fact, a bundle of religious systems without number. It comprises the religious system of Bishop Tomline, and the religious system of John Newton, and all the religious systems that lie between them. It comprises the religious system of Mr. Newman, and the religious system of the Archbishop of Dublin, and all the religious systems that lie between. All these different opinions are held, avowed, preached, printed, within the pale of the church by men of unquestioned integrity and understanding."[13]

As an expedient, therefore, to preserve the unity of the church, episcopacy must be pronounced an entire failure. And yet they of this denomination present the extraordinary spectacle of the most discordant sect in all Christendom boasting the conservative powers of their religion as its distinguishing glory, and urging a return to this, their "one body in Christ," as the only means of preserving the unity of the church!

[12] Prose Works, Vol. I. pp. 121, 122.
[13] Review of Gladstone's Church and State, Miscel. Vol. III. p. 306; Hetherington, 130, 131. Bishop Warburton says the Church, in his days, was like Noah's ark, where a few sensible creatures were crowded in a corner, quite as much annoyed by the company and the concomitants within as by the storm without.

CHAPTER XIV.

THE BENEDICTION.

I. ORIGIN and import of the rite.

It seems to have been from remote antiquity a common belief that either a blessing or a curse, when pronounced with solemnity, is peculiarly efficacious upon those who are the objects of it.[1] So common was this belief that it gave rise to the proverb, "The blessing and the curse fail not of their fulfillment." The consequences were momentous, according to the character of the person from whom the prophetic sentiment proceeded. The blessing of the aged patriarch, of the prophet, the priest and the king was sought with peculiar interest, and their execration deprecated with corresponding anxiety. Of the king's curse we have an instance in 1 Sam. xiv. 24. Saul adjured the people and said, Cursed be the man that eateth any food until the evening, that I may be avenged on mine enemies. Comp. Josh. vi. 26 with 1 Kings xvi. 34. The blessing and the curse of Noah upon his sons, Gen. ix. 25–28, and of Moses upon the children of Israel, Deut. xxviii., xxxiii., are familiar illustrations of the same sentiment, as is also the history of Balaam, whose curse upon Israel Balak sought with so much solicitude, Num. xxii., xxiii., xxiv. The blessing of the patriarchs Isaac and Jacob respectively was sought with

---

[1] Dira detestatio nulla expiatur victima.—*Hor. Epod.* 5, 90. Hence also the expression, *Thyesteae preces*, in the same ode. Comp. Iliad. 9, 455.

peculiar anxiety, as conveying to their posterity the favor of God and the smiles of his providence, Gen. xxvii., and xlviii., xlix. Comp. Deut. xxxiii. The son of Sirach expresses a similar sentiment, iii. 9: "The blessing of the father establisheth the houses of children; but the curse of the mother rooteth out foundations."

With the question relative to the prophetic character of these patriarchal benedictions we are not now concerned. It is sufficient for our present purpose that the benediction of patriarchs, of parents, and of all those who were venerable for their age or for their religious or official character, was regarded as peculiarly efficacious in propitiating the favor of God toward those upon whom the blessing was pronounced.

In addition to all this, the Aaronitic priesthood were divinely constituted the mediators between God and his people Israel. They were the intercessors for his people before his altar, and stood in their official character as daysmen between the children of Israel and Jehovah their God. In this official capacity Aaron and his sons were directed to bless the children of Israel, saying, "The Lord bless thee and keep thee. The Lord make his face shine upon thee and be gracious unto thee. The Lord lift up his countenance upon thee and give thee peace." Thus were they to put the name of God upon the children of Israel, and the promise of God was that he would bless them, Num. vi. 24–27. In conformity with this commission to the house of Aaron, it was a universal custom in the worship of the Jews, both in the temple and in their synagogues, for the people to receive the blessing only at the mouth of the priests, the sons of Aaron. If none of these priests were present, another was accustomed to *invoke* the blessing of God, supplicating in the prayer the triple blessings of the benediction, that the assembly might not retire unblessed;

but this was carefully distinguished from the sacerdotal benediction.[2]

This view of the subject may perhaps aid us in forming a just idea of the nature and import of the sacerdotal benediction. The term *benediction* is used to express both the act of *blessing* and that of *consecrating*, two distinct religious rites. The sacerdotal benediction, according to the views above expressed, seems to be *a brief prayer, offered with peculiar solemnity unto God for his blessing upon the people, by one who has been duly set apart to the service of the ministry as an intercessor with God in their behalf.*[3]

Both this and the other forms of benediction, in the acts of consecration and dedication, are exclusively the acts of the clergy. Only the higher grades of the clergy were permitted in the ancient church to enjoy this prerogative. The council of Ancyra and others restricted it to bishops and presbyters.[4] And in all Christian churches it is still a general rule that none but a clergyman is entitled to pronounce the benediction. In the Lutheran Church none but an *ordained* clergyman is duly authorized to perform this rite. The licentiate accordingly includes himself in the petition, saying, not as the ordained minister, The Lord bless *you*, etc., but, The Lord bless *us*. And if a layman is officiating, he includes the form of benediction in his prayer, varying yet again the emphasis, and saying, The Lord *bless* us, etc. Their doctrine is that the minister stands in *the place of Christ* to bless the people in his name, and that in the benediction there is an actual conferring of the blessing of God

---

[2] Vitringa, De Synagoga, Lib. 3, part 2, c. 20.

[3] According to Ambrose, the benediction is, *sanctificationibus et gratiarum vot va collatio—votiva;* quia benedicens vovet et optat.—*J. Gretseri*, Vol. V. 178, in Lib. 1, De Benedictionibus.

[4] Conc. Nic. c. 18. Ancyr. c. 13. Neo Caesari, c. 13. Constit. Apost. Lib. 8, c. 28.

upon the people—of which, however, none are partakers but those who receive it in faith.[5] Such also is the Roman Catholic doctrine of the priesthood, derived from the prelacy of the ancient church. Immediately upon the rise of episcopacy the clergy began to claim kindred with the Jewish priesthood. The bishop became the representative of the Lord Jesus Christ; and the priesthood, like that of the Jews, the *mediators* between God and man. This delusive dogma changed the character of the Christian ministry. They now became the priests of a *vicarious religion*, ministering before the Lord *for the people*, as the medium of communicating his blessing to them. This perversion of the Christian idea of the ministry, which in an evil hour was put forth as the doctrine of the church, opened the way for infinite superstitions, and did more harm to spiritual Christianity than any single delusion that ever afflicted the church of Christ. It is remarkable, however, that neither the New Testament nor primitive Christianity gives us any intimation of a vicarious priesthood.

With reference to the intercessory office of the Jewish priesthood, Christ our Mediator and Intercessor with the Father is, indeed, styled our great High Priest, Heb. iv. 14; comp. also, ii. 17; iii. 1; v. 10. His benediction he pronounced upon little children when he took them in his arms and blessed them, Mark x. 16. In his separation from his disciples at Bethany, when he was about to return unto his Father in heaven, he ended his instructions to them by pronouncing upon them his final benediction: "He lifted up his hands and blessed them; and it came to pass that, while he blessed them, he was parted from them and carried up into heaven," Luke xxiv. 50, 51. These acts, however,

[5] Witness thousands prostrating themselves to receive the benediction of the pope at Rome, and the whole house of American bishops kneeling to receive the blessing of a fellow-bishop.

have no reference to the sacerdotal benedictions of the Jewish priesthood. They are only the expressions of the benevolent spirit of our Lord; the manifestations of that love wherewith he loved his own to the end.

The apostles, also, frequently begin and end their epistles with an invocation of the blessing of God upon those to whom they write; sometimes in a single sentence, and sometimes with a triple form of expression, analogous to the Aaronitic benediction. But these, again, appear to be only general and customary expressions of the benevolent desires of the writer toward those whom he addresses. They are a brief prayer to the Author of all good for his blessing upon the persons addressed. Whatever be the form of the salutation, it is only expressive of the love and benevolence which swelled the hearts of the apostles toward the beloved brethren to whom they wrote.

But in all the writings of the New Testament we have no indication of the use of the *sacerdotal benediction*, in the Jewish and prelatical sense of the term, in the religious worship of the apostolical churches. It appears, indeed, not to have been a religious rite, either in the apostolical or primitive churches, during the first or second century. Neither the apostolical fathers, nor Justin Martyr, nor Tertullian make any mention of the sacerdotal benediction. This omission of a religious rite, in itself so becoming and impressive, is the more remarkable in the primitive Christians, inasmuch as they, in other things, so closely imitated the rites of the Jewish synagogue, in which this was an established and important part of religious worship.

In regard to the reasons of this omission writers upon the subject are not agreed. Some suppose that the secret discipline of the church afforded occasion for this omission. The doctrine of the Trinity was one of these sacred mysteries which were carefully concealed from the uninitiated. So scrupulous were the churches on this point that, for a time, even the use of the Lord's Prayer was prohibited in public assemblies for religious worship, because it was thought that it conveyed an allusion to this sacred and hidden mystery.

Others suppose that the occurrence of the sacred name of God, יְהֹוָה, to the Jews, *verbum horrendi carminis*—which none but the high-priest was ever permitted to pronounce, and he only once a year, on the great day of the atonement—that the occurrence of this awful name of Jehovah was, to the early Christians, a reason for omitting the sacerdotal benediction.[6]

But the reader, we doubt not, has anticipated us in assigning altogether another reason for the extraordinary omission of the sacerdotal benediction in the primitive church. Was it not the superintending providence of God which graciously withheld the apostles and primitive Christians from adopting a rite rendered obsolete by the great atoning sacrifice of the High Priest of our profession and susceptible of unutterable abuses, as the subsequent history of the church too clearly shows? It is another instance of those remarkable *omissions* of which Archbishop Whately has largely treated, with consummate ability, in different works. He has noticed the wise precaution with which God in his providence so ordered events that no possible trace should be found in the primitive church of any prescribed mode of church government, to the exclusion of all others; or of a creed, or catechism, or confession, or form of prayer, or liturgy upon which superstition could seize as an invariable rule of faith and practice, and abuse to support a sanctimonious religion which should conform to the letter, but disregard the spirit of his word. Such an omis-

---

[6] Siegel, Handbuch, Vol. II. S. 114. J. H. Haenen, Exercit. de ritu benedictionis sacerdotalis. Jenae, 1682, cited by Siegel. Augusti, Denkwürdigkeiten, Vol. X. S. 179, 180.

sion he regards as "literally miraculous." Copying so closely after the synagogue, and yet, against all their Jewish prejudices, dropping this rite of their synagogue-worship, the apostles must, on the same principle, be supposed to have been supernaturally withheld from taking that course which would *naturally* have appeared to them so desirable.

The apostolical benediction, then, in spirit and in import, is altogether unlike the Aaronitic benediction of the Jews or the prelatical blessing of the bishop and priest. It is nothing more than a *brief prayer, a benevolent desire, offered with solemnity unto God, for his blessing upon the people.* The several forms of expression are one in meaning, and express the desire that the blessing of God, both spiritual and temporal, may be and abide with the worshiping assembly. The clergyman alone pronounces the benediction, not in the *vicarious character of mediator or intercessor between God and his people,* but solely in conformity with the apostolic precept, requiring all things to be done decently and in order. We now return to the prelatical use of the benediction.

II. Mode of administering the rite.

The Jewish priests pronounced the blessing standing and facing the people, with the arms uplifted, the hands outspread and with a peculiar position of the fingers;[7] the congregation meanwhile standing. The attitude of the assembly and of the officiating priest was the same in the Christian church. But the words of the benediction were chanted, and the sign of the cross was given.

The sign of the cross, both in the Eastern and Western churches, was regarded as indispensable in the benediction. This sign is still retained, not only by the Roman Catholics,

[7] Vitringa, De Synagoga, Lib. 3, p. 2, c. 20, p. 1118. Vitringa, Hadria Reland, Antiq. Sac. Vet. Heb. p. 102.

but even by many Protestants. The Lutherans make use of it, not only in the benediction, but in the consecration of the elements, in baptism, ordination, confirmation, absolution, etc. The Church of England also retained the sign in baptism.[8] But how extensively it is observed at present in that church the writer is not informed.

The benediction was sometimes sung, sometimes chanted, and sometimes pronounced as a prayer. There was no general rule or uniform custom on the subject. But when offered in connection with the responses of the people, it was sung and the responses chanted. Such, according to Augustine, is still the custom of the Lutheran Church, and to some extent also of the other Reformed churches.

In many places the benediction is pronounced twice; once at the close of the sermon, and again at the conclusion of the worship.

In Catholic churches the congregation kneel or incline the head while the benediction is pronounced. The priest, arrayed in clerical robes, stands with uplifted hands and a peculiar arrangement of the fingers, speaking in the Latin

---

[8] See canon 30, where it is sanctioned and defended at length. The following is given, among many instances of the studied and superstitious formalities which have been observed to give a mysterious significancy to this sign of the cross in the benediction: "Graeci aeque atque Latini, quinque digitis, et tota manu crucem signantes benedicunt. Differunt quod Latini, omnibus digitis extensis, Graeci indice medio ac minimo extensis ac modicum incurvatis, non ita tamen, ut inter se respondeant; sed pollex directione sit, rectaque respiciens, medius, pollicis incurvatione, introrsum vergat, minimus, inter pollicem et medium dirigatur; police super annularis ad sese moderate deflexi unguem apposito id agunt. Qua se ratione et tres divinas personas, digitis nempe tribus extensis; et duas in Christo naturas; duobus ad se junctis, rentur significare."—*Leo Allatius, De Eccl. Occid. et Orient. censens.*, Lib. 3, c. 18, pp. 1357–1361, cited by Augusti.

tongue in an elevated tone and with a prolonged accent resembling a chant.

REMARKS.

1. The sacerdotal benediction was very early made the means of enhancing the sanctity of the clerical office generally, and especially of that of the bishop.

It was supposed to have a peculiar efficacy in propitiating the favor of Heaven. A mysterious, magic influence was ascribed to it. Even Chrysostom seems to have supposed that it rendered one invulnerable against the assaults of sin and the shafts of Satan.[9] Accordingly it became to the clergy a convenient means by which to impress upon the people a sense of the peculiar sanctity of their own office, and the importance of the blessings which the people might receive at their hands. Even kings reverently bowed to receive the benediction of the bishops, who especially were not slow to take advantage of this popular impression, and early claimed the exclusive right of blessing the people. The subordinate clergy having been duly consecrated by them, were permitted in their absence and as their representatives to pronounce the benediction upon the people. Still the act was virtually that of the bishops. *Qui facit per alium facit per se.* So that all clerical grace centred in the bishop, and from him, through his clergy, descended upon the people of his diocese.[10] In this way the rite became the means of exalting the office of the bishop, and of

---

[9] Imo vero, mihi ne commodes horas duas, sed tibi ipsi, ut ex oratione patrum aliquam consolationem percipias, ut benedictionibus plenus recedas, ut omni exparte securus abeas, ut spiritualibus acceptis armis invictus diabolo et inexpregnabilis fias.—*Cited by Siegel, Handbuch,* Vol. II. 8. 111, Vol. III. p. 64, C. Benedict. Ed. Paris, 1837.

[10] J. H. Böhmer, Jus. Protestant, Lib. 3, vit. 40, §§ 14 and 41.

inspiring the people with profound reverence for him and his official character.

2. The sacerdotal benediction was soon perverted from its original and simple use, and bestowed on various occasions upon a great variety of persons and things.

If the clerical benediction was attended with such benefits to the people in their religious assemblies, the same effects might be expected upon different classes of persons. Catechumens, accordingly, and candidates for baptism, energumens, penitents, etc., became the separate subjects of this rite. Persons of every description and condition pressed to receive the blessing of the priest. Even in the age of Constantine this rage for the blessing of the clergy was forcibly manifested in its manifold applications to different classes of persons.[11] To what a pitch of extravagant folly and superstition it afterward arose is sufficiently manifest in the rituals, missals and agenda of the Romish Church.

3. The perversions of this religious rite afford another illustration of the consequences of a departure from the simplicity and spirituality which become the worship of God.

Possessed with the idea that clerical grace belonged to the ecclesiastical order, and might be imparted to another

---

[11] Gretser gives the following instances, among many others, to show in what estimation the blessing of the priest was held: Cum S. Epiphanius episcopus Salaminae Cypri Hierosolymis versaretur, *omnis aetatis et sexus turba confluebat offerens parvulas* (ad benedictionem) *pedes deosculans, fimbrias vellens, ita ut gradum promovere non valens, in uno loco vix fluctus undantis populi sustineret.*—Vol. V. p. 190. So also the venerable Bede, in his Hist. Eccl. Lib. 3, c. 26: In magna erat veneratione tempore illo religionis habitus, ita ut ubicunque clericus aliquis aut monculius adveniret, gauderentur ab omnibus, tanquam Dei famulus exciperetur, et jam si in itinere pergens inveniretur accurrebant, et flexa cervice, vel manu signari vel ore illius se benedici gaudebant.—*Cited by Gretser*, as above.

by their benediction, men sought this blessing on many, and often on frivolous, occasions. It became an essential rite in almost all the ordinances of religion, and was pronounced upon all classes of persons. It also became essentially the consecrating act by which men were inducted into the different orders and offices of the church. If clerical consecration gave a religious sanctity to men, so might it also to whatever else was to be set apart to a religious use. Hence the consecration not only of the bread and wine of the eucharist, but of the church, the altar, the bell, the organ, the holy water, the baptismal water, and of almost everything that belonged to the sanctuary or could be employed in its service.

If the blessing of heaven could in this manner be imparted to man, so might it be also to his fields, his flocks, his herds and whatever else might be employed or improved for his benefit. Indeed it would be difficult to say what class of men, or what, amidst all that is devoted to the service of man, has not at some time been the subject of sacerdotal benediction.[12]

When once the mind has taken its departure from the great principles of religion, which, whether relating to faith or practice, are few and simple, it wanders, in endless mazes lost, uncertain where or upon what to settle and be again at rest. So easy and natural, and so disastrous withal, is the descent of the human mind from that which is inward

---

[12] The Gregorian Sacramentary, for example, specifies the following particulars in which the benediction of the priest was pronounced,— Benedictio domus—et novae domus.—putei—uvae vel favi—Ad fruges novas—Ad omnia quae volueris—crinis novae—agni et aliarum carnium—Casei et ovorum—Ad quemcunque fructum novarum arborum—Peregrinantium, itinerantium. To which many things have been added, such as Navis—Armorum, ensis, pilei et vexilli, turris, Thalami conjugalis, sepulchri, etc.

and spiritual in religion, and pure and simple in its manifestation, to that which is outward and formal.

4. The foregoing considerations suggest another strong objection to prelacy—its tendency to superstition.

It is indeed a besetting sin in man to give a misdirection to his religious feelings by a veneration for unworthy objects, or by an *inordinate* reverence for what is really venerable in religion. Every religious ceremony, however appropriate, is liable to degenerate into a mere form, and consequently to encourage superstition. But this danger is immensely increased by the multiplication of rites and forms. The attention given to them soon becomes inordinate, extravagant, superstitious. The tendency to superstition increases in proportion to the number and insignificance of the objects which are thus invested with religious veneration. In the episcopal system there is much to create and foster such a tendency. This profound veneration for saints and saints' days, and for things that have been the subject of episcopal consecration, this punctilious observance of festivals and fasts, this scrupulous adherence to the rubric and the letter of the prayer-book, this anxious attention to clerical costume, to attitudes and postures,—what is it all but superstition, giving a religious importance to that which has nothing to do with heartfelt and practical religion? Even the Bishop of London in a late charge, while he professedly condemns the Oxford superstitions, expresses great anxiety that the rubric should be closely adhered to, wishes all his clergy to preach *in white,* sees "no harm" in two wax candles, *provided they are not lighted,* and approves of the arrangement "lately adopted in several churches, by which the clergyman looks to the *south* while reading prayers, and to the *west* while reading lessons!"

5. Episcopacy encourages indirectly, if it does not directly inculcate, the notion of a *vicarious religion.*

Ancient prelacy transformed the minister of Christ, under the gospel dispensation, into a Levitical priest. By this means the Christian religion was changed into something more resembling Judaism or Paganism than Christianity. The priesthood became a distinct order, created by the appointment of God and invested with high prerogatives as a vicarious propitiatory ministry *for* the people;—the constituted medium of communicating grace from God to man.[13] The nature of the sacraments was changed. The sacramental table became an *altar*, and the contributions of the people an *offering* to the Lord. Papacy has held firmly to this doctrine of a vicarious religion down to the present time. Indeed no small share of the corruptions of that "mystery of iniquity" originated in its false idea of the Christian ministry.

Protestantism at the Reformation was but half divorced from this delusion, and indications of its existence are still manifest in Protestant episcopacy, The very name of "*priest*" is carefully retained; one of the second order of the clergy is not a minister, a presbyter, a pastor in the ritual, but always a "*priest.*" The bishop is a reverend or right reverend "father in God." And then that clerical grace which flows only through this appointed channel of communication between God and man, the grace that is given by the imposition of the bishop's hands, the grace imparted to regenerate the soul in baptism, the grace that establishes the soul and seals the covenant in confirmation, the mysterious grace imparted in the benediction—provided always, that the act be duly solemnized by a priest divinely appointed and episcopally ordained,—verily, all these resemble more the ministrations of the Levitical priesthood than of the pastors and teachers whom Christ

---

[13] Sacerdos constituitur medius inter Deum et populum.—*Th. Aquinas, Summa* 3, p. 22.

gave "for the perfecting of the saints for the work of the ministry."

Momentous consequences followed from the substitution of a vicarious priesthood. No church without a bishop, apostolical succession, divine right, the exclusive validity of episcopal ordination, baptismal regeneration, the mysterious efficacy of the sacraments, the grace of episcopal benediction and confirmation; truly these are awful mysteries; and they affect more or less the whole economy of grace. The natural results of such a faith are seen in the movements of the Tractarians and the Ritualists. The great object of these "unprotestantizing" reformers is to reinstate in the church the prelatical ministry of other days and to restore a vicarious religion with its endless absurdities and superstitions. Thus "the character of the church of Christ is changed. She is made to stand in the place of the Redeemer, whose work is marred. His atonement is incomplete, his righteousness insufficient. Ceremonies are multiplied, and the kingdom of God is no longer righteousness and peace and joy in the Holy Ghost. The office of the ministers is of course entirely changed and their true character lost. Thunders more awful than those of Sinai are heard. All is discouragement: the object of the Christian ministry in their hands being apparently to try how difficult, how painful, how uncertain the Christian's course can be made with that ministry, and how impossible without it?

"In a word, their steps are dark, their ministrations mysterious; suited rather to the office of a priest of some heathen mythology than of ambassadors from Christ, ministers of the everlasting gospel, whose feet are beautiful upon the mountains as those that bring glad tidings, that publish peace.

"The aspect which it wears toward those of other communions is fearful in the extreme. No purity of faith, no labor of love, no personal piety, no manifestation of the fruits of the spirit, will avail anything. Though steadfast in faith, joyful through hope and rooted in charity, they pass not through the eye of this needle, and shall not seek the kingdom of God."

The great evil of such a system is that it is a religion of forms, of mysterious rites and awful prerogatives. Heaven in mercy save us from a religion which substitutes these things for the gospel of the grace of God, through Jesus Christ our Lord! To episcopacy in any form, the one great objection which includes almost all others is this—it unavoidably, if not intentionally, encourages that besetting sin of man—*the innate propensity to substitute the outward form for the inward spirit of religion.*

We close, therefore, this protracted view of the Government and Worship of the Primitive Church with a profound impression of the greatness of that wisdom from on high, which guided the apostles in adopting an organization so simple and at the same time so efficient in promoting those great ends for which the church of Christ was instituted; which also directed them in the establishment of those simple and impressive forms of worship, which most happily promote the spirituality and sincerity in the worship of God that alone are well pleasing in his sight. Nor can we resist the conviction that the substitution of the episcopal government and worship for the apostolical was an efficient if not the principal cause of that degeneracy and formality which soon succeeded to the primitive spirituality and purity of the church. It began in the multiplication of church officers and ceremonies. Everything that could attract attention to religion by its pomp and ceremony was carefully brought to the aid of the church. It had been alleged by the heathen as an objection to the Christians that they had no solemn rites, nothing attractive, nothing imposing to command the admiration of men. To obviate this objection and reconcile the heathen to the Christian religion, not a few even of these pagan rites, with a little variation, were incorporated into the rituals of the churches. After this fatal departure from the spirit of the gospel, the progress of declension exhibited in constantly increasing ostentation and formality was easy and rapid. The elegant and forcible language of Robert Hall is the happiest expression which we can give to our view of this speedy and disastrous degeneracy: "The descent of the human mind from the spirit to the letter, from what is vital and intellectual to what is ritual and external in religion, is the true source of idolatry and superstition in all the multifarious forms which they have assumed; and as it began early to corrupt the religion of nature, or more properly of patriarchal tradition, so it soon obscured the lustre and destroyed the simplicity of the Christian institute. In proportion as genuine devotion declined, the love of pomp and ceremony increased. The few and simple rites of Christianity were extolled beyond all reasonable bounds; new ones were invented, to which mysterious meanings were attached, till the religion of the New Testament became in process of time as insuportable as the Mosaic law"

APPENDIX.

The reader will better understand the propriety of Milton's denomination of the Episcopal liturgy—"an extract of the mass translated"—by comparing some extracts from the Mass Book with corresponding portions from the Book of Common Prayer. For the sake of comparison they are set in parallel columns:

FESTIVALS.

MASS BOOK.	PRAYER BOOK.
A Table of the Festivals, which are to be observed by all the Catholics of the U. States, according to the last Regulations of the Holy See.	*A Table of Feasts, to be observed in this Church, throughout the Year.*
All the Lord's days throughout the year.	All Sundays in the Year.
Circumcision.	The Circumcision of our Lord Jesus Christ.
Epiphany.	The Epiphany.
Purification.	The Conversion of St. Paul.
St. Matthias.	The Purification of the Blessed Virgin.
St. Joseph.	St. Matthias the Apostle.
Annunciation.	The Annunciation of the Blessed Virgin.
St. Mark.	St. Mark the Evangelist.
St. Philip and St. James.	St. Philip and St. James, the Apostles.
Finding of the Cross.	The Ascension of our Lord Jesus Christ.
Nativity of St. John Baptist.	St. Barnabas.
St. Peter and St. Paul.	The Nativity of St. John the Baptist.
St. James.	St. Peter the Apostle.
St. Ann.	St. James the Apostle.
St. Lawrence.	St. Bartholomew the Apostle.
Assumption.	St. Matthew the Apostle.
St. Bartholomew.	St. Michael and all Angels.
Nativity of the Blessed Virgin.	St. Luke the Evangelist.
Exaltation of the Holy Cross.	St. Simon and St. Jude, the Apostles.
St. Matthew.	All Saints.
St. Michael.	St. Andrew the Apostle.
St. Luke.	
St. Simon and St. Jude.	
All Saints.	
All Souls.	
St. Andrew.	

MASS BO K.	PRAYER BOOK.
Conception.	St. Thomas the Apostle.
St. Thomas.	The Nativity of our Lord Jesus Christ.
Christmas.	
St. Stephen.	St. Stephen the Martyr.
St. John.	St. John the Evangelist.
Holy Innocents.	The Holy Innocents.
Easter Monday.	Monday and Tuesday in Easter Week.
Easter Tuesday.	
Ascension Day.	Monday and Tuesday in Whitsun Week.
Whitsun Monday.	
Whitsun Tuesday.	
Corpus Christi Day.	

FASTS.

The forty days of Lent.	Ash-Wednesday.
The ember days at the four seasons, being the *Wednesday, Friday* and *Saturday* of the first week in Lent; of Whitsun Week; after the 14th of *September;* and of the third week in Advent.	Good-Friday.
	Other Days of Fasting; on which the Church requires such a Measure of Abstinence as is more especially suited to extraordinary Acts and Exercises of Devotion.
The Wednesdays and Fridays of all the four weeks of Advent.	The Season of Lent.
The vigils or eves of Whitsunday; of the Saints Peter and Paul; of the Assumption of the Blessed Virgin; of All Saints, and of Christmas Day.	The ember-days at the four seasons, being the Wednesday, Friday and Saturday after the first Sunday in Lent, the Feast of Pentecost, September 14 and December 13.
All Fridays throughout the year. The abstinence on Saturday is dispensed with, for the faithful throughout the United States, for the space of ten years (from 1833), except when a fast falls on Saturday.	The three Rogation Days, being the Monday, Tuesday and Wednesday before Holy Thursday, or the Ascension of our Lord.
	All the Fridays in the year, except Christmas Day.

PREFACE.

It is truly meet, and just, right and available that we always, and in all places, give thanks to thee, O holy Lord, Father Almighty, eternal God: Through Christ our Lord; by whom the Angels praise thy Majesty, the dominations adore it, the powers tremble before it, the heavens and the heavenly virtues, and blessed Seraphim, with common joy, glorify it: With whom we beseech thee, that we may be admitted to join our voices; saying in an humble manner:—

Dearly beloved brethren, the Scripture moveth us in sundry places to acknowledge and confess our manifold sins and wickedness, and that we should not dissemble nor cloak them before the face of Almighty God, our heavenly Father, but confess them with an humble, lowly, penitent and obedient heart; to the end that we may obtain forgiveness of the same by his infinite goodness and mercy. And although we ought, at all times, humbly to acknowledge our sins before God; yet

APPENDIX. 391

MASS BOOK.	PRAYER BOOK.
	ought we chiefly so to do, when we assemble and meet together, to render thanks for the great benefits that we have received at his hands, to set forth his most worthy praise, to hear his most holy word, and to ask those things which are requisite and necessary, as well for the body as the soul. Wherefore I pray and beseech you, as many as are here present, to accompany me, with a pure heart and humble voice, unto the throne of the heavenly grace, saying:—
[The Lord's Prayer often repeated.]	[Similar repetitions.]

Gloria Patria.	*Gloria Patri.*
Glory be to the Father, and to the Son, and to the Holy Ghost; As it was in the beginning, is now, and ever shall be, world without end.	Glory be to the Father, and to the Son and to the Holy Ghost. As it was in the beginning, is now, and ever shall be, world without end. ["By this rubric," say the Commissioners of 1661, "the Gloria Patri is appointed to be said six times ordinarily, in every morning and evening service, frequently eight times in the morning and sometimes ten; which, we think, carries with it, at least, an appearance of that *vain repetition* which Christ forbids."]

The Benedicite, or Canticle of the Three Children. Daniel iii.	*Benedicite, omnia opera Domini.*
All ye works of the Lord, bless the Lord; praise and exalt him above all, for ever. O all ye angels of the Lord, bless the Lord; O ye heavens, bless the Lord.	O all ye Works of the Lord, bless ye the Lord; praise him, and magnify him for ever. O ye Angels of the Lord, bless ye the Lord; praise him, and magnify him for ever. O ye Heavens, bless ye the Lord; praise him, and magnify him for ever.
O all ye waters that are above the heavens, bless the Lord: O all ye powers of the Lord, bless the Lord.	O ye Waters that be above the Firmament, bless ye the Lord; praise him, and magnify him for ever. O all ye Powers of the Lord, bless ye the Lord: praise him, and magnify him for ever, etc.

CREEDS.

The creeds are both taken entire from the Roman Catholic ritual.

MASS BOOK.

I believe in God the Father Almighty, Maker of Heaven and Earth, etc.

PRAYER BOOK.
The Apostles' Creed.

I believe in God the Father Almighty, Maker of Heaven and Earth, etc.

THE LITANY.

The Litany is little else than a transcript and amplification of the Roman Catholic Litany of the saints, blended with the Litany of Jesus.

Lord, have mercy upon us.
Christ, have mercy upon us.
Christ, hear us.
Christ, listen to us.

Father of heaven, God, have mercy upon us.

O God, the Son, Redeemer of the world, have mercy upon us.

O God, the Holy Ghost, have mercy upon us.

Holy Trinity, one God, have mercy upon us.

Holy Mary, pray for us.
Holy mother of God, pray for us.
Saint Michael, pray for us, etc.
Be gracious to us, spare us, Lord.
Be gracious to us, hear us, God.
From all evil;
Deliver us, Lord.
From all sin;
Deliver us.
From thy wrath;
Deliver us.
From sudden and unprovided death;
Deliver us.
From the snares of the devil;
Deliver us.
From wrath, hatred and all evil desires;
Deliver us.

O God, the Father of heaven, have mercy upon us, miserable sinners.

O God, the Son, Redeemer of the world, have mercy upon us miserable sinners.

O God, the Holy Ghost, proceeding from the Father and the Son, have mercy upon us miserable sinners.

O holy, blessed and glorious Trinity, three persons and one God, have mercy upon us miserable sinners.

Remember not, Lord, our offences, nor the offences of our forefathers; neither take thou vengeance of our sins.

Spare us, good Lord, spare thy people, whom thou hast redeemed with thy most precious blood, and be not angry with us for ever;
Spare us, good Lord.

From all evil and mischief, from sin; from the crafts and assaults of the devil, from thy wrath, and from everlasting damnation;
Good Lord, deliver us.

From all blindness of heart, from pride, vain glory and hypocrisy, from envy, hatred and malice, and all uncharitableness;
Good Lord, deliver us.

APPENDIX.

MASS BOOK.	PRAYER BOOK.

MASS BOOK.
From the spirit of fornication;
    Deliver us.

From lightning and tempest;
    Deliver us.
From everlasting death:
    Deliver us.

By the mystery of thy holy incarnation;
    Deliver us.
By thine advent;
    Deliver us.
By thy nativity;
    Deliver us.
By thy baptism and holy fasting;
    Deliver us.
By thy cross and passion;
    Deliver us, Lord.
By thy death and burial;
    Deliver us. Lord.
By thine admirable resurrection;
    Deliver us.
By the coming of the Holy Ghost, the Paraclete;
    Deliver us.
In the day of judgment;
    Deliver us.

We sinners beseech thee to hear us.
That thou wouldst spare;
    We beseech thee.
That thou wouldst deign to lead us to true repentance;
    We beseech thee.
That thou wouldst deign to grant peace and true concord to Christian kings and princes;
    We beseech thee.

That thou wouldst deign to preserve the apostolical master, and all the ecclesiastical ranks in our sacred religion;
    We beseech thee to hear us.
That thou wouldst deign to humble all the enemies of the holy Church;
    We beseech thee to hear us.
That thou wouldst deign to lavish on the whole Christian people peace and unity, we beseech thee.

PRAYER BOOK.
From all inordinate and sinful affections, from all the deceits of the world, the flesh and the devil;
    Good Lord, deliver us.
From lightning and tempest, from plague, pestilence and famine, from battle and murder, and from sudden death;
    Good Lord, deliver us.
By the mystery of thy holy incarnation, by thy holy nativity, and circumcision, by thy baptism, fasting and temptation;
    Good Lord, deliver us.

By thine agony and bloody sweat, by thy cross and passion, by thy precious death and burial, by thy glorious resurrection and ascension, and by the coming of the Holy Ghost.
    Good Lord, deliver us.
In all time of our tribulation, in all time of our prosperity, in the hour of death, and in the day of judgment;
    Good Lord, deliver us.
We sinners do beseech thee to hear us, O Lord God, and that it may please thee to rule and govern thy holy Church universal in the right way;
    We beseech thee to hear us, good Lord.
That it would please thee to bless and preserve all Christian rulers and magistrates: giving them grace to execute justice and to maintain truth;
    We beseech thee to hear us, good Lord.
That it would please thee to illuminate all bishops, priests and deacons with true knowledge and understanding of thy word, that both by their preaching and living they may set it forth and show it accordingly:
    We beseech thee to hear us, good Lord.
That it may please thee to bless and keep all thy people;
    We beseech thee to hear us, good Lord.

MASS BOOK.	PRAYER BOOK.
	That it may please thee to give to all nations unity, peace and concord;
	We beseech thee to hear us, good Lord.
Son of God, we beseech thee.	Son of God, we beseech thee to hear us.
O Lamb of God, who takest away the sins of the world;	O Lamb of God, who takest away the sins of the world, grant us thy peace.
Spare us, Lord.	
O Lamb of God, who takest away the sins of the world, listen to us, Lord.	O Lamb of God, who takest away the sins of the world, have mercy upon us.
O Lamb of God, who takest away the sins of the world, have mercy upon us.	
O Christ, hear us.	O Christ, hear us.
Lord, have pity on us.	Lord, have mercy upon us.
Christ, have pity on us.	Christ, have mercy upon us.
Lord, have pity on us.	Lord, have mercy upon us.

The Episcopal Church not only observes many of the holy days, festivals and fasts of the Roman Catholic Church, but it copies from the "Mass Book," with little variation, many of the collects and lessons for those days.

Preface on Ascension day.	*Preface on Ascension day.*
It is truly meet, and just, right, and available, that we always, and in all places, give thanks to thee, O holy Lord, Father Almighty, eternal God: through Christ our Lord; who, after his resurrection, manifested himself to all his disciples, and in their presence ascended into heaven, to make us partakers of his divinity. And therefore, with the angels and archangels, with the thrones and dominations, and with all the militia of the heavenly host, we sing the hymn of thy glory; saying, without end:	It is very meet, right, and our bounden duty, that we should at all times, and in all places, give thanks unto thee, O Lord [Holy Father], Almighty, everlasting God.
	Through thy most dearly beloved Son Jesus Christ our Lord; who, after his most glorious resurrection, manifestly appeared to all his apostles, and in their sight ascended up into heaven, to prepare a place for us: that where he is, thither we might also ascend, and reign with him in glory:
Holy, holy, holy, Lord God of Sabaoth. The heavens and the earth are full of thy glory. Hosannah in the highest. Blessed is he that comes in the name of the Lord. Hosannah in the highest.	Therefore, with angels and archangels, and with all the company of heaven, we laud and magnify thy glorious name; evermore praising thee, and saying, Holy, holy, holy Lord God of Hosts, heaven and earth are full of thy glory: Glory be to thee, O Lord Most High. *Amen.*

In making the above comparison we have only used the Mass Book or Roman Catholic Manual in common use in the United States. But we have seen enough to illustrate the popish character of the liturgy of the Episcopal Church. To what extent this comparison might be carried by reference to all the liturgical books of the Roman Catholics we are not informed. But the commissioners who formed the Book of Common Prayer, under Edward VI., with Archbishop Cranmer at their head, themselves declare that "everything sound and valuable in the Romish Missal and Breviary was transferred by them without scruple to the English Communion Service and to the Common Prayer." The commissioners who were appointed by Charles II., A. D. 1661, to revise the liturgy also say: "We humbly desire that it may be considered that our first reformers, out of their great wisdom, did at that time compose the liturgy so as to *win upon the papists and to draw them into their church communion* BY VERGING AS LITTLE AS THEY COULD FROM THE ROMISH FORMS BEFORE IN USE."

From the first introduction of the English liturgy, in 1548, there was a steady return to the superstitions of Popery. So that the papists themselves boasted "that the book was a compliance with them in a great part of their service; so were not a little confirmed in their superstition and idolatry, expecting rather a return to them, than endeavoring the reformation of themselves." This return to the Popish service became so striking in the reign of Elizabeth, that a body of divines was appointed by the Lords in 1641, to take into consideration certain "Innovations in the doctrine and discipline of the Church of England." Among the "innovations in discipline" are enumerated the following:

"1. The turning of the holy table altar-wise, and most commonly calling it *altar*.

"2. Bowing toward it, or toward the east, many times, with three congees, etc.

"3. Advancing candlesticks in many churches upon the altar so-called.

"4. In making canopies over the altar, so-called, with traverses and curtains on each side and before it.

"5. In compelling all communicants to come up before the rails, and there to receive.

"6. In advancing crucifixes and images upon the altar-cloth so-called.

"7. In reading some part of Morning Prayer at the holy table when there is no communion celebrated.

"8. By the minister's turning his back to the west, and his face to the east, when he pronounceth the creed or reads prayers.

"9. By pretending for their innovations the injunctions and advertisements of Queen Elizabeth, which are not in force, etc.

"10. By prohibiting a direct prayer before sermon, and bidding of prayer."

In addition to the above "innovations," exceptions are made to the change in the vestments of the clergy, to the sign of the cross in baptism, to the absolution of the sick and the burial service—"the sure and certain hope of resurrection to eternal life."

The intelligent reader cannot fail to notice the striking similarity, we might almost say the *perfect identity*, of these innovations with those which the Ritualists are renewing in the Episcopal Church. What is all this mighty movement of that party but another revival of Popish superstition? Another return to Popery; another illustration of the strong affinities which have ever subsisted between the Church of England and the Church of Rome.

The objectionable character of those Popish affinities which have been the frequent subject of remark in the progress of this work, particularly in pp. 311-320, become strikingly apparent in these parallelisms between the Mass Book and the Prayer Book. The design and effort of the great ritualistic controversy of the age is to unprotestantize the Protestant Episcopal Church and reunite it with what Ritualists and Papists denominate the Holy Catholic Church. The Ritualists have made the discovery that it is possible to shake off the bondage of Protestantism and yet to remain in the English Church, of which they claim to be the only true and consistent members. Upon the opposite parties, which they style "Puritan," the "Broad Church," the "Establishmentarian" and the "High and Dry" sections, they lavish their contempt without measure, while they are vigorously pushing on "the great Catholic Revival" by restoring "the mysterious and symbolical pomp of a Roman Catholic church." By vestments, ornaments, attitudes and novelties without number they avow themselves to be in their forms of worship "histrionic, both almost and altogether." By these means they expect "to catholicize the church" and convert the world. The Reformation was a blunder, or a series of blunders. Protestantism is a failure; but on their minds the true light has arisen which is to enlighten the benighted regions of Protestantism. Ritualism, we are told, "is the way to overcome dissent." "The great Catholic revival is now drawing all the most earnest and most devout of the various Protestant bodies toward the church." It is a great and formidable movement, urged on with talent, zeal and energy worthy of a better cause. The power of this Ritualistic movement is another illustration of the ready assimilation of the English to the Romish Church.

"Of all Protestant churches," remarks the learned author of Horae Biblicae, himself a distinguished civilian and a Roman Catholic, "the National Church of England most nearly resembles the Church of Rome. It has retained much of the dogma and much of the discipline of Roman Catholics. Down to the sub-deacon it has retained the whole of their hierarchy; and, like them, has its deans, rural deans, chapters, prebends, arch-deacons, rulers and vicars; a liturgy taken in a great measure from the Roman Catholic liturgy, and composed, like that, of psalms, canticles, the three creeds, litanies, gospels, epistles, prayers and responses. Both churches have the sacraments of Baptism and the Eucharist, the absolution of the sick, the burial service, the sign of the cross in baptism, the reservation of confirmation, and order [ordination] to bishops, the difference of episcopal and sacerdotal dress, feasts and fasts."

We know, indeed, that the Articles of the Church of England strongly protest against the errors of Popery and assert the doctrines of the Reformation. And this is another verification of the famous declaration of Lord Chatham, that the Church of England has "a Calvinistic creed, a Popish liturgy and an Arminian clergy."

INDEXES.

INDEX OF TEXTS.

	PAGE		PAGE
Genesis ix. 25–28	373	John iv. 21, 24	301
—— xxvii	374	—— xix. 24	51
—— xlviii	374	Acts i. 15–34	52, 351
—— xlix	374	—— i. 21, 22	180
Numbers vi. 24–27	374	—— i. 23	51
—— xxii	373	—— i. 24	277
—— xxiii	373	—— ii. 4, 13, 47	323
—— xxiv	373	—— ii. 14	352
Deuteronomy xxviii	373	—— ii. 32	180
—— xxxiii	373, 374	—— iv. 7	352
Joshua vi. 26	373	—— iv. 24–31	277
1 Sam. xiv. 24	373	—— v. 4	31
1 Kings xvi. 34	373	—— v. 29	352
Psalms xxii. 19	51	—— v. 32	180
Ecclesiastes v. 6	147	—— vi. 1–8	28, 32, 53
Joel iii. 3	51	—— vi. 34	352
Nahum iii. 19	51	—— viii. 4	221
Zephaniah iii. 3	186	—— viii. 17	189, 256
Haggai i. 13	147, 148	—— viii. 25	221
Malachi ii. 7	147, 148	—— ix. 39	141
Matthew ii. 6	134	—— ix. 40	277
—— iv. 28	38	—— x. 39–42	180
—— vi. 5	280	—— x. 47	256
—— vi. 9–13	278	—— xi. 1–18	31, 32
—— ix. 35	38	—— xi. 19–24	32
—— xii. 42	141	—— xi. 26	191
—— xviii. 15–17	95	—— xi. 29, 30	31, 139
—— xx. 25–28	29	—— xi. 30, 43	11
—— xxvii. 35	51	—— xiii. 1	147, 158
Mark x. 16	376	—— xiii. 3	188
—— x. 42–45	29	—— xiii. 11	91
—— xv. 24	51	—— xiii. 15	38
Luke iv. 15, 44	38	—— xiii. 17	43
—— xi. 2–4	278	—— xiii. 40, 41	353
—— xxiii. 34	51	—— xiv. 1	38
—— xxiv. 50, 51	376	—— xiv. 23	33, 57, 61, 188
John iii. 10	148	—— xiv. 26, 27	31
—— iii. 22	141	—— xv. 1	32, 38

INDEX OF TEXTS.

	PAGE
Acts xv. 4	139
—— xv. 23–30	365
—— xv. 29–33	32
—— xvi. 25	323
—— xvii. 10	38
—— xvii. 22	353
—— xviii.	24, 26, 190
—— xix. 6	189
—— xx. 17	126, 128, 176
—— xx. 17–28	174, 198, 224
—— xx. 18	353
—— xx. 24	355
—— xx. 28	126, 224, 356
—— xx. 36	277
—— xxii, 14, 15	180
—— xxxiii. 11	180
—— xxvi. 16	180
Romans i. 13	31
—— x. 4	276
—— xii. 8	126
—— xiv. 5, 6	276
—— xvi. 8	126
—— xvi. 16	142
—— xvi. 17	94, 95
—— xvi. 21	53, 126, 143
1 Cor. i. 10	31
—— ii. 1	31
—— iii. 5	30
—— iii. 5–7	190
—— iv. 17	143
—— v. 3–5	89, 103
—— v. 4	33, 89
—— v. 11	94
—— vi. 1	33
—— vi. 5	36
—— ix. 1	180
—— xi. 1	32
—— xi. 30	92
—— xi. 13–16	31
—— xii. 12, 13	45
—— xii. 28	147
—— xiv. 1	276
—— xiv. 16	324
—— xiv. 26	127, 324
—— xiv. 29, 32, 37	147
—— xvi. 1	31
—— xvi. 3, 4	31, 32
—— xvi. 10	144
—— xvi. 19, 20	142
—— xvi. 22	93
2 Cor. ii. 6	90
—— ii. 10	144
—— vii. 10	94
—— viii. 19	57
—— viii. 23	32, 54

	PAGE
2 Cor. ix. 1	32
Galatians ii. 4	276
—— ii. 7–9	142
—— ii. 11	95
—— iii. 1	276
—— iii. 3	24
—— iv. 9	276
—— v. 17	92
—— vi. 8	92
Ephesians ii. 20	45, 147
—— ii. 3	92
—— ii. 2	147
—— iii. 5	147
—— iv. 3	45
—— iv. 11	17, 147, 285, 332
—— iv. 13–16	19
—— iv. 14	19
—— v. 19	329, 336
—— vi. 21	145
Phil. i. 1	32, 54, 143, 174, 198, 224
—— ii. 25	32, 222
—— iv. 3	54, 146
Colossians i. 7	54
—— ii. 5	276
—— ii. 11	92
—— ii. 16, 20	276
—— iii. 16	323
—— iv. 10	54, 146
1 Thessalonians i. 1	54, 143, 146
—— iii. 2	54, 143, 146
—— iv. 1	32
—— v. 12	126, 133
—— v. 21	31
2 Thessalonians i. 1	54, 143, 146
—— iii. 14	94, 95
1 Timothy i. 1	324
—— i. 3	143, 144
—— i. 20	92, 95
—— ii. 1	278
—— iii. 1–7	122, 131, 223
—— iii. 2–7	129, 132
—— iii. 8	180, 321
—— iii. 16	324
—— iv. 14	122, 129, 184, 189, 194, 198
—— iv. 17	193
—— v. 17	129, 134, 137
—— v. 21	30
—— v. 22	190
2 Timothy i. 6	188, 190, 194
—— ii. 11–13	324
—— ii. 24, 25	30
Titus i. 5–9	155, 159, 171, 198, 220
—— i. 6–10	131
Hebrews ii. 17	376
—— iii. 1	376

INDEX OF AUTHORITIES.

	PAGE		PAGE
Hebrews iv. 14	376	1 Peter v. 13	54, 146
—— v. 10	376	1 John v. 1	130, 198
—— x. 25	38	2 John i. 1	198
—— xiii. 7, 17, 24	126, 133	—— i. 10	95
James i. 25	276	3 John i. 1	198
—— i. 17	324	Revelation ii. 8	154
—— ii. 1	31	—— ii. 14, 20	95
—— ii. 2	38	—— iv. 8	324
—— ii. 12	276	—— v. 9–14	324
1 Peter ii. 2	130	—— xi. 15–19	324
—— ii. 9	76	—— xiv. 13	317
—— v. 1	198	—— xiv. 17	317
—— v. 2	356	—— xv. 3, 4	324
—— v. 2, 3	128	—— xxi. 1–8,	324
—— v. 3	30	—— xxii. 10–18	324
—— v. 12	146		

INDEX OF AUTHORITIES.

A

Aeneid VI., 635, 272, 273.
Agath. Conc. 223, 245, 272.
Allgemeine Kirchenzeit, 26.
Ambrose, Opera, 194, 195, 286, 329, 367.
Ammianus Marcellinus, 73, 360, 375, 367.
Ancyra, Conc., 95, 375.
Antioch, Conc., 72, 238, 240, 241, 242, 250, 252.
Apostolical Constitutions, 65, 241, 277.
Apostles' Spirit of, Example, 29.
Aquinas, Thos., Summa, 3, 385.
Arles, Conc., 74, 240.
Arnold's Christian Life, 239.
—— Wahre-Abbildung der Ersten. Christ., 4to., 28, 248, 250, 251, 331.
Athanasius, Apol., 168.
—— De Synodo Arimin., 236.
Augusti, Denkwürdigkeiten, 88, 285, 322, 329, 330, 331, 342, 378, 342–346.
Augustine, Ep., 63, 65, 72, 167, 280, 332, 342, 345, 346.
—— Opera, 196, 140.
Arelat. Conc., 253.
Aurel. Conc., 76, 241, 253.

B

Barcelona, Conc.,
Barnes' Apostolical Church, 145, 187.
—— Reply, 122.
Barrington's Miscel., 42.
Barrow, Dr., on Pope's Supremacy, 47, 106.
Basil the Great, 253, 293, 299, 304, 329.
Baudry's Selections, 61.
Baumgarten, Erläuter. Christ. Alt., 108, 152.
Beamish's Letter to Pusey, 320.
Bengel, Erklär. Offenbarung, 250.
Bernaldus, Constantiensis, 176.
Beza, on Acts xiv. 23, 60.
Bibles, Swiss, French, Italian, etc., on Acts xiv. 23, 60.
Bilroth. Comment., 91.
Bingham, 52, 66, 68, 71, 74, 106, 272.
Blondell, on Elections, 68, 100, 152, 153, 176, 306.
Böhmer, J. H., Diss. Juris Eccles. Antiq., 99, 100, 145, 226, 356, 386.
—— Jus. Protestant, 381.
Böhmer, W., Alterthumswissenschaft, 68, 70, 77, 223.
Bowden's Works, 130.

INDEX OF AUTHORITIES.

Bowdler's Apostolical Succession, 145, 191, 207, 260.
Bracar., Conc., 223, 246, 260.
Brown's Law of Christ, 263.
Bull, Bishop, Defensio Fid. Nic., 327.
Bunsen's Hippolitus, 244.
Burnet's History of Reformation, 203.
Burton's History of the Christian Church, 68.

C

Campbell's Lectures on Eccl. Hist., 142, 150, 154, 164, 165.
Canons, Apostolical, 239, 241.
Carthag., Conc., 68, 72, 223, 240, 241.
Chapman, in Smyth's Presbytery and Prelacy, 131.
Chalcedon, Conc., 67, 250, 264.
Chauncey, Episc., 95.
Chrysostom, Works, 53, 72, 100, 110, 140. 142, 152, 173, 174, 250, 261, 264, 303, 329, 331, 381.
Christian Observer, 309, 369.
Clarkson's Works, 68, 112, 165, 170, 185, 211, 298, 299, 304, 306.
Clement of Alexandria, 140, 159, 281, 303.
Clemens, Romanus, Ep. ad Corinth, 32, 34, 46, 60, 62, 153.
Codex Ecclesiae Africanae, 59.
Coleman's Ancient Christianity, 189, 234, 238, 239, 248, 249, 328, 368.
—— Christian Antiquities, 200, 368.
Colton, C., on Episcopacy, 124.
Conder's Non-Conformity, 189, 227, 347.
Constant., Conc., 67.
Constitutions, Apostolical, 140, 248, 250, 251, 375.
Constitutions and Canons of the Epis. Church, 212, 370.
Cyprian, 53, 64, 66, 67, 77, 83, 99–102, 104, 111, 166, 228, 237, 254, 255, 256, 368.
Cranmer, Bishop, 203.
Cyril of Jerusalem, 140.

D

Daillé, ci-dessus, 66, 102, 145.
D'Aubigné's History of Reformation, 77, 227, 237, 345, 347, 365.
Davidson's Eccl. Polity, 164.

Demosthenes, 58.
De Wette, Acts xiv. 23, 60, 89.
Diodati, on Acts xiv. 23, 60.
Du Pin, Antiqua Ecclesiae Disciplina, 49, 93, 99, 103, 107.
—— Sac. Geog. Africa., 167.

E

Echell. Abr., Eutychius Vindicatus, 200.
Edin, Rev., 181–183.
Eichhorn, Can. Recht., 236.
Epiphanius, 140.
Eliberis, Council, 238, 253.
Ephraem, the Syrian, 343.
Erasmus' Works, 138.
Ernst, Kirchenrecht, 225, 228.
Eschenburg, Versuch, Religionsvorträge, 356, 360.
Eutychius of Alexandria, 161.
Eusebius, Ecclesiastical History, 65, 97, 99, 105, 111, 140, 153, 158, 237, 246, 247, 250, 324–329, 332.
—— Vit. Const., 293, 303, 357.

F

Fathers, early, on Elections, 61.
Firmilian, 172, 226.
Fuchs' Bibliotheca, 108, 115.

G

Gabler, De Episc. Prim. Eccl. 177, 225.
Gangra, Conc., 241, 245, 250.
Gerbert, Musica Sacra, 327, 330.
Gehardi, Loci, Theolog., 187.
Gieseler, Lehrbuch, 198, 225, 227.
Gieseler, Cunningham's Trans., 56, 70, 124, 226, 227.
Goode's Divine Rule, 193, 194, 206, 225.
Gratian, 176.
Gregory the Great, 74.
Gregory Nazianzen, 65, 71, 76, 152, 175, 245, 251, 260.
Greiling, Christengemeinen, 35, 47, 52.
Gretser, De Benedictionibus, 375, 382.
Grossman, D., Ueber eine Reformation der Protestantischen Kirch. Verfass. in Königr. Sachsen, 52.
Grotius, Comment ad Act. xi. 30, 45; xiv. 23, 60, 324.
Guerike, Kirch. Gesch., 108, 223, 225, 226.

INDEX OF AUTHORITIES. 403

H
Haenen. Exercit. De Benedic., 379.
Hales' Works, 129.
Hall, Bishop, 277.
Hall, Robert, 251, 263, 388.
Hallam's Constitutional Hist., 205, 270, 271, 314, 316.
Hammond, Henr., 176.
Hardy, Rev. Th., 248, 263.
Hawes' Tribute, 216.
Hawks, Rev. Dr., 207, 211.
Hefele, C. J., ed. of Clem. ad Cor., 62.
Hegesippus, 140.
Henke, Allgem. Gesch. der Christ. Kirch., 227, 236.
Herder on Psalmody of the Ancient Church, 332, 333.
Hertzog, Encyclopedia, 38, 330.
Hetherington, Hist. of Westminster Ass., 205.
Hilary, Comment., 194, 226, 229.
Hind's Hist., 42.
Hooker's Ecclesiastical Polity, 110.
Hopkins' Hist. of Puritans, 345.
Horace, 348, 371, 373.
Horne's Introduc., 92.
Hubbard, Rev. William, 245.
Hugo, Grotius, 43.
Hüllman, Ursprünge der Verfass. in Mittelalter, 312.
H. W. D. of Philadelphia, 202.
Hume, Hist. of Eng., 216.

I
Ignatius to the Philadelphians and Smyrneans, 59, 111, 162, 165.
Iliad, XXIII., 51.
—— II., 75, 373.
Infidelity, French, 29.
Irenaeus' Works, 157, 158, 193, 226, 260.
Isidor. Pelus., 336.

J
Jahn's Archeol., 92, 93.
Jerome's Works, 67, 132, 140, 152, 171, 173, 174, 198, 229, 258, 331.
Jewel, Bishop, 193, 347.
Justinian, 74, 264.
Justin, Martyr, 155, 156, 280, 295, 326.

K
Killen, Dr. W. D., Ancient Ch., 94.

King's Primitive Christianity, 68, 96, 99, 106, 130, 164, 204.

L
Lactantius, Inst., 368.
Lampridius, Vit. Severi, 65.
Lancey, De, Bishop, 198.
Lange, Comment., 53.
—— Apost. Church, 94.
Laodicea, Council, 93, 168, 240, 245, 250.
Leo Allatius, De Eccl. Occident et Orient, 380.
Leo the Great, 67.
Leo VII., 250.
Liebetrut, Tag des Herrn, 124.
Locke, on Government, 241.
Lucian's Philopatris, 281.
Luther's first Hymn-Book, 344.
—— Works, 347.

M
Macaulay's Miscel., 215. 271.
—— Rev. of Hallam, 319.
—— Rev. of Gladstone, 372.
Magdeburg Centuriators, 112.
Marca, Peter de, 225.
Mason's Works, 130, 135, 171, 172.
Meyer, on Acts xiv. 23, 60.
Miller, Rev. Dr., Letters, 203.
Milton's Prose Works, 142, 157, 161, 162, 214, 253.
Mosheim, De Rebus Christianorum ante Constantinum Magnum, Commentarii, 4to, 34, 46, 49, 50, 56, 58, 68, 106, 108, 109, 117, 222, 226, 227, 236.
—— Can. Recht., 106.
Münscher, Handbuch der Christ. Dog., 227.
Münter, Met. Offenbar., 323, 325, 327.
Myer, Comment., 60.

N
Narbon., Conc., 260.
Neal's History of the Puritans, 271, 315.
Neander's Allgemeine Geschichte der Christlichen Religion und Kirche, 33, 46, 48, 57, 58, 60, 89, 92, 94, 108, 109, 110, 138, 201, 223, 224, 226, 237, 242, 270, 327, 331.
—— Geschichte der Pflantzung und Leitung der Christlichen Kirche, 25, 31, 34, 35, 36, 40, 54, 58, 127, 131, 136, 190, 224, 323, 356.

Neander's Introduction, 15–24.
Necessary erudition, 203.
Neocaesarea, Conc., 375.
Nice, Council, 49, 72, 238, 242, 364, 375.
Nicholas Tudeschus, 176.

O

Observer, Christian, 309, 369.
Odyss., Homeri, 51.
Onderdonk's Episcopacy Tested, 143.
Origen, against Celsus, 63, 100.
—— Homily on Levit., 65, 103, 298, 327.
—— Com. in Math., 103, 113.
—— De Orat., 148, 279.
—— Opera, 227, 279, 282, 298, 326.
Orleans. Conc., 76, 244, 253.
Owen's Gospel Church, 54, 85.

P

Paris, Conc., 78.
Paulinus, 65.
Pertsch, Canon Recht., 31, 259, 225.
—— Kirchliche Historie, Vol. I., 30, 35, 69, 70, 94, 106, 228.
Petavius, on Eutych. of Alex., 176, 201.
Pfaff, De Orig. Juris Eccl., 88, 94.
Philo, 38.
Pius of Rome, 155.
Planck, Geschichte der Christlich. Kirchlichen, Gesellschafts-Verfassung, 5, Bde., 8vo., Vol. I., 27, 30, 70, 71, 73, 108, 115, 116, 117, 118, 122, 200, 222, 223, 225, 227, 236, 237, 238, 241, 244, 245, 250, 252, 257, 258, 264.
Pliny's Letters, 97, 288, 324, 329.
—— Nat. Hist., 301.
Polycarp, Ep., to the Philippians, 96, 154, 280.
Pont. Diac. in Vit. Cyp., 66.
Pontif. Rom., 67.
Potter's Antiq. of Greece, 299.
Prideaux's Conn., 299.

Q

Quien, Le, on Eutchyius of Alexandria, 201.

R

Ranke's Hist. of Pope's, 208.
Recorder, Episc., 214.
Rehkopf, Vit. Patriarch Alex., 201.
Reland, Antiq. Sac. Vet. Heb., 379.

Renaudot, Hist. Patriarch Alex., 200.
Rheinwald, Kirchliche Archäologie, 124, 152, 198, 357.
Riddle's Christian Antiquities, 66, 68, 96, 98, 137, 152.
—— Chronology, 47, 51, 70, 72, 77, 80, 110, 236, 304, 306.
Rheinwald, Michael, 237, 357.
Rigaltius, 138.
Röhr's Kritischen Predigerbibliothek, 55.
Rothe, Die Anfänge der Christlichen Kirche, Vol. I., 25, 44, 51, 53, 54, 55, 127, 131, 136, 140, 141, 142, 146, 188.
Rufin, Hist. Eccl., 65.

S

Sack, Comment. Theolog. Inst., 31.
Salvianus, 261.
Sardica, Conc., 168, 238, 240, 375, 285.
Schaff, Apost. Ch., 94.
Schoene, Geschichtsforschungen der Kirchlichen Gebrauchen und Einrichtungen Christen, 28, 131, 166, 167, 223, 285, 296, 307.
Schroeter und Klein, Für Christenthum Oppositionschrift, I., 23.
Schoettgen, Horae Heb., 149.
Scholiast, Greek, 174.
Schroeckh, Kirch. Gesch., 264.
Scriptores Ecclesiastici, De Musica, 336.
Selden, Origines et Romae, cited, 200.
Semisch, C., on Justin, 156, 294, 326.
Severus, Alex., 64.
Sidonius Apollinar., 73, 75, 76, 261.
Siegel, Handbuch der Christlich. Kirchlichen Alterthümer, 4 Bde., 26, 30, 127, 223, 237, 240, 241, 252, 378.
Simonis, Vorlesungen über Christ. Alterthum., 77, 108.
Siricius Ep. ad Himer., 71.
Smyth, on Presbytery and Prelacy, 193.
—— Eccl. Repub., 209, 212, 234, 240.
—— Apostolical Succession, 234.
—— Presbytery and not Prelacy, 145, 203.
Socrates' History of the Church, 31, 47, 57, 65, 161, 169, 234, 258, 365.

INDEX OF AUTHORITIES. 405

Sozomen, Eccl. History, 65, 167, 168, 169, 246, 248, 343.
Spectator, Christian, 203.
Spittler, Canon, Recht., 30, 220, 225, 227.
Stillingfleet's Irenicum, 100, 152, 203, 204, 232.
Suetonius, 302.
Suicer, on χειροτονέω, 59, 60.
—— Thesaur., 220.
Sulpitius, Severus, Vit. e. Martini, 65, 253.
Symmachus, Ep., 73.
Synessii, Ep., 74, 150.

T

Talmud, Jerusalem, 143.
Tertullian's Apology, 62, 97, 98, 160, 286, 287, 296, 300, 303, 325, 357.
—— De Poenit., 104.
—— De Pudicit., 99.
—— De Fuga, 113.
—— Ad. Castitat., 111, 113, 226.
—— De Jejun., 116.
—— De Anima, 286, 325.
—— De Corona, 293.
—— De Bapt., 174, 339.
—— De Monog., 226.
—— De Praescrip., 225.
—— De Oratione, 282, 283, 303.
Theocritus, 322.
Theodoret, Eccl. History, 65, 103, 168, 330, 343.
Theodorus Mopsues., 173, 174, 329.
Theodosian, Codex, 246, 248, 257.
Thomas de Jesu, 346.
Tindal, on Acts xiv. 24, 61.
—— Rights of Ch., 94.
Toletum, Conc., 260.
Tracts for the Times, 83, 123.
Trajan's Epistle, 24.

U

Urban II., Pope 176.
Usher, Archbishop, 177.

V

Valentinian III., 75, 107, 252.
Valesius in Euseb., 52.
Vater and Henke, Allgem. Kirch. Gesch., 236.
Venema, Institutiones Hist. Eccl., 120.
Vitringa, De Synagoga Vetere, 4to, 30, 44, 88, 94, 147, 374, 375, 379.

W

Waddington's Church Hist., 154.
Walch, De Hymnis Eccl. Apost., 302.
—— Hist. der Päpste, 328, 367.
Whately's Errors of Romanism, 312.
—— Kingdom of Christ, 43, 51, 150, 184, 290, 292.
—— Hist. of Religious Worship, 48, 56.
Whitaker, 204.
Wilkins, Bp., on Gift of Prayer, 277.
Wilson, on Church Gov., 146.
Wiseman, Dr., on the Tractarian movement, 320.
Witsius, De Oratione, 306.

X

Xenophon's Memorabilia, 133.

Z

Ziegler's Versuch der Kirchlichen Verfassungsformen, 127, 225, 243, 250, 264.
Zunz, Die Gottesdienstlichen Vorträge der Juden., 149.

INDEX OF SUBJECTS.

A

Admission to the church, mode of, 114.
"Ἄγγελος τῆς ἐκκλεσίας, 147.
Alexandria, mother church, 242.
Ambrose chosen bishop, 65, 71,.
Angel of churches supposed bishop, 138; not bishop, 147–150.
Antistes, antistes sacrorum, 152.
Apollos not ordained, 190.
Apostles, their appropriate office, 180; shun the distinctions of rank, 30; disown episcopal power, 30, 138; brotherly salutations, 31; remonstrate with the church, and address them as independent fraternity, 31-33, 35; did not baptize, 137; their oversight of the churches, 142.
Apostolical succession, origin of, 204; derived from Romish church, 266; groundless, 177, 181, 219; presbyterian, not episcopal, 180.
"Ἄρχοντες ἐκκλησιῶν, 152.
Aristocracy in elections, 74; govern the church, 75: rise in the church, 224–228; conventional, unauthorized, 228.
Assumptions of episcopacy, 177.
Attitude in prayer, 299, 302.
Auretius, reader, 71.

B

Baptism by presbyters, 136; by the laity. 230, 285.
Barnabas the Evangelist, 146.
Benediction, origin and import of the rite, 373; Aaronitic, 374; apostolical, entirely unlike the benediction of the Jewish priesthood and that of prelacy, 376–379; mode of administering the rite, 379; true idea of it, 375; abuses of it, 381-383.
Bengel, on angel of the church, 156.
Bible, a republican book, 215, 248.
———, withheld from the laity, 289.
Bingham, on elections, 66, 68; on the liturgy, 292.
Bishops, their office, 22, 36; without a name in the Bible, 179, 221; their election resisted, 73; not distinguished from presbyters, 126; proof, 128, 163; plurality of, inadmissible, 129; never confounded with apostles or deacons, 130; derived from Greek, 131; titles interchanged with presbyters, 128, seq., 152; their qualifications, 132; duties the same as those of presbyters, 133; but one in a diocese, 129, 130; no official title in the Scriptures, 138, 169, 177-179; not superior in rank to presbyters, 153, seq.; according to Clement, 153; to Polycarp, 154; to Justin Martyr, 155; to Irenaeus, 157; to Clement of Alexandria, 159; to Tertullian, 160; merely presbyters, 162; pastors only of single parishes, 164; a bishop's charge originally a single congregation, 162, seq.; admitted by Episcopalians, 170, 203, seq.; all met for worship in the same place, 165; personally known to their bishop, 165, 166; limited in extent, 166; bishops in country towns, 166, 167; vast multitudes of them, 167, note; ascendency of city bishops, 167, 239; identical in rank with presbyters, according to Jerome, 171, 229; to Hilary, 230; to Chrysostom, 173, 174; to Theodoret, 174; to the Greek scholiast, 174; to Elias, archbishop of Crete, and to Gregory Nazianzen, to Isidorus Hispalensis, 175, 176; to Bernaldus Constantiensis, to Pope Urban, to Gratian, to Nicholas Tudeschus, 176; J. P. Launcelot, and to Gieseler, 176; origin of their distinction from presbyters, 198; causes of their increasing ascendency, 227; called priest, 227; their authority yielded by silent consent, 223; mildly exercised at first, 223; authority increased by councils, 235; bishops in the city, their pre-eminence, 220, 223, 249, 252; tyranny over the clergy, hold the

INDEX OF SUBJECTS. 407

revenues of the church, 245; power over the clergy, 225, 226, 240, 254; vast accumulation of their wealth, 240, 245; means of carrying their measures, 250; divine rights of, 254; their intolerance, 257; their pride, 259; their ignorance, 260, 315, 306.

C

Campbell on the Episcopate of Timothy and Titus, 142.
Canon of Valencia on elections, 67.
Carthage, discipline by the church of, 100, 102.
Causae ecclesiasticae, 245.
Catechetical instructions, 238; favor Episcopacy, 238.
Catholics, multitude of their bishops, 263.
Chalcedon, council, 67, 250, 264.
Christ, his example, 29: his instructions, 29; his spirit, 29; worshiped as divine in primitive psalmody, 325-327.
Christianity, paganized by papacy, 274; suffers no alliance, with the state, 251, 263.
Christians, styled Jews, 39.
Chrysostom chosen bishop, 65; on bishops and presbyters, 130.
Church, primitive, first formation, 25; addressed by the apostles, 31, 32; modeled after the synagogue, 21, 33, 37-44; according to Neander, 41; Vitringa, 43; Whately, 43; name derived from synagogue, 40; kept pure, 84; one in a city, 150, 163; a religious society, for religious ends, 229; no connection with state governments, but adapted to any, 208, 251; restraints upon the clergy, 231; guarded against sectarianism, 209; gave scope to ministerial zeal, 210; preserved harmony in the clergy, 210; formed an efficient ministry, 211; made an efficient laity, suited to our free institutions, 214; sovereignty destroyed, 244; begins to inherit property by will, 240, 245, 246; corruptions of, 259.
Church government popular, 25, 37, 108, 178; simple, 26, 28, 45; changed, 77; church and state united, 222-225.

Church and State, 245, 252, 263.
Church, "holy catholic," 237, 274.
Churches, formed alike, 60; bond of union in the apostles, 142; care of them by the apostles, 142; apostolical, their ascendency, 222-225.
Churchman on liturgies, 309.
Clemens the Evangelist, 146.
Clement of Rome, cited, 62, 153.
Clergy, nominations in elections, 67; opposed by the people, 72; deposed by the church, 106; discipline by them, 115-117; not prosecuting officers in the church, 121; two orders, 129, 154; subject to restraint by the church, 209; depressed by the bishop, 241, 245; unjust privileges, 285; distinctions observed with care, 269; party spirit of, 241, 249; sycophancy of, 250; civil and ecclesiastical powers, 251; appeals to the emperor, 252; mercenary spirit, 252; claim divine right, 254, 256; persecuting spirit, 257; ignorance, 260, 306.
College of presbyters, 20, 224.
Collection sent by Saul, 139.
Conder, on ordination, 139.
—— on congregational singing in England, 347.
Confederation of the churches, 116, 235.
Confusion of titles of bishop and presbyter, 127, 138. 179, 180.
Congregation, meaning of, 41.
Congregational singing, 338-342; in Germany, 339.
Consignat, 194, note.
Constantinople, council, 67.
Cornelius, chosen bishop, 67.
Correspondence of the churches and bishops, 237.
Council of the churches with the apostles, 32.
Councils, their authority denied, 48; at Jerusalem, 135; result, not by James, 135, 136; their influence in forming episcopal government, 116, 235.
Creeds, primitive, none, 292.
Cross, sign of, 368, 379.
Cyprian on elections, 66, 68; on discipline by the church, 99-102.

D

Daillé on elections, 66.
Deacons chosen by the church, 53; their office, 127; induction to office, 187; distinguished from presbyters and bishops, 153.
Declension, religious, caused by episcopacy, 244, seq.
Delegates sent by the churches, 33, 54; their character, 54.
Delegation from Antioch to Jerusalem, 139.
Delegatus ecclesiae, 149.
Delitzsch, Dr., on the angel of the church, 148, seq.
Devotional influence of sacred song, 341-347.
Διάκονοι, 127, 156.
Diocese, 169.
Diocesan episcopacy, 239-242; disfranchises the laity, 239; destroys the discipline of the church, 242.
Discipline by the church, 33, 36, 37, 87; argument from Scripture, 87, 89; from the early fathers, 95, seq.; from ecclesiastical writers, 107; from analogy, 109; usurped by the priesthood, 115; authorities, 107-114; at Carthage, 102; at Rome, 102; in the Eastern church, 102; right of lost, 118; the right inherent in the church, 119; advantages of, 119, seq.; not punitive, 119; neglected in the Episcopal Church, 119, 122, 261; moral efficacy of it, 120; administered by bishops, 237, 117, 268; destroyed. 242, 261.
Discipline neglected, 121-124.
Disciplina Arcani, 237; is an argument against a liturgy, 304.
Disfranchisement of the laity, 239, 242, 246.
Disputes decided by the church, 33.
Divine right, 69, 117, 177, 181, 204, 227, 236, 254, 270; guidance, 76, 117, 191.
Doctrinal truth enforced by psalmody, 341-349.
Donatists, multitude of their bishops, 167.
Du Pin on discipline by the church, 107; on primitive episcopacy. 167.
Duties of bishop and presbyter identical, 133.

E

Edinburgh Review on apostolical succession, 182, 183.
‘Ηγέ’ομαι, 133.
‘Ηγούμενοι, 126.
Elections by the church, 32, 34, 53, 54; loss of, 68-79; of an apostle, 51; by the brethren according to Mosheim, Neander, Grossman, Röhr, 52; Chrysostom, 53; of the deacons, 53; of the delegates, 54; of the presbyters, 55; usual mode of. 60; mode of resistance by the bishops, 70; tumultuous proceedings, 71; efforts to correct them, 73; controlled by the bishops, 71; canonical, apostolical, 78; right of every church, 79; preserves balance of influence, 80; foundation of religious liberty, 79; safeguard of the ministry, 83; of the church, 84; promotes mutual endearments between pastor and people, 85; produces an efficient ministry, 85.
Emperors, Christian, mistaken efforts to extend Christianity, 262, 263.
Episcopacy, primitive, 132. See bishops. Illustrated, 163-169; fallacious reasoning of, 169; rise of, 228-230; causes of it, 220; summary of its rise, 259; anti-republican characteristics, 223-233; growth in this country, 233; illustrates the rise of American Episcopacy, 233; divine right of 69, 117, 177, 236, 270; introduced irreligious men into the ministry, 248; oppressive to the laity, 239, 244-248, 268; creates unjust distinctions among the clergy, 269; intolerant, 269; impairs the efficacy of preaching, 212, 311, 365, 368; hindrances to ministerial usefulness, 212; wanting in liberality, 213; fails to preserve the unity of the church, 371; its tendency to superstition, 365, 384; encourages the idea of a vicarious religion, 384; encourages a disposition to substitute the outward form for the inward spirit of religion, 387.
Episcopacy anti-republican, 232.
Episcopalians concede the identity

INDEX OF SUBJECTS. 409

of bishops and presbyters, 202; the validity of presbyterian ordination, 184–207; unsupported by argument, 177, 181.
Ἐπίσκοποι, 22, 126, 150, 153.
Ἐπισκοποῦντες, 130.
Ἔφοροι, 152.
Eraclius chosen bishop, 65.
Eustathius chosen bishop, 65.
Excommunication by the church, 91, 93; by the bishops, 115.
Elections, ancient fathers on, 62–65.

F

Fellowship of the churches, 46, 142; encouraged by the apostles, 142; interrupted by episcopacy, 242.
Firmilian on ordination by presbyters, 192.
Forms of prayer opposed to the spirit of Christianity, 275; to the example of Christ and the apostles, 277, 278; contrary to the simplicity of primitive worship, 279; unknown in the primitive church, 285; opposed to gospel freedom, 279; opposed to the simplicity of primitive worship, 285, 294; at first indited by any one, 300–303; prepared for the ignorant, 307; not adapted to the desires of the worshiper, 308; wearisome by repetition, 309; not in harmony with the subject of discourse, 310; adopted from pagans, 312.

G

German psalmody, 339.
Gifts, miraculous, 189.
Government of the church by the members of it, 109; changes through which it passed, 234, 263.
Guidance, divine, claimed by the bishops, 254, 204, 228, 76, 259.

H

Hall, Robert, on church and state, 251, 263.
Hands, laying on of, 187–189.
Harmony in the church, 27.
Hawes' tribute, 216.
Hegesippus, character of James, 140.
Heresies punished with great severity, 257; greatly increased, 84, note, 258, 363, 371.
Heretics and heresies, 248, 257, 371.

Hierarchy, origin of, 225; further development, 227; metropolitan, 242; influence of, on the laity, 244; on the clergy, 248; on moral state of the church, 261.
High church, 204, 269, 369.
Hilary on primitive worship, 285; on presbyterian ordination, 194; on the rise of episcopacy, 230.
Homilies in the primitive church, 351; discourses of Peter, 351; of Paul, 353; characteristics of their preaching, 354; homilies in Greek church, characteristics, 360; causes of the forming of this style, 362–364; homilies in the Latin church, 365; causes productive of their characteristics, 366–368.
H. W. D., of Philadelphia, 202.
Hymns of human composition forbidden, 334.

I

Identity of bishops and presbyters, 126. See under each term bishop and presbyter.
Ignatius, his epistles suspected, 162; interpolated, 162; do not support episcopacy, 163.
Ignorance of the clergy, 260, 306, 366.
Imposition of hands, 141, 144.
Independence of the churches, 34, 45, 49; asserted by Mosheim, 48, 49; by Dr. Barrow, 46; by Riddle, 47; by Whately, 48, 49.
Innocent, 111; arrogant pretensions, 78.
Instrumental music in churches, 335.
Interventors in elections, 72.
Irenaeus, identity of bishops and presbyters, 157, 158.

J

James not bishop at Jerusalem, 139; reasons for his residence there—his character, 140.
Jerome on elections, 67; on bishops and presbyters, 132, 197; on the rise of episcopacy, 229.
Jerusalem, council at, 135; seat of the Christian religion, 135–139.
Judgment, private right of, infringed, 247, 244.
Jury of the church, trial by, 120.
Justin Martyr cited, 155; on primitive worship and ordinances, 294.

35   S

410   INDEX OF SUBJECTS.

K

Κυβέρνησις and διδασκαλία, 18.

L

Laity, 230; disfranchised, 239, 246; oppressed, 239; baptize, 226, 230.
Laity and clergy, balance of power between, 80; disfranchised, 117; injustice to them, 239, 268; loss of their spiritual privileges, 246; indifferent to the interests of the church, 246; to their Christian fellowship, 264; lose control of revenues, 245.
Layman's Bible, 342.
Lapsed, censure of, 115.
Laws enacted by the people, 49, 110, 117–119; right taken from them, 247.
Legatus ecclesiae, 147.
Letters addressed to the church, 110; missive by the church, 111.
Liberty, religious, loss of, 81.
Litigations settled by the church, 37.
Liturgy formed by each bishop, 303; unknown in the primitive church, 288; no relics of any, nor record of such as found at this time, 292; appeal is made to tradition for such forms as belong to the liturgy, 293; liturgies the production of a corrupt age, 306; for an ignorant priesthood, 306, 307; wearisome by repetitions, 309; encroach upon the time which should be allotted to the sermon, 311; exalt the inventions of man above the word of God, 311; English liturgy of popish and pagan origin, 312; erroneous in doctrine, 313–320.
Lord's Prayer not a prescribed form, 278; unknown as such by the apostles and apostolical fathers, 279; summary of conclusions respecting it, 280; unsuited to the Christian dispensation, 284; varied phraseology, 278, 284.
Luther a reformer by his musical powers, 346.

M

מַלְאָךְ, 147.
Mark the Evangelist, 199, 200.
Martin of Tours chosen bishop, 71.
Mason, Dr., on equality of bishops and presbyters, 135; cited, 130.
Maximianists, their bishops, 167.
Μετά, meaning of, 141.
Miletius chosen bishop, 65.
Milton's Prose Works cited, 150, 142, 157, 161, 162, 215, 253, 371.
Ministers, none superior to presbyters, 137.
Mosheim on elections by the church, 58. See Index of Authorities.
Metropolitan government, established, 242, 243; means of its establishment, 244; results, 244.
Music sacred, power of, 338–342.

N

Necessary erudition, 203.
Neander on the two great parties in the church, 288. See Index of Authorities.
Nice, Council, on elections, 66.
Nightingale of Wittenberg, 345.

O

Offices of clergy multiplied, 290, 248, 367.
Officers of the church, 35, 36.
Omissions providential, 290, 311, 376, 370, 378.
Onderdonk on office of Timothy, 143.
Orders, but two in the priesthood, 153.
Ordination claimed by bishops, 255; by presbyters, 159; import of it, 189, note; right of presbyters according to Firmilian, 192; to Irenaeus, 193; to Hilary, 194; to Jerome, 197–199; to Eutychius of Alexandria, 161, 200; to Planck, 201; to Neander, 201; to Blondell, 201; to the Canons, 202; to Dr. Miller, 203; various Episcopal authorities, 202–207; by Cranmer, 203; Necessary erudition, 203; Whittaker, Usher, 204; Stillingfleet, Forbes, King, 204; Goode, 206; Bowdler, 206; Summary, 206; Clarkson, 169; by divine right, 255.
Organs in church music, 335.
Origen as a preacher, 360; on discipline, 103.
"Οση δύναμις αὐτῷ, of Justin, 296–299.
"Οχλοις τοῖς, 73.

INDEX OF SUBJECTS. 411

Outward religion, 287, 369, 382, 387, 388.
Overseers, name, 35.

P

Paganism in papacy, 272-274.
Papal government, 265.
Parochial bishops, 163; parochial system, 220-223.
Passive obedience, 270.
Pastor not a prosecuting officer, 121.
Pastores, 152.
Patres ecclesiae, 152.
Patriarchal government, 264.
Paul and Barnabas ordaining presbyters, 60; in council at Jerusalem, 135; his ordination, 191.
Peace of the church by discipline, 121.
Pearson on elections, 66.
Penance, system of, 116; promotes the bishop's power, 238.
Penitents restored by the church, 104.
People overreached in elections, 77; people govern themselves in everything, 109; rights abridged by councils, 235, 236.
Persecution under Trojan, 27.
Placet, visum est, 236.
Planck on divine right, 254-256. See Index of Authorities.
Ποιμαίνω, 134.
Polycarp, cited, 96, 165, 166.
Pontificale Romanum, 67.
Popish affinities in the liturgy, 272-299, 254, 301, 312-320.
Popish and pagan affinities, 272, 312, 314, 315, 319, 320, 362, 386.
Praepositi, 152; praesides, praesidentes, praesules, 152.
Prayers of the primitive church, 275. See forms of prayer, prayers of Christ and the apostles, extempore, 278, 297; Lord's Prayer, 278; attitude in, 302.
Prelacy injurious, unjust, 268-271.
Presbyters, their office, 21, 36, 126; choice of them, 55: titles, 126, 152; equality with bishops, 126-178; addressed as bishops, 128; term derived from Jews, 131; appellations interchanged with bishops, 126, 151; qualifications, 132; duties identical with presbyter, 133, 162; teachers of the church, 134; counselors, 135; administer ordinances, 136; ordain, 137; distinguished from deacons, 153; equal to bishops, according to Clement, 152; to Polycarp, 154; to Justin Martyr, 157; to Irenaeus, 155; to Clement of Alexandria, 159; to Tertullian, 160; ascendency of those in a city, 221; their right to ordain, 169; according to Firmilian, 192; to Hilary, 193, 226; to Jerome, 197; to Eutychius of Alexandria, 201; to Planck, 201; to Neander, 201; to Blondell, 203; to Dr. Miller, 203; to various Episcopal authorities, according to Chrysostom, 173, 174; to Theodoret, 174; to the Greek scholiast, 174; to Elias of Crete, and to Gregory Nazianzen, 175; to Isidorus, to Bernaldus, to Pope Urban, 176; to Nicholas Tudeschus, to J. P. Launcelot, and to Gieseler, 176; College of, 224.
Πρεσβύτεροι, 127, 135, 152.
President of presbyters, 195, 224, 229, 231.
Priesthood, Jewish, disowned by the church, 43; divine right of, 54, 69, 244, 254, 204-227, 236, 270.
Priesthood, discipline by, 115.
Priests, bishops so-called, 227; claim to be divinely appointed, 227, 235, 253.
Proclus, 76.
Πρόεδροι, 155.
Προεστώς, 168, 169, 148, 156, 295.
Προεστῶτες, 149, 152, 160, 137.
Προϊστάμενοι, 126, 152.
Προΐστημι, 133.
Προστάται, 152.
Προφῆται, 147.
Protest against secular power, 78; of Free Church in Scotland, 81, 82.
Psalmody of the primitive church, 321; the first disciples indited and sang songs, 324: fragments of such in the New Testament, 324; songs of primitive Christians, 327; Christ the subject of their songs, 325; one primitive hymn remains, 327; mode of singing, 328, 325, 329; no instrumental music, 328; responsive singing not general; all the congregation sang, 330;

delight of primitive Christians in it, 331; power of ancient psalmody, 332; changes in ancient psalmody, 333–337; claimed by the clergy, 337; means of propagating doctrinal truth, 341; of moral discipline, 347; importance of simplicity in it, 348.
Purgatory of pagan origin, 273.
Puritans, origin of the name, 315; their wisdom and piety, 215; by Hume, 216; their legacy to us, 217; defection from their religion, never, 218; objections to Prayer-Book, 315.
Purity of the church by discipline, 121.

R

Receive the Holy Ghost, 188, 201, 256, 317; origin of the term, 256, 317.
Republic of the church, 45, 48, 214, 234, 270.
Revenues of church held by bishops, 245; taken from the laity, 246.
Riddle on elections, 68; on presbyterian ministry, 137.
Right divine of bishops, origin of, in the Episcopal Church, 204, 318; in the ancient church, 270.
Ritualism and ritualists, 212, 312, 365, note, 368, 369, note, 371, 384, 387.
Ritualists' boast, 319.
Rock of the church, 113.
Roman government tolerated all religions, 26.
Romans ritualists, 299, 312.
Romanizing germs in the Prayer-Book, 318.
Romish Church, corruption of, 266.
Ruler of the synagogue, 44; his duties, 149.
Russell, Lord J., on ritualism, 267.

S

Sacrament, how administered primitively, 294.
Σάρξ, 92.
Scottish Free Church, 81.
Scriptural exposition, importance of, 358–360.
Secular music corrupts the worship of the church, 336.

Secular power, interference, 72, 77.
Seniores, seniores plebis, 152.
Shepherd, office of bishop and presbyter, 134.
Silas the Evangelist, 146.
Simonis on discipline by the church, 107.
Singers in a choir in the fourth century, 336.
שְׁלִיחַ צִבּוּר, 22, 147–151.
Sovereignty of the church destroyed, 244.
Spirit's guidance claimed, 228, 259.
Stillingfleet on rise of episcopacy, 231.
Stuart, Prof., on the angel of the church, 148, seq.
Submission passive, doctrine of, 138, 173, 225, 236, 253–257.
Succession, apostolical, absurdity of, 181, 182; origin of, derived from the Romish Church, 266, 267; only in person, 185.
Succession, apostolical, and divine right, 48, 69, 117, 177, 181, 201, 204, 227, 236, 244, 254, 256, 270, 274, 285, 382, 386.
Suffrage, universal, 56; right of, 81. See Elections.
Sycophancy of the clergy, 250.
Sylvanus the Evangelist, 146.
Synagogue, endeared to the Jew, 37; ruler. 44; popular in government, 44.
Synods, power over the church, 117.

T

Temple-service unsuited to the church, 37; discarded, 43.
Tertullian, discipline by the church, 98; on elections, 62; on baptism by laity, 226; on primitive order, 288; on primitive worship and ordinances, 299; Antagonisticus, 288; on the Lord's Prayer, 281.
Testimonio adepti, 62.
Timothy, supposed bishop, 144; not bishop of Ephesus, 142; Timothy an evangelist, 143; travels with and for the apostle, 143; entreated to remain at Ephesus, 145.
Titus, supposed bishop, 145; not bishop at Crete, 146.
Tractarian movement admired by Catholics, 320.

INDEX OF SUBJECTS. 413

Tractarians assign origin of liturgies to the fifth century, 305.
Tradition of forms, 293.
Trajan on songs of primitive Christians, 324, 329; to Pliny, 97.
Truth, religious, its simplicity gives it power, 308.
Tumults of elections, 73.

U

Union of church and state, 251, 252, 308.
Unity of the church unknown in apostolical age, 45; absurd, 371; influence in establishing the episcopal government, 237.
Unprotestantizing efforts, 267.
Usage, apostolical, 112.
Usurpation of the bishops in elections, 76; in discipline, 118.

V

Valens, presbyter, defection of, 96.
Valesius on discipline by the church, 107.
Veto of metropolitan, 72.

35 *

Vicarious priesthood, 384.
Visitors at elections, 74.

W

Wealth of the clergy, 246, 253.
Westminster Divines, Hetherington's, 215.
Whately on omissions in Scripture, 290, 291, 311, 370, 376, 378; on apostolical succession, 183, 184.
Whitgift on divine right, 205.
Whitby, Dr., on the office of Timothy and Titus, 146.
Wilkins, Bishop, on gift of prayer, 277.
Wiseman, Dr., on the Tractarian movement, 320.
Worship of the church simple, 38, 300–302, 332; does not tolerate disorder, 276, 288; primitive and ordinances, 294.

X

Χαρίσματα, 189.
Χειροτονηθείς, etc., 59.
Χειροτονεῖν, meaning of, 58, 59, 61.
Χειροτονήσαντες, 57, 61, 188.

Coleman's Manual on Prelacy and Ritualism.

THE

APOSTOLICAL AND PRIMITIVE CHURCH,

POPULAR IN ITS GOVERNMENT, SIMPLE AND INFORMAL IN ITS WORSHIP.

BY LYMAN COLEMAN, D.D.

J. B. LIPPINCOTT & CO.,
PUBLISHERS, PHILADELPHIA.

(From the Preface.)

"The object of the author in writing this work is to commend to the consideration of the reader the admirable simplicity of the government and worship of the primitive church, in opposition to the polity and ceremonials of prelacy.

"In the prosecution of this object he has sought, under the direction of the best guides, to go to the original sources, and first and chiefly to draw from them. On the constitution and government of the church none have written with greater ability, or with more extensive and searching erudition, than Mosheim, Planck, Neander and Rothe. These have been his principal reliance; and after these a great variety of authors.

* * * * * * * *

"In the preparation of this work the author has studiously sought to write neither as a Congregationalist nor as a Presbyterian exclusively; but as the advocate of a free and popular government in the church; and of simplicity in worship, in harmony with the free spirit of the Christian religion. It is enough for the author, and, as he would hope, for both Congregationalists and Presbyterians, if the church is set free from the bondage of a prelatical hierarchy, and trained, by simple and expressive rites, to worship God in spirit and in truth. In opposition to the assumptions of prelacy, there is common ground sufficient for all the friends of popular government in the church of Christ to occupy. In the topics discussed they have equal interest, whether they would adopt a purely democratical or a representative form of government as the best means of defending the popular rights of the church. We heartily wish indeed for all true churchmen a closer conformity to the primitive pattern in government and in worship; but we have no controversy even with them on minor points, provided we may still be united with them in the higher principles of Christian fellowship and love."

NOTICES OF THE WORK.

REV. DR. COLEMAN—

Dear Sir: The inspection of the new edition of your work on "The Apostolical and Primitive Church" brings back into fresh view the winter of 1843, when we were together at Berlin, and you were prosecuting your studies with signal diligence in reference to the work, and were enjoying the society and counsels of Dr. Neander and other eminent historians. You certainly deserve a rich reward for your perseverance in *finishing* the work which you then so enthusiastically *began*. The improvements which you have introduced into the new edition seem to me important, and will much augment the value of the work. It may be used very advantageously as a text-book in our theological seminaries. A large part of a professor's lectures is lost for want of a text-book on the subject of those lectures. Although oral lectures are indispensable, still the printed text-book has some advantages over them. When students were confined to text-books without lectures, they acquired a kind of discipline which they do not acquire from lectures without text-books. They were apt to be more accurate and thorough; their knowledge was more fundamental and deep, although they were less enthusiastic in their studies than now and their attainments were less extensive. There are so many principles stated in your work, and they are illustrated by so many references to historical fact, that it must be a valuable book for *study* as well as for *reading*, and for recitation as well as for study.

I hope that your long-continued labors on the constitution of the Primitive Church will be followed by those results which you have aimed to secure—a diligent and candid attention of good men to the subject, and an ecclesiastical practice regulated by well-established principle. Yours, faithfully,

ANDOVER, *February* 3, 1869. EDWARD A. PARK.

PRINCETON, N. J., *February* 12, 1869.
REV. DR. COLEMAN—
Dear Sir: * * * This revised edition of your book on the Primitive Church is eminently seasonable in this day of tendency to ritual religion, and when the taste for the showy and specious and external is becoming so prevalent. Your main position is one that cannot be refuted. The hierarchy of later times, with its elaborate ceremonial, finds no precedent in the Christian Church until long after the days of the apostles. It is highly important, in view of the pretension with which the opposite is assumed, that all classes should have easy access to the proof of that fact.

I have already introduced into my lectures many references to your book, and intend to recommend it as often as I traverse the field of its discussion.   Yours, very truly,
JAMES C. MOFFAT.

UNION THEOLOGICAL SEMINARY, NEW YORK, *February* 27, 1869.
REV. DR. COLEMAN—
My Dear Sir: I have spent some time in looking over the plate-proofs of your work on the Apostolical and Primitive Church, and am free to say that I am greatly pleased with it. It is careful and thorough in its method, and sound and solid in its conclusions. The time must come, though it may not come very soon, when honest controversy with respect to the polity and worship of the early Church must cease. You certainly have done your part toward bringing about that issue. I trust your book may be not only widely read, but closely studied.
Yours, very truly,   ROSWELL D. HITCHCOCK.

(*From* THE EVANGELICAL MAGAZINE, *London.*)

"We hail with unmingled satisfaction the seasonable publication of this masterly volume. It is emphatically a book for the times. * * * It proceeds from the pen of a Christian and scholar, who has made himself known advantageously to the American and British public by his invaluable work on the 'Antiquities of the Christian Church.' * * * We know no volume in our language in which the scriptural parity of Christian ministers is more firmly asserted and more satisfactorily proved."

(*From* THE CHRISTIAN EXAMINER, *London.*)

"No minister of any denomination ought to remain without this volume for a day. From it alone he can obtain arguments more than sufficient to overturn the petulant heresy of the age."

(*From* THE PATRIOT, *London.*)

"This work forms an admirable text-book upon the whole subject of church government; and the cheap form in which it is presented to the English public will place it within the reach of every dissenting minister and student, to whom it will be of especial value."

(*From* THE NONCONFORMIST, *London.*)

"It has avoided the popular errors of being verbose and overlaid, and is transparent, learned, concise, convincing. Few writers can say so much in few words as Mr. Coleman."

(*From* THE REV. DR. MILLER,

Late Professor of Ecclesiastical History and Church Government in the Theological Seminary, Princeton, N. J.:)

"I feel myself very much your debtor for the instructive and able manner in which you have executed your task. You have in my opinion fully *demonstrated* that Prelacy can find no support whatever, either in Scripture or primitive usage. It is not, I am deliberately persuaded, more indubitably plain, from the word of God and from early Christian antiquity, that *Transubstantiation* and the *Worship of Images* are mere human inventions, than you have made it clearly to appear that *diocesan* episcopacy was superinduced on *parochial* episcopacy by clerical pride and ambition long after the apostolic age. So far as the general scope of your volume goes, I entirely concur with you, and rejoice in its appearance as a publication of importance and of sterling value."

(*From* THE REV. DR. COX, in the *New York Evangelist.*)

"I greet with pleasure, and have perused with profit, the excellent volume of Mr. Coleman's. It evinces cool research, rich and various learning, historical accuracy and conclusive argument. I value it as a truly useful, excellent and seasonable manual on the important topics of which it treats, for authentic reference as well as entertaining perusal. I can only say that I have been so gratified with its contents that I have a good conscience and free pen in commending it to the private as well as the public libraries of our countrymen."

(*From* THE CHRISTIAN REVIEW.)

"This work is one which will attract much attention, and serve as the storehouse of argument and authority on the subject of which it treats; it abundantly redeems the promise of the title-page. The various parts are stated with great clearness, and every material point is sustained by the confirmation of the Fathers.

"While the book is one of great value in reference to the controversy on church polity, it contains also much information relating to the organization and worship of the early churches, which will make it acceptable to the general reader."

www.ingramcontent.com/pod-product-compliance
Lightning Source LLC
Chambersburg PA
CBHW030556300426
44111CB00009B/1005